DEMOCRACY AND SOLIDARITY

POLITICS AND CULTURE
James Davison Hunter and John M. Owen IV, Series Editors

DEMOCRACY AND SOLIDARITY

On the Cultural Roots of America's Political Crisis

JAMES DAVISON HUNTER

Yale

UNIVERSITY PRESS

New Haven and London

Published with the assistance of the Institute for Advanced Studies
in Culture, University of Virginia.

Published with assistance from the Mary Cady Tew Memorial Fund.

Yale University Press books may be purchased in quantity for
educational, business, or promotional use. For information, please
e-mail sales.press@yale.edu (U.S. office) or sales@yaleup.co.uk
(U.K. office).

Set in Janson type by Integrated Publishing Solutions.
Printed in the United States of America.

Library of Congress Control Number: 2023940466
ISBN 978-0-300-27437-0 (hardcover : alk. paper)
ISBN 978-0-300-28489-8 (paperback)

A catalogue record for this book is available from the British Library.

Authorized Representative in the EU: Easy Access System
Europe, Mustamäe tee 50, 10621 Tallinn, Estonia,
gpsr.requests@easproject.com

10 9 8 7 6 5 4 3 2 1

For
Honey

Man's capacity for justice makes democracy possible;
but man's inclination to injustice makes democracy necessary.

—REINHOLD NIEBUHR,
The Children of Light and the Children of Darkness, 1944

[The Founders had established the proposition that all men
were created equal] so that the enforcement of it might follow
as fast as circumstances would permit. They meant to set up a
standard maxim for free society, which should be familiar to all, and
revered by all; constantly looked to, constantly labored for, and even
though never perfectly attained, constantly approximated, and thereby
constantly spreading and deepening its influence, and augmenting
the happiness and value of life to all people of all colors everywhere.
. . . Its authors meant it to be, thank God, it is now proving itself,
a stumbling block to those who in after times might seek to turn a
free people back into the hateful paths of despotism. They knew the
proneness of prosperity to breed tyrants, and they meant when such
should re-appear in this fair land and commence their vocation they
should find left for them at least one hard nut to crack.

—ABRAHAM LINCOLN,
speech on the Dred Scott decision, June 26, 1857

Notwithstanding the dark picture I have this day presented of
the state of the nation, I do not despair of this country. "The arm
of the Lord is not shortened," and the doom of slavery is certain.
I, therefore, leave off where I began, with hope.

—FREDERICK DOUGLASS, July 5, 1852

Contents

Preface

Liberal Democracy at the End of the American Century

DEMOCRACY IN AMERICA IS in crisis. The heart of this book tells a story—different from others—about why it is so.[1]

The story I tell revolves around the *cultural* sources that have underwritten liberal democracy and how, through conflict, these sources have evolved over the course of two and a half centuries. I argue that the specific configuration of cultural sources that underwrote American democracy—what I call America's hybrid-Enlightenment—sought to provide an ethical vision for the reconstitution of public life. It not only made certain ideas and ideals intelligible but, in the process, provided sources for solidarity or cohesion that, by virtue of their opacity, could contain democracy's many internal disagreements.

The Problem of Solidarity

The critical question is: solidarity on what terms?

This is an important question because solidarity, even one that depends on opacity, *always* has limits; that is to say, solidarity is always set within boundaries that define a line between inclusion and exclusion. What makes this story historically and ethically compelling is the way in which those sources—and thus the boundaries of inclusion and exclusion—have been contested over many generations. That contestation is an ineradicable feature of liberal democracy in America not least because of fundamental contradictions present

xi

within the hybrid-Enlightenment at the start: namely, the promise of freedom and equality and universal justice and yet the denial of those goods to large swaths of the American population. The hope of a vibrant political solidarity implied in America's hybrid-Enlightenment was always set against contradictions intrinsic within itself, contradictions that have guaranteed and continue to guarantee tension, conflict, and, at times, violence.

The story I tell here is how those contradictions within America's hybrid-Enlightenment have been repeatedly "worked through." The process of "working through" (*durcharbeiten* in German, from which the concept originated) those contradictions certainly and often dramatically altered the character of the hybrid-Enlightenment over the years, but invariably in ways that have remained recognizable to successive generations. At least until the present, when those efforts are being abandoned by leading factions on the right and the left.

But that's not quite the whole story either, for solidarity is not just about the will to come together to do the work of democratic politics. It is about the cultural preconditions and the normative sources that make that coming together possible in the first place.[2] These sources, it would seem, have largely unraveled. I bring the story to a conclusion by calling into relief the complex and rather dark place to which American political culture has brought us. The sources of solidarity drawn from America's hybrid-Enlightenment have partly disappeared from shared memory and practice, but they also partly have evolved into deformations of their highest and best ideals. More troubling still, they seem to have been replaced by an alternative and, frankly, nihilistic culture logic—one that is, ironically, shared across our political and partisan divisions—that not only renders democratic solidarity impossible but creates the conditions in which the authoritarian impulse becomes impossible to restrain. Simply put, the authoritarian impulse becomes manifest in the attempt to address the absence of solidarity. If solidarity cannot be generated organically, it will be imposed coercively.

A Caveat

Here, a caveat: I am not arguing that partisans in the contemporary culture war are the same in these respects. That would be a terrible misreading of my argument. This is *not* an argument for the moral equivalence of the Left and Right in the ways nihilism is manifest nor in the ways that authoritarian tendencies find expression. Efforts to place culpability in these ways misconstrue the nature of the relationship of political agency and culture in history. To speak of culture is to speak of the frameworks of meaning and understanding and how they are interpreted and put into practice in people's lives and in the institutions around them. These vary considerably. As they bear on the ways the cultural logic of nihilism and its consequences have become manifest, partisan positions at the least will reflect different, changing, and often asymmetrical positions within the contested and ever-evolving configurations of power. My argument is that all partisans are drawing—albeit differently—from the same cultural sources in the never-ending contest over position. How could they not?

A Reflection on Method

In telling this story, I hope to contribute to a fresh synthesis of American political history along the lines suggested by the historian Daniel Walker Howe and practiced by such luminaries as David Brion Davis, David Hackett Fischer, and T. J. Jackson Lears. Howe encouraged a "new cultural history of politics" that would not exclude economic conditions and motives but would see economic interests and political ideology both as artifacts of membership in a community of shared beliefs and values and as material factors that reinforce cultural dispositions and commitments. The symbolic and the material are interrelated and mutually dependent. This approach, as Howe rightly observed, vindicates the perception of progressive historians that American history is one not of simple consensus but one of profound conflict, resistance, invention, accommodation, appropriation, and contestation over authority and power.[3]

I push the cultural turn further along than perhaps Howe and others might have had in mind. There is a tendency to focus upon the observable elements of culture, such as the values, beliefs, folklore, and folkways of people and perhaps their cultural institutions. Of even greater significance, in my view, are "the deep structures of culture," *the tacit assumptions and latent frameworks of meaning embed-*

ded within the structures of social life. These are the cultural antecedents of political life, and it is from the resources of these tacit assumptions and latent frameworks of meaning that liberal democracy
has been able to change and yet maintain a thread of continuity.

This is partly why I use the word *solidarity* as opposed to *consensus* or *unity.* "Consensus" suggests conscious rational agreement,
placing great store on reason and rationality to the exclusion of the
affective and sociological dimensions of human experience. To be
sure, a certain degree of consensus is necessary among those who
make and enforce the law and procedures for determining the law—
policymakers, judges, law enforcement, and the like—otherwise, the
concept of "the rule of law" would have no meaning. But its applica-
bility tends to be narrow, limited primarily to those who are technically and administratively proficient in the law. Consensus, in this
sense, may radiate outward from this space into opaque ideals that
can be shared by large portions of the citizenry. To apply the concept of rational consensus to the general public can be warranted, but
as a rule, it sets untenably high expectations. Instead, in this context,
solidarity serves as a more useful concept by signaling that there are
other things that bind us together besides our capacity to rationally
argue and deliberate. It further suggests a predilection toward a cohesion or concord that is capable of transcending or folding within
it any particular disagreements. The power of solidarity is found in
the unspoken, often vague or fuzzy resonances of shared identity,
shared affections, shared challenges, and a shared destiny.

Thus, if Americans are divided politically, it is because they are
divided culturally at this level. If there is little or no common political ground today, it is because there are few if any common assumptions about the nature of a good society that underwrite a shared
political life. If we cannot find a way beyond our political stalemates,
it is because we cannot find the cultural sources of common hopes
or a common vocabulary for articulating those hopes in ways that
transcend those impasses and lead us beyond them.

Much the same, of course, can be said of the crises of democracy beyond American shores. Authoritarian tendencies have always
been present in the shadows of all modern nations and have now
(re-)emerged publicly in democracies long thought to be immune
from those tendencies. Scanning the range of crises, we can certainly

find common themes. Given the power of globalization and its inter-connectivity, how could we not? Yet there are also important differences among nations that are rooted in the irreducible particularities of history, region, and circumstance.

The present reflection, then, is a case study focused on understanding the *cultural roots of the crisis of American democracy*. It is not the whole story, but it is one that addresses elements that are almost wholly ignored in public discourse and in the scholarly literature. The central premise of this approach is that one cannot take the full measure of the crises of democracy in the late modern world—both here and abroad—without understanding the nature and dynamics of its cultural antecedents. Understanding those cultural antecedents will not only highlight factors not usually considered, it will also bring us to a more sober reckoning with the crisis we face.

My concern with the deep structures of culture—their nature, how they are changing in the late modern world, and the consequences of those changes to everyday life—animates and unites virtually all of my work. Indeed, a while back, I wrote about the deep structures of cultural conflict in my 1991 book *Culture Wars: The Struggle to Define America*.[4] This current story is its bookend. It concerns the sources of solidarity deep within the cultural architecture of liberal democracy and their fate.

Though this is a longish book, I think of it more as an extended essay because it is neither a systematic *theoretical* treatment of American democracy nor a comprehensive *historical* treatment of American political culture over the last two and a half centuries. The work is exhaustive in neither of these ways; nor does it aspire to be. Rather, the heart of this book is a selective and interpretive history of American public and political life over the last two and a half centuries, intended to highlight particular themes relevant to and illustrative of my argument. In making my case, I lean more upon existing knowledge than new research, following Howe, not in order to summarize what we already know but rather to reconceptualize our understanding.

I should note that one way my selective interpretation takes expression is in my effort to highlight the thought of a number of important figures: David Walker, Angela Grimké, Lyman Beecher, Phoebe Palmer, Frederick Douglass, John Dewey, Reinhold Niebuhr,

Walter Lippmann, Martin Luther King Jr., Richard Neuhaus, Richard Rorty, and Chantal Mouffe, among numerous others. I invite them into the historical narrative not to provide a comprehensive view of their thinking nor to trace the thread of an intellectual history. Rather, they appear in the story as leading cultural indicators. Each of these figures was remarkable for his or her recognition of how the cultural dynamics underwriting liberal democracy in America were changing in their time and what was at stake in the challenges they sought to address. They signify (and in some cases understood themselves) the ways that culture underwrites democracy. Moreover, they exemplify the difficult struggle of "working through" those cultural sources to renew democracy in their time. Whether we would agree with them or not, these "intellectuals," broadly defined, have illuminated the dynamics of America's collective efforts to work through the difficult and seemingly intransigent contradictions embedded in America's hybrid-Enlightenment.

The Achievement of Liberal Democracy

I have written this book for several reasons, not least of which is my concern for the fate of liberal democracy. The authoritarian alternatives, whether in the reactionary or revolutionary modes, operate with false coherences that encourage a malignant thoughtlessness in the sense that Hannah Arendt described.[5] Worse still, of course, these false coherences invariably lead to the injury, mistreatment, or even ruin of all who stray beyond their dogmas.

For all of its many horrific historical failures and ongoing defects—none of which should be swept under the rug—I still hold liberal democracy to be among the greatest achievements of human history. The great statesman Tomáš Garrigue Masaryk—a man who well knew what the alternatives looked like—declared that democracy was the political form of the humane ideal. Democracy not only provides the regulative ideal and practical hope of human freedom so central to human flourishing, it also embodies the principle of resistance to government *within* the principle of government itself.[6] The ideals and practices of liberal democracy recognize, affirm, and within their cultural logic, possess the inherent potential for self-correction, often against massive odds. And yet all depends upon a modicum of solidarity because common goods depend upon at least some common understandings, common loves, or common purposes.

The possibilities for an ever-more humane common life within a regime of liberal democracy are slow in coming, and they are certainly anything but inevitable. Yet unlike the alternatives, they are both imaginable and can be approximated within liberal democracy's framework. That potential is always at risk, but it seems to me especially true today when the din of the authoritarians in our midst grows ever louder.

PART I

Introduction

CHAPTER ONE

The Cultural Crisis
of Liberal Democracy

T HE CRISIS OF DEMOCRACY in America is apparent to all.
Ordinary Americans of all backgrounds and convictions
recognize that the entire political ecosystem—not only
its leadership and its governing institutions, but also its
leading ideas and ideals—is failing. This predicament is made worse
by the fact that Americans themselves are increasingly fragmented
and polarized, unable even to converse across their differences, much
less find a way to work together in solidarity to address what is a
common crisis.

The questions that follow are as urgent as they are obvious. Just
how deep are the problems facing American democracy? And can
they be fixed?

The Apparent Problem

If we take politicians, political activists, journalists, and the most im-
passioned citizens as our guides, we will tend to see the problems we
face in contemporary political life as rooted in the corruption, bad
decisions, or flawed ideology of a particular leader or party. It's the
Democrats' fault. No, it's the Republicans' fault. Partisans of all stripes
see things this way: the leaders and the parties of the opposition are

nearly always portrayed as beyond the pale—a threat to decency, civility, justice, fairness—indeed, a threat to America. The news media reinforce this polarization when they report—often with manifest prejudice—on the ups and downs of political fortune by this candidate or that, this party or that, this issue or that. For most activists, commentators, and citizens, the crisis of democracy is not a common crisis, but one caused by the other side. The question of how to restore democracy, then, comes down to mobilizing our political will in a new election or new referendum, voting the wrong party out and the right party in. It's as simple as that.[1]

More astute observers of American political life today recognize that the problems are deeper than any particular politicians or any particular election cycle, but even their accounts tend to locate the concern about democracy *within politics itself*—for example, in the weakening of America's voting system through voter suppression or bureaucratic challenges to the independence of state election procedures and personnel. Others point to the growing alienation and cynicism of the public toward the government. Still others highlight the fragmentation and polarization within the electorate and among political parties. They instance the increase in vulgarity, incivility, and extremism in political discourse as well as the abuse of basic ethics in governing. Some cite the excessive power of the state, while others lament its declining power and effectiveness.

The more compelling of these accounts go further, relating the political problems to broader social pathologies, including a growing individualism and the loss of social capital—the bonding and bridging relationships in public and private life that foster trust and cooperation. Such accounts make note of the increasing "us versus them" factionalizing of identity politics, the polarizing effects of social media in the political process, and the growing economic inequality dividing the interests of the privileged from those of the poor. And all are unanimous that civic life is being coarsened through the commercialization of absolutely everything.

Political Remedies

Remarkably, despite the difficult realities surrounding our troubled democracy, we still tend to conclude that whatever the problems we face, they are, in the end, *fixable*. The ideas proposed are nearly always constructive, even if not entirely practicable.

By these accounts, *we can address the deeply fractured and dysfunctional nature of our Republic* by reviving the mediating institutions of family, community, schools, churches, charities, and local associations and local markets.[2] *We can renew the depleted social capital* that withers the bonds of our communities and endangers the effectiveness of schools, the safety of neighborhoods, equity in taxation, day-to-day honesty and trust, and even our health and happiness through education, work-based initiatives, and community service programs.[3] *We can address the alienation of the electorate* from the government, of the poor from the rich, and of minorities from majorities through new or renewed government programs and reforms.[4] *We can overcome our debased and factionalized public discourse* by examining our own blind spots, by rejecting the dehumanization of our political opponents and recognizing that the purpose of political discourse isn't to score partisan points or even to be proven right, but rather to better ascertain truth and reality.[5] *We can moderate a polarizing internet* that has helped to produce a polarized body politic by inducing the corporations of the new media to foster informational diversity.[6] *We can remedy the inadequacies of our administrative state and our hyper-individualism and, in turn, reinvigorate civic life* if we can recover the republican virtues that once characterized public philosophy in America and renew the civic institutions that support them.[7] *We can rediscover the common good* through subordinating personal identity into a unified citizenship concept if we can prioritize political action over preaching ideology and legislative battles over appeals to rights. In this way, we can help to rebuild a sense of common feeling among Americans, and a sense of duty to one another.[8] In effect, the remedy amounts to creating, affirming, and committing to a new social covenant.[9] *We can even address the spiritual dimensions of this political crisis* and America's broader decline through a Christian revival in America.[10]

One could point to many other analyses of our political crisis, many of which are exceedingly astute.[11] What they tend to share in common is the belief that any remedy comes down to a matter of political will and smart public policy. The general sense is that if we are just a little more clever or try just a bit harder by mobilizing our individual and collective political resolve, we can rebuild the social fabric that gives life to democracy.[12] As one observer put it, "Americans have revitalized their culture of democracy many times before, and we can do it again."[13] Though concern about the fate of democracy is acute, particularly after the Trump presidency, Americans still cling to a long-held belief in their nation's resilience: because America has faced far more daunting challenges in the past, it will surely overcome its present challenge.

Such confidence is the popular expression of the American philosophical tradition of pragmatism, a tradition that sees the truth of things in their usefulness. From the esoteric to the ordinary, from leaders to citizens, from scholars to ordinary folk, Americans of all backgrounds and beliefs tend to seek ideas that cash out in constructive practical consequences.[14]

But What If . . . ?

To be sure, one should never give into despair. Not to hope and not to think creatively and practically for solutions to the range of troubles facing us seems nothing less than a blasphemy.[15]

Yet it is also important to remember that while institutions, even as they evolve, tend to be stable and enduring, no human institution is permanent. No institution is infinitely fixable. Under the circumstances, it is worth considering whether contemporary American democracy can be fixed. What if the political problems we are rightly worried about are actually symptoms of a deeper problem that has no obvious or no easy remedy, certainly not one that is a matter of public policy?

That deeper problem, I contend, is historical and cultural. It is rooted in the highly fragile and contingent circumstances in which modern democracy—and American democracy in particular—came into being. The democratic revolutions of the eighteenth and nineteenth centuries in Europe and North America were the offspring of the Enlightenment—that is, of the broadly rationalist intellectual and institutional revolutions of the seventeenth and eighteenth centuries—and they all reflected the Enlightenment's highest ideals, contradictions, hopes, and inconsistencies. This was nowhere more true than in the American case. When Henry Steele Commager subtitled his book *Empire of Reason* "How Europe Imagined and America Realized the Enlightenment," he may have overstated the case, but the point had ample merit. The Enlightenment, and the American adaptation of it in particular, underwrote the project of modern liberalism that, for all of its voluminous flaws and appalling failures, can fairly boast of achievements that stand among the greatest in human history.

With the advantage of early twenty-first-century hindsight, we can now see that the Enlightenment project has been unraveling for quite some time. We might reasonably ask whether the problems we are witnessing today are the political consequences of that unraveling. If so, any possibility of "fixing" what ails late modern American democracy has to take the full measure of this fundamental transformation in the deep structures of American and Western political culture.

Part II: E Pluribus Unum?

A Different Take on Culture

There is no shortage of scholarly and journalistic work examining the ways culture works on the surface of political life. The story I want to tell, by contrast, begins with a different understanding of culture and of the relationship between culture and politics, one that is stronger and deeper.[16]

The leading accounts in the social sciences see culture as a reflection of economic and political relations. A more aggressive version would say that culture is merely the sum of those artifacts derived from or reflecting the struggle for power and privilege, the chief purpose of which is to justify existing social arrangements. A more benign version of this approach relates the social and political "values" reflected in public opinion to the interests of ordinary people, interests rooted in such material conditions as their social class, educational level, gender, race, region, age, and the like. These, in turn, are predictive of different political positions and actions. In both instances, however, the symbolic and expressive dimensions of social life as well as the institutions that sustain them are, in the materialist epistemology that underlies them, basically "epiphenomenal" to the "real" dynamics of partisan power and economic privilege. Culture, then, is both *distinct from* economics and politics and *subordinate to* them. In this sense, politics is thought to be prior to culture—both in the sense of being determinative of and of greater importance than culture.[17]

On the Priority of Culture over Politics

I take a different approach that sees the symbolic and expressive elements of culture as fully integrated within and encompassing of the totality of human experience. Because language and the meanings it makes possible are constitutive of all human experience and activity, culture is also constitutive of life's patterns or "structures"—from the ordinary configurations of private life to the powerful institutional establishments of social life. Like the air we breathe, culture permeates all things human. The symbolic expressions of a culture provide a picture of the world, the logics by which it works, and thus the structure within which individual and collective action is interpreted and taken. In short, culture provides the means by which the world around us, in all of its complexity, is made comprehensible. It functions to orient human belief, thought, and action, both individually and collectively.

This means that the most materially "real" phenomena in human experience—not least a society's political economy—are themselves culturally constituted: they are underwritten by a culture's symbolically formulated assumptions, and they grow, ramify, and find sustenance through various organizational, linguistic, and imaginative resources. As the old platitude has it, there is no "outside" of culture. Culture is determinative precisely because it is definitional.

For this reason, culture is not separate from power. Rather, it is the most elemental form of power precisely because it possesses the capacity to define reality. Thus, it stands to reason that culture is not distinct from the economy—it is the centermost part of the economy, enabling the whole system and its parts to work. Likewise, culture is not and could not be separate from politics, for it is what makes politics intelligible because it provides the frameworks of meaning and understanding within which political institutions and political action make sense. Culture, then, is not prior to power because it is itself a form of power, but it is prior to politics. While it is true that politics is mainly about the use and administration of power, for it to be about more than power—for example, about justice or freedom or equality—it depends upon a realm that is relatively independent of politics. This is why, in the end, culture is prior to politics.[18]

By this account, if we find political solidarity within a regime, it is because it rests upon a cultural solidarity, a solidarity of at least some shared meanings and practices. *Mutatis mutandis*, if there is social and political conflict, culture is often the deepest part of that conflict—again, because culture is definitional, providing the terms by which conflicting interests and worldviews are defined. In sum, the political dynamics of a society always operate against a symbolic backdrop that frames the meaning of institutions and actors and, of course, the actions that take place among them.

Surface and Depth

In this more robust approach, culture operates at two (analytically distinct) levels.

On the surface, culture refers to ideas, values, beliefs, attitudes, ideals, tastes, ideologies, arguments, objects, and other artifacts of human society. It includes modes of symbolic expression that are observable, accessible, and more or less manipulable. What is distinctive about the surface of culture is that we are conscious and intentional about it. On the surface of culture, we have agency. We can talk about it, analyze it, build upon it, and destroy it. Both individually and collectively, we knowingly employ various symbolic resources to devise and enact strategies of action or to justify action, and we do so from within the most mundane parts of everyday life to the grand schemes generated by such major institutions as the government, the military, the corporation, the university, the hospital, and the like. It is precisely because culture at this level is observable and useable that this is what most people think about when they think about culture.

But culture operates below the surface as well.[19] Culture at its deepest level is the *implicit* order underneath the *apparent* order of things, and it typically manifests itself as the *unspoken* rules, schemas, and resources that organize the overall forms of linguistic—and by extension cultural—expression and practice.

Indeed, if the power of culture is the power to define reality, then the power of culture is measured by the degree to which its meanings are taken for granted. This is to say that the picture of the world that culture presents and the logics by which it operates are most powerful when they are buried within our collective unconscious. It doesn't fully matter whether our world-picture meets some rational criteria of internal coherence; the world seems to be that way to us—more or less rational, more or less coherent, more or less compelling. The world as we understand it is simply the world as it is. It doesn't need to be explained. Reality is simply given. It is self-evidently what it is.

To say that culture operates at an implicit level, then, is to recognize that it is not fully articulable. Culture, at this level, often takes shape in dispositions and sensibilities, sometimes a mood or a temperament that, in turn, provides the basis for inference, speculation, and conjecture. Thus, even if the world is not always explicitly interpreted, it doesn't need to be because we have a strong sense, rooted in our intuitions and dispositions, that it is interpretable.

Furthermore, culture at this deeper and implicit level is by no means formless; it has structure. Indeed, I would contend that the deep structures of culture provide *an implicit view* of the nature of *reality*, the nature of *knowledge* (how we come to know things), the nature of *human persons* with whom we live, the nature of our *social obligations*, and not least, the *ends toward which meaningful individual and collective action is oriented*. Every culture implicitly poses and addresses (in various ways) these proto-philosophical questions—the questions of metaphysics, epistemology, anthropology, ethics, and teleology.[20] The key word here is *implicit*. Few people are aware of such large labyrinthine puzzles, much less dwell upon them. Clearly, most people are not philosophers. Yet these are the categories that form the backdrop of the world within which individual and institutional actors live, work, and have their being. All civilizations (and in turn all social orders), whether they are aware of it or not, address these puzzles in one way or another. For each, they define *the background frameworks* of understanding, knowledge, interpretation, and imagination that frame *the foreground realities* of day-to-day life.

Mythos—The Story We Tell about Ourselves

Together these elements are woven into a shared and often implicit narrative or *mythos* that provides a loosely coherent account of the nature of the world, the nation's (or a group's or a people's) self-understanding, its common aims, purposes, and dreams, and the lives of its heroes and villains. *A mythos is the story that a people tells about itself—past, present, and future.* It is a story of collective self-understanding, but it is more than that. It also possesses the qualities that Charles Taylor has called a "social imaginary," or what Richard Weaver once called a "metaphysical dream of the world," an intuitive and integrative sense of the world, how it works, how everything fits into it, and the hopeful possibilities toward which it is moving.[21]

A mythos, then, is not defined by its historic accuracy or careful hewing to facts; indeed, the picture it presents of the world, however opaque or vivid, is largely beyond the reach of countervailing facts or perspectives. The power of a mythos—any mythos—is found in its resonance with experience, its coherence, and its practical effect—that is, its capacity to inspire, motivate, and mobilize people toward common ends, both immediate and long term. The mythos, while larger than politics and a background framework to politics, is also its animating vision because it provides the motivation and aspiration toward which collective life and its politics are oriented.

Cultural Logics

I use this term throughout this book. It manifests itself in the foreground of what is legible, but its force derives from the background of what is assumed.[22] Cultural logic is a kind of reasoning, but its standard is rarely internal consistency or cohesiveness or validity based upon empirically verifiable evidence. Rather, it is *a form of meaning-making* that is rooted in premises that cannot themselves be authenticated or validated. To those who operate within particular cultural logics, the world makes sense, as do the range of actions that follow from them.

To take a simple and obvious case: if you believe that there is a benevolent god-creator who is sovereign over life and history, then you will be compelled to follow the teachings of that god. Or, closer to earth, if a fetus is a human child as much as any newly born child, then it makes sense to oppose a law that gives legal sanction to abortion, and if a fetus is not, then it makes sense that there would be laws making abortion legal. Or, if you assume that the federal government is corrupt and the system is rigged against you, then it makes sense to oppose that system and its outcomes. And so on.

It is important to highlight that *what follows* those premises is, typically, a limited range of alternative ways of understanding or behaving. Given our picture of the world and the premises that make it real, we often cannot imagine any other ways of seeing the world or envisioning any alternative courses of action. This is to say that *cultural logics are logics of necessity.* At the level of experience, there is pressure or a compulsion or obligation to think or act in certain ways because we cannot see how it could be otherwise.

The Politics of Culture and the Culture of Politics

We can highlight a more robust view of public culture by drawing a further distinction between the "politics of culture" and the "culture of politics."[23]

The politics of culture refers to the contest of power over cultural issues. This would include the mobilization of parties and rank-and-file support, the organization of leadership, the formation of special-interest coalitions, and the manipulation of public rhetoric on matters reflecting the symbols or ideals at the heart of a group's collective purposes. This is what most people think about when they use the term *culture war.* In this case, the culture war is the accumulation of conflicts over issues like abortion, gay and transgender rights, church/state issues, funding for the humanities and arts, and so on. Though culture is implicated at every level, *the politics of culture is primarily about politics.*

The culture of politics, by contrast, is a nod toward the deep structures of culture. It refers to the symbolic environment within which political institutions are embedded and political action occurs. This symbolic environment is constituted by the implicit frameworks of meaning that make particular political arrangements understandable or incomprehensible, desirable or reprehensible. As Michael Oakeshott famously wrote, "While politics can give expression to and defend a particular social order, it cannot direct it. Political activity may have given us the Magna Carta and the Bill of Rights, but *it did not give us the contents of these documents, which came from a stratum of social thought far too deep to be influenced by the actions of politicians*."[24] These basic frameworks of implicit meaning constitute what I call the culture's "deep structure."[25] Without these deep structures, the form, function, and ideals of political institutions and practices simply do not make any sense. The culture war has also unfolded at this level.

Culture and Liberal Democracy

So it is with liberal democracy. Though there are conservative and progressive interpretations of this tradition, its ideational centerpiece is constituted by the premises and principles of individual and collective freedom and representative self-government. It further recognizes that a society is inherently diverse in its interests, ideas, values, and commitments, and yet it provides the mechanisms for addressing these differences in ways that can lead to common goods. Indeed, it valorizes those differences in order to prevent any one set of interests or ideologies from dominating others.

And yet, following Oakeshott, politics did not invent the value of individual freedom or the idea of representative self-government. Neither did it create the value of toleration or the hope of a common good in the midst of highly divisive differences. Nor did politics generate the concepts of justice, equality, equity, decency, civility, or the temperament to long for these things. These too came from a stratum of social thought far too deep to be influenced by the actions of politicians. It is that deeper "stratum of social thought" that mainly interests me here.

It is obvious to everyone that the surface manifestations of late eighteenth-century American culture are very different from present-day culture. This is also true (even if not as obvious) as it bears on the deeper manifestations of culture. It only follows, then, that the nature of solidarity has changed as well. But rarely without a fight.

That tension and conflict are built into the paradox of America's national motto: *E Pluribus Unum*, Out of Many, One. Americans like to say that they enthusiastically affirm diversity—the *pluribus*—but diversity always has limits or *boundaries that demarcate the lines of inclusion and exclusion*. The boundaries of "tolerable difference" have evolved over decades and centuries. Chapter 2 explores the nature of "boundary work," both how boundaries are drawn and maintained and how they are contested and ultimately change. Chapter 3 explores the substance of solidarity, of which there are two kinds. One kind is *negative solidarity*, a coming together born in reaction to the presence of an enemy or, perhaps, in response to a crisis. The nation coming together after the 9/11 attacks is an obvious illustration of this. It is a powerful form of solidarity, but it tends to be ephemeral, as it was in 2001. There is also *affirmative solidarity*, which is a solidarity of common understanding and common affections. Fourth of July parades and Memorial Day remembrances held in towns and cities across the country are meant to be rituals of affirmative solidarity. Political theorists have discussed affirmative solidarity at a "meta" level for quite some time, but while of great importance in its own right, the subtext of this academic debate is about how thick or thin common beliefs or affections need to be and how explicit the articulations of those affirmations need to be. In times of stability, people take commonalities for granted. The habits of political thought and practice are enough. But in times of crisis there is always a need for the giving of reasons—given explicitly and given publicly. The legitimacy of any governing authority depends upon it. So what are they?

Part III: "Working Through" America's Hybrid Enlightenment

Historical Reflections

The aim of this book, in a nutshell, is to provide an account of the deeper cultural sources, how they have been "worked through" over the generations to address successive challenges, and where this long and difficult process has led us to today.

The story begins with the Enlightenment itself as a historically contingent cultural revolution that provided the cultural infrastructure for modern liberal democracy. It provided the sources out of which were forged an ethical vision for the reconstitution and reformation of public life. Across the disparities found in its French, Scottish, and German expressions, the common thread of the Enlightenment was that the standards of truth, justice, and rationality were universal and therefore generally available to all reasonable persons. Through the light of reason, these standards would be so apparent that no rational human being could deny their authority.[26]

In America, the strata of social thought that underwrote liberal democracy took shape as a hybrid-Enlightenment, a blending of cultural sources that drew from many different tributaries of thought and practice. As an ethical ideal, the hybrid-Enlightenment was generative and powerful, to be sure, but also greatly flawed.

I argue that within the deep and surface structures of American political culture, there were profound contradictions that have laid bare the inadequacies of America's hybrid-Enlightenment as a source of liberal democratic solidarity. So much of the story to renew democracy since its founding is a story of the effort to revise, reconstitute, and revivify the hybrid-Enlightenment and the cultural logics that have rendered liberal democracy intelligible and coherent, even against its own weaknesses, contradictions, and failures. I call this a process of "working through" culture.

The largest part of this book is the historical narrative. It begins in chapters 4 and 5 with a sketch of the contours of the hybrid-Enlightenment. Drawing as much from Calvinism as it did from classical Republicanism and Lockean individualism, it was a complex and fairly thick cosmology from which a powerful and generative mythos would take shape. Yet it was also deeply contradictory. It would fuel a century of nation-building, but it also deepened the contradictions by doubling down on the boundaries of exclusion, most egregiously against the aboriginal tribes of the continent and African-born slaves, but also against Roman Catholics, Mormons, and Jews.

But this is just the start of a story that continues in chapters 6 through 10, running through the Civil War and its aftermath in the dissolution of the "Christian Republic," the secular turn of the Progressive Era in the early decades of the twentieth century, mid-twentieth-century humanism, and the evolving culture wars of the late twentieth and early twenty-first centuries to the present. Along the way, the hybrid-Enlightenment was worked through again and again in ways that changed it dramatically, yet also in ways that were entirely recognizable with its past. Through tension and conflict, the boundaries of inclusiveness in America did slowly expand while still somehow maintaining enough solidarity across its differences.

There are clear signs, however, that we are now in a period of exhaustion. The endlessly worked-through sources of the hybrid-Enlightenment are depleted and no longer have traction. For some, those sources have been forgotten. For others, they have been distorted beyond recognition to serve partisan interests. For still others, they are seen as *the* fundamental problem with America. No matter the case, they have unraveled as sources of solidarity.

Part IV: Late-Stage Democracy

This doesn't mean that all solidarity has disappeared or that everything has fallen apart. Far from it.

Making Sense of Our Current Dilemma

As I argue at the start of chapter 11, solidarity, in part, remains in localities across the nation. Despite their differences, people in neighborhoods, towns, and cities *are* working together to get things done and to solve common problems.

Even at the national level, there is still a solidarity rooted in the procedures of law and the Constitution that competing sides, even if reluctantly, still abide by. These have been sorely tested in recent times, most notably through the Trump years and their aftermath, but so far they have proven to be more or less resilient. What the Trump years did was to reveal just how fragile this kind of solidarity actually is.

It is also true that many Americans recognize the problem and have rolled up their sleeves to do something about it. There are literally hundreds of ambitious initiatives, mostly local in character, that seek to address polarization and the absence of solidarity in American public life. Organizations such as Stand Together, Bridge the Divide, and Reunited States all seek to bring ordinary citizens together to mend the deep divisions in the nation. The problem is the massive chasm between the local and the national and between the hopes of ordinary citizens and the institutional interests of activists and leaders. Against the forces of powerful national organizations and the new communications technologies, it is not likely that citizen initiatives will make much headway. The corrosive and polarizing discourse of national life has already seeped into the discourse of local life, and that seepage is likely to continue.

Solidarity remains and goodwill can be found everywhere. But it is also clear that the hybrid-Enlightenment as the evolving source of much of America's solidarity has unraveled at its deepest levels, and we have not yet seen the full consequences of that development. This leaves us with fundamental questions about the very possibility of liberal democracy in our time.

The Dilemma Restated

So here is our dilemma: if, in fact, the frameworks of meaning and interpretation and the cultural logics that defined the hybrid-Enlightenment in turn created the conditions for the birth of liberal democracy and, in some debatable measure, have sustained it over time, what now? What happens when those frameworks of meaning lose their authority? *Can an Enlightenment-era political institution— liberal democracy—survive and thrive in a post-Enlightenment culture?* Is there anything from the hybrid-Enlightenment project that remains? That is salvageable or renewable? What, if anything, can be reconstructed from this deconstructed culture? Or, if (for some) salvaging the hybrid-Enlightenment project is neither possible (sociologically) nor desirable (politically or ethically), then what cultural resources will sustain liberal democracy going forward?[27]

The answers to these questions are not obvious. Neither is it obvious that there *are* answers. We have long wanted to believe not only in the durability and stability of American democratic institutions but also in their long-term vitality. Democracy in America has survived for two and a half centuries, meeting and mediating severe disruptions to the social order along the way. Why shouldn't it survive well into the future?

Perhaps it will, but in no way is this guaranteed.

The assumption of the enduring vitality of liberal democracy in

America is challenged not only by the unraveling of the deep structures of the hybrid-Enlightenment, but also by what appears to be
filling the void.

Underneath the polarization a different common culture has
emerged, but tragically not one that fosters unity. Rather, it is one
that, by its nature, turns in on itself and destroys. It is a culture of
nihilism, driven by a cultural logic of *ressentiment*, a narrative of injury that seeks revenge through a will to power. Its negations lead, as
Philip Rieff put it, to "a nothingness that can be both radical and
reactionary at the same time."[28]

As we see all around us, the challenge of maintaining a meaningful and effective governing under these conditions is difficult, if not
impossible. Add to this the multiple crises of global poverty, rogue
states with nuclear weapons, climate change, mass immigration, an
increasingly unstable international order, and the like, and the stakes
are high indeed.

The Ongoing Experiment

From its earliest years, American democracy was understood as a
"grand experiment" in constructing a *novel* political order upon a *new*
foundation.[29] American democracy, then, was an exercise in hope—
hope that the world and the lot of ordinary people could be made
different and better through a liberal democratic political order. Yet
experiments can fail, and hopes can be dashed. The contention of
this book is that we are at a moment when the answer to the fundamental question about the vitality and longevity of liberal democracy can no longer be assumed—though not because we are polarized, but because we no longer have the cultural resources to work
through what divides us.

PART II

E Pluribus Unum?

CHAPTER TWO

The Boundaries of Solidarity

A T THE HEART OF our dilemma is a tension reflected in America's national motto: *E Pluribus Unum.* Out of Many, One. How, exactly, does that work? What kind and how much diversity—the *pluribus*, the many—is possible while still maintaining some kind of oneness or commonality—the *unum*—that defines our solidarity? And commonality on what terms? Where do we, in our vast differences, find commonality and, in turn, solidarity?

Diversity and Its Limits

In any society, difference is a given and it is irreducible. And while this is true, it is equally true that in any society there are limits to the difference that society is willing or able to tolerate.

Let me put it differently. Every civilization, every society, every social group—without exception—draws *boundaries*, boundaries between what people love and hate, approve of and disapprove of, countenance and oppose, and on the basis of those boundaries, determines whom we recognize and include and whom we exclude within those groups, societies, or civilizations—those we adulate, accept, or at least tolerate, and those we find more or less repugnant and therefore reject.[1]

The boundaries that both unite us and divide us are rooted in what we judge or at least imagine to be good or bad, acceptable or unacceptable, decent or indecent, safe or dangerous—moral judgments that are comprehensive without being consciously so. The range of things to which these judgments can be applied are infinite—they can be various ideas, beliefs, or values (for example, religious theologies or political ideologies) or social and economic interests (such as degrees of wealth or poverty) or physical attributes (such as racial and ethnic attributes or physical disabilities) or social practices (like dietary habits) or places of origin (countries or regions of ancestry).

Boundaries are a given and inescapable because they are *constitutive of identity*—it is through the drawing of boundaries that we are defined and define ourselves. This is to say that both personal and collective identity presuppose a clear differentiation from others. Thus, membership in *any* group, whether a family, a religious organization, a club, a political party, or a nation, presumes that others are not members. It only stands to reason that activities that are acts of social inclusion are, at the same time, acts of social exclusion. In short, all civilizations, all societies, all social groups, to one extent or another, have a certain "tribal" character by virtue of what they cherish and abhor, embrace and reject, and these things shape the way in which they regard and treat those who think or believe or act or value or look differently.

Just as the drawing of boundaries is universal in every human society, community, institution, and group, so too is *boundary work*. Boundary work is simply another term for social control—the means by which order and cohesion in a society or group are maintained; in practical terms, boundary work is how wayward, unruly, recalcitrant, or transgressive members of a group or society are brought back into conformity. Its most obvious manifestations are in law: those who break the law violate the formal rules or boundaries of a society or community and, when caught, they are subject to legal consequences as a way of both bringing rebellious members back within the boundaries of legal acceptability and of warning others what will happen to them if they too breach the boundaries. Depending on the nature of the violation, the lawbreaker pays a fine, is put on probation, is sent to jail, or in the extreme, is put to death.

In the realm of culture (narrowly defined), the process is the same: those who transgress its boundaries are punished to bring them back into the fold and to be an example to others of what happens if they do the same. Culture and the law do overlap, but because culture also involves the *informal* rules or boundaries of acceptability and unacceptability—what scholars in the field call mores, customs, codes, traditions, and the like—the penalties for breaching boundaries also range: from shunning and ostracism to ridicule and shaming to scolding and reprimand to torture and death.

Infamous cases of the most extreme forms of boundary work are too numerous to mention, but they are illustrative of the principle. Thus, early in Western history, one thinks of the 1486 Catholic theological treatise *Malleus Maleficarum*—the "Hammer of Witches"—which elevated sorcery and witchcraft to the criminal status of heresy and endorsed the torture and extermination of witches as the most effective remedy for witchcraft. Early Puritan settlers in America, of course, had their own version of this in the late seventeenth century, in what is popularly known as the Salem witch trials, in which thirty were found guilty and nineteen were executed. Other cases are found in the often-brutalizing legacy of the Congregation for the Doctrine of the Faith, an office founded by the papacy in 1542 for the purpose of defending the Church from heresy.[2] And when American colonists Anne Hutchinson and Roger Williams challenged the leading ideas of the Puritan divines in the 1630s, they were, predictably, banished for the crime of heresy and sedition. Boundary work can be bloody business.

Lest anyone imagine that harsh measures of social control are the province only of the passionately religious, there are innumerable cases on the equally passionate secular left. Prominently, one can recount the torture and murder of Rosa Luxemburg and Karl Liebknecht in 1919, the imprisonment of Antonio Gramsci in 1926, and the exile and eventual murder of Leon Trotsky in Mexico in 1940 with an ice axe in his head. And then, of course, there are the Stalinist purges of the mid-1930s, in which at least 750,000 dissenting members of the Communist Party were executed and more than a million others were sent off to the gulags. The effort to discredit and defame alleged Communists in the McCarthy-era purges in the United States in the 1950s were mild by comparison, of course, but damaging to those who endured it.

Boundary work plays out in international affairs: most obviously in war, but also in the various sanctions—economic, military, and diplomatic—those nations impose upon one another. It is ubiquitous in national politics in the ways that each party seeks to punish, embarrass, discredit, or coerce the other and its individual representatives.

It is also pervasive in the actions of every social movement that has ever existed. In our world today, is this not the meaning of "political correctness" and "cancel culture"? They are simply tools of social control that function to police the boundaries of competing moral and political visons of collective life. Conservative judicial decisions or legislative acts in favor of restrictions on abortion, transgender bathrooms, or gay marriage have been powerful impediments to progressive interests just as the potential for being labeled a racist or sexist or a homophobe is a powerful deterrent against violating the progressive norms of equity. Movements even do boundary work on their own people, as evident in the purging of moderate Republicans from leadership of the party in recent times or the exclusion of gay police in gay pride celebrations.

Boundary work is ubiquitous because it is inherent in the nature and maintenance of any and all social orders. It is the means by which ideas or people are included or excluded from the group. People can pride themselves on being tolerant and inclusive, but toleration and inclusivity always operate within a certain limited range. People can celebrate diversity, but the diversity they celebrate is always proscribed by certain parameters. There are always some people and some ideas that are outside the bounds of how a culture defines what is "normal," "tasteful," "reasonable," "truthful," "ethical," "believable"—and therefore allowable. And because boundaries are never permanent, but rather constantly challenged and contested, people who may be on the "right side" of social consensus one day may find themselves on the "wrong side" another day.

Boundary Work and Democracy

At a deeper level, boundary work has the more important function of maintaining the solidarity and cohesion of the group or institution or society and reaffirming the authority of those who draw the boundaries—whether that authority is of the pope, priests, or clergy, of the führer, the supreme leader, the *generalissimos*, of the courts, the commissars, the managers, the bureaucrats, the technocrats, or even the authority of the mob.

Culturally speaking, the rudimentary puzzle of democracy is determining how expansive those boundaries of difference and inclusion should be and—given the ways that difference often provides the preconditions of conflict—*defining the terms of solidarity capable of uniting us in spite of our differences. E Pluribus Unum* is an inspiring national motto, to be sure, but it has always been easier said than done.

Easier said than done because it is constantly contested and evolving. Especially in the modern and now late modern world, the *pluribus* expands, seemingly without end. Moreover, there is increasing fluidity of the values, roles, attachments, networks, tastes, and interests that constitute the boundaries of social life in the first place. For many, there is a liberation that comes from the weakening of the bonds of social and ethical commitment, but liberation is often accompanied by confusion and uncertainty.

Working Through the Contradictions

All of this bears on the puzzle of understanding the boundaries of solidarity that underwrite liberal democracy in America. That culture in its deep structures is, of course, continuous within the bounds of history. Yet its boundaries have always been contested and with that contestation has come change. The evolution of the deep structures of culture occurs for many reasons, not least of which are the sheer contingencies of history and human action. Yet in America, they have also changed in response to contradictions present within the nation's own cultural logics.

The fundamental contradiction at the root of American democracy is, on the one hand, the promise that all are created equal, but then, on the other, the practice of excluding wide swaths of humanity. Lines have been drawn and reinforced that have included some and notoriously rejected others. These lines have, most notably, excluded African Americans, but also Native Americans, certain religious communities, immigrants from various parts of the world, the poor and working classes, women, and so on. The fundamental historical challenge of American democracy has been to overcome those contradictions on terms that nevertheless maintain some level of unity, comity, and solidarity.

Durcharbeiten as Boundary Work

But how? As I have noted, the story I want to tell here is one of how, over time, the cultural logics of the Enlightenment in America have been successively worked through to achieve new interpretations of itself. Solidarity and its cultural sources, then, are by no means static.

The term *working through* loosely derives from psychoanalytic theory and I employ it analogically—not literally, of course, but to show how cultural processes parallel the psychoanalytic. So what does it refer to?

Sigmund Freud introduced the concept of durcharbeiten, the process of "working through," to describe the efforts a patient makes in order to become aware of, confront, and ultimately overcome repressed memories and experiences that hinder healthy ego development.[3] Although in psychotherapy, hypnosis can be an effective technique in bringing to light repressed memories, in the end, hypnosis circumvents those repressions rather than taking them on directly. In other words, at its best hypnosis can identify the trauma but it cannot address it therapeutically. It's just a first step.

By contrast, "working through" is a conscious and deliberate process that entails what Freud calls "a will to remember" and ultimately a will to overcome and remedy damage done. The process is done not by the patient alone but rather dialectically, through interaction with a therapist. Invariably, there is pushback and resistance, even to the point that the patient acts out the pathology, even on the therapist him- or herself. Needless to say, the process of working through repressed memories of trauma does not happen quickly or all at once. It takes time and, as I say, it can get very unpleasant. But ideally, the end of all of this effort is a new framework of self-understanding achieved by working through besetting problems of the past as a way of confronting the present and future. The process is "arduous" and conflictual, but if successful, the ego is refashioned in ways that are not perfect, to be sure, but healthier all the same. As a process, it "effects the greatest changes in the patient."[4]

In a similar way, long-standing contradictions (by rough anal-

ogy, the *trauma*) inherent within a cultural logic (*ego*) eventually challenge the coherence of the mythos (*self-understanding*) that cultural
logic has created. The contradictions themselves generate "a course
which cannot be avoided nor always hastened."[5] The plausibility and
legitimacy of that mythos are finally undermined, creating a crisis
within traditional understandings of collective life. The crisis is one
of interpretation, typically between the interests of those wanting to
maintain and those wanting to challenge the dominant mythos. Out
of this dialectic, older cultural understandings are worked through
to address and overcome those contradictions. Over time, *the past,
with all its problems, is made intelligible in light of the present and the
present is made comprehensible in historically recognizable ways.* In this
way, older and established ways of seeing and interpreting collective
life are not lost—indeed, they are retained—but they come to mean
something different. In its net effect, the boundaries of tolerable and
intolerable are reconstituted. The line between inclusion and exclusion shifts or is redrawn.

It is important to note that none of this unfolds in ways that
quickly resolve conflict. More often than not conflict persists, especially if resolution is forced through law or the coercive power of the
state. In such instances, there is an attempt by partisans to impose an
ethical reckoning on a social order whose institutions have not integrated the terms of that reckoning in its patterns of thought and
practice and thus whose populace has not had the time to make those
patterns of thought and practice its own. All sorts of distortions can
follow.

As Theodor Adorno reflected on the catastrophe of National
Socialism in Germany from 1933 to 1945, the process of working
through is emphatically not to "close the books on the past" or "to
remove it from memory" altogether.[6] But he also saw the ways in
which history was reinterpreted to downplay the malevolence of the
regime and its innumerable atrocities: "The terribly real past is triv-
ialized into merely a figment of the imagination." In addition, he witnessed a kind of performative process of working through displayed
in dishonest psychological reactions—surely including a "fictitious
guilt," but also "defensive postures where one is not attacked, intense
affects where they are hardly warranted by the situation, an absence
of affect in the face of the gravest matters, not seldom simply a re-

pression of what is known or half-known." Ultimately, the failure to
work through the past of National Socialism in Adorno's day was
due to an inability to address the conditions that created it in the
first place, for in his view, "the past will have been worked through
only when the causes of what happened . . . have been eliminated."
In this, Adorno remained hopeful, to be sure, but also perhaps naïve.

Working Through as Sociology

As Freud and Adorno make clear, the process of working through
the historic contradictions—psychologically and institutionally—is
far from an academic exercise. Against the temptation to see history
exclusively through the lens of ideas, one must never forget that ideas
are always situated in relational and institutional contexts, both limited and empowered by the financial, organizational, and social network resources available. It is here where we see the often-grubby
dynamics of competition over status, economic interest, legal privilege, state power, and the like play out. In short, ideas are *always*
situated within cultural economies, and the success or failure of any
particular set of ideas is largely determined by the outcome of the
conflict over competing cultural economies and the interests that
drive them. This means that durcharbeiten is not just a process of
"collective psychology," as in a working through of the broadly shared
attitudes and opinions of a people over time, but a sociological process involving the interplay of large institutional forces, the leadership and resources they constitute, and the narratives that justify
their actions in the world.

The dynamics by which cultures work through their contradictions historically and sociologically, then, are enacted by individual
and organizational actors operating within different social and institutional arenas. A central part of this story thus plays out in an interaction *among* elites as well as *between* elites, the institutions they lead
or represent, and their publics (in this case, the general citizenry).

Intellectuals as Leading Cultural Indicators

Intellectuals, *broadly defined,* are thus an especially important part
of this story. I take the category of "intellectuals" inclusively here as

those who have a disproportionate capacity to define and shape the symbolic universe of a community or society. Theirs is the power of articulacy. They certainly would include scholars, journalists, lawyers, judges, the clergy, movement activists, and educators as well as leaders in business, philanthropy, politics, and the like who have a significant public platform for addressing the affairs of the day. In this very broad sense, intellectuals include all those who generate, intellectualize, translate, and promote ideas about the ordering of the social and political world. These actors matter because they have a disproportionate capacity to interpret the world for others. Out of their influence, they provide the reasons for the granting or withholding of legitimacy to the powers that be. Authority, as John Patrick Diggins once put it, represents the intellectual expression of power, and the problem of authority remains the problem of men and women of ideas.[7]

There are among them, however, those who are particularly noteworthy for their insight into the deeper cultural issues implicit in the challenges we face and for their ability to make them explicit. As I mentioned in the preface, throughout the story I tell here, I highlight many of these figures, some well known—Adams, Jefferson, Douglass, Dewey, Niebuhr, Lippmann, and King, for example, and others who may be less so—David Walker, Angelina Grimké, Phoebe Palmer, Richard Neuhaus, and Richard Rorty, among others. In their moment in history, they understood with uncommon clarity the contradictions inherent within liberal democracy and, from their unique perspective, gave voice to what was at stake. Their insight and power of articulation made them critical to the process of working through these stubborn contradictions. For good or ill, they were all engaged in the boundary work of pushing out, narrowing, or simply defending lines of inclusion and exclusion. For the purposes of my account, these observers and the speech acts for which they are known also help us see the thread of continuity in the changing cultural undercurrents animating liberal democracy. In this respect, we can see them as something akin to leading cultural indicators.

Cultural Economies

The efficacy of the authority that movements claim and the success of the boundary work in which they are engaged are measured by the degree to which the claims made by those in power or who aspire to power, as well as the justifications they give for the use of power, are received by the public as self-evidently real and true. This is made possible in part by the persuasiveness of the ideas, but perhaps even more so by the scale, effectiveness, and stability of the cultural economy that surrounds and promulgates those ideas—the dense networks of individuals and institutions (the writers, editors, newspapers, tracts, publishing houses, television production companies, public relations and advertising firms, social media outlets, and so on) that produce and popularize a particular world-picture and turn it into everyday practice.

When citizens regard a political system as legitimate, public and political stability follow. There may be irritability, complaint, and protest, but citizens will generally consent and comply with decisions made. Things get done. When citizens distrust their government, are cynical of their leaders' motives, or feel alienated from the political system that rules them, at the very least, it becomes difficult to address basic political problems. Over time, these are the circumstances that lead to conflict.

This is, of course, where American public culture has been moving for quite some time. It is polarized not only in its values and beliefs or in its competing world-pictures. This is obvious enough. It is also polarized by competing cultural economies that sustain those contested beliefs, values, and world-pictures. The polarization of different cultural infrastructures, then, entrenches and sustains the polarization of values and beliefs, creating the conditions where the legitimacy and authority of any governing rule or reigning administration—whatever it happens to be—are permanently delegitimized.

Only on the surface, then, is the question of the "center" or the "unum" a question of public opinion or of the arithmetic mean of popular sentiment on particular issues at any particular time. At its deepest levels, it is a question of authority, and less formal authority than informal authority, less the formal structures of authority than the framework of reality and moral good upon which those structures are based. Mediating all these cultural dynamics are the organizational and institutional dynamics of a cultural economy, and if this is contested, so will everything else.

In Sum

The questions, once again, are: What are the boundaries of tolerable difference? Who is and who is not included within that background consensus? Despite many differences, who is recognized as a legitimate participant in the work of collective solidarity and who is not?

The process of sorting these questions out is inherently conflictual, involving powerful institutions, interests, and egos. Yet, as we will see, the resolution is rarely found in law or politics alone or, even less, in the exertions of raw power, state-sanctioned or otherwise, even though in contemporary times it tends to be the strategy of first choice among the key actors involved. The consequences of the attempt to resolve boundary matters through law or brute force are very often and unintentionally tragic or at least counterproductive to the ends these actors hope to achieve. Such means create the appearance of change when little substantive change may have actually taken place; thus, it may create only a simulacrum of solidarity when real solidarity is a long way from being realized.

CHAPTER THREE

The Sources of Solidarity

THE IDEA OF A set of shared understandings and sensibilities that contains our differences and disagreements is not a tired formulary but a basic requirement of democratic life. However bitterly polarized disputes over certain policy issues may be and however ideologically, economically, or racially factionalized we as a people may become, any kind of meaningful democratic politics presupposes at least some minimally shared understandings and commitments that are prior to political action.

Solidarity, Not Consensus

Yet here let me be clear: I am not at all suggesting these shared understandings require a formal consensus over policy questions, the kind measured daily by public opinion polls. The American people have always been divided about such things. Solidarity, as I say, is a richer term than mere consensus. Where consensus suggests conscious and deliberate assent, what more typically binds us together in solidarity is the complex interweaving of the rational, affective, psychic, and sociological elements of human experience, things that cannot always be put into words. At some level, it would include some common ideas or ideals, but it would also include such intangibles as intersubjective resonance and intuition, things that are at least every bit as affective as they are cognitive. Altogether, these elements provide sources of a common recognition, a sense of "we-ness" or "us-ness" that carries with it an element of mutual obligation. Solidarity in this more capacious sense defines a *framework of cohesion within which legitimate political debate, discourse, and action take place.*

But what is that framework?

Negative Solidarity: The Uses of a "Good Enemy"

It is a commonplace of social theory that solidarity can be generated through *shared opposition* to something, someone, some group, or some idea that is seen as hostile. In opposing an adversary—whether real, exaggerated, manufactured, or imagined—communities are drawn together and are united as a collectivity. In the process, a clarity is achieved about those ideals or characteristics that make one's group distinctive and admirable and one's opponent and adversary repugnant and therefore intolerable. In short, identity and solidarity are reinforced through antagonism and resistance. These dynamics are especially important during times of social and political change when the boundaries that define shared identity are blurred and ambiguous. Social groups uncertain about who they are, are "reminded" by their participation in acts of collective opposition to a threat, whether internal to the group or external. The "latent functionality," as sociologists say, of standing together to oppose or punish an adversary is a ritual reaffirmation of the community's identity in the face of what may be a far greater adversary, its own internal moral disintegration. In fact, during times of cultural uncertainty, communities may even fabricate a threat to their existence or well-being just to oppose it. Solidarity always depends, at least in part, upon a "good enemy."

"Negative solidarity," then, is a common feature of social life, and it plays an integral role in its history. In the ongoing struggle to define America—what it has been, what it is, and what it should be—there have been an array of reliably "good" enemies. The presence and imperial ambitions of King George III were of critical importance in uniting the colonists in their struggle for independence. Hostility toward the aboriginal tribes of North America was essential (or so it was thought) to unity in the national mission of westward expansion. The swaggering militarism of Kaiser Wilhelm II and the German armies proved a worthy enemy uniting America and its allies during World War I, as were Hitler, Mussolini, and Hirohito and their armies during World War II. Not least, the global ambitions of the Soviet Union during the Cold War brought most factions in American political life together over the last half of the twentieth century. With the attack on the World Trade Center and the Pentagon on September 11, 2001, Americans came together again— even if only briefly—in their shared hostility to Islamic radicalism. The same can be said of how Americans came together in opposition to the Russian invasion of Ukraine in 2022, as did, of course, a large number of nations in NATO. Negative solidarity can be very powerful.

So much so that even when there are no plausible external enemies, social groups tend to find them internally, among themselves. In American history this dynamic has also been prominent. Groups that have been viewed as pariah people, such as Blacks, Catholics, Jews, Asians, and Muslims, all, at various times and in various ways, represented the "enemy within" and thus opposition to these groups at different points in time served the same function of generating and sustaining collective solidarity among many of the country's white and Protestant inhabitants. So too did those Communists who had purportedly infiltrated the American government in the 1950s. Racism and bigotry in American history also served the purposes of negative solidarity.

Fear and loathing, then, are effective sources of solidarity and can provide a framework through which political discourse and action can take place. Yet negative solidarity is always limited in its effectiveness. Absent any other shared beliefs and commitments, not to mention shared affections and hopes, it will be a weak framework and, more often than not, ephemeral, lasting only so long as an enemy seems a threat.

The great virtue of an enemy and the solidarity it does generate is that it can remind people of what values, ideals, and convictions they *do* embrace and are willing to defend, yet there have to be at least *some* positive, community-affirming ideas or sympathies that people share in common.

Affirmative Solidarity—Common Understandings, Common Loves

What kind? They can run the gamut. At one end of a continuum, they might include a binding consensus over certain ideals that define the identity and aspirations of the political regime. At the other end, there would be agreements over the administrative processes, procedures, and rituals that mediate political action. It is upon these agreements—however simple or elaborate, substantive or procedural—that social and political solidarity in democratic life is found and through which it evolves.

The various kinds of shared understandings talked about in America have been wide ranging. In popular terms, these understandings have been collectively referred to as "the American dream." In scholarly treatises, this has been framed as "the American creed," America's "civil religion," America's "public philosophy," and "the vital center." In narrower, legal-rational terms, it has been discussed in terms of the binding power of the Constitution. Each of these ideas implicitly conveys an ethical ideal for the composition of public life. Yet importantly, each of these terms is also opaque enough for people in all of their diversity to read their own beliefs into them. At the same time, they are symbolically promising enough for people in their diversity to find them compelling. In these ways and over many generations, these terms have taken on a life of their own.

The Nature and Constitution of the "Unum"

The importance of *some* shared understandings that ground *some* basic agreements at the source of democratic vitality has been recognized from the beginning. After all, the Constitution of the United States begins with "*We*, the People." Its preamble goes on to explain the logic of why it was essential to formalize those agreements into the nation's Founding document: in short, it was "to form a more perfect *Union*, establish *Justice*, ensure domestic *Tranquility*, provide for the *common defence*, promote the *general Welfare*, and secure the Blessings of *Liberty to ourselves and our Posterity*." The aspirational goods that democracy was to ensure were understood to be *shared in common*. As a legal formulation of those aspirational goods, the Constitution was singularly important.

Yet the Founders also knew that while important, such a document was, as Madison put it in Federalist 48, but a "parchment barrier" to tyranny without the beliefs and commitments of the new nation's citizens. Law rested upon some shared normative understandings. In the early years of the Republic, it was widely thought that "the only foundation of a free constitution is pure virtue" (Adams); that "virtue or morality is a necessary spring of popular government" (Washington); and that it was a "chimerical idea" that "any form of government will secure liberty or happiness without any virtue in the people" (Madison).[1] This still seemed true a generation after the Founding period when Tocqueville argued, "There is no country in the world in which everything can be provided for by the laws, or in which political institutions can prove a substitute for common sense and public morality," and "Morality is the best security of law and the surest pledge of freedom."[2]

In today's world, such statements are red meat for certain political actors who might hope to force such sentiments ham-fistedly into public policy and educational practice. At the very least, people don't talk that way anymore, and many appear not to believe that way either. More profoundly, a word like *virtue* would have little real meaning to any group of political actors today. Maybe the problem is as simple as that, but I doubt it. The reason is, of course, that cultural history never repeats itself and thus *we are left with the question of what possible shared normative understandings and agreements are required, much less possible, today for a functioning, if not vital, democracy.* Out of many, one. But what is it that makes us one? What, if any, are the cords that hold us together? Are there any shared understandings that transcend our differences, binding us together?

An Old Academic Debate with Real and Current Political Consequences

Political theorists have devoted a great deal of work to asking about the nature of the unum, the commonality among citizens that makes democracy possible. But what is the nature and constitution of that agreement and how much agreement is necessary? The academic discussion has drawn in the most significant political philosophers of our time—among them, figures such as John Rawls, Jürgen Habermas, Charles Taylor, Richard Rorty, Judith Shklar, Seyla Behabib, Ronald Dworkin, Michael Sandel, Chantal Mouffe, and many others. The literature is, as one would expect, voluminous. It can also be esoteric.[3]

The long-standing academic debate is worth lingering over for a moment. Theory represents an abstract ordering of reality, and while the abstractions of political theory rarely translate precisely into public discourse, those abstractions have implications for it all the same. What are always lost in the move from academic to public discourse are the nuances, the fine lines of distinction and disagreement made by political philosophers themselves. Yet out of these intellectualizations and out of the debates that produce them emerge the broad categories by which judges judge, politicians contend, civic leaders lead, and young people are formed as citizens. Just as important, *these debates are themselves expressions of culture and as such reflect broader historical dynamics within political life*. Political theory, in short, is a cultural artifact and needs to be understood as such.

It is important to note upfront that this is an evolving debate. There is now a major innovation in this field that will be an important part of my argument later on in this essay. But for much of the past century, there were roughly three relatively distinct camps of political theory on this question, with each camp holding a number of distinctive views and positions that sometimes modify and sometimes extend these orientations. In short, the academic debate takes place within a lumpy continuum between "foundationalism" and "proceduralism," with "communitarianism" somewhere in the middle.

FOUNDATIONALISM

Although *foundationalism* is marginal in the modern academy, it has been the default theory of political legitimacy for most of human history. Foundationalists believe that all governing regimes depend for their legitimacy on an authority that transcends politics. For some, this authority is a god or gods; for others, a permanent human nature or the laws of nature itself; for others still, the dictates of universal reason. What all these authorities have in common is that they are not chosen by human political actors but are, rather, self-justifying. They provide a standard of justice or basis for a vision of the common good that looms over the political process, holding a regime's decisions and actions to account. For foundationalists, then, only those regimes that conform to these rudimentary claims of God or reason or human nature or nature itself are legitimate.

There is considerable variation within the foundationalist camp, most of it ranging within a theological spectrum. It figures most prominently, of course, on the theological right, such as one would find in political Islam, of which Iran is a prominent example.[4] In the Western tradition, there is no equivalent to Shari'a, and those within the Christian tradition who approximate these views today are few in number and extremely marginal.[5] Yet foundationalist themes can also be found on the theological left as well as within mainstream Christian political theology.[6] On the political left, there are Marxists who believe that society should be founded on the truth embodied in absolute historical laws and emancipatory anthropology. Marxists who believe in democracy think that these truths can be realized democratically, through the expression of the will and interests of the masses as they create the conditions for a pure Communism.

And yet the mainstream of foundationalist political thinking within politically liberal societies is found in the natural law tradition. The new natural law theory developed by the Catholic philosophers John Finnis, Germain Gabriel Grisez, Joseph Boyle, and Robert George provides a relatively broad and generic set of normative principles that its proponents argue are independent of the reasoner, true by nature. As Finnis put it, "Moral norms are a matter of objective reasonableness, not of whim, convention, or mere 'decision.'"[7] These principles are legitimate and authoritative because they are embedded in the natural order and are accessible to anyone by thinking clearly. More recent natural law advocates like to quote a maxim favored by two old natural lawyers, Saints Augustine and Thomas Aquinas: *Lex iniusta non est lex*, an unjust law is not a law. If a government's decrees violate the natural law, citizens should disregard them.

At the same time, because the principles derived from natural law are relatively few in number and lack specificity, human reason is invariably implicated. The world in its complexity must be interpreted. Legislators, then, very typically find themselves without any fully specified moral norm to guide them and therefore have to exercise their own powers of practical reason to determine what sort of law satisfies the requirements of the basic human goods under given circumstances.[8]

Human reason, then, is necessarily entwined in interpretation. Yet the foundational truths are found in the natural order, they are objective and therefore universal, and they are far-reaching in their claims. For natural law theorists, it is in a commitment to the truths embedded in the natural law where democracy finds solidarity. The "unum" comes not through fiat but through shared belief. But here democracy also finds its legitimacy, for if we can all know these truths through our reasoning, then the members of a democratic public can work together to align public policy with the absolute truth.

PROCEDURALISM

The decline of organized religion and the expansion of pluralism in late modernity have rendered substantive understanding and agreements difficult if not impossible to find. These new circumstances have sent many democratic theorists in search of alternatives. As early as the early modern period, in part inspired by bloody wars over transcendent doctrines, the so-called social contract tradition sought to ground political legitimacy in a free agreement among members of society. Although many social contract theorists retained foundationalist elements in their thinking—Locke, for example, believed that political authorities must respect the natural rights that God had given man—the very idea of grounding political legitimacy in a contract, a voluntary agreement among ordinary human beings, already represented a decisive move away from foundationalism and toward *proceduralism*.

Proceduralists believe that political legitimacy is grounded in the process of political decision-making. Whereas foundationalists think that a political community is bound together by a set of shared ideas about divine law or human nature, proceduralists believe that solidarity can be founded on a shared *commitment to a method* for working out disagreements, a set of rules for living together peaceably. Proceduralism is thus well suited to a moment like ours in which agreement on transcendent truths can be hard to come by, to say the least. Proceduralist political philosophers since Locke have hoped that this more down-to-earth concept of legitimacy might allow people who disagree fundamentally about eternal truths to share a country and a government in peace.

Proceduralism's frank recognition of a growing pluralism and the diminishing likelihood that we will find any robust agreements about transcendent political authority have made it attractive to a varied group of contemporary political philosophers.

The question of solidarity was central to the intellectual project of the great political philosopher John Rawls, who put it this way: "How is it possible for there to exist over time a just and stable society of free and equal citizens who remain profoundly divided by reasonable religious, philosophical, and moral doctrines?"[9] In response, he developed a relatively thin proceduralism in his 1971 opus, *A Theory of Justice*. His argument was intended to describe and defend a liberal, rights-based political order in terms that would be acceptable to any reasonable person—not just those with a prior commitment to liberal values. In this way, he hoped to secure widespread political agreement among people with conflicting moral cosmologies.

To arrive at this neutral system, Rawls performed a now-famous imaginative exercise, asking what "principles of justice" citizens would choose from behind a "veil of ignorance" that kept them from knowing the social position they would occupy under the new order. In chapter 1 of *A Theory of Justice*, he explained that "we are not to think of the original contract as one to enter a particular society or to set up a particular form of government. Rather, the guiding idea is that the principles of justice for the basic structure of society are the object of the original agreement. They are the principles that free and rational persons concerned to further their own interests would accept in an initial position of equality as defining the fundamental terms of their association."[10]

Without knowledge of their own social position, Rawls thought, individuals would choose a set of principles that would be fair for all. This theory was proceduralist because it grounded political justice not on a divine command or a scientific revelation about human nature but on the choice of "free and rational persons concerned to further their own interests." Rawls hoped to reframe the problem of justice in terms of an ideal of justice as fairness; an ideal that presupposes the possibility of "society as a system of fair social cooperation between free and equal persons."[11] If we can agree on certain abstract, universalizing principles about fairness (for example, the availability of opportunity and the distribution of advantages) derived from equally abstract and universalizing procedures everyone would accept as reasonable, we would have an overlapping consensus upon which the work of government could legitimately proceed. Legitimacy would derive from the neutrality of the procedures by which decisions are made and from the impartiality of the structures and policies of the regime.

However, Rawls's critics responded that he had loaded the dice in favor of his own political opinions. In a famous critique of *A Theory of Justice*, Rawls's Harvard colleague Michael Sandel, discussed below, argued that the procedure embodied in the "veil of ignorance," far from abstracting away from all controversial political assumptions, actually relied on a controversial picture of the human individual as radically autonomous and independent. In other words, Rawls's thin procedure still presumed a good deal of substantive agreement on the nature of the good life—agreement that might not exist in an ideologically diverse society.

In response, Rawls would try to escape from substantive metaphysical claims in his second major work, *Political Liberalism*. Rawls's solution was to offer a more thoroughly proceduralist justification for his doctrine of justice as fairness. In the introduction, he acknowledged that human reason would not lead everyone to the same place, even under ideal conditions.

Rawls now argued that fair negotiations among holders of "reasonable yet incompatible" comprehensive doctrines could generate an "overlapping consensus," a modus vivendi agreed upon by all. This marked a political and pragmatic turn in his thinking.[12] In this light, disagreement could be mediated by reference to what people in our society *in fact* believe, insofar as they can be said to hold any settled beliefs. Those "settled beliefs" constitute a historically contingent consensus derived "from fundamentally *intuitive* ideas implicit in the public political culture and abstract[ed] from comprehensive religious, philosophical, and moral doctrines."[13] Those "fundamentally intuitive ideas implicit in the public political culture" gesture toward what I call the "deep structures." Authority is no longer metaphysically based upon claims about the nature of human beings (that is, their reasonableness); rather, it is situated precisely in the consensus-producing procedural norms themselves, which are oriented toward the pragmatic needs of the political system. This does not mean that justice as fairness is amoral—only that it is concerned exclusively with *political* morality.[14] In sum, Rawls depicts his political conception of human nature as entirely historically contingent but politically binding *for that reason:* because it is proper to us.

Rawls's political turn is emblematic of democratic theory's struggle with pluralism in the last third of the twentieth century. But he is not alone. Another prominent account came from the German philosopher Jürgen Habermas, who argued that solidarity, and thus democratic legitimacy, could be achieved through a decision process whose outcomes would be normatively binding.[15] In other words, a norm has to be acceptable to everyone and—this is the distinct contribution of Habermas's discourse ethics—it must not simply spring from the head of a philosopher like Rawls, but be agreed upon in a practical discourse among real, live participants with real interests. Habermas's discourse ethics, relying as it did on real discussion in the real world, may have been more grounded and concrete, but in the end, it was no thicker or more metaphysical than Rawls's political theory. There have been other proceduralist accounts as well.[16]

COMMUNITARIANISM

Rawls's bold declaration of a new liberal system in *A Theory of Justice* and the problems attending it helped to inspire *communitarianism*, an intellectual movement that sits somewhere on the spectrum between proceduralism and foundationalism.

Communitarians believe that pure procedure is not enough to form the basis for human life together. In his critique of *A Theory of Justice*, Michael Sandel argued that Rawls's procedure relies on a curiously stunted idea of the human person. Rawls's conception of persons as "free and rational," utterly unencumbered by any attachment other than their own interests and, at the same time, isolated from the deep and often unchosen commitments that make them who they are, posited people who simply do not and cannot exist: "Can we view ourselves as independent selves, independent in the sense that our identity is never tied to our aims and attachments? . . . I do not think we can, at least not without cost to those loyalties and convictions whose moral force consists partly in the fact that living by them is inseparable from understanding ourselves as the particular persons we are—as members of this family or community or nation or people, as bearers of that history, as citizens of this republic."[17]

Politics necessarily entangles us in dependencies, and when these dependencies are entirely independent of our preexisting constitutive attachments, we can no longer be said to be self-governing. In the end, the procedural conception of government banishes moral language from public discourse and so denies us important resources for making political judgments, at the expense of an abstract notion of liberty.[18]

In the end, the communitarians argue that proceduralists are trying to build a common way of life on an insubstantial understanding of persons and culture, one that is parasitic on the strong social and cultural sources that it hopes to replace. As Charles Taylor put it, the communitarians believe that "a democratic society needs some commonly recognized definition of the good life."[19] By asking citizens to set aside their most cherished commitments in favor of a neutral, universally acceptable set of bare procedures, the proceduralists are restricting their ability to engage in serious and substantive political discourse about the things that matter most to them. Communitarians, then, want a renewed acknowledgment in public life of the self and of culture as multiply-constituted in ways that take the fact of pluralism for granted.

In this way, communitarians seem to resemble foundationalists, who asserted that something more than a common decision procedure was required to bind citizens together. But communitarians differed from the foundationalists in their reluctance to take a stand on what kinds of binding agreements would do the job. Their agnosticism on the question of *what* that commonly recognized definition should be calls to mind President Eisenhower's famous observation, "[o]ur form of government has no sense unless it is founded in a deeply felt religious faith, and I don't care what it is."[20] Communitarians talked about patriotism and shared national ideals, which they hoped could unite disparate groups in a pluralist society, rather than about philosophical or religious claims, which would be more difficult for a diverse citizenry to agree on.[21] What this meant in practice was that thick cultural narratives were not authoritative in themselves—as they would be within foundationalism—but were rather instrumental in the larger work of building and defending a livable social order.

Where Things Stand

This overview is obviously a distillation, and as such, it doesn't intend to be anything other than a sketch that would define a range of thought in this arena. One can add and subtract, debate who is important and who is not, and dispute the finer points, as scholars have.[22] I will later consider a new perspective taking shape in the debate, one that is currently called "agonism." In the end, these categories are only more or less useful as a preliminary tool for sorting through the rich and complex theoretical landscape.

With this in mind, it is entirely fair to say that foundationalism is a marginal position among scholars, and the more robust and otherworldly the foundations of a political regime are, the more marginal they are. This is, undoubtedly, a reflection of the loss of credibility of traditional religious beliefs among elites and the overwhelming secularity of the dominant institutions they inhabit.

Yet significantly, foundationalism (in its variety) is a relatively important way of thinking in the larger population and for the opposite reason—a more or less religious populism in the general public operates within an institutional web that accommodates and even encourages those convictions.

Needless to say, the academic distinctions are lost in public discourse, but lest anyone be tempted to imagine that the broader distinctions are irrelevant, they in fact constitute some of the underlying terms of conflict in our public culture.

So, what is the subtext of this academic debate?

Subtext

Thick and Thin

More will be said later about how these ways of thinking play out in our public culture, but for now, it is worth noting that the contentions among various theorists are, in certain respects, *artificial*, or at least overstated. In one significant way, the protagonists in this debate are closer to each other than they imagine.

The important question everyone is really debating is just how thick or thin the agreements and commitments that underwrite a democracy need to be to sustain democracy and to make it vital. For the strong foundationalist, those agreements need to be thick as chowder. They believe that questions about the basis of knowledge and authority, of personhood, of ethics and teleology, and so on, require answers. For the post-metaphysical liberal proceduralist, those agreements can be as thin as broth. Proceduralists believe that we will not likely find agreements over such important philosophical questions or, if we do, they will be minimal; that the most we have are certain rational procedures by which we can mediate our disagreements rooted in contingent yet implicit cultural agreement. Among the communitarians in the middle, the view is that those questions are essential and cannot be avoided, but we need a politics that will create the space to allow them to be integrated within our public discourse and political system.

So, for all the disagreement, no one disputes that there have to be *some* shared understandings, *some* common affections, *some* agreements as the basis of solidarity. That those agreements operate out of a shared language and are oriented toward some ethical ends (such as justice)—however vague—means that consensus is more than merely technical or administrative; that those agreements are rooted in practice means that solidarity is not merely ideal or ideological. However thin or thick—minimal or maximal—those agreements and commitments need to be, in principle they are supposed to provide a framework within which legitimate democratic power is contained and managed.

It is critical to emphasize that these understandings and these agreements are fundamentally normative in character and aspirationally authoritative. When thick, the bonds people share are *overtly* ethical in nature. Obligations are deeply felt and carry a binding force on those who are socialized into those agreements. When thin, those agreements may only be oriented toward creating conditions in which people, in theory, could *generate* the moral or ethical.

Because they are normative or presuppose an emergent normativity, they provide a "center" that delineates the margins of justifiable political behavior and thought; frames the limitations and horizons of legitimate political aspirations; asserts and defines the boundaries of individual rights, collective recognition, and national identity; and provides the foundations of a solidarity that transcend individual and group differences. *These are the agreements that contain*

all of our disagreements. Even when paper thin, the minimal function
of this cultural agreement would be to define what is transgressive;
what citizens respond to with outrage and thus what individuals,
groups, institutions, and the nation itself cannot, should not, and
will not condone in public life. In principle, such agreements are the
cultural substructure of a democratic polity and regime.

The question again is, what is enough? How thin can an unum
be without a political order unraveling? And by the same token, what
is too much? How thick can a consensus be without it being repressive or discriminatory to those on the ideological, racial, and religious margins of social life?

Articulation

And how *explicit* do these agreements need to be? Partly because the
issues at stake translate into law and policy, most speak of the "center" in terms that can be made explicit. It is important that the formation of public culture be articulable. As Craig Calhoun put it, "In
this 'polyphonic complexity of public voices,' the giving of reasons is
still crucial. Public reason cannot proceed simply by expressive communication or demands for recognition, though the public sphere
cannot be adequately inclusive if it tries to exclude these. The public
sphere will necessarily include processes of culture-making that are
not reducible to advances in reason, and which nonetheless may be
crucial to capacities for mutual understanding. But if collective will
formation is to be based on reason, not merely participation in common culture, then public processes of clarifying arguments and giving reasons for positions must be central."[23]

Most of what constitutes a culture, though, is implicit: what is
assumed by contending factions in public debate. To be sure, the
question of the "center" could be about political ideals like liberty
or justice or it could be about positions on public policy. But at the
deepest levels, the question surrounding the center is about the subtle unspoken assumptions, sensibilities, and dispositions people have
toward public life, the grounds upon which people assume these to
be real and true and thus about the meaning and use of the words
and symbols that constitute a public discourse. These assumptions,
sensibilities, and dispositions define what most people experience as

an intrinsic understanding of what can be said and not said, what is done and what is not done (much less imagined!), and as such they possess a moral and justificatory force quite independent of their formal recognition in any explicit contract.[24]

Some scholars make allusions to this level of cultural reality. Rawls, for example, speaks of the foundational importance of "settled convictions," the "shared fund of implicitly recognized basic ideas and principles."[25] Habermas makes repeated reference to the necessity of a large "background consensus" rooted in shared, intersubjective lifeworlds for the stability of democratic discourse.[26] And Michael Sandel defines the public philosophy in these very terms: "the political theory *implicit* in our practice, the *assumptions* about citizenship and freedom that inform our public life."[27] Many operating within the proceduralist camp have long assumed that even in the natural evolution of social life, the "settled convictions" that make sense of democracy's rituals and procedures would remain "settled"; that the "background consensus" of shared assumptions and implicit agreements that make discursive practice fair and reasonable would remain stable.

But What If the "Background Consensus" Is Not Stable?

Put simply, how thick and explicit does the unum need to be to satisfy the requirements of political solidarity in a liberal democracy? Every social order requires some defense, at times at great personal risk; and every political order requires some sacrifice in its defense. In 1780, Abigail Adams wrote to her son Quincy Adams, "Justice, humanity and benevolence are the duties you owe to society in general. To your country the same duties are incumbent upon you with the additional obligation of sacrificing ease, pleasure, wealth and life itself for its defense and security."[28]

Where do those duties come from? And what values or ideals or commitments would obligate anyone to sacrifice ease, pleasure, wealth, and life itself for their defense and security? What is the common good for which people are willing to endure sacrifice? The answers to these questions may have been self-evident in late eighteenth-century New England, but they are no longer.

If we presume that truth is accessible and reasonable, that public reason is recognizable as such, that human justice is genuinely possible, that citizenship and thus self-rule is meaningfully attainable, that individual freedoms can be guaranteed, and that unpopular religious, social, and political opinion can be tolerated, it still leaves many obvious questions unanswered. Whose truth? Justice on what terms? Reasonable (or unreasonable) by what public standards? Tolerance for whom? Citizenship toward what end? And where are the boundaries between individual freedom and the public good and how are they balanced?

In American history, these questions have always been contested, but within linguistic and moral boundaries that have been at least intelligible, if not generally approved, by most, if not all, factions. This is not mere theory. Wide-ranging conflicts over social and political issues have tended to unfold within a cosmology that constituted a legitimate authority for working through such conflict. *Any* legitimate exercise of political power has depended upon *some* shared authoritative institutions and, undergirding these, some more or less authoritative values, standards, and narratives.

Even through the culture wars of the last half century— or much of them, anyway—a politics rooted in competing moral visions may have been incommensurable and unreconcilable, *but it was still mostly intelligible to opponents.* Even if distorted by slanderous caricature, our contested politics still drew from legible traditions of political theory and practice and operated within a framework of political institutions, authority, and ritual that were lawful and legitimate.

But what remains of this complex of shared ideas, practices, and authority now? What are the threads that tie us together? Are there sources of shared agreements and hopes upon which we all stand, and if so, what are they? How thick or thin, explicit or implicit do they need to be?

The Waning Sources of Solidarity?

There is nothing like a good enemy to generate solidarity—sociologically speaking. But opposition to an enemy is effective as a catalyst to solidarity only if the group opposing has enough shared understandings, ideas, values, ideals, or characteristics that would define it as distinct. And even then, negative solidarity tends to be short-lived in its effectiveness.

There must be more. But what "background consensus," to use

Habermas's concept, or "settled convictions," to use Rawls's term, is there? What shared sources are there to draw upon capable of binding us together in common understanding and purpose? And how much and what kind of an unum or cultural substructure is necessary to make liberal democracy viable and even vital?

The contention of this book is that the frameworks of meaning and interpretation, that is, the cultural logics of a very specifically American adaptation of the Enlightenment project, provided the *cultural conditions* for the emergence of liberal democracy in America—among other things, a framework of "tolerable difference" and thus also of consensus and solidarity. Precisely because of its unique adaptation, flexibility, and opacity it could *in principle* contain within itself many, if not most, of the contentious differences present at the time of the Founding and could more or less evolve and adapt to historical circumstances over two centuries. In reality, of course, that adaptation has proved a rather rocky road.

Even so, from all that we can see, those conditions are no longer present. Indeed, for quite some time, the culture that has underwritten liberal democracy in America (and in Europe too) has been unraveling. The cultural sources that made it possible in the first place have, in the most elemental ways, dissolved, and all of the efforts to reconfigure and revivify those cultural sources over the decades, while well intended and at times unifying, have just as often been profoundly deficient and at times injurious. More troubling still, there are signs today that the task is being abandoned, replaced by a different and much darker cultural logic.

If this is right, what cultural sources—however minimal—could possibly provide enough "background consensus" or "settled convictions" to keep the project of liberal democracy viable? What could be enough to do the work? And what would be the consequences if the effort to work through these questions is abandoned?

How this gets sorted out will be answered not by scholars but by history and the powerful institutional dynamics by which it moves. And history is providing a more profound set of challenges of which we have not taken full measure.

Thus, if past is prologue, then it is to the past that I now turn to begin making sense of the circuitous and often tortured path that has led to the present crisis.

PART III

"Working Through" America's Hybrid-Enlightenment

CHAPTER FOUR

America's Hybrid-Enlightenment

T HAT THE ENLIGHTENMENT UNDERWROTE the great democratic revolutions of the eighteenth and nineteenth centuries is well known, as are the ways in which the variation of political outcomes across Europe and North America reflected the philosophical differences of this broad intellectual and cultural revolution.[1] It is not an accident, for example, that the radical Enlightenment centered in Paris created conditions for the Reign of Terror and the guillotine, and the moderate Enlightenment in America, drawing from Scotland and England, did not. What is far more interesting is to see just how historically contingent, uneven, and varied these intellectual and cultural developments were and how fragile their political outcomes. Reading the letters of John Adams, one sees how chaotic and inchoate events and decisions were. Every decision was contested, and the results were often "decided by the vote of a single state and that vote was often decided by a single individual." The unfolding of events was, in Adams's words, "patched and piebald."[2]

Such fragility and contingency are, perhaps, especially interesting in America, where the "Enlightenment project" was not one thing, but rather a cluster of embryonic and historically provisional ideas and convictions, often inconsistent with one another. These drew from many and assorted sources, most prominently biblical, classical, and Whiggish, and were synthesized philosophically, in large part, by the commonsense realists of the Scottish Enlightenment. To see these evolving affinities and confluences is to recognize that the great democratic revolutions of the eighteenth and nineteenth centuries—including the democratic revolution in America—were anything but inevitable.

Yet within that emergent, contested, complex, and fragile collection of assumptions, ideas, and beliefs, we find the animating cultural logic of a new social and political order. Needless to say, it was a profoundly flawed social and political order. The blight of slavery and the shame of Native American genocide are unavoidable facts of American history and culture and they have left an indelible stain of contradiction. But in its time and against the backdrop of the absolutism of the British monarchy and the global and totalizing vision of the Roman Catholic Church, the emerging social and political order could make justifiable claims to be both liberal and democratic, celebrating above all the ideals of freedom, equality, justice, and tolerance. Even under the dim light of its many oppressive manifestations, these were not just empty slogans but substantive ideals with deep meaning forged from the experience of systematic and sustained political and economic oppression. The affirmation of those ideals and commitment to them provided a foundation and framework of solidarity within which people and associations with different interests and vantage points could come together. Underlying this framework were assumptions about the existence of truth, the knowability of the reality of the world through reason, observation, and experience, the meaning and purpose of history, and the capacity of citizens to shape it.

As Adam Seligman argued in his brilliant treatment of the idea of civil society, the cultural logic of the Enlightenment was an attempt to provide a vision for the reconstitution of public life. It comprised an ethical ideal for a flourishing society that would reconcile individual liberties (among them the freedom to pursue personal interests) and the public good. It was a vision of freedom, but also of interdependence, sympathy, mutuality, and benevolence, supported by such civic virtues as loyalty to the community, knowledge of public affairs, civility, and restraint in the conduct of deliberation. As a system of political institutions and practices, democracy was not coterminous with that vision of the public good, but rather served it, supported it, and, in these respects, gave political expression to it.[3]

The cultural logic of the Enlightenment also provided the sources of authority by which to adjudicate disputes and dilemmas of every kind, the central ideas for collective identity, the boundaries by which claims and actions could be deemed legitimate or illegitimate, and the ground rules for political engagement. "Right Reason," rooted in the universal laws of nature and reflected in the constitution of the human soul, would be the final arbiter of ethical and moral dilemmas. This was an ancient idea that found new life in the neoclassicism of the Enlightenment elite. Cicero's rendering gave poignant expression to the ideal: "There is in fact a true law—namely right reason—which is in accordance with nature, applies to all men and is unchangeable and eternal. By its commands it summons men to the performance of their duties; by its prohibitions it restrains men from doing wrong. Its commands and prohibitions always influence good men but are without effect upon the bad. To invalidate this law by human legislation is never morally right, nor is it permissible ever to restrict its operation, and to annul it wholly is impossible."[4]

This tradition was long in the making and it evolved along the way. It had been appropriated by the church fathers of the patristic age. It matured in the medieval theology of Thomas Aquinas and later in the natural law philosophy of Hugo Grotius and Samuel von Pufendorf.[5] Through the late seventeenth and eighteenth centuries, it was mediated by the reformist thinkers, writers, and preachers of the English and Scottish Enlightenment—figures such as Isaac Newton, Thomas Hobbes, John Locke, Anthony Ashley Cooper (the third Earl of Shaftesbury), Thomas Reid, Adam Smith, Francis Hutcheson, Adam Ferguson, and David Hume (among many others). Altogether, the idea of natural law, drawing from and evolving within both classical and biblical sources, formed the backdrop for the political innovations that were to come in America.[6]

The influence of the British Enlightenment was especially significant for what was to unfold in America.[7] There was, of course, significant intellectual cross-pollination between France and England. The English and the Scots shared with the French *philosophes* a commitment to the natural rights of equality and liberty, the authority of reason and science, and through them the belief in human progress. Yet the British intellectuals gave precedence to what they believed to be the natural or innate social virtues of sympathy, mutuality, prudence, charity, and benevolence as well as disgust and resentment. Not least because a disproportionate number of the American colonists had roots in the British Isles, it was the distinctive "moral philosophy" of the Scottish and English Enlightenment that found hospitable soil in the thirteen colonies in which to grow. What is more, because so many of the early American colonists in New England and the mid-Atlantic had also been religious dissenters—Puritans chief among them—the soil would be especially conducive to appropriating this cultural logic in ways favorable to religious faith.[8]

A *Hybrid*-Enlightenment

The Enlightenment in America, then, was not a unitary and triumphant movement of secular rationality, as polemicists might have it.[9] Nor was it a revolution that uncomfortably coexisted with the fading legacy of Puritanism. The Enlightenment in America was, in fact, a lively and evolving syncretism.

This is not to say that there weren't tensions between the more secular Enlightenment thinkers and Protestant divines and the worldviews they each espoused. Indeed, they distrusted each other, often reviled each other, and argued endlessly with each other. Given the Enlightenment's naturalist epistemology within science and law and its overriding commitment to dispassionate reason against the numinous mysteries of supernatural faith, tensions were inherent and thus ever-present. And yet secular Enlightenment thinking in America was also sympathetic to the *forms and ethos* of traditional Protestant faith.

On the one hand, Enlightenment ideas and perspectives *were understood religiously*. As Henry May put it, "Men of the late eighteenth century, whether they were Calvinists or Arminians, deists or atheists, seldom thought about any branch of human affairs without referring consciously to some general beliefs about the nature of the universe and man's place in it, and about human nature itself. In this sense Jefferson and Paine were as religious as any New England Congregationalist. The denials and defiances of Enlightenment skeptics and materialists are denials and defiances of religious doctrine, usually religious in their own intent."[10]

At the same time, Protestant faith, especially in New England, was intensely rationalist in the earnest attempt to reconcile Calvinist faith to emerging Enlightenment ideologies and sensibilities. As one minister put it, "There is nothing in Christianity that is contrary to reason. God never did, He never can, authorize a religion opposite to it, because this would be to contradict himself."[11] In this view, revelation was not the antithesis of nature but a complement to it. Properly understood, the Bible was always rational and moral.

This general view reflected a larger aspiration held by many in the seventeenth and eighteenth centuries to find a balance between science and religion, reason and passion, logic and desire, authority and freedom and a political order that could embody that equilibrium. But even where this aspiration broke down, there was a common and unqualified ethical commitment shared by both the party of faith and the party of reason to live more moral lives and build better societies. Neoclassical and republican language was transposed by people of faith: the Republic was a Christian commonwealth, virtue was piety, vice was sin, and liberty was the opportunity for righteous living.[12] Providentialist language had an extensive sympathy with the ideals of liberty defined by the eighteenth-century Whig tradition. In this way, late eighteenth-century clerics could call for incessant prayer that "the spirit of true republican government may universally pervade the citizens of the United States."[13]

Likewise, the Enlightenment in America carried a Calvinist moral sensibility, even when it repudiated its doctrines of original sin, the divinity of Christ, the Trinity, the existence of miracles, and the like. The reason was that everyday personal and social ethics were essentially the same. One very prominent illustration is what is now called *The Jefferson Bible*—a new rendering of the life of Christ Jefferson created in 1803. Entitled "The Morals of Jesus," this version of the Bible eliminated all the supernatural references of the Gospels, leaving only Christ's ethical teaching. "To the corruptions of Christianity I am opposed," he wrote Benjamin Rush, "but not to the genuine precepts of Jesus himself," to which he was "sincerely attached . . . in preference to all others."[14] Indeed, in their private morals, deists were often as puritanical as Calvinists.[15]

In the end, the hybrid-Enlightenment in America was a broad enough and opaque enough amalgamation to encompass substantial diversity and the tensions that diversity implied. Enlightenment ideas certainly had greater traction in the urban middle and upper-middle classes, and yet they also spread fairly widely, even to the small-town and agrarian populations to the extent that they accommodated Christian ideas and morals.

The Question of Authority

Perhaps no figure was more influential on the thinking of the Founders of the American Republic and its public culture than the English philosopher John Locke. His influence on Jefferson was especially significant, shaping his views of individual rights, the responsibilities of citizens and popular sovereignty, the nature and duties of government, the separation of powers and, above all, the centrality of reason in the formation of free societies.

But as Seligman observed, Locke was a transitional theorist in the early development of this hybrid cultural logic. Locke drew upon the natural law philosophers in many ways, not least in his view of the transcendent preconditions of his theory of civil society. The ontological status of the rights and privileges that were at the basis of civil society derived not only from the traditions of natural law but also from a Christian, and specifically Calvinist, reading of the relationship of humankind to God. As Locke put it in his *Two Treatises of Government* (book II, section 6), "The state of nature has a law of nature to govern it, which obliges everyone: and reason, which is that law, teaches all mankind who will but consult it, that being all equal and independent, no one ought to harm another in his life, health, liberty or possessions. For men being all the workmanship of one omnipotent and infinitely wise Maker—all servants of one sovereign Master, sent into the world by His order, and about His business—they are His property, whose workmanship they are, made to last during His, not one another's pleasure, and being furnished with like faculties, sharing all in one community of nature, there cannot be supposed any such subordination among us."

Thus freedom and equality, as Seligman put it, "were not rooted in a psychological, historical or logical *a priori* but in a Christian, and more particularly Calvinist, vision of a community of individuals under God's dominion."[16]

In this cultural logic, there was no *worldly* authority that could be intrinsically legitimate. Indeed, for Locke, all authority in this world was derived ultimately from God. The different structures of political authority found in the world were all derived from the individual's own executive and legislative authority in the state of nature, which individuals hold in their "capacity of agents of God." In Locke's vision, the idea of a community of saints was no longer a viable social model; a community of individualized moral agents pursuing the social good in conformity to the "will of God" was. In all of this, "Locke's vision was grounded theologically in axioms whose ontological status was not given to empirical evidence or questioning."[17]

With the Scottish Enlightenment, the relation between worldly/human reason and God's will as the sources of the moral order began a reorientation. By the eighteenth century, the transcendent aspects of the Lockean vision were being replaced by the ideas of moral sentiments and natural sympathy (reason and the passions) as the source of the moral order. The social order was grounded in and guided ethically by the human propensity toward innate mutuality. In an intellectual climate defined by deism, the transcendent grounding of the social order had lost a measure of credibility for elites. While divine revelation and Godly benevolence were in no way absent from an understanding of human affairs, they were, nevertheless, operating at a greater distance.[18]

This broad orientation took form in the midst of significant and ongoing disagreement. Yet the general consensus that emerged held that the dictates of "Right Reason" were in accord with the laws of nature. As such, reason embodied universal principles that were valid for all people, in all contexts, at all times. The universality of reason would bridge the distinction between private and public, between the individual and the collective, between egoism and altruism, between the ever-perplexing relationship of personal interests and the social good. How so?

In terms of the private interests of individuals, reason offered certain universally applicable rules of conduct. By following these rules, the individual would be able to ascertain his or her own benefit. Among these benefits, the three most important for the working of society were the stability of possessions, their transfer by consent, and the performance of promises.[19] Whatever else the rules of reason might mean and whatever else they might accomplish, individuals would follow the rules if only to maximize their self-interest.

Reason both governed the passions and guided them toward the public good. For some, reason brought us to a true understanding of the providential designs for the world. For others, reason was itself an element of the natural affections, the combined effect of which always led to mutuality and cooperation. Reason was thought to be the source of our common and inalienable rights—the right to freedom, equality, and justice. Reason and nature made these rights, and the ideals they represented, coherent to all people and provided the means by which those ideals could be realized.

The continuing point of synthesis between the Reformed Christian and secular Enlightenment traditions over the eighteenth century was an epistemology of transcendence. Even though it was understood in radically different and somewhat competing ways, the notion of transcendence at play was sufficiently capacious as a concept and sufficiently opaque as a sensibility that it could absorb a plurality of views, opinions, and traditions. In this way, it provided a common framework for understanding the significance of the individual in the world, offered a common language and a common grammar for recognizing the natural affections and moral sentiments shared by all humanity, grounded reason within nature (which was read by Calvinists as expressive of the will of God), and made the ethical principles and ideals to which reason pointed universal. Though plagued by internal contradictions, this remained a transcendent moral order that, nevertheless, embraced both individual and collective spheres equally and reconciled one to the other. Thus, the seeds of social solidarity could be found in human sentiments, the public good within private interests, the universal within the individual.

This synthesis represented a radical transformation from traditional providentialist accounts of the ancien regime in which all authority in public and private life was mediated by the ritual practices, hierarchical structures, and institutional processes of the Catholic or Anglican Church. This was a new model of the moral order in which authority was now grounded within a society of individuals who, in principle, shared the moral ties of sentiments and sympathy as well as a vision of universal truths. This applied as much to the strident Calvinist, whose individuality (her life and conscience) was defined in an unmediated relationship to God, as it did to the most skeptical free-thinking deist, whose individuality was measured by the dictates of conscience and Right Reason. Not only was the status of the individual transformed by imbuing her with a new autonomy and agency, the nature of the ties between individuals—that is, the nature of society itself—was also transformed. These ties were defined no longer by an ascriptive membership determined by the geography, family, or faith one was born into, as they had in the ancien regime, but by the ties of moral sentiment, reason, and common, though voluntary, belief in shared ideals.

It is essential to note that this was not a facile civil religion or a faith defined by the least common denominator fabricated from compromise for the purposes of political legitimacy. It was a synthesis informed by rich traditions of thought and practice, drawing as much from the Bible as from the philosophical traditions of natural law; indebted as much to Revelation as to reason, this hybrid-Enlightenment provided the framework for the emergence of democratic life that was different from anything before seen.

It was for precisely this reason that, though cultural tensions persisted, the Enlightenment project in America found fertile soil in the vitality of popular religion; not only in the more intellectual Calvinism of New England but in the various communities of folk Protestantism that predominated throughout the colonies in the late eighteenth century and within the new Republic in the first half of the nineteenth century. Though the political philosophy of the Founders was post-Lockean, large portions of the American people were still operating within the providentialist sensibilities of the Lockean world. Thus, within the habitus of these faith communities, authority in worldly affairs, no less than in the churches they inhabited, largely remained rooted in a particular model of communal identity based on covenantal commitments to church, community, and nation.[20]

The New Idea of Citizenship

Nowhere were these hybrid-Enlightenment ideals more crystallized than in the reappropriation of the classical republican idea of citizenship. Citizenship is an old idea with roots in Greek and Roman antiquity. Then, of course, only the tiny number of the landed nobility was included. In the late eighteenth and early nineteenth centuries, the application was still severely limited, yet in the American revolutions, citizenship became a possibility imaginable for common men; indeed, more than ever before, with the possibility, written into the Founding documents, that more yet could possess it.

Citizenship meant membership in a political community that provided legal benefits of protection of person and property but assumed public responsibilities of participation. In Aristotle's terms, citizenship was an *office* and a central, if not the highest, part of the vocation of a human being. More than a legal designation, citizenship was an ideal that conferred the dignity of self-rule. But now here, in this unprecedented moment in modern history, ordinary men had the agency to determine the frameworks of public life. With the legal designation came the ethical burden of participating in the unfolding of history. To be a citizen was, in the sweep of history, a rare and precious privilege.

Underwriting the "rights of man" was a shared anthropology. A citizen was, for one, a possessor of reason. Reason was innate to the human soul, integral to a person's natural affections, and central as well to what it meant for others to be made in God's image. As such, citizens were capable of reasoned discourse about the public affairs that affected them.

A citizen was also a bearer of virtue, expected to honor obligations, be respectful of persons irrespective of beliefs or station in life, and show loyalty to the larger community to the point of willingly sacrificing personal interests in recognition of their common fate. In this way, citizens worthy of the name possessed a disposition of benevolence toward the community with whom they shared a common destiny.

Human beings shared an innate mutuality and were thus given to sociability. For this reason, citizens were understood to be by nature members of a community and, as Adam Ferguson put it in 1782, "no longer made for [themselves]." A citizen "must forego his happiness and his freedom, where these interfere with the good of society. . . . He is only part of a whole . . . and if the public good be the principal object with individuals, it is likewise true that the happiness of individuals is the great end of civil society."[21]

Human beings "are united by instinct," acting in society "from affections of kindness and friendship," not merely motivated by interest. But even in Adam Smith's famous version, the pursuit of private interests would, through the magic of the Invisible Hand, convert into the public good. Being part of the whole gave us a love of the whole and would compel us to put the good of the whole above the good of the parts. As Adam Seligman put it, "The ties of solidarity are found within the logic of citizenship itself."[22]

"To be an American citizen," as Sean Wilentz has said, "was by definition to be a republican, the inheritor of a revolutionary legacy in a world ruled by aristocrats and kings."[23] Yet these political transformations did not occur in isolation or without the bolstering dynamics of competitive markets and a growing religious populism. All of these dynamics were mutually reinforcing.[24]

Citizenship, Faith, and the Antinomian Ethos

The relationship between religion and politics as it bore on citizenship was especially significant. On the one hand, democratization in the political sphere transformed American religion, providing, as it did, the conditions for what was to become the Second Great Awakening. As in the political sphere, ordinary Christians in the early decades of the new Republic rejected the inherited distinctions between elites and ordinary people and, specifically, those between the clergy and an unsophisticated laity. Doing so, they grew to reject the authority of a cultivated and learned theology in favor of a more accessible religious vernacular. They increasingly cast aside the wisdom of tradition in favor of the spiritual passions and experiences of the present. A new class of religious leaders "short on social graces, family connections, and literary education" reflected the pious enthusiasms of ordinary believers and shaped movements aligned with the values and priorities of common folk.[25] This religious transformation was reflected in a demographic transformation that terrified the leadership of established denominations. According to Nathan Hatch, "By 1820 Methodist membership numbered a quarter million; by 1830 it was twice that number. Baptist membership multiplied tenfold in the three decades after the Revolution; the number of churches increased from five hundred to over twenty-five hundred. The Black church in America was born amidst the crusading vigor of these movements and quickly assumed its own distinct character and broad appeal. By the middle of the nineteenth century, Methodist and Baptist churches had splinted into a score of separate denominations, white and Black. In total these movements eventually constituted two-thirds of the Protestant ministers and church members in the United States."[26]

Religious revivalism and populism, born out of this revolutionary spirit, became a defining and enduring impulse in American life in this period, one that would in turn spill out of the religious sphere back into the political.

Indeed, if democratization in the political sphere helped spawn religious populism, it is also true that religious populism became a means by which popular sovereignty in the civic realm was nurtured. Relocating religious authority within the experience of the believer was profoundly empowering to ordinary people, not least to women, who dominated the revivals and the swelling rolls of church membership. As it bore on their eternal fate, people knew themselves to be responsible agents, capable of thinking for themselves and making their own decisions.

This was no less the case as it bore on their political future—people had to think for themselves about freedom, equality, and representation, all reinforced by the democratic rhetoric of liberty. The democratic hope of living a better (and godlier) life and building a better world was pervasive. To be sure, there was an antinomian element woven within both religious and political democratization that would prove, many generations later, to be subversive of all authority and solidarity.[27] Yet, at this point, despite its inherent sectarian tendencies, the populism and revivalism of the post-revolutionary period was the source of the spread of Christianity in America as well as the foundation of nearly all social reform prior to the Civil War.[28] It was "a powerfully integrating and cohesive force."[29]

"To Begin the World over Again"

Among the almost creedal principles of the Enlightenment was the idea of progress, bolstered by a widely shared hope for the future. This ethos was more than a vague consciousness about the movements of human advancement in the world. Rather, it was an electrifying sense that a new world was dawning, a world with no limits on what was possible. Through the advancements of reason and science, humanity could overcome superstition and intolerance and, in time, war, disease, and other forms of human suffering.

Those who lived in this time had the sense that a new world was in the making and that it was theirs to make—which is why hope was also suffused with anxiety. There was nothing about the circumstances in which they lived that suggested a better world was inevitable or that its coming into being could avoid hard work, struggle, and suffering. Everything was at stake. Against the still-powerful vestiges of the ancien regime, it was possible to create a new society, and with it new systems of government oriented toward achieving the flourishing for which people everywhere longed.[30]

Nowhere was that sense of hope and possibility more tangible than in America, where a new kind of nation was actually being forged. The most radical meaning of the American Revolution, Henry May once observed, came from the fact that it happened at all.[31] With its success came the palpable awareness that something new and real was emerging against the backdrop of an old world. Writing in the first year of the War of Independence in an essay "Addressed to the Inhabitants of America," Thomas Paine declared in *Common Sense*, "We have it in our power to begin the world over again. A situation, similar to the present, hath not happened since the days of Noah until now. The birthday of a new world is at hand."[32]

The global significance of this opportunity was not lost on Paine or his audience: "The cause of America is in great measure the cause of all mankind."[33] The sentiment was ubiquitous. Six years later, in 1782, the great seal, *Novus Ordo Seclorum*, was designed, giving expression to this sensibility. The Founding of America marked the beginning of a new era in the human drama. That same year, in letters widely read in England and on the Continent, the French immigrant Crèvecoeur described the American as "a new man, who acts upon new principles . . . new ideas . . . new opinions."[34]

The hopefulness was not diminished by years of war. In a letter to Jefferson, Caesar Rodney wrote: "The Revolution of America, by recognizing those rights which every Man is Entitled to by the laws of God and Nature, Seems to have broken off all those devious Tramels of Ignorance, prejudice, and Superstition which have long depressed the Human Mind. Every door is now Open to the Sons of genius and Science to enquire after Truth. Hence, we may expect the darkening clouds of error will vanish fast before the light of reason; and that the period is fast arriving when the Truth will enlighten the whole world."[35]

Across the spectrum of Christian behavior, the same event was understood in eschatological terms. The revolutionary conflict was a cosmic struggle between God's elect and the Antichrist. American liberty was God's cause and British tyranny was the Antichrist's. To win the war would set the conditions for Christ's thousand-year reign.[36]

At least compared to the Old World—and however imperfect it still was—America stood for political freedom, equality before the law, economic opportunity, religious toleration, and popular sovereignty through representative government.

The breathless optimism of the Enlightenment project in America was rooted in part in the fact that the new Republic hadn't inherited from Europe many of the traditional preconditions of nationhood. It is true that most of the immigrants of the new colonies were British, yet as David Hackett Fischer demonstrated, the differences among them were more radically distinct than countries in Europe were different from one another.[37] These differences multiplied as the numbers of immigrating Germans, Scandinavians, Dutch, Italians, and others grew. Americans had to invent themselves as a nation, and the possibilities seemed boundless.

Every bit as important was how this secular hope for a new age not only paralleled but fused with biblical millennialism. Within the legacy of Puritanism, America was still a nation chosen, a mythic ideal that had not diminished in resonance from the early years of the colonial period although now the myth was coming to have new meaning. The revolutionary Enlightenment had its polemicists, its moral absolutes, and its emotional enthusiasm, which all resembled the prophets, the creeds, and the passions of popular religion. Even that "infidel" Thomas Paine made extensive use of the language and imagery of the Old Testament in his pamphlet *Common Sense*, which might account for the fact that it was so widely read from the pulpit.

Civic and religious millennialism, then, were mutually supportive. During the fight for independence, it was well understood (not least by the British) that the most unified and effective supporters of sedition were the "black-coated regiment" of the Calvinist clergy, especially in New England.[38] Though the clergy were often divided doctrinally and theologically, they were united politically and organized accordingly.[39] Even more, for most Calvinists, there was divine meaning in the War of Independence and the Founding of the new Republic. Jonathan Edwards's grandson and president of Yale, Timothy Dwight, matter-of-factly believed that America was the future site of the Christian millennium and, in the meantime, the home of free government, reason, progress, and the "rights of man."[40] These hopes were further fueled by an increasingly popular postmillennial theology of end times laid out by Edwards himself. Postmillennialism not only argued that the Second Coming of Christ would come about at the end of a thousand years of peace, it lay a burden upon believers to do all they could to bring about that peace through social and moral reform.

Across so many social, geographic, political, and philosophical differences, then, was a shared sense of a common destiny, a shared obligation to labor together on its behalf, and a shared urgency about this epic task—beginning with independence itself. "Every day," Paine wrote, "convinces us of its necessity."[41]

Thick and Overlapping

To those for whom all is difference, all is struggle, there is no dispute here: the years leading up to and following the Founding of the American Republic were contentious—riven with religious schism, philosophical and ideological division, political and economic conflict and competition—not to mention racial, ethnic, and national violence. The strife was pervasive, even if not ubiquitous, and questions of power and identity were always central. This factionalizing often brought out the worst in people and communities, not least jealousy, animosity, belligerence, slander, insult, corruption, violence, and even genocidal savagery. It would be an act of fantasy, then, to describe this period as the halcyon pastoral depicted so inspiringly in the Hudson River School. All social orders are underwritten by violence or its threat, and as the historian Bernard Bailyn has extensively documented, America in this Founding period was no exception.[42]

Yet it would be equally illusory to say that there were no shared understandings, shared aspirations, or shared culture. There was, in fact, an essential, even if precarious, commonality in American public culture, despite all the forces of disunity, within the powerful hybrid ideals of the American Enlightenment and the civic/religious practices they both reflected and inspired.[43] It was overlapping, diffuse, and all things considered, fairly thick: substantive enough to contain many, if not most, disagreements. As Bailyn put it, this hybrid-Enlightenment provided a comprehensive but also functional theory of the political order. It certainly provided the grounds for an oppositional politics at the heart of the American Revolution, but also a "harmonizing force" capable of unifying the discordant factions across the political spectrum.[44]

Perhaps one reason for this is that in important ways (as Nietzsche first noted), the secular Enlightenment was a rewriting of Christian metaphysics, ethics, and teleology in naturalist language—its novel philosophies were a secularized faith, its cheerful belief in progress a secularized hope, its humanitarianism a secularized charity.[45] And beyond this, the Enlightenment substituted the immortality of the soul with the immortality of reputation and replaced religious saints with its own hagiography of Newton, Bacon, Locke, and so on. It has been said that pieties never die, they just change their objects of worship, but there was much more substantive overlap than might be apparent at first glance.

In the foreground of America's hybrid-Enlightenment were the ideals of freedom, equality, justice, and toleration, ideals that were by no means uncontested, complete, or universal. While their meaning was opaque enough to compel interminable political dispute over what these terms actually meant and how they should be applied, they were not empty of substance. They were, in fact, rich with meaning and ideological force. They translated into this novel idea of citizenship.

In the background, framing the meaning and experience of these ideals, was a shared providentialist understanding of the cosmos. Religiously and doctrinally, of course, Americans were endlessly divided, but this was not a secular culture and, though rationalist and liberalizing, the Enlightenment elements in that culture did not fundamentally undermine a taken-for-granted belief in God or the recognition of transcendence working in the world. For most Americans—

whether deist or Calvinist, rationalist and intellectual or revivalist and
popular, high church establishmentarian or sectarian—there was a
God more or less active in the universe and in human affairs. Indeed, this God was, for most, Christian and, even more, Protestant.
Though hegemonic and certainly oppressive to those who dissented,
this belief nevertheless provided a language and an ontology that
framed understandings of both public and private life. And yet this
was also a culture, following Weber and so many others, that was
inner-worldly in its orientation and ascetic in its general ethical disposition, an ethic that shunned extravagance, opulence, and self-
indulgence and prized hard work, discipline, and utility. In ethics it
was individualistic, to be sure, but informed by biblical and republican traditions that tempered individual interest and moved it toward
the public interest and common goods.[46] Not least—and long before John O'Sullivan came up with the phrase "manifest destiny" in
1839—this was a public culture defined by a shared understanding
of America under divine guidance and purpose. This was a uniquely
American adaptation of the Enlightenment vision of a world made new.

The Hybrid-Enlightenment Personified

The tense and difficult but also profoundly generative interplay between these two elements of the American idea was symbolized by
the well-known but fraught relations between two of the early Republic's greatest statesmen: Thomas Jefferson and John Adams. The
two joined forces and ideas to help build a new political order, but
for a while it seemed as if their differences might be unresolvable in
the long run. Their eventual reconciliation pointed to the possibility
of a deeper basis for unity between Adams's more traditionalist and
religious sensibility and Jefferson's progressive rationalism.

The two men were, of course, both leading advocates for American independence from Great Britain, and Adams was part of the
subcommittee that appointed Jefferson to draft the Declaration of
Independence. Once the crisis of the Revolution had passed, however, the common struggle gave way to an ordinary political contest
for power, and the differences between Jefferson and Adams took on
greater importance.

Adams's ardent support for the Revolution notwithstanding, his political disposition was broadly conservative. He was a firm believer in the permanence of social hierarchy, and he was suspicious of attempts to establish egalitarian political orders.[47] Consequently, he favored more aristocratic forms of constitutionalism, insisting that Britain's constitutional monarchy was a kind of republic and that post-1788 America, with its unitary executive, was a kind of monarchy; in the 1790s, he even began to argue in favor of hereditary governing institutions.[48] And although Adams shared the disbelief in miracles and the Trinity that was common among the American elite of his time, he maintained a kind of reverent, mystical awe toward traditional faith, and he worried about attempts to sever religion completely from public life. According to the historian Gordon Wood, Adams arrived over the course of his life at a kind of ecumenical regard for the various forms of Christianity practiced in the early Republic, and he talked about even the doctrines he rejected with what Wood, quoting him, calls a "sense of humility in an 'inscrutable and incomprehensible' universe . . . his deeply held belief that Christianity was 'Resignation to God.'"[49] In short, Adams carried a great deal of the mystical and traditionalist sensibility of eighteenth-century American religion into the constitutional and political debates of the post-revolutionary period.

Jefferson, who was wholeheartedly devoted to the ideas of the Enlightenment, differed from Adams on each of these points. Despite his own aristocratic background and his maintenance of an enormous slave plantation at Monticello, he was a staunch defender of political egalitarianism. His constitutional theory stressed the sovereignty of the people, and he rejected the hierarchical "estate theory" of political representation by social class that Adams continued to favor.[50] As for religion, Jefferson was, as we've seen, a rationalist through and through. He preserved none of Adams's humble respect for traditional religion; instead, he ridiculed crucial points of Christian doctrine. In contrast to Adams, he found the more mystical doctrines of the faith utterly repugnant. Yet even Jefferson's highly redacted version of the life of Jesus, which removed every supernatural element from the Gospels, can be read as a concession to the public's religious sensibilities—as a demonstration that he had not abandoned Christianity altogether.[51]

Inevitably, these differences cashed out in fierce personal and political disagreements as the two men assumed leading roles in the politics of the young country. Matters came to a head in the closely contested presidential election of 1800, which pitted the incumbent Adams against Jefferson. Adams's conservative Federalist Party faced off against Jefferson's more progressive Democratic-Republican Party in what can only be called a kind of early culture war. The Federalists wanted closer ties with hierarchical Britain, and they warned darkly about the dangers posed by popular government. The Federalist-controlled Congress even showed itself ready to tolerate substantial abridgements of the freedom of speech, passing a Sedition Act that criminalized "false, scandalous, or malicious" criticism of the government. Jefferson and the Republicans, meanwhile, were inspired by the French revolutionaries' attempts to establish a far more radically egalitarian form of government than had been attempted in America, and they wanted the United States to pursue closer ties with France rather than Britain, which they saw as reactionary and unenlightened. And they were outraged by the Sedition Act, both on principle and because they (not unreasonably) saw it as an attempt to censor their attacks on Adams and his government.

These differences became the chief themes of an acrimonious campaign. The Republican press attacked Adams as a reactionary and a monarchist, accusing him of seeking to undermine hard-won American freedoms by bringing the country back into Britain's orbit. In one private letter, Jefferson accused Adams and his allies of attempting "to bring back the times . . . when ignorance put everything into the hands of power & priestcraft."[52] Meanwhile, the Federalists accused Jefferson of atheism and the Republicans of seeking to bring the guillotine and general lawlessness of the French Revolution to the United States. The radical ideals of the Enlightenment were clashing directly with the conservative mores that were still favored by much of the American public.

Yet Jefferson and Adams famously reconciled, corresponding extensively over the last years of their lives before dying on the same day—July 4, 1826. That they were able to forgive one another points back to the unity that they and other members of the ideologically diverse Founding generation had been able to find amid their deepest differences. Adams may have favored more hierarchical forms of rule but, like Jefferson, he was firmly committed to the rule of law—a commitment that set the new American regime apart from almost every government in the history of the world.[53] Jefferson may have scorned traditional religion, but like Adams, he believed in a supreme divine power ordering the universe and making it intelligible. While both men sometimes descended to ad hominem, including in their exchanges about and with one another, they were also lovers of argument and reasoned intellectual consistency, as evidenced by Adams's extensive writings on political theory and Jefferson's love of philosophy. And although Jefferson was sometimes tempted by Continental opulence and Adams by monarchical grandeur, the two shared a deep affection for the culture of unpretentious simplicity and honest virtue that constituted so much of the self-conception of the early Republic. Jefferson's and Adams's passage from friendship to bitter rivalry and back dramatized the fertile tension between the religious and the secularist, the conservative and the progressive, the mystical and the rational tendencies in the American hybrid-Enlightenment. The unlooked-for success of their greatest project, just as much as their final reconciliation, demonstrated that this union of apparent opposites could be surprisingly resilient.

An Overlapping Solidarity

From the earliest days, America's hybrid-Enlightenment provided the cultural sources within which American democracy took form and matured. It provided a framework and the logics within which action and deliberation could unfold and, perhaps more important, a structure within which controversy, antagonism, and disagreement could be worked through.

Boundary Work

To be sure, this overlapping solidarity was aided by the presence (and memory) of "useful enemies": not least the large number of Native American tribes from the colonial period through the westward expansion and then, of course, King George III and his armies leading up to and during the War of Independence and then through the War of 1812. In their political aspirations, Americans shared an equal disdain for the religious superstitions of Roman Catholic popery on the Continent and the infidelity and violence of the Jacobins in France.[54] Solidarity was aided as well by the ethnic and religious similarities of a largely white and Protestant population drawn mainly from Great Britain but also northern Europe. And it was aided still further by the generally agrarian and mercantilist economy and division of labor that defined the everyday experience and habits of work, family, and community for most Americans.

No one would make the case that a thick conception of moral and political authority and, upon that, a consensus of constitutive ideas and ideals would alone provide the solidarity upon which the experiment in democracy could be sustained. Even from the outset, the Founders were skeptical of that. Early in his life, for example, John Adams had held out the hope that America could be a "Republic of Virtue," a nation in which the baser tendencies of humankind could be tempered by the higher ideals of virtue, benevolence, and duty. But after the revolution, he realized that neither the people nor its leadership "could be trusted as guardians of the republic."[55] Elites were driven by ambition, the masses were driven by their appetites, all were guided by self-interest, and none possessed the virtue for self-rule. As Adams put it in a letter to Jefferson in 1781, "I have been long settled in my opinion that neither Philosophy, nor Religion, nor Morality, nor Wisdom, nor Intellect, will ever govern nations or parties, against their Vanity, Pride, Resentment or Revenge, or their Avarice or Ambition. Nothing but Force and Power and Strength can restrain them."[56] Alexander Hamilton echoed the point. "Why has government been instituted at all?" he asked. "Because the passions of men will not conform to the dictates of reason and justice without constraint." James Madison too regarded control of passions as the central problem of politics. In his view, avarice and ambition were the prevailing motives of men, and neither personal virtue nor religious faith—nor reason, for that matter—could be counted on to keep them in check.[57] They were right, of course. At the very least, as Adams put it, "power must be opposed to power, force to force, strength to strength, interest to interest as well as reason to reason, eloquence to eloquence, and passion to passion."[58] They found that opposition in the constitutional articulation of the balance of powers. A common agreement over the institutional forms, procedures, and constraints of this dispersion of power would have to do its work.

Yet with that said, no one would dispute how important the ideas of liberty and equality and self-rule at the heart of the Enlightenment conception of civil society would continue to be for national identity and purpose. For ordinary Americans, this was the hope of America, the preconditions of the possibility of greater human flourishing. Because of the freedom the nation aspired to, the equality of opportunity, and the value placed on hard work and talent, one could start from almost anywhere and become anything. It was a mythos that made sense of sacrifice, self-denial, hard work, and obedience to the rules. Neither would anyone dispute the providentialist sensibilities that grounded reason, pictured human beings, and framed the future. Intellectually, ideologically, and dispositionally, "the United States has been," as Arthur Mann put it, "the land of the enduring Enlightenment."[59]

Enduring, perhaps, but far from static.

CHAPTER FIVE

Mythos and Nation-Building

THE CIVIC SOLIDARITY AMERICANS found in the ideals of freedom, equality, justice, and toleration were anything but free-floating abstractions or formal categories transcending place and time. Rather, the content of these ideals was underwritten by a shared, though mostly tacit, understanding—a constellation of givens—that was defined by a uniquely American adaptation of the Enlightenment. Their meaning was situated within a social, political, and cultural context long in the making.

On the surface of public life, of course, there was endless disagreement about what these ideals meant among different religious, political, and economic factions and interests. Yet underneath the surface—within the tacit structures of the hybrid-Enlightenment—there was a cohesion anchored by a religious imaginary that provided assurance that America was a nation existing under the guidance of Providence and moving toward the millennial hope of a world made new. Though this imaginary was overwhelmingly Protestant in character, it was still broad enough and opaque enough for people and communities of widely different backgrounds, experiences, convictions, and interests to find their place and contend within it. This tacit public culture contained these surface differences and made them intelligible, even if not always persuasive. Even those who were hostile or indifferent to the doctrines of the Calvinists found common ground in a culture that was populist, suspicious of hierarchy, ethically ascetic, and pragmatic. This tacit public culture also framed the obligations of public life. The frontier idyll of the early American rugged individual notwithstanding, Americans understood presumptively that they were not made merely for themselves but were given to a sociability recognizing that the fate of any one was inescapably linked to the fate of all. Cooperation in the task of building a nation and building a future was not an option—it was a necessity. And as creatures who were blessed by God with the power of reason, it was through public reason that they would contend toward that future.

As I've emphasized, the public culture of America's hybrid-Enlightenment took shape historically in ways that were highly contingent and riven with contradiction, often barely acknowledged. Even so, it was durable enough to provide the cultural resources for a century of nation-building. All of the elements were present at the beginning, but most important in the late eighteenth and early nineteenth centuries was a millennialism—both religious and secular—in which it was assumed that America played a redemptive purpose in human history.

The durability of these cultural resources certainly speaks of continuity, but it should not imply inertia. Through the first half of the nineteenth century, the cultural logic of America's hybrid-Enlightenment was, in fact, "worked through" but in ways that exaggerated the religious elements of the Founding period and diminished its classical, secular, and deistic elements. Its net effect was a reconfiguration of the Enlightenment project in America into a mythos of America as a "Christian Republic." But this reconfiguration was only the start. What were the implications of this mythos for addressing the contradictions of democratic life?

Mythos

We have seen hints of this mythos already—the groundwork for it was laid long before the nineteenth century. An important pre-revolution moment in its unfolding, however, was marked by the publication of John Adams's *A Dissertation on the Canon and Feudal Law* in 1765. This was Adams's first effort to understand the significance of New England and of America more broadly in history. His starting point was a reflection on human nature, history, and the struggle for freedom. As he put it, "Human nature [was] chained fast for ages in a cruel, shameful, and deplorable servitude" to two systems of tyranny that flourished in Europe. Those systems encompassed the temporal and spiritual, the political and religious. Tyranny, in short, derived from the various monarchies that dominated the nations of Europe and from the Roman Catholic Church that overspread Europe itself. Liberation from these tyrannies began with the Reformation. "One age of darkness succeeded another," Adams wrote, "till God in his benign providence raised up the champions who began and conducted the Reformation. From the time of the Reformation to the first settlement of America, knowledge gradually spread . . . and in proportion as that increased and spread among the people, ecclesiastical and civil tyranny seem to have lost their strength and weight."[1]

In this view, the discovery of America by Europeans, the Enlightenment itself, and eventually the American Revolution would be seen as a succession of victories on behalf of human liberty that traced back to the sixteenth century. These developments, in Adams's view, represented a continuation of the work of the Reformation. Importantly in this succession, what began in the religious sphere extended into the civil sphere. The freedom that ordinary people required in the realm of faith would become the freedom they required in politics. Thus, as with faith, the civil rights of citizens "cannot be repealed or restrained by human laws—Rights, derived from the great Legislator of the universe."[2]

As Adams reflected in the original draft, "I always consider the settlement of America with reverence and wonder, as the opening of a grand scene and design in Providence for the illumination of the ignorant, and the emancipation of the slavish part of mankind all over the earth."[3]

The Founding of this new Republic and the building of the nation were, then, apocalyptic events marking an important moment in an ongoing struggle that would establish a new nation, justify its territorial expansion, and spawn nearly every reform movement of the nineteenth century.

A half century later, this understanding was reiterated by Adams's son, John Quincy Adams, in 1821. At the time Adams (the son) was secretary of state and four years from becoming president himself.

In a Fourth of July celebration address, he echoed the moral and political view of the Protestant establishment that dominated the United States for the whole of the nineteenth century. He reminded his audience that for seven hundred years, people had lived under a "portentous system of despotism and of superstition" by which in the conflict "between the oppressions of power and the claims of right . . . man had no rights. Neither the body nor the soul of the individual was his own." The religious Reformation represented "an improvement" and "an advance" "in the progress of man": "From the discussion of religious rights and duties, the transition to that of the political and civil relations of men with one another was natural and unavoidable; in both the reformers were met by the weapons of temporal power. . . . Released from the fetters of ecclesiastical domination, the minds of men began to investigate the foundations of civil government."[4]

What followed was the Declaration of Independence. This document and the birth of nationhood it represented, for Adams, "stands, and must forever stand alone, a beacon on the summit of the mountain to which all the inhabitants of the earth may turn their eyes for a genial and saving light, till time shall be lost in eternity. . . . It stands forever, *a light of admonition to the rulers of men; a light of salvation and redemption to the oppressed.*" The principles of the Declaration "must be recognize[d] . . . as eternal truths," he wrote, the duty of all citizens "to pledge ourselves and bind our posterity to a faithful and undeviating adherence to them."[5]

Lyman Beecher

One of the most interesting figures to emerge on the scene in this moment was Lyman Beecher. Beecher was born in New Haven just a year before America declared independence and grew up in the bracing early decades of the new Republic. As a young man, he studied at Yale under Timothy Dwight, president of the university and the grandson of Jonathan Edwards. For the better part of three decades, he pastored churches in Long Island and Connecticut. In 1832, at the age of fifty-seven, Beecher took his message to heart by becoming president of Lane Seminary in Cincinnati with the mission of training ministers to serve the westward expansion. He and his successive wives also raised thirteen children. All seven sons followed him into the ministry, including the famous abolitionist Henry Ward Beecher. Among his six daughters were the educational reformer Catherine Beecher, the suffragist Isabella Beecher Hooker, and the novelist and abolitionist Harriet Beecher Stowe.

Beecher is important for the ways he captured the energy of the new nation and became one of the most renowned and compelling apologists for the millennial hopes of America. He admitted at first that he was dubious about Jonathan Edwards's claim that the millennium would originate in America. He called the idea "chimerical." And yet the evidence all around him suggested otherwise. "If it is by the march of revolution and civil liberty, that the way of the Lord is to be prepared, where shall the central energy be found, and from what nation shall the renovating power go forth? . . . In the providence of God" America was "destined to lead the way in the moral and political emancipation of the world. . . . There is not a nation upon earth which, in fifty years, can by all possible reformation place itself in circumstances so favorable as our own for the free, unembarrassed application of physical effort and pecuniary and moral power to evangelize the world."[6]

This theme was set first in a sermon he gave in Plymouth, Massachusetts, "in commemoration of the landing of the Fathers" on December 22, 1827.[7] He began with an observation about the abundance of the world, affirming that the earth was capable of sustaining a thriving population and it was only "the perversion of her resources and of the human faculties, which has made the misery of man so great." The great civilizations in Egypt, Greece, Rome, and Europe had all demonstrated ingenuity but also ultimately a corruption that led to the failure to meliorate the condition of humankind and to "disenthrall the nations." But in America, moral renovation was underway that would "change the character and conditions of men." Not partial, not temporary, and not only for the wealthy and powerful, this renovation would be "the last dispensation of heaven for the relief of this miserable world, and shall bring glory to God in the highest, and upon earth peace and good will to men." This renovation required the democratization of private property for ordinary people against "the monopoly of the soil" by the few, the suffrages of freemen against the monopoly of power by the few, and the rights of conscience against tyranny. "Where," he asked, "could such a nation be found" where these conditions existed? "Look now at the history of our Fathers," he exclaimed, "and behold what God hath wrought." The Puritans, he argued, "lay the foundations of a new empire. And now, behold their institutions; such as the world needs, and, attended as they have been by the power of God, able to enlighten and renovate the world." These institutions "recognize the equal rights of man—they give the soil to the cultivator, and self-government and the rights of conscience to the people. They enlighten the intellect, and form the conscience, and bring the entire influence of the divine government to bear upon the heart." The history of the nation, he argued, was indicative of "some grand design," a history "of perils and deliverances, and of strength ordained out of weakness" that included the "wars with the savage tribes, and with the French, and at last with the English." But "if it had been the design of heaven to establish a powerful nation, in the full enjoyment of civil and religious liberty, where all the energies of man might find scope and excitement, on purpose to show the world by experiment, of what man is capable; and to shed light on the darkness which should awake the slumbering eye, and rouse the torpid mind, and nerve the palsied arm of millions; where could such an experiment have been made but in this country, and by whom so auspiciously as by our Fathers, and by what means so well adapted to that end, as by their institutions?"

In Beecher's view, the moral energy of nation-building was generated out of the revivalism of the Second Great Awakening. "The revivals of religion which prevail in our land among Christians of all denominations," he said, "are without a parallel in the history of the world and are constituting an era of moral power entirely new." These revivals "declare the purpose of God to employ this nation in the glorious work of renovating the earth." But if the moral vitality of revivalism was the fuel of nation-building, its engine was constituted through the "concentrated benevolence" of voluntary institutions.

> Voluntary associations of Christians were raised up to apply and extend that [moral and religious] influence. . . . And now we are blessed with societies to aid in the support of the Gospel at home, to extend it to the new settlements, and through

the earth. We have Bible societies, and Tract societies, and associations of individuals, who make it their business to see that every family has a Bible, and every church a pastor, and every child a catechism. And to these have succeeded Education societies, that our nation may not outgrow the means of religious instruction. And while these means of moral culture are supplied, this great nation from her eminence, begins to look abroad with compassion upon a world sitting in darkness; and to put forth her mighty arm to disenthrall the nations, and elevate the family of man.

Much of the rest of Beecher's sermon was given to the need "to cherish and extend our religious institutions." Much, in his view, was at stake. The "universal extension of our religious institutions, is the only means of reconciling our unparalleled prosperity with national purity and immortality. . . . Unless we can extend the power of religious institutions through the land, dark clouds will soon obscure [God's] glory, and his descent to a night of ages will be more rapid than his rising."

The story Beecher told about America reflected the substance and tone of literally thousands of sermons, tracts, and treatises produced by many others over the nineteenth century on the subject of the millennium and America's place in it. This literature demonstrated how central and utterly commonplace a millennial understanding of national identity and purpose was.[8] Like Beecher, these nation-builders were not blind. Obstacles preventing Christian perfection were many and serious in their minds. Even so, Americans understood themselves, in the words of one New England pastor, as "a people peculiarly favored of Heaven."[9] The hope born out of this conviction was enacted in moral reform and echoed repeatedly. In 1847, we hear the theme yet again in the famous tract by Horace Bushnell, *Barbarism the First Danger*: "The wilderness shall bud and blossom as the rose before us; and we will not cease, till a Christian nation throws up its temples of worship on every hill and plain; till knowledge, virtue and religion, blending their dignity and their healthful power, have filled our great country with a manly and happy race of people, and the hands of a complete Christian commonwealth are seen to span the continent."[10]

The Evangelical Turn

From the Adamses, father and son, through the Beecher family, Horace Bushnell, and thousands of others in between and long after, the story that Americans would tell about their nation as a Christian Republic was far from a fringe idea perpetrated by religious eccentrics or hoary, backwoods reactionaries. The language and imagery of this mythos were familiar to Americans everywhere. Its proponents were established and influential leaders in the mainstream of American society, and as the nineteenth century wore on, most of them, in their context, were progressives.

For ordinary folk living at the time, the experience was mainly one of continuity.[11] The public culture then would not have seemed so different from the Founding period. Among the leadership classes of the Founding generation, however, the heritage of classical antiquity was also ubiquitous. Certainly, they all knew the Jewish and Christian Scriptures, but beyond this, a general knowledge of the classical authors was "universal among colonists with any education."[12] Knowledge of Plutarch, Livy, Cicero, Sallust, and Tacitus provided a window into the political history of Rome from the early first century to the end of the second. This was an epoch that provided inspiration because of the virtues of simplicity, patriotism, integrity, and love of justice and liberty characteristic of its early years, but also prompted caution due to the venality, cynicism, corruption, and oppression of its latter years. Even if this literature was illustrative, and the learning behind it superficial, it provided an anchoring and widely recognizable authority.

But organized deism largely evaporated in the early years of the nineteenth century. It had its stalwarts, of course, but they became increasingly marginal voices through these decades, and any movements rooted in free-thinking tendencies were all but swept aside by religious enthusiasm.[13] Looking back, we more easily see that the saturation of the mythos of the early American Republic by Protestant Christian language, metaphor, and imagery represented an initial "working through" of the cultural logic of America's hybrid-Enlightenment through a widening of its religious tributaries and, in effect, a damming up of its secular, deistic, and free-thinking tributaries. The proponents of the evangelical turn would have also believed themselves justified as a matter of principle, for even John Locke, in his *Letter concerning Toleration*, had argued that atheists should not be tolerated, at least not in public affairs. In Locke's words, "Those are not at all to be tolerated who deny the being of a God. Promises, covenants, and oaths, which are the bonds of human society, can have no hold upon an atheist. The taking away of God, though but even in thought, dissolves all; besides also, those that by their atheism undermine and destroy all religion, can have no pretense of religion whereupon to challenge the privilege of a toleration."[14]

Though Locke wrote this *Letter* in 1689, for most Americans its concerns seemed to be validated by the radical and violent tendencies of the French Revolution. Free thinking in America, then, wasn't absent, but it wasn't native to the early decades of the Republic either.

The growth of higher education in the early nineteenth century was another window into the ways the evangelical turn was crystallized and hardened. By 1860, 182 permanent colleges had been founded in the United States and of these, 175 were under denominational control.[15] It wasn't just that the secular influence of the Enlightenment had been displaced. Rather, in many ways it was routed with disparagement. As one foreign observer put it in 1837, "The Jews are tolerated in America with the same liberality as any other denomination of Christians; but if a person were to call himself a Deist or an Atheist, it would excite universal execration."[16]

Some scholars have suggested that it wasn't at all inevitable that Protestantism would become hegemonic in the way that it did.[17] True, but the odds were certainly in its favor. One reason was surely demographic. According to the 1790 census, all but a small fraction of the population had originated from Protestant countries, and of these, 83.5 percent had come from England and 6.7 percent from Scotland.[18] They brought their faith with them—the majority of churches in post-revolutionary America were Episcopalian or Presbyterian, along with the churches from the nonconforming Congregationalist, Methodist, and Baptist denominations. Depending on the region, these, along with Lutheran, the Dutch Reformed, and Disciples of Christ churches were, more often than not, the most stable and most prominent institutions in every village, town, and city in America. What is more, their clergy were, more often than not, the dominant intellectual class. They were, as a rule, better educated and more literate than most others in their communities, and through their sermons, they were among the chief purveyors of authoritative knowledge and opinion.

Importantly, these churches provided the means of transforming a geographically scattered population into communities as places to meet, socialize, worship, and ritually mark the traumas and transitions of life, from birth to death. The life experience of individuals was circumscribed by the expectations of a whole community: infants were not simply born, they were baptized; children didn't merely grow up, they were catechized; men and women didn't come together, they were married with the blessings of the church.[19] Not only did churches provide places of common belief, they offered belonging for a scattered population.

Protestant Christianity came to exert an outsized influence in America's hybrid-Enlightenment because it grew rapidly; it did so (as I noted in the previous chapter) because of a transformation of its ethos. Leading up to the nineteenth century, American Puritanism had evolved from a formal intellectual and establishment Calvinism to a more populist and experiential evangelicalism, an evolution that was cemented by the Second Great Awakening. The doctrines and beliefs remained very much the same, but the interpretations, rituals, and practices were different. Rather than a faith rooted in rational proposition, the evangelical turn favored personal conversion through an emotional encounter with the Holy Spirit. "Genuine" Christianity would now reside in the authenticity of individual and personal experience. And whereas traditional Calvinism, through its doctrine of predestination, had been somewhat passive regarding social reform, nineteenth-century evangelicalism actively sought to subordinate social and political institutions to divine judgment and to rationally and self-consciously reform them accordingly. This was an empowering faith that was more appealing to the yeoman and merchant classes of the early nineteenth century. Fueled by the emotional intensity of revivalism—yet another source of solidarity—the evangelical ethos swept through America in the first half of the nineteenth century, its influence manifested in all the leading Protestant denominations.

To be sure, not all Protestants were aligned with this transformation. Ethnically based confessions that included German Lutherans, Dutch Calvinists, Old School Presbyterians, and Antimission Baptists, along with Unitarians, Roman Catholics, and the unchurched, were at least leery of revivalism, if not forthrightly critical of it. And much of their defiance was rooted in their resolve to preserve their historical identity and practice. Yet in their broader cosmology, dissenters still had more in common than not with the evangelicals, not least in their shared tendencies toward moral perfectionism in personal life and utopian hope in social and political life. Consequently, revivalist evangelicalism came to dominate the cultural logics of public life in this period. Through the evangelical turn, religion became a more powerful political force in the first half of the nineteenth century than it had been even at the time of the American Revolution.[20]

The Paradox of Religion and National Life

Still another reason Protestant Christianity came to exert an outsized influence in nineteenth-century America was its novel solution to the paradoxical relationship between religion and the state. The constitutional conditions were conducive to its spread.

For centuries, the idea of an official national religion established by law at public expense had been normative, and yet in America, by the close of the eighteenth century, the idea had been all but abandoned. It's true that a few state establishments (in Connecticut, New Hampshire, and Massachusetts) remained, but they too were given up in the early decades of the century.[21] Sectarian quarrels made even a softened form of religious establishment unmanageable. What had *not* been abandoned, however, was the conviction that societies required a unifying faith and a broadly accepted system of morality. This conviction remained as strong as ever.

The paradox was, in effect, addressed through an innovation: "American civilization" would be undergirded by Christian faith and morals, not through legal mandate but rather through free will and voluntary effort. In short, an establishment by other means—cultural, not legal. A formal and legal wall of separation would exist between church and state, but religion and civic life would come together to form the religious and moral foundations of the Republic. The bridge between these two spheres would be forged through voluntary discipline, not by the authoritarianism of traditional societies. It was, as Daniel Walker Howe described it, "the functional equivalent of an established church" that would serve the ideal of a Christian society.[22]

In light of historical precedent, this resolution was quite remarkable. Writing in 1837, Francis Grund, an émigré from Austria—sometimes called the "Jacksonian Tocqueville"—highlighted the point in his book *The Americans, in Their Moral, Social and Political Relations*. After recording the number of churches in America (15,477 by his count) served by the number of ministers (12,127), he observed, "When we reflect that no tax is imposed for the support of ministers, or the building of churches, and that, consequently, all those establishments are the result of voluntary contributions of the people, the conviction will certainly be forced on our minds that the Americans are deeply impressed with the importance of religious instruction, and that together with their freedom, they prize nothing so high as the sacred truths of Christianity. No more satisfactory evidence is required on this subject than the fact that they are willing to *pay* for it; which is certainly a singular coincidence when contrasted with the political position of other countries."[23]

The vast number and variety of churches in America, Grund observed, were voluntary associations that survived and grew on resources they could generate themselves. On this basis, most Protestant leaders in the range of denominations simply assumed that the Christian character of the nation would expand and be sustained through voluntary means. Freed from the corruptions that had long marred state ecclesiastical hierarchies, America would become *more* Christian than ever. Religious freedom and the political freedom promised by democracy would be mutually reinforcing.

Faith itself was a medium of solidarity, a shared cosmology rooted in transcendence, grounded in a common and authoritative Scripture—however much people disagreed on the particulars. But the primary source of solidarity was morality. As the argument went, without religiously infused moral standards, civilization would simply fall apart. Grund saw it clearly:

The religious habits of the Americans form not only the basis of the private and public morals, but have become so thoroughly interwoven with their whole course of legislation, that it would be impossible to change them, without affecting the very essence of their government. . . . The deference which the Americans pay to morality is scarcely inferior to their regard for religion, and is, in part, based upon the latter. The least solecism in the moral conduct of a man is attributed to his want of religion, and is visited upon him as such. . . . They see in a breach of morals a direct violation of religion; and in this, an attempt to subvert the political institutions of the country.[24]

For these reasons, ministers were quick to admonish their parishioners. It was only a rhetorical ploy for the Reverend Jesse Appleton, president of Bowdoin College, to ask, as he did in 1814, "Do you believe that any State, community, or nation can be powerful, tranquil, and permanently happy, if their morals are extensively depraved? Would not the most alarming depravation of morals result from a general disbelief in the Christian religion? Would the happiness of families, would property or life be secure in a nation of deists? If Christianity is the most powerful guardian of morals, are you not, as civilians, bound to give it your support and patronage?"[25]

To his audience, the answer was obvious.

The "Benevolent Empire"

The renowned historian Winthrop Hudson observed that by the 1860s, "the ideals, the convictions, the language, the customs, the institutions of [American] society were so shot through with Christian presuppositions that the culture itself nurtured and nourished Christian faith."[26] Through the march of human events, the work of the Holy Spirit would bring salvation to many, would extend the work of mercy and care and, in the process, cleanse America of its sin. But in the lead-up to the millennium, there was work to do. As the Reverend Julian Sturtevant exhorted his fellow Yale alumni in 1861, "There is to be a long reign of peace on earth. But it is not to be ushered in by leaving crime unpunished, and unoffending virtue unprotected, and giving up this present world to men of violence and blood, to tyrannize over it to their heart's content; but by effecting such changes in the social, political and moral condition of the world, through the dissemination of freedom, instruction, and a pure Christian faith, as shall render a long reign of peace and justice possible. In the present state of the world, it is not possible."[27]

To Sturtevant and his contemporaries, this was an age of benevolence and America was a "benevolent empire," yet there was still much work to be done. This vision would be realized through the expansive and interlocking network of organizations committed to social and moral reform, the effect of which would extend near and far, but whose vital and animating center were the cities.[28]

The hard work of benevolence implicit in Sturtevant's admonitions was not an adornment to evangelical commitment but central to ethics of moral perfection. As such it defined another critical element in the national mythos of the time. This moral perfectionism was rooted in the assumption that as citizens and as a nation, America and its people existed in a covenantal relationship with God, akin to Israel's relationship to God described in the Old Testament. The idea meant that Americans were morally responsible before God to make their country exemplary in service to God's purposes of establishing his kingdom on this earth. Blessings and curses were linked to how well they lived up to that calling.[29] The work of benevolence, then, was spiritually urgent.

The Reformist Impulse: The Example of Phoebe Palmer

Thus, when Lyman Beecher gave his sermon "The Memory of Our Fathers" in 1827, championing voluntary societies as the engine of moral reform, he was promoting something that had already started to unfold and that was to become a vast network of voluntary associations oriented toward a broad variety of specific reforms.[30] Indeed, Beecher was among the founders of the most prominent of these associations. Among the earliest and largest were the American Board of Commissions for Foreign Missions (1810), the American Education Society (1815), the American Bible Society (1824; this organization consolidated hundreds of Bible societies around the country founded as early as 1808), the American Sunday School Union (1824), the American Tract Society (1824), the American Home Missionary Society (1826), and the American Temperance Society (1826). These were all national in vision and ambition and, with their local auxiliaries, the number of such organizations totaled in the thousands. Of the American Temperance Society, there were over eight thousand local chapters. Organized benevolence around the "reformation of morals" ranged even further to include societies that discouraged travel, work, and recreation on the Sabbath, profanity, idleness, dishonesty, gambling, horseracing, cockfighting, dueling, drunkenness and intemperance, and "all pernicious habits," as well as educational societies that served the common schools, associations oriented toward prison reform, asylums and schools for the care of the deaf and mute, and eventually, societies that promoted abolition. A few of these were national in scope, some were regional or statewide, and many, many more were local auxiliaries of these larger organizations.[31]

An exemplar of this vision was Phoebe Palmer. She was born in New York City into a middle-class family of devout Methodists in 1807. She was the fourth of sixteen children, though only eight reached the age of maturity.[32]

To say the family was "devout" doesn't quite capture the intensity and rigor of piety common in the early nineteenth century. Each morning, every day, a bell was sounded to announce morning prayers, giving her family time to prepare for the day. At the second bell, a half hour later, morning prayers began with her father reading verses from the Bible and explaining them, followed by songs sung from a hymnal and then prayers for the day ahead and for the needs of others. The entire family was expected to be present for this ritual, which was repeated in the evening.

Given this background, faith was real to her, but also commonplace. In 1835, now in her late twenties, Palmer experienced a profound renewal of her faith that set her, along with her physician husband, on a path toward leadership in the wave of urban revivalism. She became active in the Tractarian movement of lay evangelism, developed into a prolific author (*Entire Devotion to God, Faith and Its Effects, Promise of the Father, The Way of Holiness*), and became the owner and editor of the magazine *Guide to Holiness*. She also traveled extensively in the United States, Canada, and Great Britain, speaking at camp meetings and revival services, and, beginning in 1840, she led the Tuesday Meeting for the Promotion of Holiness out of her home in New York City. The Tuesday Meeting was the locus of the holiness movement in New York, and over four decades, it spawned nearly 250 similar meetings as far away as New Zealand and India.

Palmer exemplified the centrality of evangelism to moral reform. Aligned with the classical Christian theology on the subject, she believed that all people are made in the image of God, that inside every person, whether rich or poor, strong or weak, is a "gem of priceless value"—a soul that had been diminished by rebellion against God. "His manliness of form, his intellect, his precious soul, made in the image of God, are well-nigh lost from human vision— buried beneath the rubbish of sin." Yet Christ sees the worth of every human being and "purchased him with His own blood."[33]

Belief in the *imago Dei* was the critical motive behind Palmer's labor on behalf of the poor. The work of salvation, in her view, was a part of a benevolent cycle in which care for the soul led to the care for the conditions of a person's life. People needed to be fed, clothed, educated, and freed from the influence of alcohol. And they needed jobs—and to keep those jobs, they needed to be sober, honest, and upright, which meant that they needed salvation. In this, she was animated by the words and example of Christ. For Palmer, Scripture taught that God desires that the poor be cared for and treated justly. "We speak of the poor as objects of God's special regard, for he presents them as such."[34] On this she was fond of quoting the Gospel of Matthew (in the King James Version): "In as much as ye have done it unto one of the least of these, my brethren, ye have done it to me." In this way, humanitarian relief and evangelism were inextricably linked.

It was out of this well-spring of conviction that Palmer participated in most of the local work of evangelism and moral reform in New York City. Besides her involvement with the Tract Society, the Female Assistance Society, and the women's temperance movement, she took an active part in prison ministry in the Tombs in Manhattan, helped establish Hedding Church, a mission to the poor, supported an orphanage, became a foster parent to a number of children herself, and most significantly, founded the Five Points Mission in an area comparable only to London's East End as the most squalid slum in the Western world. There, she led the effort to build a chapel, parsonage, baths, schoolrooms, and a settlement house with apartments for twenty families, mostly single mothers, to live without charge. With this came food, clothing, and jobs.

Phoebe Palmer was a remarkable woman, but she was only one of innumerable people involved in the work of moral reform. As voluntary benevolent associations proliferated, they provided ways to unite people from different backgrounds in common purpose. And their production of tracts, articles, and sermons was prodigious. In the absence of an established church, what else could guarantee religion, piety, and moral conformity? As important were its social and political implications. As Jacob Rush put it, "All immorality tends in its very nature, and by inevitable consequences, to the overthrow and ruin of society."[35]

To be sure, the net effect of this broad network of voluntary organizations oriented toward moral reformation was the creation of a lower threshold of agreement than religious doctrine. It was easier to find solidarity on matters of social welfare and civilizational purpose among Unitarians, liberals, and orthodox evangelicals than on matters of theology. Membership in a moral society was open to men of every confession and party who, as one minister put it, were "willing to maintain a sober moral life." In the process, the Puritan morality of the colonial period was transformed into evangelically infused republican virtue in the post-revolutionary period.

Cultivating Republicanism

In their totality, the moral reform movements of the first half of the nineteenth century nurtured the mythos of the Christian Republic, and the growth of these movements in villages, towns, and cities expanded their institutional reach. Yet there was no initiative more central to this ambition than the effort to educate the young through the common school movement.

The backdrop was conducive. America's Founders had fully recognized the necessity of education to the stability and proper functioning of the Republic. They believed it to be the principal means of securing and perpetuating the experiment in democracy. To a person, the Founders held that the quality of a democracy hinged in some large part on the thoughtfulness, intelligence, and virtue of its people. Jefferson, for one, argued that "to protect individuals in the free exercise of their national rights," to "guard against degeneracy," and to prevent tyranny from its leaders, it was necessary "to illuminate as far as practicable, the minds of the people" through "liberal education."[36] Education, he argued, would render "the people the safe . . . and ultimate guardians of their own liberty."[37] Benjamin Rush, in his "Thoughts upon the Mode of Education Proper in a Republic," had argued that schools would be "nurseries of wise and good men."[38] Noah Webster likewise believed that "education . . . forms the moral characters of men and morals are the basis of government."[39] Such convictions were championed consistently through the early decades of nation-building.[40] Education would be the means by which the knowledge, civic virtue, and true moral character necessary for citizenship in a republic would be accomplished.

Jefferson, however, recognized that most families could not afford to educate their children. That task, he had written in his 1779 bill to the Virginia legislature, "A Bill for the More General Diffusion of Knowledge," must fall to the government.[41] Yet making education free and universal as a matter of law and public policy was by no means a foregone achievement. Through most of the nineteenth century, state legislatures demonstrated a stubborn reluctance to fund public education through tax revenues. It took more than a century before Jefferson's ambitions were fulfilled, and public education, at least for the elementary grades, became mandatory in all fifty states.

In the meantime, the general education of the young took form through a partnership of public and denominational schools. In all of them, there was never any debate about the essential role religion would play in the formation of citizens. In the Founding period, Benjamin Rush gave voice to what was to become the standard view: the "only foundation for a useful education in a republic," he said, "is to be laid in religion. Without this, there can be no virtue and without virtue, there can be no liberty and liberty is the object and life of all republican governments."[42] His rhetoric was provocative: he said he would "rather see the opinions of Confucius or Mohammed inculcated upon our youth than see them grow up wholly devoid of a system of religious principles." Nevertheless, the faith he recommended for schooling was "the religion of Jesus Christ." As Rush put it, "A Christian cannot fail of being a republican, for every precept of the Gospel inculcates those degrees of humility, self-denial, and brotherly kindness which are directly opposed to the pride of monarchy and the pageantry of a court. A Christian cannot fail of being useful to the republic, for his religion teacheth him that no man 'liveth to himself.' And lastly, a Christian cannot fail of being wholly inoffensive, for his religion teacheth him in all things to do to others what he would wish, in like circumstances, they should do to him."[43]

In addition to reading, writing, arithmetic, and religion, students would also be taught "the general principles of law, commerce, money and government"—"all necessary for the yeomanry of a republican state."[44]

Yet during this period of nation-building and through the transformations entailed in the movements of moral reform, the interdenominational Protestant cast of general education became fully entrenched.[45] The missionary zeal of Protestantism and the building of a republic were aligned in the task of citizen formation. Throughout the country, but in the westward expansion in particular, Protestant ministers understood the establishment and oversight of schools and colleges as a religious obligation. A "free school for every settlement, and a grammar school for every hundred families," declared a missionary to Oregon in 1848.[46] Alexis de Tocqueville's observation that "almost all education is entrusted to the clergy" made sense in light of the campaign to build a Christian republic.[47]

Boundary Work

This "benevolent empire" represented the sum and substance of the evangelical turn that occurred in the first half of the nineteenth century. This turn represented both *continuity with* and a significant *transformation of* America's hybrid-Enlightenment. On the one hand, it reinforced, popularized, and promulgated the political mythos of a nation in covenantal relationship with God. In an age of nation-building, this provided cultural sources and moral energy not only for extraordinary growth and expansion but for solidarity along the way. But the consequences of the evangelical turn were also substantial for the ways Americans attempted to address the enduring contradictions of exclusion in a civilization that promised inclusion. The boundaries dividing "in" from "out" were reinforced certainly through law and custom, but often through violence. For all the good intentions to build a benevolent empire in covenant with God, those efforts also exposed the contradictions more openly, bringing their darker consequences more and more into relief.

And Its Consequences

The accounts of these contradictions are well known, especially to scholars of the period. But for those who are unfamiliar, it is worth recounting some of the highlights to illuminate the tortuous ways Americans attempted to work through the range of contradictions embedded so deeply in the nation's cultural logic. This will also bring into relief the failures inherent in the evangelical turn in America's hybrid-Enlightenment. Boundary work was bloody business.

NATIVE AMERICANS

To the American settlers, the aboriginal tribes of North America had always been a threat. Their skin was dark, their language was foreign, their habits of life were unfamiliar, and their beliefs were alien. They were, in the words of the Declaration of Independence, "merciless Indian Savages, whose known rule of warfare, is an undistinguished destruction of all ages, sexes and conditions." Even though their numbers were diminished severely over the course of the nineteenth century, the tragic irony was that the so-called Indian problem only grew.

The "problem," of course, was that they controlled so much land. Until 1812 or so, the demands of the settlers had been relatively modest and the cessions of land from various tribes were relatively small. At the turn of the nineteenth century, most of the land west of Pennsylvania, Tennessee, Ohio, North Carolina, South Carolina, and eastern Georgia and north of east Texas and Louisiana belonged to the hundreds of indigenous tribes, the largest among them the Cherokee, Creek, Seminole, Chickasaw, Navaho, Arapaho, Comanche, Apache, Sioux, Cheyenne, Pawnee, Crow, Blackfeet, Seneca, Delaware, Osage, Shoshoni, and Ute. By 1820, however, it was clear that the indigenous tribes were simply obstacles to the expansionary interests of the benevolent empire. As William Henry Harrison, then governor of the Northwest Territory, put it, "Is one of the fairest portions of the globe to remain . . . the haunt of a few wretched savages, when it seems destined by the Creator to support a large population and to be the seat of civilization?"[48] The question was rhetorical. It was clear to most everyone that Providence had placed upon America the burden of governing the immense sweep of a beckoning continent. And so a land grab of unprecedented proportions was on.

Decades before, in 1787, the U.S. Congress had famously promised in article 3 of the Northwest Ordinance that "utmost good faith shall always be observed toward the Indians; their land and property shall never be taken from them without their consent."[49] Over 350 treaties followed, all based on the idea that each tribe was a separate nation with the right of self-determination and self-rule.[50] Needless to say, the number of promises broken are too many to count. Though the Indian nations resisted, often violently, they were divided, unorganized, outnumbered, and poorly armed and thus never strong enough to successfully oppose their segregation, extermination in certain cases, and involuntary removal from their ancestral lands.

The process was neither easy nor straightforward. The government sanctioned literally hundreds of raids, attacks, and wars on the Indian tribes, and by the 1870s, most of that land that was to become the continental United States had been ceded to the government.[51] In the process, of course, the native tribes were forcibly evicted, their tribal life and culture eviscerated. This happened many times in different regions, most egregiously as a consequence of the Indian Removal Act of 1830, which resulted in roughly one hundred thousand Cherokee, Seminole, Chickasaw, and Choctaw Indians being marched at the point of a bayonet from the Southeast to lands west of the Mississippi. The story of the Trail of Tears caused by greed and cruelty is well known; thousands died along the way.

There were an estimated 900,000 aboriginal natives in the area that was to become the United States at the time of Columbus, but by 1876, there were only about 280,000 left. Until 1887, most Native Americans were ineligible for citizenship, and birthright citizenship was granted to Native Americans only in 1924.

CATHOLICS

The story of Roman Catholics is very different. In the early days of the Republic, Catholics were viewed as more of a tolerable oddity than a threat. The reason was mainly demographic: at the time of the first census, just under 1 percent of the population (roughly 35,000 out of 4 million) was Catholic, and many of these were English, well-educated landowners dwelling in Maryland and Pennsylvania. Over the next forty years, the number increased to 600,000, and by 1850, the number had swelled to 1.75 million. Between 1845 and 1850 alone, the U.S. population shifted from about 95 percent to 90 percent Protestant. The trends continued through the 1850s, with immigration accelerating, adding an additional 2.6 million inhabitants—accounting in that single decade for 51 percent of all who had immigrated since 1820. They came from the German states, eastern Europe, Italy, and elsewhere, but the lion's share—nearly 30 percent—came from Ireland. And these "hordes," as they were sometimes called, were overwhelmingly Catholic.[52] They were driven to America by famine and poverty and so, naturally, they were mostly poor and illiterate, expanding the ranks of unskilled labor. They concentrated in the slums and shantytowns of the great eastern and midwestern cities of Baltimore, Philadelphia, New York, Boston, St. Louis, and Chicago. One observer described the phenomenon as "a peaceful invasion by an army, more than twice as vast as the estimated number of Goths and Vandals that swept over Southern Europe and overwhelmed Rome."[53]

Catholics, of course, and the priests who represented them were, in the minds of the Protestant establishment, bearers of all the superstitions, oppressive doctrines, and authoritarian edicts that Protestants had fled in the first place. But more than that, the Catholic Church had also long been viewed by Protestants as having conspiratorial ambitions of world domination, by coercive means if necessary. Catholicism already held sway in French Canada to the north and in Mexico, Haiti, and Puerto Rico to the south and now it had designs on infiltrating America to expand its influence.[54] The issue that settler nativists repeated again and again was that the nature of authority in the Roman Catholic Church meant that it could never be democratic. As Samuel Morse, inventor of the telegraph and a nativist of the first water, put it in 1835, "Our religion, the Protestant religion, and Liberty are identical, and liberty keeps no terms with despotism. . . . Let Papists separate their religious faith from their political faith, if they can, and the former shall suffer no political attack from us."[55] Lyman Beecher emphasized the point: "A religion which never prospered but in alliance with despotic governments, has always been and still is the inflexible enemy of liberty of conscience and free inquiry and at this moment is the main stay of the battle against republican institutions. A despotic government and despotic religion may not be able to endure free inquiry, but a republic and religious liberty CANNOT EXIST WITHOUT IT."[56]

Simply put, anti-Catholic nativism found roots and justification in fear for the Republic.[57]

But, of course, there was more to it. Woven within this cultural logic was a conviction that Catholics were alien and Catholicism was an alien faith—differences that were accentuated by poverty, illiteracy, language, and ethnicity. Immigrants from France and Spain were considered "swarthy," and those from southern Italy and Sicily, Black. More threatening still, Catholics were given to "low morals" and "bad habits," chief among them the tendency to drink.

Anti-Catholic sentiment was pervasive and justified the creation of settler nativist organizations such as the American Protestant Association in 1842, the goal of which was "to see the Protestant interests of the country united in a peaceful, enlightened, and vigorous opposition to the aggressive movements of the Papal Hierarchy against the civil and religious liberties of the United States." The group "respectfully, but firmly" pressed civil authorities "to resist every attempt which this *foreign power* may make to interfere with the *civil rights* of the American People."[58] A decade later, in 1854, popular opinion intensified to the point of giving birth to the American Party, also called the Know-Nothing Party, which championed limitations on immigration and draconian restrictions on citizenship and officeholding.

Among the Protestant clergy, the intent may have been peaceful, but the rhetoric of settler nativism surely created conditions conducive to a regular occurrence of mob aggression—the burning of the Ursuline Convent in Charlestown, Massachusetts, in 1834; the "Bible riots" in Philadelphia in the summer of 1844; nativist riots in St. Louis in 1844, 1849, 1852, and 1854; the Cincinnati Riots of 1853 and 1855; the Bloody Monday Riot in Louisville in 1855; the Lager Beer Riot in Chicago in the spring of 1855; the Know-Nothing Riots in Baltimore in 1856 and in Washington and New York in 1857—in all, reaping a promiscuous loss of life, copious injury, and damage and destruction of property, including to churches and seminaries.

MORMONS

There were many exotic offshoots of the religious fervor of the early 1800s, including the Millerites, Unitarians, Spiritualists, and the first Black denominations. But perhaps the most disturbing to the Protestant establishment was Mormonism. Mormonism was founded in 1830, and while its theological beliefs and practices resembled Protestantism to a certain degree, on certain particulars they were heretical and offensive. Among the offenses were the practice of polygamy, the addition of Scripture in the Book of Mormon, the belief that Jesus had visited America, the existence of modern prophets, belief in the literal gathering of Israel in the restoration of the Ten Tribes, and the belief that Zion will be built on the North American continent. But even discounting the heresy, there was simple incredulity that such a religion existed. As Horace Bushnell put it in his famous tract of 1847, "Who could have thought it possible that a wretched and silly delusion, like that of the Mormons, could gather in its thousands of disciples in this enlightened age, build a populous city, and erect a temple, rivalling in grandeur, even that of the false prophet at Mecca?"[59] Mormonism was not Christian orthodoxy, and therefore public opinion was not welcoming.[60]

Hostility to the Latter-Day Saints began by calling its founder, Joseph Smith, a madman, a fraud, and an imposter and Mormonism a delusion and deception—a false religion and therefore a menace to true faith, rather than a new variety of Christianity. From western New York, members of the church meandered through the central Midwest, from Kirtland, Ohio, to various places in western Missouri to western Illinois. Trouble followed them all the way as every effort to settle was followed by eviction. The animosity between Mormons and their neighbors reached a head in the summer and fall of 1838 when tensions erupted in armed conflict.[61] By the end of October, Missouri's governor, Lilburn Boggs, issued an executive order: "Mormons must be treated as enemies and must be exterminated or driven from the state if necessary, for the public peace their outrages are beyond all description."[62] Three days later, a Missouri militia attacked a Mormon settlement, killing and mutilating eighteen Mormons, including children—just one atrocity in the great Mormon war. A few years later, in 1844, Joseph Smith and his brother Hyrum were murdered by a mob.

AFRICAN SLAVES

African slaves and their descendants were long regarded as categorically different from white Europeans and their American progeny. And not just different but inferior. Jefferson said it succinctly in 1785 in his *Notes on the State of Virginia:* "Blacks, whether originally a distinct race, or made distinct by time and circumstances, are inferior to the whites in the endowments both of body and mind."[63]

Not to be outdone, Southern clergy often shared and gave biblical sanction to the prejudices of slaveholders in sermons, tracts, reviews, and books such as "Slavery and the Bible" (1850), *The Duties of Christian Masters* (1851), *The Political Economy of Slavery* (1853), *Scriptural and Statistical Views in Favor of Slavery* (1856), and *An Inquiry into the Law of Negro Slavery* (1858).[64] Yet very few of these apologies for slavery were as authoritative as the one provided by Dr. Samuel Cartwright, who made a moral, theological, and political defense of slavery on the basis of medical science.

Cartwright was not a rube. In his day, he was one of the most distinguished and outspoken medical leaders of the antebellum South. Eventually appointed by Jefferson Davis to be assistant surgeon general of the Confederate States, he was given the task of chairing a committee of four medical doctors appointed by the Medical Association of Louisiana, whose findings resulted in "Report on the Diseases and Physical Peculiarities of the Negro Race," published in the *New Orleans Medical and Surgical Journal* in 1851.[65] Cartwright presented "facts" of physiological differences between whites and Blacks— that the latter's "brain is a ninth or tenth less than other races," that "the ganglionic system of nerves are larger in proportion than in a white man"—meaning that the Black man "partakes of sensuality, at the expense of intellectuality." This "deficiency of cerebral matter in the cranium, and an excess of nervous matter . . . has rendered the people of Africa unable to take care of themselves. It is the true cause of their indolence and apathy, and why they have chosen, through countless ages, idleness, misery and barbarism to industry and frugality,—why social industry, or associated labor, so essential to all progress in civilization and improvement, has never made any progress among them."[66]

This was also "why, in America, if let alone, they always prefer" what "we call, slavery, . . . which is actually an improvement on the government of their forefathers, as it gives them more tranquility and sensual enjoyment, expands the mind and improves the morals, by arousing them from that natural indolence so fatal to mental and moral progress." Give them liberty and they "would relapse into barbarism."[67]

Blacks are, he concluded very much "like children"—they "are easily governed by love combined with fear, and are ungovernable, vicious and rude under any form of government whatever not resting on love and fear as a basis"; they "love those in authority over them," indeed, "the negro can no more help loving a kind master, than the child can help love her who gives it suck." "The love they bear to their masters, [is] similar in all respects to the love that children bear to their parents." And finally, "Like children, they require government in everything; food, clothing, exercise, sleep—all require to be prescribed by rule, or they will run to excess." This is why the Black man "is unfitted . . . for the responsible duties of a free man, but like the child, is only fitted for a state of dependence and subordination."[68]

Cartwright argued that everyone benefited from a slave economy. Without the labor of the negro "cultivating these burning fields in cotton, sugar, rice and tobacco, . . . would go uncultivated and their products lost to the world." "Both parties are benefitted—the negro and his master." But "a third party benefitted—the world at large. The three millions of bales of cotton made by negro labor, afford a cheap clothing for the civilized world."

In his mind, Cartwright's medical and scientific evidence showed the fallacy of

the dogma that abolitionism is built on; for here, in a country where two races of men dwell together, both born on the same soil, breathing the same air, and surrounded by the same external agents—liberty, which is elevating the one race of people above all other nations, sinks the other into beastly sloth and torpidity; and the slavery, which the one would prefer death rather than endure, improves the other in body, mind and morals; thus proving the dogma false, and establishing the truth that there is a radical, internal or physical difference between the two races, so great in kind, as to make what is wholesome and beneficial for the white man, as liberty, republican or free institutions, etc., not only unsuitable to the negro race, but actually poisonous to its happiness.[69]

In the end, he affirmed that what the Founders held forth in the Declaration of Independence—that all men are created equal—was "only intended to apply to white men."[70]

Cartwright's work gave expression to new developments in racial theory taking place in Europe and the United States, evolving from an older form that viewed racial difference as a matter of dissimilar faculties (what Jefferson referred to as "endowments of body and mind") to a scientific racism.[71] This hardened racial differences into rational and empirical taxonomies and did so with the authority and prestige of modern science. Thus it further entrenched the institution of slavery with "enlightened" rationalizations for unspeakable cruelty.

Brutalizing labor was only the beginning of the indignities slaves endured. The privations of food, clothing, shelter, and medical care; the separation of families; the wearing of chains; and the arbitrary torture that came in the forms of beating, flogging, cat-hauling, paddle-torturing, scalding, branding, and burning were undeniably common. The murder of slaves occurred without culpability, for no Black person could stand as a witness against a white person. The Reverend William T. Allan, who grew up the son of a slaveholder in Huntsville, Alabama, recounted that "at our house, it is so common to hear their [the slave's] screams, that we think nothing of it and lest anyone should think that in general the slaves are well treated, let me be distinctly understood:—*Cruelty* is the *rule* and *kindness* the *exception*."[72] "The slaves," he said, "are neither considered nor treated as human beings," but rather as brutes. The word *brute* in the eighteenth and nineteenth centuries denoted "beast" or "bestial," something "savage," "untamed," "irrational"; something lacking human qualities.[73]

A Less Than Benevolent Empire

The brutal irony of these contradictions is brought into relief by the palpably optimistic vision of the benevolent empire. Horace Bushnell, in his thundering polemic *Barbarism the First Danger*, published in 1847, painted a picture of the burden he and his generation sought to bear:

> To save this mighty nation; to make it the leading power of the earth; to present to mankind the spectacle of a nation stretching from ocean to ocean, across this broad continent; a nation of free men, self-governed, governed by simple law, without soldiers or a police; a nation of a hundred millions of people, covering the sea with their fleets, the land with cities, roads and harvests; first in learning and art, and all the fruits of genius, and, what is highest and best of all, a religious nation, blooming in all the Christian virtues; the protector of the poor; the scourge of oppression; the dispenser of light, and the symbol to mankind, of the ennobling genial power of righteous laws, and a simple Christian faith—this is the charge God lays upon us, this we accept and this, by God's blessing, we mean to perform, with a spirit worthy of its magnitude.[74]

The mythos, refined and crystallized through the reworking of America's hybrid-Enlightenment in the early years of the nineteenth century, provided a story of expanding benevolence. The "benevolent empire" would be realized not by violence but by good works, not by ruthless conquest but by compassion and munificence.

This vision seemed achievable or at least plausible to those who lived it. Though far less effective than its members hoped or imagined, the vast network of benevolent societies accomplished much real good. Through local home missionary and tract societies, denominational organizations and local churches, food, clothing, and money were distributed to the poor, and settlement homes were founded for indigent families and orphans. The unemployed were helped with job placement, and legislation was introduced to protect workers from unfair competition. Hospitals and free medical dispensaries were built in cities to care for the sick and dying, and tens of thousands of children were brought to literacy and numeracy through various Sunday school unions. Prominently, temperance societies proliferated, not in a starchy effort to regulate personal behavior but to reform society in ways that dealt with what they believed was a prime cause of poverty and the destruction of the family. All the while revivalist preaching railed against "the love of money" and the abuses of wealth. Most importantly, the abolitionist movement grew in membership, geographic reach, and persuasive power.[75]

The jolting reality was that the expanding nation and its institutions as well as its growing economic and political power were achieved in large measure through the exploitation of its native and Black inhabitants. Not only exploited but unwelcomed; and not just unwelcomed but forbidden by law from participating in or enjoying the fruits of their labor and natural wealth. The benevolent empire, through various strategies of boundary maintenance, in fact denied them liberty, prosperity, and all the rights and protections of citizenship. The benevolence so earnestly and sincerely sought after clearly was, with the exception of a small but growing abolitionist movement, blind to its own limitations. In the name of national unity and political compromise, it accommodated these contradictions, reinforcing its boundaries of exclusion symbolically, economically, legally, politically, and violently.

A Deepening Crisis in the Cultural Logic of America's Hybrid-Enlightenment

There are at least two points that are important to highlight. The first is that the contradictions that played out in this period were not remotely accidental. They were systemic, and not just in the sense of organized and enduring. The contradictions were systemic by virtue of being built into the deep structures of the reigning world-picture—its metaphysics, its epistemology, its anthropology, its ethics, and its teleology—and, in its totality, its mythos, the story the nation was telling about itself. Just as the good works of social reform were rooted in the cultural logic of this iteration of America's hybrid-Enlightenment, so too were its grotesque and inhumane contradictions.

The second point concerns the cultural logic by which these contradictions were managed and justified. Largely under the guidance of the clergy—the leading intellectuals of the day—and the varied institutions they built, Americans worked through their hybrid-Enlightenment, refashioning their own conception of the unum. No one who reads the primary sources of the period could conclude it was a cynical ideology. It was, rather, a matter of deep passion and conviction, and as such, it possessed the moral energy to build a nation.

But just as every culture orients its inhabitants to see it and themselves as "good," so too every culture creates boundaries, and in these ways, nineteenth-century America was no different. Under the moral pressure of the theological and constitutional promise of freedom and equality, the various contradictions demanded a religious accounting. Everything that followed was framed by, interpreted in light of, and morally and theologically evaluated through its reigning cosmology.

Consider first the ways the Protestant establishment managed the boundaries with Native Americans. In the early decades of the nineteenth century, Americans tended to agree that so many atrocities had been committed by both the government and settler militia, on the one hand, and the Indians on the other that mutual coexistence was impossible. Accounts from travelers buttressed these conclusions. In 1833, Timothy Flint, a Harvard-educated itinerate minister who traveled extensively through the western territories, wrote, "In the unchangeable order of things, two such races cannot exist together, each preserving its co-ordinate identity."[76] Native populations were, in the minds of most Americans, unassimilable. The pragmatic conclusion was to restrict contact between white settlers and Indians. A removal policy became inevitable. It was possible because the number of Native Americans was so small.

A similar logic was applied to Black Americans. Even among many abolitionists, as early as the 1770s, there were proposals to expatriate free Blacks to the western frontier or back to Africa. By the 1820s, the American Colonization Society settled on West Africa in what was to become Liberia. Dozens of local colonization societies sprung up in the years that followed, raising money for the cost of transportation and resettlement. The idea never really gained traction, however. African Americans themselves viewed colonization as forced removal disguised as voluntary emigration, and so it is no surprise that between 1820 and 1856, only 9,502 Black Americans emigrated to Liberia.[77]

After being evicted so many times from so many communities, the Latter-Day Saints finally removed themselves of their own accord. The murder of Joseph Smith and his brother Hyrum was the last straw. Brigham Young led the Mormons outside of the existing union of the United States to the Utah Territory, a region that did not achieve statehood until 1896. As for Catholics, they were too numerous to be excluded, but it is fair to say that the majority of Protestant Americans wished that Catholics had never left Europe in the first place.

Where separation and removal were impossible or impractical, members of the dominant culture pursued a strategy of partial inclusion, always and irrevocably on the terms of the Protestant majority. That strategy was assimilation through Christianization. As Josiah Strong put it, "Nothing can save inferior races but a willing and pliant assimilation."[78] Of the white Protestant majority he wrote, "Is there any room for reasonable doubt that this race, unless devitalized by alcohol and tobacco, is destined to dispossess many weaker races, assimilate others, and mold the remainder, until, in a very true and important sense, it has Anglo-Saxonized mankind?"[79]

This managed assimilation was the deliberate strategy of the federal government in dealing with native populations from its earliest years. Numerous missionary societies were formed after the Revolution to evangelize and civilize natives. In 1819, the government even provided a civilization fund to teach farming, literacy, and all the values and ways of life requisite to productive participation in society. The goal in all cases was to convey "the benefits of civilization and the blessings of Christianity" so that we "may look forward to the period when the savage shall be converted into the citizen . . . and the fruits of Industry, good order, and sound morals, shall bless every Indian dwelling."[80]

Christianization had taken hold in the slave population, and as early as the 1820s, Black Americans were forming their own denominations. Catholics were Christians, of course, but the wrong kind. Assimilation through conversion to Protestantism met with little success, leaving Catholics and Protestants in a standoff. The reigning Protestant majority was not about to budge. Few laid out the case for attrition more coherently than Lyman Beecher in his *Plea for the West*. Since the invasion of barbarians into Rome, he wrote, "the world has never witnessed the rush of such a dark minded population . . . as is now leaving Europe and dashing upon our shores. . . . Clouds like the locusts of Egypt . . . are coming down to settle on our fair fields." Catholics were the "inflexible enemy of the liberty of conscience and free inquiry," and they sought "the subversion of our institutions." That said, he opposed "the violation or abridgment of their civil and religious rights" and opposed "any attempt to cast odium upon Catholics." He would have their "property and rights protected with the same impartiality and efficacy . . . as any other denomination" and would abhor any "lawless violence against the rights and property of Catholics" as much as he would against any Protestant. Yet it was essential to oppose the Catholic Church until it had become "liberalized and assimilated." Of this outcome he was fairly confident: "As republicans and Christians, we certainly hail the day when the Catholic church shall be reformed . . . [having] renounce[d] the past unscriptural and anti-republican claims, maxims, and deeds of the church of Rome."[81]

In short, it was essential to oppose the Catholic Church until Catholics had assimilated to the (Protestant) Christian Republic.

The Fraying Lines of Inclusion

In sum, the mere existence of these communities represented a threat to the reigning Protestant establishment, and anything that threatened it was thought best to be removed, converted, or otherwise assimilated. These were the tactics of boundary work, the terms of inclusion into the unum.

To be sure, there were sharp political differences in this overarching cultural consensus, but these differences operated *within* a shared cosmology. Where we see enduring political differences, we see them rooted in fundamentally different moral and ethical evaluations emanating from the deep structures of this culture. In the case of the Catholics and Mormons, the rudimentary difference was over truth. In the case of Black and Native Americans, the rudimentary difference was over anthropology—the judgment that such people were not fully human. Policy differences reflected these more rudimentary disagreements.[82] Nowhere were these differences more important and consequential than in the debate between the defenders of slavery and the abolitionists. For the first sixty years of the nineteenth century, Americans were willing to live with these differences for the sake of national unity. But peace in the face of differences as fundamental as these, and the jarring contradictions that underwrote them, were not, in the end, sustainable.

CHAPTER SIX

The Unmaking of
the Christian Republic

THE STUBBORN PERSISTENCE OF these contradictions—declared equal but denied equality, declared free but denied freedom—was, as I have argued, generated and sustained by a larger mythos whose roots were found in America's hybrid-Enlightenment—that mythos that was then crystallized over the course of the nineteenth century through the millennialist aspirations and moral perfectionism of the "Christian Republic." The plights of Native Americans, Black Americans, Mormons, and Catholics were all implicated in this logic; all were outside the boundaries of inclusion for reasons of race, religion, or religion interwoven with race and ethnicity, and the violence done to them was justified (and at times even encouraged) by this mythos. And yet no people were more definitively outside the unum and its bonds of solidarity than enslaved African Americans.

Contradiction and Compromise

The evangelical turn in America's hybrid-Enlightenment in the early nineteenth century had the net effect of doubling down on the boundaries of inclusion and exclusion, reinforcing and intensifying these long-standing contradictions. For all practical purposes, these contradictions were mostly ignored or suppressed at the Founding of the Republic and in the decades that followed. Lyman Beecher's iconic articulations of the American mythos in the 1820s and 1830s, for example, never once mentioned, much less addressed, the conditions of the enslaved Black people or Native Americans and the inhumane way many white Americans treated them.

In the name of unity, there were political efforts to find compromise on the most egregious contradiction: the matter of slavery. These efforts took shape in the Three-Fifths Compromise in 1787, the Missouri Compromise in 1820, the Talmadge Amendment, the Compromise of 1850, and the Kansas-Nebraska Act of 1854, and yet, in the end, they only heightened tensions in the nation rather than diminished them.

But how did this play out culturally in the years leading up to the war? The emerging institution of public education provides a window on these undercurrents.

The School as a Benevolence; the School as a Cudgel

As we have seen, in the early to mid-nineteenth century, education emerged as a carrier of republican virtue and formation second only to the church. The school was seen as a nursery for citizenship in the Republic and the means by which consensus over America's public philosophy would be reproduced for generations to come. Through the prism of public education in its early years, we can see how the contradictions of marginalization and exclusion played out for ordinary Americans.

The emergence of common and public education in early nineteenth-century America was, in all practical effects, coterminous with the evangelical turn in America's hybrid-Enlightenment. Education was overwhelmingly Protestant and sectarian in ways that to its proponents could not have otherwise been imagined. Protestant clergy, as we have seen, were tireless in the founding of schools. The Protestant King James Version of the Bible was the foundational spiritual and moral authority.

Good intentions abounded, but for Native Americans, schools

were a tool of assimilation and subjugation. For Catholics, who had long valued education, the public schools were also tools of assimilation and subjugation, but they understood them as such and had the wherewithal to resist. The great Catholic school wars in New York and Philadelphia, for example, attest to this: riots in Philadelphia led to five churches being burned to the ground, thirteen people killed, and the bishop fleeing the city for his life.

African Americans, who had no access to schooling, long understood that education was empowerment, that it was a bedrock of citizenship and, along with voting, the symbol and substance of membership in a democratic political community. It was a substantive measure of inclusion in the American experiment in democracy. They *also* understood that, as David Walker, a free Black man, put it in 1829, "The major part of white Americans, have, ever since we have been among them, tried to keep us ignorant. . . . For colored people to acquire learning in this country, makes tyrants quake and tremble on their sandy foundations. . . . The bare name of educating the colored people, scares our cruel oppressors almost to death."[1]

White people, racist and nonracist alike, also understood the empowering nature of education for the Black population. The discrimination against African Americans was staggering on this count: in 1850, only 2 percent of all Black children were enrolled in schools, compared to roughly two-thirds of all white children.[2]

Overt discrimination in education was worst in the South. In the first half of the nineteenth century the legislatures of Virginia, South Carolina, North Carolina, Georgia, Alabama, Louisiana, Mississippi, and Missouri all either outlawed or imposed severe legal restrictions against reading and writing for Blacks, whether enslaved or free. Even in Northern states, where slavery had officially ended at the time of the Revolution, harsh restrictions were imposed on access to the common schools. Laws varied. In some states, such as Delaware and Indiana, Black children were simply excluded from public schools. In other states, such as New York, Massachusetts, Connecticut, Rhode Island, Ohio, and Pennsylvania, segregation was the rule of the day— education for Black children was permitted, but typically in separate schools. And while public funding for public education was contested through most of the nineteenth century, Black schools consistently received little or no public support.[3]

The Prophetic Grievances of David Walker

David Walker, a thirty-three-year-old African American, well under-stood how whites kept Blacks from learning. His observation about discrimination in education was just a snippet from a long pamphlet that he published in 1829. Indeed, that pamphlet was one of the most important polemics of the early nineteenth century; in its time, it was a statement as radical as any of the Revolutionary period. His *Appeal, in Four Articles; Together with a Preamble, to the Coloured Citizens of the World* was a scorching rebuke of the grotesque and unacknowledged contradictions at the heart of the new Republic.[4] His condemnation of white educational discrimination was just the beginning of his grievances.

Walker was born in 1796 and raised in the Carolinas. Though his father had been enslaved and, by some accounts, had died before his birth, his mother had been freeborn, by virtue of which he himself was free. As a young man, he traveled extensively through the country. In the South he witnessed slavery in all of its manifestations, finding those who lived under it "degraded, wretched, abject."[5] He became a clothes merchant, eventually settling in Boston. He was also a devout Christian and a committed member of the Methodist Church as well as of the Prince Hall Freemasons, both of which fueled his rage against slavery and his active involvement with the still-nascent abolitionist cause. That commitment found full expression in his *Appeal*.

Walker accused white Christians of being an "unjust, jealous, unmerciful, avaricious and blood-thirsty set of beings, always seeking after power and authority." On the whole, white Christians are "cruel . . . ten times more cruel, avaricious and unmerciful than ever [pre-Christian Europeans] were."[6]

> They beat us nearly to death, if they find us on our knees praying to God. If they find us with a book of any description in our hand, they will beat us nearly to death—they are so afraid we will learn to read, and enlighten our dark and benighted minds— . . . they brand us with hot iron—they cram bolts of fire down our throats—they cut us as they do horses, bulls, or hogs—they crop our ears and sometime cut

off bits of our tongues—they chain and handcuff us, and while in that miserable and wretched condition, beat us with cow-hides and clubs—they keep us half naked and starve us sometimes nearly to death under their infernal whips and lashes—they put on us fifty-sixes and chains, and make us work in that cruel situation, and in sickness, under lashes to support them and their families . . . and to crown the whole of this catalogue of cruelties, they tell us that we (the blacks) are an inferior race of beings! Incapable of self-government!!—We would be injurious to society and ourselves, if tyrants should loose their unjust hold on us!!! That if we were free we would not work, but would live on plunder or theft!!!! That we are the meanest and laziest set of beings in the world!!!!! That they are obliged to keep us in bondage to do us good!!!!!![7]

"In all of history," he concluded, "no people have been treated worse."[8]

If things weren't bad enough on their own terms, this tragedy was made all the more glaring and bitter against the backdrop of the ideals of American democracy. When Walker wrote that his objective is "to awaken in the breasts of my afflicted, degraded and slumbering brethren, a spirit of inquiry and investigation respecting our miseries and wretchedness in this *Republican Land of Liberty!!!!!!*" his mockery is unmistakable: "Did not God make us all as it seemed best to himself? What right, then, has one of us, to despise another, and to treat him cruel, on account of his colour, which none, but the God who made it can alter? Can there be a greater absurdity in nature, and particularly in a free republican country?"[9] America is a "land of oppression but pretended liberty."[10] "See your Declaration Americans!!!," he declares.

Do you understand your own language? Here your language, proclaimed to the world, July 4th, 1776—"We hold these truths to be self-evident—that ALL men are created EQUAL!! . . . " Compare your own language above, extracted from your Declaration of Independence, with your cruelties and murders inflicted by your cruel and unmerciful fathers and yourselves on our fathers and on us—men who have never given your fathers or you the least provocation!!!!!!

... Now, Americans! I ask you candidly, was your sufferings under Great Britain, one hundredth part as cruel and tyrannical as you have rendered ours under you?[11]

Walker recognized the national contradiction in the duplicity of Jefferson himself, expressing incredulity that "a man of such great learning, combined with such excellent natural parts, should speak so of a set of men in chains."[12]

It was out of a framework defined by the Hebrew and Christian Scriptures and the Constitution—sources so central to the cultural logic of America's hybrid-Enlightenment—that Walker could write against those who have "held us up as descending originally from the tribes of Monkeys or Orang Otangs," asserting that "we and our children are not of the HUMAN FAMILY" but "an inferior race of beings." On this foundation, Walker could declare with complete conviction and integrity that "we are MEN, and not brutes, as we have been represented and, by millions, treated."

> Throw away your fears and prejudices then, and enlighten us and treat us like men and we will like you more than we do now hate you. . . . (You are not astonished at my saying we hate you, for if we are men we cannot but hate you, while you are treating us like dogs.) . . . Treat us like men, and there is no danger but we will all live in peace and happiness together. . . . Treat us then like men, and we will be your friends. And there is not a doubt in my mind, but that the whole of the past will be sunk into oblivion, and we yet, under God, will become a united and happy people. The whites may say it is impossible, but remember that nothing is impossible with God.[13]

Everything else, he rightly believed, would follow. To acknowledge the Black man's humanity is to acknowledge that "freedom is [our] natural right." And so, he wrote, "We ask [white people] for nothing but the rights of man, viz. for them to set us free, and treat us like men. . . . If they do, there will be no danger, for we will love and respect them, and protect our country."[14]

At the end of the day, he concluded, America "is as much ours as it is the whites"—more so, for "we have enriched it with our *blood and tears.*"[15] Walker understood in ways that white people were blind to that the expansion of the nation was in part made possible by slave labor.

This tragedy was made even more appalling because the crime of slavery was being perpetrated by Christians—or rather "pretenders to Christianity," as he called them. The system was justified, he charged, by "pretended preachers of the gospel": "Have not the Americans the Bible in their hands? Do they believe it: Surely, they do not see how they treat us in open violation of the Bible!!" Here too, the hypocrisy was as extreme as it was contemptible: "Can anything," he wrote, "be a greater mockery of religion than the way in which it is conducted by the Americans?"[16]

Walker's *Appeal* was incendiary. He printed it with his own money and found an informal distribution system for it, relying on Black sailors, pursers, and stewards sailing out of Boston who were sympathetic to the cause. Wherever it turned up, the pamphlet inspired the enslaved and was denounced by whites. There were rumors that thousands of dollars in bounty had been offered to anyone who would capture or kill him. Friends encouraged him to leave the country for Canada. Untroubled, he carried on his work, but in 1830, in the midst of publishing the third edition of the *Appeal*, Walker was found dead, crumpled up near the door of his shop, most likely the victim of poisoning.

The Black Church

A martyr to the cause of freedom, David Walker marked the transition from the gentle suasion of the Quakers to the more aggressive and confrontational demands of the abolitionist movement. Yet he spoke out of a tradition and a community in which such thoughts as his, while rarely uttered so publicly, were commonplace.

Protestant Christianity had become established in the African slave community as early as the 1750s. Black Protestants found the turn from traditional Calvinism to the emotional and experiential warmth of revivalism agreeable, and in the years that followed, their numbers grew dramatically. Just as the church was the most powerful and pervasive institution in the lives of ordinary white Americans in the nineteenth century, so it became in the slave and freeborn Black population. Evangelicalism in the nineteenth century was not a white religion. Black and white Protestants shared the same faith, and in this way, Black Christianity became established as a movement within a movement, a community within a community, a cosmology within a cosmology, albeit one, as Walker indicates, in opposition.[17]

The relationship between white and Black Christianity was awkward and uncomfortable, but also generative. Of course, the backdrop of social mores among whites at that time meant a deep antipathy toward incorporating Blacks into the mainstream of society. Yet as Donald Mathews argued, evangelism by its very nature entailed the inclusion of everyone into the sacred community, including those regarded as a pariah people. Conversion had egalitarian implications insofar as the gospel was a gift to all people, regardless of their station in life. All believers—indeed, all people—were equally loved and valued by God, and thus, despite racial stereotypes, anxieties, and fears, conversion provided an authentic sign of God's grace and a demonstration of the humanity of all Black people. Ironically, at the same moment that perhaps the most erudite and urbane of the American revolutionaries—Thomas Jefferson—declared that Blacks could never be fully integrated into America, evangelical Christianity had sowed the seeds for a breakdown of social distance between white and Black.

To be clear, the *intent* of white Christianity may not have been revolutionary egalitarianism—at least, not at first—but in its net effect it was just that.[18] "God," the Christian Scriptures taught, "was not a respecter of persons" (Acts 10:34). And Jesus announced that he had come into this world "to preach good news to the poor, to proclaim release to the prisoners and . . . to liberate the oppressed" (Luke 4:18–19). This was a message that resonated especially among the Quakers and Methodists, leading many to declare slavery "contrary to the laws of God, man, and nature, and hurtful to society, contrary to the dictates of conscience and pure religion," proclaiming slaveholding a "villainy" that violated "all the laws of Justice, Mercy, and Truth."[19] This conviction was at the heart of what was to become the abolitionist movement.

It was also a conviction taken to heart by Blacks themselves. The sin against African slaves was morally reprehensible on its own terms but made more so by the fact that they were innocent of anything that could possibly justify their exploitation. In this light, Christianity, even more than the Constitution, offered enslaved and freeborn Blacks justification for their claim to the respect and care of their brothers and sisters in Christ. As Walker's *Appeal* made clear, anything less than that moral, spiritual, and legal recognition demonstrated the hypocrisy that white Americans were willing to abide.

Additionally, Christianity offered a biblical narrative of freedom rooted in the story of the Israelites, who had been enslaved and oppressed by Egypt but who were delivered and taken to a promised land of freedom. It was a narrative that the Puritans and colonists themselves had appropriated not so many years before in fleeing the religious and political oppressions of the British Empire. Christianity thus represented a faith shared in common, but within the Black population, it was a faith that would be subversive of the reigning social order.

It was partly because of the subversive nature of their common faith and common theology of personhood and liberation that white Christians were ambivalent in their welcome of their Black brothers and sisters. Blacks still had no voice in the life of the church, dramatized by a segregation that relegated them to the back of the church or to its gallery. They lived on the periphery of white Christianity and were dependent upon it. But eventually the Black church, led by freemen, broke off, formed both local congregations and national denominations, and became places of independence, mutual care, and encouragement—and also empowerment.

Importantly, the Black church became *the* means by which African Americans began to create a public life for themselves. Here, as perhaps nowhere else, they found themselves within the logic of America's hybrid-Enlightenment. Richard Allen, a slave from Delaware who eventually bought his freedom and, under the tutelage of the famous Methodist revivalist Francis Asbury founded the African Methodist Episcopal Church in 1816, gave voice to this. Just before his death, he would write, "This land, which we have watered with our tears and our blood, is now *our mother country* and we are well satisfied to stay where wisdom abounds, and the gospel is free."[20]

Abolition, Angelina Grimké, and
"the First Charter of Human Rights"

The struggle against slavery was not one that the Black church and the people they served had to fight alone. Coming alongside was a growing movement of Black and white abolitionists. There was a range of perspectives in this movement, though participants would have generally agreed, as one abolitionist put it in 1834, that "the holding of slaves is not only sinful, unjust, inhuman, and immoral, but impolitic in the highest degree. It is a heavy curse that hangs over our country; a shame and disgrace to a Republican government; a blot or foul stain on the fair face of our boasted land of liberty. All orations on liberty should cease, while two million of our fellow beings are groaning in slavery. . . . If something be not speedily done to deliver us from the evil, it will, ere long, be the downfall of our Republic."[21]

An abolitionist voice had been present since the seventeenth century, mainly within the small Quaker community in the Northeast. Though it began to grow louder in the late eighteenth century, the cause was scattered and disorganized until the early 1830s, when it finally began to gain traction as a movement. The record of nearly endless brutality is well summarized by newspapers and periodicals such as the African American–owned *Freedom's Journal* (1827), William Lloyd Garrison's the *Liberator* (1831), the *American Anti-Slave Reporter* (1834), the *Emancipator and Journal of Public Morals* (1834), the *Quarterly Anti-Slavery Magazine* (1835), the *Philanthropist* (1836), *Mirror of Liberty* (1838), the *National Anti-Slavery Standard* (1840), and Frederick Douglass's *North Star* (1847). It also gained traction through the American Anti-Slavery Society (1833), the Liberty Party (1839), and the American and Foreign Anti-Slavery Society (1840). To give an idea of the scale of this movement in the 1830s alone, the number of auxiliaries to the American Anti-Slavery Society grew from 75 to 1,348 between the years 1833 and 1838.[22] This transformation of the abolitionist cause was, in no small part, a result of the leadership that Angelina Grimké and her sister Sarah brought to it.

Angelina Grimké was born in 1805 in Charleston, South Carolina, the fourteenth and last child of John and Mary Grimké.[23] The family came from rare privilege. Though a colonist, the father had been sent to Oxford to study law, returning soon after to cast his lot with the revolutionaries against England. After the war he practiced law, served in the state legislature, and soon became a senior associate justice of the South Carolina Court of Common Pleas. Among other holdings, the family owned a large plantation and the slaves to work it.

Though a dutiful daughter, it was Sarah, Angelina's older sister by thirteen years, who was the original rebel in the family. From an early age, Sarah had found the system of slavery viscerally repugnant. She was even chastened by her father when he discovered that she, as a twelve-year-old, had been teaching one of the household maids to read—against the laws of the state. In 1821, now in her late twenties, Sarah moved to Philadelphia and joined the Society of Friends, and there her opposition to slavery deepened. Impressed by her sister's faith and theology of nonviolence, Angelina eventually followed her sister's footsteps into Quakerism and abolitionism and, in 1829, followed her to Philadelphia.

In 1836, Angelina wrote a thirty-six-page, densely argued pamphlet entitled *An Appeal to the Christian Women of the South*.[24] Written with the hope that Southern women would be persuaded by one of their own and would in turn influence their husbands, the *Appeal* laid out an ethical, theological, and political case against slavery. The style was passionate and personal—"It is true, I am going to tell you unwelcome truths, but I mean to speak those *truths in love*, and remember Solomon says, 'faithful are the *wounds* of a friend.'"[25] Like David Walker, Angelina integrated the liberal political theory of the Constitution with biblical analysis in straightforward articulation of the hybrid-Enlightenment.

Her opening gambit grounded her argument in the affirmation of human equality in the Declaration of Independence. "If it is a self-evident truth," she writes, "that all men, everywhere and of every color are born equal, and have an *inalienable right to liberty*, then it is equally true that no man can be born a slave, and no man can ever *rightfully* be reduced to *involuntary* bondage and held as a slave, however fair may be the claim of his master or mistress through wills and title-deeds."[26]

Anticipating the common rebuttal that "the Bible sanctions Slavery, and that is the highest authority," she affirmed that "the Bible is my ultimate appeal in all matters of faith and practice, and it is to *this test* I am anxious to bring the subject at issue between us." What followed was a tour de force of biblical exposition that began with the Creation story in Genesis, worked through the Noahide covenants, the life of Abraham, and the laws of the Jewish dispensation bearing on servitude. In all, she concluded, "the code of laws framed by Moses with regard to servants was designed to protect them as men and women, to secure to them their rights as human beings, to guard them from oppression and defend them from violence of every kind." The laws and practices of slavery in the South clearly fell far short of this standard.[27] As she argued, the "Code Noir of the South robs the slave of all his rights as a man, reduces him to a chattel personal, and defends the master in the exercise of the most unnatural and unwarrantable power over his slave. . . . The attributes of justice and mercy are shadowed out in the Hebrew code; those of injustice and cruelty, in the Code Noir of America. Truly it was wise in the slaveholders of the South to declare their slaves to be 'chattels personal'; for before they could be robbed of wages, wives, children, and friends, it was absolutely necessary to deny they were human beings."[28]

From here, Grimké moved on to the ethics of Christ and St. Paul to conclude that the "first charter of human rights . . . was given by God, to the Fathers of the Antediluvian and Postdiluvian worlds, therefore this doctrine of equality is based on the Bible."[29]

Recounting the courage of women from biblical times through the Reformation and Counter-Reformation and to the abolitionist cause in Great Britain, she called upon her sisters in the South to show similar courage. "The women of the South can overthrow this horrible system of oppression and cruelty, licentiousness and wrong."[30]

The *Appeal* was widely distributed by the American Anti-Slavery Society, and among abolitionists, it was received with broad approval. From Grimké's intended audience in the South, however, the reception was considerably chillier—in her hometown of Charleston and in other cities throughout the South, the *Appeal* was publicly burned. It was, in every way, bad form for a woman to speak out in public, not least against slavery. Her friends wrote her, warning of the mob violence she would likely face if she returned to Charleston. The mayor himself spoke to her mother, informing her that the police had been instructed to prevent her daughter's landing and that if she made it to shore, she would be arrested and imprisoned.[31]

Thus began Angelina Grimké's public campaign to end slavery. She and her sister moved to New York and formally became activists for the cause. Both began a speaking tour, addressing packed audiences. But precisely because they were women, linking the rights of the enslaved with the rights of women, they had also irritated the religious and abolitionist authorities everywhere, including the abolitionist leader Catherine Beecher. The Quaker leader John Whittier asked them, "Is it not forgetting the great and dreadful wrongs of the slave in a selfish crusade against some paltry grievances of our own?" to which they responded, "What then can women do for the slave when she is herself under the feet of man and shamed into silence?"[32] As they were challenging the boundaries of race, they were challenging the boundaries of gender as well.

Within a year, Angelina followed the *Appeal* with *An Appeal to the Women of the Nominally Free States*.[33] In the spring of 1838, she lectured to thousands at Odeon Hall in Boston and then testified against slavery at a committee of the legislature of the state of Massachusetts, the first woman to do so. Later that year, she married the abolitionist Theodore Dwight Weld, and as their first project together they, along with Sarah Grimké, scoured through Southern newspapers to gather evidence about the conditions and atrocities of slavery. The result was *American Slavery as It Is: Testimony of a Thousand Witnesses*, published the following year—a volume that would inspire Harriet Beecher Stowe's *Uncle Tom's Cabin*.[34] After this, Angelina pulled back from public life to become a teacher and mother, but her stamp on abolition and women's suffrage had been firmly and enduringly established.

"The Underlying Conception of Man"

For all its vitality in bringing a nation into being and sustaining it through its first eighty years or so of nation-building, by the late 1850s, the solidarity generated by America's hybrid-Enlightenment could not abide the inherent contradictions of racism and slavery any longer.

The boldness of Frederick Douglass's Fourth of July "Oration" in Rochester, New York, in 1852 echoed the outrage of David Walker two decades earlier.[35] "What have I . . . to do with your national independence?" he thundered. "Are the great principles of political freedom and of natural justice, embodied in that Declaration of Independence, extended to us?" The fact, of course, was that they were not: "I am not included within the pale of this glorious anniversary! Your high independence only reveals the immeasurable distance between us. The blessings in which you, this day, rejoice, are not enjoyed in common. The rich inheritance of justice, liberty, prosperity and independence, bequeathed by your fathers, is shared by you, not by me. The sunlight that brought life and healing to you, has brought stripes and death to me. This Fourth July is yours, not mine. You may rejoice, I must mourn." The hypocrisies were flagrant. "America," he argued, "is false to the past, false to the present, and solemnly binds herself to be false to the future. Standing with God and the crushed and bleeding slave on this occasion, I will, in the name of humanity, which is outraged, in the name of liberty, which is fettered, in the name of the constitution and the Bible, which are disregarded and trampled upon, dare to call in question and to denounce, with all the emphasis I can command, everything that serves to perpetuate slavery—the great sin and shame of America!"

The constitutional and biblical contradictions were obvious enough, but what made them both insoluble and combustible was that they were beyond the reach of law, reason, politics, and religion. They were rooted in more fundamental disagreements—disagreements in the substrata of America's hybrid-Enlightenment.

Those disagreements were not found in competing understandings of ultimate reality. In fact, people in the North and the South believed equally in a creator God whose hand was active in history. In both the North and the South, people were confident about God's purposes in America. Neither were there differences in the ways of knowing the world; there was no dispute over the source of authoritative knowledge about human affairs. As Walker acknowledged, people in the North and South were equally confident in the Bible and how it spoke to the moment and the rightness of their cause. For both sides, the Bible was plain in its meaning and, to all, self-interpreting.[36]

Thus, abolitionists such as Daniel Alexander Payne, the presiding bishop of the African Methodist Episcopal Church, could declare in 1861 that the "great deliverance" of abolition would be brought about by "the Lord; the Lord God Almighty, the God of Abraham, Isaac and Jacob," for only God "couldst have moved the heart of this Nation to have done so great a deed for this weak, despised and needy people."[37] And with equal confidence, apologists for the regime of slavery, such as the Southern Methodist minister J. W. Tucker, could boldly pronounce to his Confederate audience a year later that "your cause is the cause of God, the cause of Christ, of humanity."[38]

How could they be so sure? Both sides pointed to Scripture as the final authority in these matters. "There is not a word in the New Testament," declared the abolitionist theologian Tayler Lewis, "about buying and selling slaves," against which the Reverend Henry Van Dyke could respond, "When the abolitionist tells me that slaveholding is sin, in the simplicity of my faith in the Holy Scriptures, I point to this sacred record, and tell him, in all candor, as my text does, that his teaching blasphemes the name of God and his Doctrine."[39]

Underneath these competing interpretations of Scripture and the will of God in history were fundamentally different *anthropologies* and their *ethical* implications all operating within the deep structures of America's hybrid-Enlightenment. David Brion Davis summarized the problem lucidly: "The *fundamental* problem of slavery," he wrote, "lay not in its cruelty or exploitation, but in the underlying conception of man as a conveyable possession with no more autonomy of will and consciousness than a domestic animal."[40]

In his famous overview of slavery law in 1827, Judge George Stroud wrote, "The cardinal principle of slavery,—that the slave is not to be ranked among *sentient beings*, but among *things*—is an article of property—a chattel personal,—obtains as undoubted law in all . . . states. In South Carolina it is expressed in the following language: 'Slaves shall be deemed, taken, and reputed and adjudged in law to be *chattels personal* in the hands of their masters, owners, and possessors, and their executors, administrators and assigns, *to all intents, constructions and purposes whatsoever.*'" As Judge Stroud put it, "Absolute despotism needs not a more comprehensive grant of power than that which is here conferred."[41]

In the end, Black people were not quite human—at least not in the same way that white people were. With this as the background of consensus, one could, with impunity, treat Blacks no differently than a domestic animal. And of course, in the regime of slavery, they were. As one abolitionist observed, "Every kind of cruelty has been exercised upon them that the most brutal tyranny could desire, or savage barbarity invent. And what is the reason of all this? Why? because . . . 'they are guilty of being born with a coloured skin,'— and hence many conclude, that they are intended by nature to be made subservient to those who have the good fortune to be born white."[42]

The purported inferiority of Black people had been enshrined in national policy in 1787 with the Three-Fifths Compromise, which counted three-fifths of each state's slave population toward the state's total population for the purposes of representation and taxation. It revealed the ambivalence of the government's position. It was a compromise, after all. National sentiment regarding the enslaved population had been divided from the beginning. The Three-Fifths Compromise was a settlement between those who justified slavery on the grounds of the economic utility of slave labor and those who believed that liberty was central to the identity and aspirations of the new Republic. The so-called compromise also revealed the priority the Founders gave to unity over justice, but unity only in a formal sense. The ambivalence surrounding slavery never went away. Indeed, the end of the international slave trade in 1808 may have closed one particular chapter of inhumane practice, but it also lessened abolitionists' urgency to work for the end of slavery even as the institution was expanding and its depredations were deepening.

Indeed, although the transatlantic slave trade ended in 1808, the number of slaves in America actually grew. According to census data, there were just under 1.2 million slaves in the United States in 1810. By 1860, just fifty years later, there were 3.95 million, a growth mainly due to an extraordinarily high birth rate. All the while, the internal slave trade prospered. Moreover, the number of slave states increased, from nine in 1800 to twelve in 1821 to fifteen states and three territories (that were to become Oklahoma, New Mexico, and Arizona) by 1861. Slavery had become a massive industry, and the slave trade leading up to the Civil War was a rapidly expanding market. Slavery had become more, not less, integral to Southern identity, economy, and international trade.

The actual growth of the slave trade *in* America even after the transatlantic slave trade ended highlights the salience of political economy in the regime of slavery and the vested interests at stake. Slavery was the foundation of an immensely profitable system of labor and the heart of an entire legal, economic, and political apparatus that defined the social and institutional order of the South—an apparatus, not incidentally, in which powerful Northern institutions in the sectors of banking, finance, shipping, and trade were entirely complicit. For the wealthiest Bostonians and New Yorkers, the status quo was more profitable than justice. Along with Southerners, certain sectors of the North had little motivation to change the structure of political and economic incentives.

But it was the anthropology of racial difference that was the root source of the conflict and the reasons why the status quo did not hold. This was made clear by those abolitionists who, operating within the lingua franca of biblical authority and exegesis, made the case that *there was a difference between slavery as described in the Bible and the regime of slavery of the American South*. For example, in the aftermath of his famous debates with Stephen Douglas, Abraham Lincoln himself called out this distinction when he observed that there were those "trying to show that slavery existed in the Bible times by Divine ordinance. . . . Douglas knows that whenever you establish that Slavery was right by the Bible, it will occur that Slavery was the Slavery of the *white* man—of men without reference to color."[43] Lincoln was replicating the subtle arguments of a number of abolitionist theologians and churchmen such as John Fee, who in his book *The Sinfulness of Slaveholding Shown by Appeals to Reason and Scripture* conceded that the New Testament never condemned the Roman enslavement of "Germans, Gauls, Spaniards, Grecians, Egyptians, Carthaginians, Syrians, Armenians . . . and the many provinces of Asia Minor." But "what was the complexion of these nations? Most were as white or whiter than the Romans themselves."[44]

If they were true to biblical authority, then, advocates of the slavery regime would have to sanction the slavery of white people too.[45] But this was unthinkable because underwriting the political economy of slavery was the settled conviction that Black men and women were simply not full members of the human community and therefore not worthy of its rights and protections.

In the end, Southern intellectuals were not put off by this line of argumentation. The myth of Black African inferiority was reinforced in the popular imagination by the centuries-long interpretation of the Scriptures of Judaism, Christianity, and Islam asserting that Africans suffered under the curse of Ham. As the story goes, Noah's youngest son, Ham, discovered his father drunk and naked. When Noah awoke and learned of this embarrassment, he cursed his son and grandson, saying, "Cursed be Canaan! The lowest of slaves will he be to his brothers" (Genesis 9:18–27). Despite the hermeneutical contortions involved, which strain all credulity, it became the near-universal opinion in the Christian world that "the sufferings and the slavery of the Negro race are the consequence of the curse of Noah."[46] In this way, it was possible for Southern Christians to concede that all people were made in the image of God, and yet simultaneously believe that "the Negro race was an accursed race." But this was by no means a universally held view.

Justice Roger Taney

By the early 1850s, Frederick Douglass could decry the implausibility of the fiction of Black subhumanity. In his July 4 "Oration," he asked,

> Must I undertake to prove that the slave is a man? That point is conceded already. Nobody doubts it. The slaveholders themselves acknowledge it in the enactment of laws for their government. They acknowledge it when they punish disobedience on the part of the slave. There are seventy-two crimes in the State of Virginia, which, if committed by a black man, (no matter how ignorant he be,) subject him to the punishment of death; while only two of the same crimes will subject a white man to the like punishment. What is this but the acknowledgement that the slave is a moral, intellectual and responsible being? The manhood of the slave is conceded. It is admitted in the fact that Southern statute books are covered with enactments forbidding, under severe fines and penalties, the teaching of the slave to read or to write. When you can point to any such laws, in reference to the

beasts of the field, then I may consent to argue the manhood of the slave. When the dogs in your streets, when the fowls of the air, when the cattle on your hills, when the fish of the sea, and the reptiles that crawl, shall be unable to distinguish the slave from a brute, then will I argue with you that the slave is a man! For the present, it is enough to affirm the equal manhood of the negro race.[47]

Douglass may have been right in a technical sense, but he was wildly premature otherwise. The common humanity of Black and white people had by no means been conceded; far less had its ethical implications been acknowledged. This was made abundantly clear in the majority opinion of the Supreme Court in the Dred Scott decision of 1857.

In a case that centered on the citizen rights of the slave Dred Scott and his wife, Harriet, Chief Justice Roger Taney posed the question: "Can a negro, whose ancestors were imported into this country, and sold as slaves, become a member of the political community formed and brought into existence by the constitution of the United States, and as such become entitled to all the rights, and privileges, and immunities, guarantied [*sic*] by that instrument to the citizen?" Taney was a prominent and accomplished attorney who had served as attorney general and later secretary of the treasury in Andrew Jackson's administration. In 1835, he succeeded John Marshall as chief justice of the Supreme Court. Though highly and widely respected across parties, he was also from a wealthy, slave-owning family in Maryland and not without personal interests at stake.

Justice Taney's answer to his own question was an emphatic no. "We think," he wrote, that slaves "are not . . . included, and were not intended to be included, under the word 'citizens' in the Constitution, and can therefore claim none of the rights and privileges which that instrument provides for and secures to citizens of the United States." He quoted the Declaration of Independence, acknowledging that the words proclaiming the equality of all men "would seem to embrace the whole human family." "But it is too clear for dispute," he argued, "that the enslaved African race were not intended to be included, and formed no part of the people who framed and adopted this declaration . . . for if the language, as understood in that day, would embrace them, the conduct of the distinguished men who framed the Declaration of Independence would have been utterly and flagrantly inconsistent with the principles they asserted; and instead of the sympathy of mankind, to which they so confidently appealed, they would have deserved and received universal rebuke and reprobation."[48] These were great men, he asserted,

> high in literary acquirements—high in their sense of honor and incapable of asserting principles inconsistent with those on which they were acting. They perfectly understood the meaning of the language they used and how it would be understood by others; and they knew that it would not in any part of the civilized world be supposed to embrace the negro race, which, by common consent, had been excluded from civilized Governments and the family of nations, and doomed to slavery. They spoke and acted according to the then established doctrines and principles, and in the ordinary language of the day, and no one misunderstood them.[49]

Taney was undoubtedly right in his description of the frame of mind of the Founders. In 1775, the enslavement of Blacks was legal in all thirteen colonies. But he went further to address why they (and the Supreme Court over which he presided) held these convictions. At the time of the Founding of the new nation, he declared, Africans were "considered as a subordinate and inferior class of beings," an "unhappy black race . . . separated from the white by indelible marks . . . never thought of or spoken of except as property," "beings of an inferior order and altogether unfit to associate with the white race, either in social or political relations; and so far inferior, that they had no rights which the white man was bound to respect." Indeed, the negro "was justly and lawfully . . . reduced to slavery"—"bought and sold and treated as an ordinary article of merchandise and traffic, whenever a profit could be made by it"—all for his own benefit.[50]

Taney's admissions are startling. Whatever rights and privileges a slave might have could be stripped away at any moment and with impunity. As "an article of merchandise and traffic" a slave could be (and often was) sold, whipped, and put to death at whim. In this way, the slave lived in perpetual vulnerability.

The majority opinion in *Dred Scott v. Sandford* emboldened the cause of slavery and its defenders. On March 21, 1861, just twenty-two days before the outbreak of the Civil War, the Confederate vice president, Alexander H. Stephens, asserted that the philosophical "cornerstone" of the new Confederate States of America was the natural and God-ordained inequality of the races. The ideas entertained by the Founders that "the enslavement of the African was in violation of the laws of nature," he declared,

> were fundamentally wrong. They rested upon the assumption of the equality of races. This was an error. It was a sandy foundation, and the government built upon it fell when the "storm came and the wind blew." Our new government is founded upon exactly the opposite idea; its foundations are laid, its corner-stone rests, upon the great truth that the negro is not equal to the white man; that slavery subordination to the superior race is his natural and normal condition. This, our new government, is the first, in the history of the world, based upon this great physical, philosophical, and moral truth. . . .
>
> Many governments have been founded upon the principle of the subordination and serfdom of certain classes of the same race; such were and are in violation of the laws of nature. Our system commits no such violation of nature's laws. With us, all of the white race, however high or low, rich or poor, are equal in the eye of the law. Not so with the negro. Subordination is his place. He, by nature, or by the curse against Canaan, is fitted for that condition which he occupies in our system.[51]

Upon this foundation the Confederate States of America was formed.

The Culture War Becomes a Shooting War

At a fundamental level, then, the conflict that gave rise to the Civil War was over the questions "Who is a person?"—made concrete by the presence of racial difference—and "How should human beings treat other human beings?"—rendered jarringly tangible by the brutalizing realities of slavery.

Highlighting the anthropological tensions within the cultural logic of America's hybrid-Enlightenment does not, in any way, diminish the importance of other cultural factors—particularly sectional differences—in the looming conflict.[52] Though evangelical Christianity pervaded both the North and the South, differences in regional self-understanding had emerged and hardened over these decades. White Southerners, as a rule, held the ideal of the Christian Republic as a romanticized *gemeinschaft*—an agrarian community of organic interdependence that was hierarchical and honor-based, made possible by an enslaved African American labor force. By contrast, the North understood itself and the America it aspired to build as a modernizing society populated by self-made rational and independent individuals. It prized individual freedom, moral discipline, equality of opportunity, and progress. Each side could read the Bible and the Constitution within its own vision and each believed its vision of the Christian Republic to be vastly superior to the other. Ultimately, these amounted to competing visions of the meaning of America—the nature of the Union and its future.

And yet underneath these competing conceptions of collective identity was the pivotal disagreement over race-based slavery. By the late 1850s, this had come to symbolize all that was either good or bad about the Southern states. To preserve their identity, economy, and way of life, eleven states ultimately seceded from the Union. America's hybrid-Enlightenment wasn't strong enough to hold the Union together, particularly as slavery was set to extend into the western territories.

The inability to resolve these contradictions in national life either rationally, constitutionally, or theologically meant they could be resolved only coercively, through military strategy and might. The boundary work in reestablishing solidarity would be carried out through war.

The benevolent empire, of course, was supposed to be a peaceful empire. God's kingdom is, as all would affirm, ruled by love and truth. But conflicts in a culture tend to foreshadow violent clashes, for cultural logics provide the underpinning reasoning and theoretical defense of the subsequent violence. As Samuel Harris, a former president of Bowdoin and later professor of theology at Yale, argued retrospectively, "The kingdom of darkness is always in antagonism to the kingdom of light. It is founded and perpetuated in selfishness, and therefore powerful interests become enlisted in perpetuating its abuses, and in resisting the progress of the truth. . . . In reference to this our Saviour said: 'I came not to send peace, but a sword.'"[53]

The slaughter of whites and Blacks in Nat Turner's rebellion and its suppression in 1831, the series of violent confrontations between pro- and anti-slavery forces often called "bleeding Kansas" between 1854 and 1859, and John Brown's violent raid on the federal armory at Harpers Ferry in 1859 were merely preludes to greater mayhem to come. With North and South each believing the other to represent the "kingdom of darkness," the contradictions could neither be ignored nor suppressed any longer. War seemed inevitable, and a war unlike anything seen before on the continent, with one of five Southern men and one in ten Northern men dying as a result of the war.[54] The human costs were catastrophic.

Through this promiscuously bloody conflict, the cultural logics of America's hybrid-Enlightenment and the contradictions inherent within it would again be worked through, however poorly and imperfectly.

The Reconstitution of Slavery by a Different Name

What Justice Taney and the Supreme Court tried to accomplish, in effect, was solidarity through legal fiat. Consensus on the matter of slavery was imposed by law—and it obviously failed. Cultural conflict is rarely if ever successfully addressed through the power of the state. It took the bloodiest war in American history, the Emancipation Proclamation in 1863, and the Thirteenth, Fourteenth, and Fifteenth Amendments to the Constitution (between 1865 and 1869) to finally undo the legalities enshrined by the Dred Scott decision.

But not quite . . .

While legally and politically important and socially empowering to millions of Black Americans, these massive changes *also* represented an attempt to create normative and political solidarity through the coercive power of the state. These legal and constitutional achievements, however, *did little to change the cultural dispositions that made the Dred Scott case plausible and possible in the first place.* They did not change the deep structures of the culture of slavery.

In this light, it is little surprise that the Thirteenth, Fourteenth, and Fifteenth Amendments were slowly and largely abrogated through state and local Jim Crow laws that enforced racial segregation in the South; through the Slaughter-House Cases of 1873 that neutered many of the Fourteenth Amendment civil and political protections within individual states; through new state constitutions that devised poll taxes, residency rules, and literacy tests for voting privileges; and through the 1896 *Plessy* decision, which enshrined the "separate but equal" principle at the heart of segregation. Reinforcing these reversals was the rise of the Ku Klux Klan, the Red Shirts, and the White Man's League—well-organized and well-armed associations that used intimidation and violence to repress the civil and voting rights of Blacks. As a further means of reestablishing white control, lynching emerged in the South in the late 1870s—over 1,750 Blacks were lynched between 1882 and 1900, with thousands more in the twentieth century.[55]

Southern whites created economic conditions against the newly enfranchised citizens that made it nearly impossible for the latter to pull themselves out of poverty. Local and statewide Black codes were reinforced to control when and where former slaves could work and how much they could be paid. In the agrarian South, slave labor was replaced by its functional equivalent, sharecropping. Lincoln's vice president, Andrew Johnson, was a Unionist, but also a former slaveholder from Tennessee. Exercising his executive authority after Lincoln's assassination, he rescinded orders giving Black farmers tracts of land that had been confiscated from Confederates. And without the ability to get credit from banks, Blacks were unable to buy land. With no other options, most Black laborers worked farms owned by whites in exchange for a share of the crop at harvest, minus the expenses for land, lodging, supplies, and food. They typically lived in the same dwellings they had occupied as slaves.[56]

Reconstruction led to the period appropriately called the Nadir. C. Vann Woodward argued compellingly that under the Jim Crow laws of the 1890s, segregation achieved even greater racial separation after Reconstruction.[57] Woodward wrote that abolition blurred the lines of a system of clear-cut domination.[58] It created ambiguity and that ambiguity was terrifying, especially to lower-class white people. This resulted for Black Americans not only in the obvious political and economic depredations but also in myriad everyday indignities. As Isabel Wilkerson chronicled in her book *The Warmth of Other Suns*, in the Jim Crow South, one could find laws requiring separate seating on all public transportation as well as segregated theaters, restaurants, public pools, schools, jails, and homes for the elderly. "There were white elevators and colored elevators (meaning the freight elevators in the back); white train platforms and colored train platforms. There were white ambulances and colored ambulances to ferry the sick and white hearses and colored hearses for those who didn't survive whatever was wrong with them."[59] There were white and colored restrooms, drinking fountains, telephone booths, taxicabs, cemeteries, and entrances to buildings. Workers in the same company would use different water buckets, cups, pails, dippers, and glasses depending on race. African Americans were forbidden to enter public parks and to live in certain white neighborhoods.

The Inefficacy of Law

What David Brion Davis said about slavery, then, was no less true for Reconstruction and the years that followed. The fundamental problem was the conception of the human being—and the law, political parties, and the state, in all their power, could not adequately touch this. The public and private culture of the South, embedded in powerful economic, political, and cultural institutions, continued to be underwritten by the presuppositions of unequal humanity. These were now joined by new scientific hypotheses of Black inferiority rooted in Darwinian theory that regarded Blacks as members of a more primitive human type. W. E. B. Du Bois was certainly right that Reconstruction made more significant progress than may initially appear, but that progress was set against a cultural logic fundamentally opposed to its highest ideals.[60] The intransigence of the contradictions within that cultural logic meant that the most rudimentary elements of the old slave regime were simply reconstituted. The post-Reconstruction South simply reproduced the effects of slavery under a different name. The old caste regime of racial inequal-

ity remained in place, and the marginalization and disenfranchisement of Blacks from complete equality remained fully and comprehensively in place.

Mythos and Solidarity

Even through—perhaps especially through—the evangelical turn
in America's public culture in the early years of the nineteenth century, it was the framework of America's hybrid-Enlightenment that
provided the cultural logic by which Americans attempted to work
through its own inherent dehumanizing contradictions.

There were outliers, of course, as there always are, but overall,
the public culture of America was still a very religious one in which
God continued to be seen as the *foundation of reality* and Scripture,
in principle, the means of *knowing God and seeing the world*. Though
North and South disagreed fundamentally on the humanity of Black
people and the ethical obligations whites should have toward them,
they agreed on the question at stake, and they sought to address it
through this religious cosmology. Not least, the mythos of providential favor on America remained firmly entrenched in public culture as well—a point worth dwelling upon.

War, Reconstruction, and Mythos

For both sides, the Civil War had been a holy war, but the North's
victory was a vindication of divine favor. From the vantage point of
the winners, the war bolstered the long-standing millennial hopes
of the Union as a Christian Republic. The suffering people endured
was terrible and tragic, but worth it in light of God's plan for America. Many could resonate with the closing refrain of Julia Ward
Howe's anthem "The Battle Hymn of the Republic," first published
in 1862: "As He died to make men holy, let us die to make men free /
While God is marching on."

This was not just a war over a moral issue, even one as important
as slavery; it was a war over the hope for humanity; the devastations
of the conflict were a divine judgment upon the national sin of slavery. Lincoln's famous supplication in his Second Inaugural acknowledged this tragic sensibility with weariness and resignation. "Fondly

do we hope," he wrote, "fervently do we pray, that this mighty scourge of war may speedily pass away. Yet, if God wills that it continue . . . until every drop of blood drawn with the lash shall be paid by another drawn with the sword, as it was said three thousand years ago, so it must be said, 'the judgments of the Lord are true and righteous altogether.'"

For the religiously faithful, the war had also been the means by which Providence would further refine the character of the American people. The American Israel would survive, unified and strengthened by the experience. The Civil War, then, was an ennobling war, in which national unity and mission were even further galvanized.[61] As one Presbyterian minister preached toward the end of the war in 1864, "God has been striking and trying to make us strike at elements unfavorable to the growth of a pure democracy; and these and other facts point to the conclusion that he is at work, preparing in this broad land a fit stage for the last act of the mighty drama, the consummation of human civilization."[62]

That consummation would remain a dream, but at the time, the hope of it had been greatly enhanced in the North and for Black Americans by the Northern victory.

Mythos during the Nadir

Perhaps the strongest indication of the enduring power of this mythos would be found in its embrace by those most implicated in the war and its aftermath—the African American community.[63] The Black church remained its strongest institution, its clergy its most powerful intellectuals. This community was awash with biblical symbols, imagery, and authority. Here too, the framework produced by America's hybrid-Enlightenment provided the cultural logic by which Black Americans worked through the contradictions of being declared equal but seen and treated unequally. They interpreted history and experience in vastly different ways, but in short, the disenfranchised sought enfranchisement within the same cultural framework as those who had disenfranchised them in the first place; the excluded sought inclusion through the same cultural logics as those who had excluded them at the outset.

In the confusing aftermath of the war, there were different ideas among Black leaders of how to make sense of Black bondage. Even so, the language and framework of biblical millennialism, in particular the identification with ancient Israel and the hope for a Promised Land, was pervasive. God was in control of history, and the future was moving toward a reign of peace and justice.

Probably the dominant strand in the African American community was more or less aligned with the dominant mythos in the country that asserted America was a "redeemer nation" where racial equality and harmony would abound. The AME bishop R. H. Cain wrote in 1886:

> Happy for the great country, happy for the negro and the nation when the great principles upon which our government is founded, when the genius of liberty as understood by the fathers, shall permeate this whole land, mold the opinions of statesmen, fix the decrees of judges, settle the decisions of Supreme Courts and executed by every law officer of this broad land; then there will need be no more discussion as to what of the negro problem. . . . There will be one homogenous nation governed by intellectual, moral worth and controlled by Christian influences. Then there will be no East, no West, no North, no South, no Black, no White, no Saxon, no Negro, but a great, happy and peaceful nation.[64]

The coming age would be worked out through the completion of democratic and republican ideals in harmony with the Anglo-Saxon race, inspired by the ideals of "the fatherhood of God and the brotherhood of men." In the same denomination two years later, J. Augustus Cole echoed this hope. "The American Negro," he wrote, "has a share in the New World. He need not rush out of the land which he bought with two hundred and fifty years of servitude to find his destiny in Africa. . . . In the case of the Negro, he is entitled to America as he is to Africa. In the plan of Providence, America seems to be reserved as the future home of the surplus of all races. Asia was allotted to Shem, Europe to Japheth and Africa to Ham. But America was given to no race."[65]

Yet there were others who understood the coming millennium in more prophetic terms. Theophilus Steward, an AME minister and teacher, was one of the prominent voices in this tradition. His book *The End of the World—or, Clearing the Way for the Fullness of Gentiles* was written in response to a triumphalist version of the millennial vision.[66] Against that view, Steward argued that judgment would come to Anglo-Saxon civilization due to its pride, militarism, and betrayal of true Christianity. In this picture, the descendants of Africa would be spared judgment. In this, "the darker races" would move from curse to blessing, from servitude to leadership into the body of "the Universal Christ." Here again, disagreement was contained within a framework of shared teleological assumptions.

The Naïve Enthusiasms of Josiah Strong

The mythos of America's providential place in history continued to be the dominant interpretive frame in the broader public culture, though white Protestant clergy were certainly the most enthusiastic advocates, progressives just as much if not more so than conservatives. These clergy were by no means marginal figures; rather, they were among the most prominent public intellectuals in the country. In their rendering, slavery and the incomplete reckoning of the Civil War was now in the past and was now owed only passing reference. They seemed pleased with slavery's formal end and were ready to put it behind them and to move on. In their assessment, this was a civilization that they, aligned with God's purposes and blessing, had built and of which they were quite satisfied. Their intent, at this point, was to simply make it "still more Christian." "God has always acted by chosen people," Yale theologian Samuel Harris declared in 1874. "To the English-speaking people more than to any other the world is now indebted for the propagation of Christian ideas and Christian civilization."[67]

Perhaps the apogee of this confident and self-satisfied zeal in the Gilded Age came with the publication and popular success of *Our Country: Its Possible Future and Its Present Crisis*, written by Josiah Strong in 1885.[68] A Congregational minister, Strong was a progressive and a well-respected voice of the Protestant establishment; indeed, he was one of the prominent leaders early in the social gospel movement.[69] As had so many before him, he believed the meaning of America was to be found in its destiny. The historical record in light of biblical revelation makes it clear that "the world is evidently about to enter on a new era, that in this new era mankind is to come more and more under Anglo-Saxon influence, and that Anglo-Saxon civilization is more favorable than any other to the spread of those principles whose universal triumph is necessary to that perfection of the race to which it is destined; the entire realization of which will be the kingdom of heaven fully come on earth."[70]

In this light, the "Anglo-Saxon holds in his hand the destinies of mankind for ages to come." It is in the United States, however, where we find "the home of this race, the principal seat of his power, the great center of his influence." Citing Matthew Arnold, he declared, "America holds the future."[71]

The case he built drew from a statistical overview of the superior material resources of the country, the physical prowess of its inhabitants, the nation's wealth-generating capacities, and its massive production of crops of every kind. More interestingly, he found evidence in recent social and political achievements as well, including "honor to womanhood, whose fruitage is woman's elevation," the abolition of slavery, and "the enhanced valuation of human life" through the humanization of law.[72]

All of this, however, was the natural outgrowth of the republican ideal of individual liberty, "which finds its root in the teachings of Christ and has grown up slowly through the ages to blossom in our own."[73] It was the melding of the great ideas of individual liberty and "pure spiritual Christianity" that differentiated the Anglo-Saxon.[74]

In the end, "there [was] no doubt that the Anglo-Saxon [was] to exercise the commanding influence in the world's future."[75] In all of this, he saw not only the hand of God but also the workings of natural selection. For this insight, he invoked Darwin in his *The Descent of Man*: "There is apparently much truth in the belief that the wonderful progress of the United States, as well as the character of the people, are the results of natural selection; for the more energetic, restless, and courageous men from all parts of Europe have emigrated during the last ten or twelve generations to that great country, and have there succeeded best.[76] Indeed, citing Darwin again, "civilized nations are everywhere supplanting barbarous nations."[77]

Strong's rhetoric soared. "We stretch our hand into the future with power to mold the destinies of unborn millions." What was at stake in this calling is nothing less than the kingdom of God: "It is fully in the hands of the Christians of the United States, during the next fifteen or twenty years, to hasten or retard the coming of Christ's kingdom in the world by hundreds, and perhaps thousands, of years. We of this generation and nation occupy the Gibraltar of the ages, which commands the world's future."[78]

The paean to America's millennial promise continued to be invoked through the end of the century. Strong's colleague in the social gospel movement, Washington Gladden, closed out the nineteenth century with a confident summation of the now utterly familiar point: in America, he declared, "the problems of history are to be solved; here, if anywhere, is to rise that city of God, the New Jerusalem, whose glories are to fill the earth."[79] This theme was reiterated in Senator Albert Beveridge's now infamous speech in favor of the American Empire on the floor of the U.S. Senate on January 9, 1900. Speaking of America's providential duty, Beveridge bellowed:

> He [God] has made us the master organizers of the world to establish system where chaos reigns. He has given us the spirit of progress to overwhelm the forces of reaction throughout the earth. He has made us adepts in government that we may administer government among savage and senile peoples. Were it not for such a force as this the world would relapse into barbarism and night. And of all our race, He has marked the American people as His chosen nation to finally lead in the regeneration of the world. This is the divine mission of America, and it holds for us all the profit, all the glory, all the happiness possible to man. We are trustees of the world's progress, guardians of its righteous peace.[80]

As we've seen, Protestant theology and practice (high-brow Calvinism before the Revolutionary War and low-brow revivalism later) were aligned with and extended civic republicanism from the late colonial period through the early decades of the nineteenth century. In the vision of Strong, Gladden, and Beveridge, we see the thread of alignment continue, now a full century on. As George Thomas demonstrated in his superb treatment, *Revivalism and Cultural Change*,

Protestant faith and republican political ideals were now reinforced by a pervasive market individualism. These interwoven threads defined the leading elements in the cultural fabric of the late nineteenth century. Populist Protestantism "framed rules and identities of the expanding market and the national polity," thereby articulating a cultural order centered on the individual citizen as the key actor. It was commonplace to believe that rational moral action by citizens would establish "national morality and transform American civilization into the Kingdom of God on earth."[81] In this way, the mythos of American public culture and its constitutive deep structures, in place for over a century, remained embedded within its most prominent and powerful institutions.

This mythos, animated by millenarian purpose, provided a compelling story that had made sense of the work of nation-building through the nineteenth century—its territorial expansion, its demographic increase, and the growth in size, power, and reach of its institutions, most importantly the market, republican polity, and faith. Given the institutional compatibility of this mythos with both the market and republican polity, it is not surprising that echoes of this story resounded through the end of the century and into the next: from Theodore Roosevelt's vision to spread Anglo-Saxon civilization around the world through Woodrow Wilson's ambition to create a global democratic order through the League of Nations, in which the United States would lead in the "redemption of the world."

And yet something was amiss. Had they been attentive, Strong, Gladden, Beveridge, Roosevelt, and Wilson would have sensed that their bravado was masking a mythos that was far more fragile than it appeared.

The Dismantling of the Christian Republic

And yet as pervasive as the cosmology of Protestant Christianity was in American public culture throughout the nineteenth century, something profoundly important had changed. It is fair to say that it was unwitting and went mostly unnoticed for the simple reason that the language of faith—in form, if not in substance—continued to be widespread in public and private life right through the end of the nineteenth century. *What had changed was that its authority had been vastly diminished.*[82]

The End of the Religious Interpretation of the World

Alfred Kazin once observed that the age of belief reached its culmination with Lincoln's Second Inaugural Address.[83] This sounds about right. Kazin positioned his observation with a funny story that illustrated the point. A group of abolitionist and Transcendentalist ministers from New England visited Lincoln in the White House. Their purpose was to tell Lincoln that they were carrying a message from God himself: that the war was God's own justice and therefore they demanded an immediate and total emancipation for all slaves. To which Lincoln replied, "Don't you think, gentlemen, He might have spoken first to *me?*"

The war was devastating in its tragic loss of human life and yet behind it was the unshakeable conviction of God's Providential design. It was a conviction embraced by Northerners and Southerners alike and for both, that conviction seemed to make the sacrifices worth it. People in both the North and the South, Lincoln said in his Second Inaugural Address, given on March 4, 1865, "read the same Bible and pray to the same God, and each invokes His aid against the other." Yet, he declared, "the prayers of both could not be answered— that of neither has been answered fully."

By taking sides so prominently in the war and having intensified the moral stakes of the conflict, *biblical faith*, in effect, *had discredited itself as a source for interpreting and directing policy matters and directly influencing public life*. And not only this: along with the collapse of Christianity's moral authority and the confidence in its assumptions came a diminution of Christianity as a credible source of knowledge, ethics, and collective moral purpose for the nation. Indeed, the heart of the nation's long-standing mythos, the story Americans would tell of the nation as an emerging Christian Republic and thus the fulfillment of God's millennial purposes, lost credibility. The blood of tens of thousands of Americans was demonstration enough of the point. Importantly, the discrediting of Protestant Christianity and of religious faith more generally in national affairs occurred long before urban industrialization, the triumph of Darwinian evolution, and the effects of modernism in theology.

In short, the Civil War, the cultural contradictions that led up to it, and its aftermath had profound, enduring, yet ambivalent consequences for the coherence and credibility of America's hybrid-Enlightenment and the solidarity it sought to sustain. The working through represented by the Civil War and its immediate aftermath had not only failed to expand the *pluribus* in any meaningful way, it also failed to redefine the *unum*—a problem only intensified in the new century by the unresolved contradictions of Jim Crow segregation; the discrimination against Irish, Italian, Jewish, and Chinese immigrants; and the ongoing struggle for women's suffrage. The promissory note of liberty and equality in the Constitution, and the hybrid-Enlightenment that underwrote it, remained glaringly unfulfilled.

CHAPTER SEVEN
A Secular Turn

T o say that the end of the Civil War marked the end of the religious interpretation of the world—at least in ways that were public and authoritative—would not describe the experience of most Americans of the time. In the early decades of the twentieth century, most Americans—white, Black, and new immigrant alike—continued to understand life religiously. Even if experienced with greater ambivalence and doubt and even when contradicted by the dualism inherent in modern everyday life, a religious imaginary continued to frame the cosmic order as well as life's major mileposts—birth, death, marriage, and the assorted rites of initiation. A religiously infused moral imaginary defined the folkways of family, work, commerce, local civic life, and personal meaning. This was, perhaps, especially true in the Black community, whose view of the world remained deeply and conservatively religious and pious long after many white Americans had abandoned their faith.[1] Among the reasons for the ongoing vitality of religious imaginaries was that the church, the parish, and now the synagogue continued, as they had through the last half of the nineteenth century, to be influential institutions in local communities. The clergy in these contexts continued to enjoy wide respect. And while far from halcyon idylls, these faith communities continued to do the work of binding people together in friendship, obligation, care, and mutual support.[2]

An Emerging Cleavage

By the start of the twentieth century, average Americans, if paying attention, might have heard the rumblings of the social gospel and of modernism in theology, the latter in particular as progressive theologians and clergy sought to reconcile more traditional Christian theology with the discoveries of modern scientific inquiry. At stake was the authority of the biblical tradition. The challenge came not only from the likes of Charles Darwin and Thomas Huxley but from the broader breakthroughs in astronomy, psychology, sociology, and philosophy. Preeminent was the challenge of reconciling increasingly literalistic interpretations of the Bible with the methods of modern intellectual investigation. Historicism and higher criticism were powerful intellectual movements in European scholarship, and as they filtered into the discourse of the American academic community, they could not be ignored by people of faith. The net effect of all these pressures was a re-symbolization of the traditions that de-emphasized the supernatural and miraculous aspects of the biblical narrative, replacing these with a near-exclusive emphasis upon its ethical aspects. These theological innovations not only allowed progressive Protestant churches to keep pace with the intellectual currents of the period, they also provided much-needed intellectual justifications for their new programs of social activism.

These emerging conflicts were most prominent within white Protestantism. Some Black Protestant elites were also influenced by the developments of the social gospel movement, but rather than embracing the larger social agenda of that movement, their focus tended to be fixed on addressing racially entrenched economic and political disparities facing the Black community.[3] Given the aggressive and brutalizing segregationist policies of the Jim Crow regime, recurrent incidences of lynching, and the everyday indignities facing Black Americans everywhere, it was an agenda they couldn't avoid, not least because it aligned with the pressing need of the average Black congregant.

Catholicism and Judaism also struggled with their own versions of these challenges as they grappled with the pressures of assimilation to a modernizing culture still very Protestant in its character. Within Catholicism, progressive initiatives came in the 1890s through a concern with the rights of labor and a desire to cooperate with Protestants in social amelioration. Progressives also led an Americanist movement that sought to phase out what they considered arcane Romanist traditions: in short, Americanizing the new immigrant population through language and custom under the American principle of religious liberty. Underwriting it all were progressive views of biblical, theological, and historical authority similar to trends in liberal Protestantism and a celebration of democracy and scientific progress, all in the effort to reconcile the authority of revealed truths with the modern age. Likewise in Judaism, the progressivist impulse took form in ideas for what was to become Reform Judaism: a shortened and vernacular worship service, the end of the segregation of men from women in worship, and a decisive move away from traditional belief and ritual observance toward an ethical idealism.[4]

By the first decades of the new century, conservative religious leaders and theologians from all three traditions were beginning to react to these progressive—for some, heretical—changes within the traditions. Among Protestants, the first ambitious response came in the publication and distribution of *The Fundamentals* in 1910 (from which the concept of "fundamentalism" derives), a twelve-volume work of theological and biblical exposition that systematically catalogued and defended the major doctrines and authority of traditional biblical faith. Summarizing all of the major archeological evidence in support of the historicity of the Old Testament stories, it attempted to refute the methods of higher criticism.[5] Traditionalist Catholics and Jews also reacted defensively in their own distinct ways. By 1923, when the Princeton theologian J. Gresham Machen published his defense of orthodoxy—*Christianity and Liberalism*—the conflict was no longer an academic or theological matter but one that had found its way into weekly preaching, Sunday school lessons, and the religious press.[6]

From the vantage point of our own time, the disputes that played out among the theologians and the clergy of all three traditions over a century ago may appear puzzling if not unintelligible, but those disputes contained within them fundamental debates over key elements of the deep structures of culture: the makeup of ultimate reality, the foundations of knowledge in the modern age, and the ethical obligations of a social order increasingly defined by industrialization and urbanization and the meaning of progress. These tensions would eventually erupt into the culture war that would unfold toward the end of the twentieth century.[7] In their time, these disputes were part and parcel of a broader intellectual transition occurring among all men and women of letters and within the institutions they inhabited; they were at the heart of tensions within the cultural logic of America's hybrid-Enlightenment.

A Secular Uprising

The backdrop of this transition in American religious culture was a reconfiguration of the larger cultural economy. As Christian Smith's research has demonstrated, this reconfiguration was not inevitable; it was actively cultivated within the dominant culture-producing institutions of the time.[8]

An obvious and dramatic indication of this broader shift was evident in the changes taking place in higher education. From the founding of Harvard College in 1636 through the last decades of the nineteenth century, the overwhelming majority of colleges in America had been established and funded by religious denominations, were governed by religious leaders, and were substantively oriented to a religiously integrated ideal of knowledge and morality. As late as 1861, about 60 percent of college presidents and about 40 percent of college and university trustees were drawn from the ranks of the Protestant clergy. By 1890, this structure of governance was being supplanted so rapidly by lay faculty, administrators, and boards that by 1918 the process was all but complete. As Thorstein Veblen wrote in 1918, "Within the memory of men still living it was a nearly unbroken rule that the governing boards of . . . higher American schools were drawn largely from the clergy and were also guided mainly by ecclesiastical . . . notions of what was right and needful in matters of learning. . . . That phase of academic policy is past. . . . For a generation past . . . there has gone on a wide-reaching substitution of laymen in place of clergymen on the governing boards . . . so that the discretionary control in matters of university policy now rests finally in the hands of businessmen."[9]

For corporate leaders who had founded and funded their own universities—including Johns Hopkins, Andrew Carnegie, James Duke, Leland Stanford, John D. Rockefeller, and Cornelius Vanderbilt— and for the large assemblage of business leaders who filled the trusteeship of colleges and universities everywhere, the secular turn was a pragmatic one, influenced in large measure by the practical needs of an industrial economy. The new social order no longer needed gentlemen who had been classically trained in the literature of antiquity. Rather, industry required young adults who were technically and professionally proficient in engineering, finance, management, law, and the like: young people who had the energy, competence, and skill to build the edifice of a rapidly modernizing society.[10]

Among the intellectual classes, however, the secular turn was more ideological, rooted in a desire for greater autonomy from religious authority and the constraints of conformity implied by earlier religious establishments. At the same time, the traditional sources of authoritative knowledge that had validated theistic models for understanding the world simply could not measure up to the triumphalist scientism of Auguste Comte (popularized in the English-speaking world by John Stuart Mill) and the evolutionary theories of Darwin applied and popularized by Herbert Spencer.[11] Nor could a theistic moral imaginary stand up to the challenge of historicism in the social sciences or the individualism, subjectivism, and experimentation of literary modernism. Even where these progressive academic movements were at cross-purposes, all of them shared a fundamental hostility to external authority, be it tradition or providence, and to the restrictions on thought placed by those authorities.

The secular turn in higher education and among intellectuals broadly only reinforced the powerful secularizing tendencies in other areas of social life. During the last decades of the nineteenth century and the early decades of the twentieth, journalism underwent rapid professionalization.[12] Seeking the prestige enjoyed by other professions, journalism aspired to become "a dignified occupation espousing an ethic of service, organized into an association, and practicing functional science" insofar as it sought ways to appropriate for itself the methods that would lead to objectivity.[13] In this new framework, religion effectively migrated to the periphery of news reporting: in part, religion was considered less and less as a topic of serious consideration; in part, it was eclipsed by what was considered the more pressing topics of politics, industry, labor, and international affairs.

In the realm of law and jurisprudence, the ascendance of legal positivism insisted on the autonomy of law and its processes quite independent of any grounding in or justification from religion, morality, and history. Judges were no longer tethered to religious or local ethics in rendering decisions from the bench. As religion increasingly became a personal matter, the wall of separation between church and state rose higher.

In the world of work, industrialization fueled the migration of ever-larger numbers from farms to cities, disrupting rhythms of small-town life and weakening the institutional authority of families, churches, and other local associations. Likewise, early twentieth-century management theories, with their emphasis on scientifically regulating time and motion and bureaucratically organizing manufacturing and administrative processes, certainly provided greater efficiencies in economic production and distribution, but they also carried into the workplace an overriding stress on the inner-worldly values of function, utility, proficiency, yield, and so on.

Accompanying these economic and managerial transformations was a spectacular growth of local and national advertising. This remarkable development surely signaled the transition from a producer to a consumer mode of capitalism in America, but here too these institutional changes were the carriers of a subtle but important cultural shift from a concern with spiritual well-being to physical and psychic well-being. As Jackson Lears has argued, the new modalities of modern advertising promised ordinary middle-class Americans a way to address the increasingly common complaints of dysphoria, depression, and neurasthenia. The expansion of marketing in these therapeutic ways went far toward turning ordinary people from a concern for salvation to one of self-realization.[14]

This turn in the normative ethos of the public sphere was reflected no less in politics in the most important social movement of the time—women's suffrage. Throughout the latter half of the nineteenth century, the pursuit of equality for women had been framed within the mythos of the Christian Republic. The stories of Angelina and Sarah Grimké, Lucretia Mott, Mary Ann M'Clintock, Susan B. Anthony—devout Quakers all—as well as the indomitable Sojourner

Truth, established the work of women's rights within the ethical ambitions of abolition and then temperance. The bond between feminism and a religiously infused moral reform remained strong through the very end of the century.[15]

The symbolic end of this alliance was marked by two events. The first was the publication of Elizabeth Cady Stanton's book *The Women's Bible* in 1895. Stanton was persuaded that any progress on the rights of women required a challenge to traditional Christianity and its understandings of the role of women. Of Scripture she declared, "I know no other books that so fully teach the subjection and degradation of woman"; of the clergy she pronounced, "No other class of teachers have such prestige and power, especially over women."[16] The book's publication splintered the movement. Even her closest collaborator, Susan B. Anthony, demurred: "I have worked 40 years to make the [women's suffrage] platform broad enough for atheists and agnostics to stand upon, and now if need be, I will fight the next 40 years to keep it Catholic enough to permit the straightest Orthodox religionist to speak or pray and count her beads upon."[17]

In the heat of the moment, Stanton's efforts were rebuked by the National American Woman Suffrage Association, but she had caught something of the national mood that would eventually carry the day.

The second event was the death of Frances Willard in 1898. Willard, a devout Methodist, was a tireless, charismatic, and politically savvy organizer who led the Women's Christian Temperance Union from 1879 to the end of her life. Under her leadership, the WCTU forged a strong alliance with women's suffrage under the conviction that if women had the right to vote, they would purge the nation of drink, gambling, prostitution, and other sins. With her passing, religion began to fade into the background of the movement.

The net effect of the secular turn in intellectual and academic life—operating within the secularizing ethos established through industrial capitalism—was a successful challenge to the monopoly long held by the Protestant establishment over the legitimate interpretation of the world. Complacent with the power and privilege that had once accompanied its leadership over America's public institutions, the Protestant establishment now found itself marginalized from the centers of cultural influence and on the defensive, stripped of the status and credibility to define reality authoritatively to the world.

The Self-Immolation of the Protestant Establishment

Against the backdrop of this secular turn, the schism between modernist and traditionalist movements in Protestantism grew wider. By and large, liberal Protestantism lay prostrate before the secular juggernaut, offering little thoughtful interrogation of what was unfolding and no meaningful resistance. Indeed, if anything, it actively celebrated the faith's "coming of age." On the other hand, conservative tendencies in Protestantism morphed fully into a fundamentalist movement. This movement flexed its muscles in the realm of *public ethics* through the Anti-Saloon League, which brought about the passage of the Volstead Act of 1919, prohibiting the manufacture, possession, use, and sale of any alcohol over .5 percent by volume. Nearly six years later, in July 1925, it flexed its muscles in the realm of *public epistemology* through the Scopes trial, pursuing a conviction of John T. Scopes for teaching evolution in the public schools of Dayton, Tennessee. The prosecution brought in former secretary of state and three-time presidential contender William Jennings Bryan to make the case. Given that the trial was in rural Tennessee, it was effectively over before it began. Siding with Bryan, the court found Scopes guilty, though the conviction was overturned on a technicality.

Together, the efforts of traditionalists represented the last gasps of the aspiration of nineteenth-century evangelicalism to establish a Christian Republic. While these initiatives succeeded legally, they failed culturally, their cultural logics facing resistance, resentment, and ridicule.

One of the keenest and most caustic observers of the time, H. L. Mencken, captured the ironies well. Of prohibition, he observed that none of the great benefits of the Eighteenth Amendment had actually come to pass. In fact, he noted, "There is not less drunkenness in the Republic, but more. There is not less crime, but more. There is not less insanity, but more. The cost of government is not smaller, but vastly greater. Respect for law has not increased, but diminished." As for the Scopes case, Mencken's daily reports to the *Baltimore Evening Sun* provided extravagant descriptions of the trial as "a religious orgy"; the locals as "yokels," "morons," "local primates," "poor ignoramuses," and "poor-half-wits"; and William Jennings Bryan as "a walking malignancy," an "imposter," a "wrecked and preposterous charlatan," "a man of consuming hatred," and "a fanatic, rid of sense and devoid of conscience." "Bryan," Mencken wrote, "was a vulgar and common man, a cad undiluted. He was ignorant, bigoted, self-seeking, blatant and dishonest. Imagine a gentleman," he wrote, "and you have imagined everything he was not." "He came into life a hero . . . now he was passing out a pathetic fool." As to fundamentalism itself, Mencken described it as "theological bilge," "rubbish," "nonsense," "buncombe," a pack of "bafooneries" and "imbecilities," and a "superstition" known for its "bigotry" and "hatred."[18]

More satire than reportage, Mencken's scalding prose certainly made for an entertaining read, but his message was serious and its target unmistakable. That message of derision soon became diffused into the judgments of the broader cultural zeitgeist. Even to those who remained within the movements of traditional Protestantism, the secular turn was, for all practical purposes, complete. In part, the conservative (now called fundamentalist) elements of American Christianity were chased out of a formative role in American public culture, having taken imprudent positions on mostly unpopular issues. In their humiliation and defeat, they became culturally alienated, theologically sectarian, and intellectually stagnant. Just as true, fundamentalist Christianity retreated from the public sphere as its members sought to be separated from a modern culture that seemed ever more worldly and sinful. Their strategy of civic privatism would remain in place through the 1960s. Together, these factors worked to isolate and marginalize their influence from this point on. Any kind of cultural authority traditional Protestantism once had was now subjected to derision and contempt. Though there would be credible voices that would, from time to time, find a public platform, never again would traditional Protestant Christianity provide the background cultural consensus for a country changing as quickly as America was in the twentieth century.

The Dislocations of Industrial Capitalism

The ethical implications of this secular turn were as significant as the epistemological implications. The backdrop was the expansion of industrial capitalism in the late nineteenth and twentieth centuries, an expansion that created brutalizing dislocations for the lower eche-

lons of the American class system. The often abysmal conditions of
unregulated labor, the inadequacy of decent and affordable housing,
the growing numbers living in poverty, the lack of healthcare, and
the fragility of living conditions, not least for the rural poor migrating to big cities, are all well known.

Equality before the law is a public good, but is it enough when
vast numbers of fellow citizens live only at subsistence level or worse?
Political freedom is a public good, but what does it mean when large
segments of the population are imprisoned by want of basic life chances?

The traditional ways of addressing the needs of the vulnerable—
private and religious charity and almsgiving, poor farms and work-
houses, orphanages, and the like—were simply inadequate for problems of this scale. Social gospel theology was an early but ultimately
insufficient response to what was, in effect, the indifference of a system of privilege and power to the needs of the poor, the indebted,
and the disadvantaged.

The same question was at stake in the women's movement. The
tension between the principle of equality before the law and the effective exclusion of women simply could not be sustained. What could
political freedom possibly mean when half the population was barred
from voting?

Dewey's Burden

The ethical and epistemological challenge to traditional religious authority was comprehensive. It was both intellectual and institutional.
The work of articulating and advocating this turn fell to thousands
of scholars, novelists, poets, journalists, and writers, none more important than John Dewey.[19] His life, spanning just shy of a century—
from just before the Civil War in 1859 to just after World War II in
1952—was witness to the great economic, political, and social transformations to high modernity. Dewey's audacious objective was to
light the way forward.

Dewey's modest start in life in what were then the regional back-
waters of Burlington, Vermont, would not have suggested these
possibilities. His parents each came from three generations of New
England farmers, a family culture that was said to be iconically in-
dustrious, shrewd, independent, thrifty, self-reliant, unpretentious,

morally upright and, on his mother's side, deeply pious. Yet he rose to be America's premier philosopher of democracy and perhaps the most distinguished exemplar of the liberal intellectual tradition. Though he was a famously dull and difficult writer and speaker, what he lacked in style he made up in ambition, productivity, and sweep of vision. At the end of Dewey's life, Henry Steele Commager wrote of him that "no major issue was clarified until Dewey had spoken."[20] His extensive writings during professorships at the University of Chicago and later Columbia were a prism through which one can see the foreshadowing of change in the cultural logic of America's hybrid-Enlightenment.

Reconceiving the Sources of Liberal Democracy

No less than the most ardent of patriots, Dewey viewed America as an exceptional nation, not least in its potential for fraternity, love of neighbor, and social justice. And yet he was supremely aware that the original formulation of America's public philosophy was not only incapable of addressing the old challenges of religious, ethnic, and racial tension, it was helpless before the new challenges brought about by industrialization, growing income inequality, and global financial instability. This was made graphic and tangible to him as a young professor first arriving by train in Chicago in July 1894—the precise moment of the famous Pullman Strike—to take up his new position at the University of Chicago. He recognized that under new and evolving social and economic conditions, liberalism had morphed from an ideal virtue grounded in legitimate claims for political and economic liberty into what he regarded as the self-serving ideology of a powerful capitalist class against the weak and disenfranchised. "The tragic breakdown of democracy is due to the fact that the identification of liberty with the maximum of unrestrained individualistic action in the economic sphere, under the institutions of capitalistic finance, is as fatal to the realization of liberty for all as it is fatal to the realization of equality. It is destructive of liberty for the many precisely because it is destructive of genuine equality of opportunity."[21] In this sense, liberal democracy for Dewey had become misdirected in ways that made it anti-democratic and counter to its own original ends.

The early decades of the twentieth century were, in Dewey's

estimate, "days of transition" in America and in philosophy. "Old sources of religion and art . . . have been discredited."[22] Dewey knew that democracy did not perpetuate itself automatically. He believed that "we now have to recreate by deliberate and determined endeavor the kind of democracy which in its origin one hundred and fifty years ago was largely the product of a fortunate combination of men and circumstances."[23]

Dewey was acutely aware of the depth of the problem and what was at stake. He understood that even more than a political system, democracy was a belief system; that democracy was underwritten by culture, and that more than a century after the Founding, the cultural framework upon which early twentieth-century democracy rested was inadequate to the challenges of the day. He understood that a comprehensive reconstitution of America's public culture was needed. In his words, this would be nothing less than the task "*of creating a genuine culture.*"[24] Nothing less than the survival of democracy depended upon it. That challenge entailed the work of self-consciously "humanizing industrial civilization, of making it and its technology a servant of human life."[25] Dewey was remarkable for how precise and self-conscious he was in understanding the problem. He was even more remarkable for taking on its burden.

But on what terms could American democracy rebuild its cultural infrastructure? Dewey shared with the Progressive movement of the late nineteenth and early twentieth centuries a common opposition to the natural law and natural rights arguments of the Declaration of Independence in favor of a political science rooted in Darwinian evolution and Hegelian historicism. Dewey was aligned with this program. Though he was known as a rationalist and pragmatist, mere proceduralism wasn't enough for Dewey. "Creating a culture" in part implied a new belief system, the heart of which was the conviction that a rationally based civic life would generate the values that would, in turn, lead to individual self-realization. Again, more than a political system, Dewey viewed liberal democracy as a way of life, "the full realization of the possibilities of human society."[26] Like the Founders of the Republic, he insisted that democracy was a moral and metaphysical aspiration whose values and beliefs rested on truth.

Dewey's vision was, at root, Jeffersonian, though only up to a point. He shared Jefferson's dispositions toward a philosophical naturalism as well as his belief in progress through scientific achievement, popular enlightenment through education, and reform through practical experimentation. And yet Dewey sought to adapt the Jeffersonian sensibility to the transforming conditions of an industrial age.

In doing so, he radicalized naturalism, severing it entirely from any association with the various forms of deism or theism. The reasons were, for him, self-evident: the claims of religion were false on their own terms. Supernaturalism, in his view, was obviously irrational. But what was worse was that in all of its expressions, it tended to translate intellectually into absolutism and institutionally into authoritarianism. As he put it, "The association of religion with the supernatural tends, by its own nature, to breed the dogmatic and the divisive spirit."[27] Clearly, then, traditional faiths were in conflict with the methods of scientific inquiry and the aims of constructive democratic collegiality.

What was required for the reconstitution of America's hybrid-Enlightenment as a reworked source of solidarity was "nothing less than a revolution in the '*seat of authority*'" that would foster a world in which "new methods of inquiry and reflection have become for the educated man today the final arbiter of all questions of fact, existence, and intellectual assent."[28] In the end, the authority upon which democratic life would rest came down to the self-correcting methods of pragmatic and experimental reasoning over against the dogmas of irrational religious belief. To search for ideals of justice and equality and fraternity in the authority of God was, in effect, a quest for a certainty that did not exist. For Dewey, there could be no compromise; "the opposition . . . is not to be bridged."[29] More significant, in this critical moment in history, he couldn't "understand how any realization of the democratic ideal as a vital moral and spiritual ideal in human affairs is possible without" abandoning the very foundations of supernatural faiths.[30]

Though the secular turn in America's hybrid-Enlightenment was overpowering both intellectually and institutionally, it was not without opposition.[31] G. K. Chesterton was just one of many voices arguing that democracy could remain viable only if undergirded by Christian faith. After his trip to the United States in 1921, Chesterton concluded that "there is no basis for democracy except in a dogma about the divine origin of man. . . . Every other basis is a sort of sen-

timental confusion, full of merely verbal echoes of the older creeds. . . .
So far as that democracy becomes or remains Catholic and Christian, that democracy will remain democratic. . . . Men will more and
more realize that there is no meaning in democracy if there is no
meaning in anything; and that there is no meaning in anything if the
universe has not a centre of significance and an *authority* that is the
basis of our rights."[32] Dewey, citing this passage in an essay defending naturalism, argued that Chesterton's cynical and pessimistic
view of human nature was at the root of all criticisms of naturalism
as a foundation for democracy. "The fact of the case," Dewey argued,
was that "the worth and dignity of men and women founded in human
nature itself, in the connections, actual and potential, of human beings with one another . . . is a much sounder one than is . . . alleged
to exist outside the constitution of man and nature."[33]

Though he had spilled ink by the gallons laying out his case for
a renewed public philosophy, the culmination of his efforts to redefine the sources and terms of democratic solidarity came together
in his Terry Lectures at Yale, delivered in January 1934 and published later that year as *A Common Faith*.[34] For someone so stridently
opposed to traditional religion, it is, on the face of it, a curious title
and argument.

Yet the paradox is revealing.

Dewey drew a distinction between "religion" and the "religious"
in the effort to rescue the "religious" from "religion." "I am not proposing a religion," he argued, "but rather the emancipation of elements and outlooks that may be called religious."[35] The religious is
present in human experience itself, he argued, and can—and should—
be separated from the myths, doctrines, creeds, deities, and rituals
of organized religion. The "religious," then, is a wholly natural and
thus empirical phenomenon: the best values of religion—"affection,
compassion, and justice, equality and freedom"—are simply the natural "impulses" of human beings; thus, the idea of God simply "represents a unification of ideal values."[36] Faith, in its universalizing
essence, is "not confined to sect, class or race" but represents the po-
tentialities of all human life pursued through action, and it functions
to integrate the self and improve life. "Such a faith," he concluded,
"has always been implicitly the common faith of mankind. It remains
to make it explicit and militant."[37]

The heart of Dewey's common faith and the cultural sources upon which he sought to underwrite liberal democracy derived not from any transcendent authority but from what America is by itself: America in action, as it were. The common faith would be based upon the self-evident "goods of human association, of arts, and of knowledge. . . . We need no external criterion and guarantee for their goodness. . . . They . . . exist as good, and out of them we frame our ideal ends."[38] Democracy, then, is the place where liberty and experimental rationality come together. Given the pace and scale of technological and industrial change, the need to reconstitute the foundation of democracy in this way was urgent. "The cause of liberty and of the human spirit," he wrote, "the cause of opportunity of human beings for full development of their powers, the cause for which liberalism enduringly stands, is too precious and too ingrained in the human constitution to be forever obscured. Intelligence after millions of years of errancy has found itself as a method, and it will not be lost forever in the blackness of night. The business of liberalism is to bend every energy and exhibit every courage so that these precious goods may not even be temporarily lost but be intensified and expanded here and now."[39]

The paradox of *A Common Faith* was that while Dewey stridently denied the substance of traditional faith, he embraced its form and its ethics. Arguably, *A Common Faith* goes even further to make explicit what was always implicit: that his naturalist treatment of the religious attitude and the qualities it promotes was the culmination of his entire philosophy.[40] Human beings, he believed, were part of the totality of nature and, while dependent upon the natural world, they were also capable of intervening in its development in ways that imaginatively direct it toward new ends. What he called "natural piety," then, rested "upon a just sense of nature as the whole of which we are parts, while it also recognizes that we are parts that are marked by intelligence and purpose, having the capacity to strive by their aid to bring conditions into greater consonance with what is humanly desirable."[41]

This kind of natural piety finds its fullest expression in the life of community, because it is through community, embodied in democracy, that the values and ideals we share can be realized.

So, while Dewey categorically rejected theism of any sort, he still oper-

ated within the cultural logic of the hybrid-Enlightenment, framing science,
pragmatic reasoning, and the naturalism that underwrote it in phrasings
that were distinctly religious. In such a way he believed one could reestablish the foundations and frameworks of a meaningful history.

Rebuilding Solidarity through Education

Dewey was remarkable not only for the sheer scale of his intellectual
project but for his own personal activism in making his progressive
vision a reality. He worked in settlement houses to help assimilate
immigrants, he marched in support of women's suffrage, he founded
such organizations as the American Humanist Association, the American Association of University Professors, and the New York City
Teachers Union. He helped lay the groundwork for the founding of
the National Association for the Advancement of Colored People
and the American Civil Liberties Union.

It's not surprising, then, that Dewey's herculean efforts to work
through the hybrid-Enlightenment philosophically gained force
through his work to build an operable philosophy of education. He
sought not only to rework the sources of solidarity but to create the
institutional conditions for reproducing it into the future.

Dewey's educational reforms were possible in part because the
ground had been prepared by Horace Mann more than a half century
before. In his day, Mann had been repeatedly faulted for attempting
to secularize public education, an accusation that was, in his own
view, "without substance or semblance of truth."[42] At the same time,
Mann insisted that "our Public Schools are not Theological Seminaries. . . . They are de-barred by law from inculcating the peculiar
and distinctive doctrines of any one religious denomination amongst
us. . . . Our system earnestly inculcates all Christian morals; it founds
its morals on the basis of religion; it welcomes the religion of the
Bible; and, in receiving the Bible, it allows it to do what it is allowed
to do in no other system—to speak for itself. *But here it stops because*
it disclaims to act as an umpire between hostile religious opinions. The very
terms, Public School, and Common School, bear upon their face,
that they are schools which the children of the entire community
may attend."[43]

The reforms Mann promoted entailed the moral demands and

aspirations of an earlier Calvinism without its accompanying theological beliefs so that they would be more universal in their appeal. The moral foundations of his educational philosophy were akin to a natural ethics, and Mann indeed called them that.[44] In their net effect, Mann's innovations in the mid-1800s laid greater emphasis on the training of citizens than on the training of Christian disciples. By universalizing the foundations of education, he also secularized them.[45]

A half century later, the idea that public education should be secular in its underpinnings had become a given for Dewey. He wrote voluminously about education in works such as "My Pedagogic Creed" (1897), *The School and Society* (1900), *The Child and the Curriculum* (1902), and his magnum opus on the subject, *Democracy and Education* (1916).[46] Naturally, his contributions to the field were an extension of his philosophical reflections, but his innovations were also born out of practical experience—he taught at both the high school and college levels, wrote curricula, consulted, and established the University of Chicago's Lab School as an experimental site for working out his philosophical innovations.

As with his other philosophical work, the guiding ethical imperative was the revivification of democracy. As we've seen, democracy was more than a system of government. It was a community that embodied a system of belief and a way of life. Schools were democracies in microcosm. Every school, he argued, should become "an embryonic community life, active with the types of occupations that reflect the life of the larger society, permeated throughout with the spirit of art, history and science. When the school introduces and trains each child of society into membership within such a little community, saturating him with the spirit of service, and providing him with instruments of effective self-direction, we shall have the deepest and best guarantee of a larger society which is worthy, lovely, and harmonious."[47]

Schools adequate in a modern democracy must reflect the ideals and practices of democracy, but they bear an even larger responsibility. For Dewey, they must also be the catalyst for the renewal of democracy and community in America. On this he was emphatic. In his "Pedagogic Creed," he put it bluntly: "Education is the fundamental method of social progress and reform" and "The teacher always is the prophet of the true God and the usherer in of the true kingdom of God."[48]

In brief, for Dewey, the school would become command central for the social and political reform of modern democratic societies. He acknowledged that the "school cannot by itself alone create or embody this [democratic] idea." But it would accomplish its progressive democratic alchemy by "creat[ing] individuals who understand the concrete meaning of the idea with their minds, who cherish it warmly in their hearts, and who are equipped to battle in its behalf in their actions."[49] Schools would cultivate inquiring and engaged students who would then be equipped to change the world.

None of these ends were possible in traditional models of education, which focused almost exclusively on the passive reception of content through a mastery of facts and rigid discipline through the use of rewards and punishments. In Dewey's mind, this was nothing more than indoctrination, the sole purpose of which was to instill conformity to the prevailing social order.[50] Traditional forms of pedagogy operated with an exaggerated respect for authority, offering no space for the exchange of ideas, authentic student participation, or active and experimental engagement with real-life problems.

The alternative Dewey envisioned would teach young people how to think, not what to think. For this, students would need to take part as decision-makers in their own learning in classrooms that were collaborative, practical, problem-oriented, and experimental.[51] "The society of which the child is to be a member is . . . a democratic and progressive society. The child must be educated for leadership as well as for obedience. He must have power of self-direction and power of directing others, powers of administration, ability to assume positions of responsibility. This necessity of educating for leadership is as great on the industrial side as it is on the political side. . . . Moreover, the conditions of life are in continual change."[52]

Precisely because the political and economic conditions of life in America were so fluid, education had to respond in kind through a pedagogy committed to creative and collaborative experimentation. In short, the school simply could not be preparation for life in a thriving and evolving democracy unless it reproduced within itself the conditions of a thriving and evolving democracy. The success of democracy, then, rested on an educational practice that itself exemplified the nation's highest democratic ideals.

Dewey's Achievement

Dewey captured much of the moment and rendered it intellectually and publicly intelligible. Over the course of his life, the radically naturalistic humanism that he had so ardently championed became more or less commonplace among his peers. The turn was significant for many reasons, not least by opening a new cleavage between the intellectual classes and the majority of Americans, one that would persist through the twentieth century and beyond.

Dewey's political philosophy, moral psychology, and educational theory unmistakably resonated with the enduring ethos and mythos of America's hybrid-Enlightenment. Yet it also represented a significant attempt to work through its cosmology: transforming its *metaphysics* into a radical naturalism, reducing its *epistemology* to the determinations of science and practical experience, and revising religious *teleology* into a hopeful progressive evolution achieved through incremental and pragmatic improvement. It affirmed a *universalizing humanistic anthropology* and an *ethics* oriented toward those left behind by industrialization, driven by the conviction that Americans, as citizens, could grow toward their full potential and reason together toward truth. Americans would thus be able to find the meaning of America in the *mythos of progress* and expanding liberty.

Left unanswered was the question of how this reworking of the hybrid-Enlightenment could cultivate the bonds of cohesion and solidarity against a world dominated by industrial production, growing inequality, a fragmenting pluralism, the solvents of mass communications, and the vastly weakened institutions of the family and local community.

Niebuhr contra Dewey

Dewey published *A Common Faith* at age seventy-five, certainly at the crest of his influence. His argument was bold, its tone self-confident, his reputation virtually unassailable. But undaunted was a forty-year-old theologian, Reinhold Niebuhr, who, in 1932—just prior to the Terry Lectures—had published *Moral Man in an Immoral Society*. Niebuhr called Dewey out by name in the introduction, not as a conservative but as a fellow progressive.

Niebuhr's credibility was hard won. He was a second-generation German immigrant who had followed his father into the Lutheran ministry. The massive disruptions accompanying global capitalism—the financial panics of 1901, 1907, 1920, and 1929, the rise of labor unions, unemployment, and the stark inequalities of wealth and life chances—were palpably real and formative to Niebuhr, who had spent the first thirteen years of his career as a pastor of a working-class, German-speaking Lutheran parish in Detroit.[53]

As a man of the Left, though unapologetically Christian, Niebuhr represented a distinctive voice coming from the religious side of America's hybrid-Enlightenment. A full generation younger than Dewey, Niebuhr admired the aging philosopher for his ambition, his practical application of intellectual work, and his personal and intellectual commitment to social reform. He also shared Dewey's critique of the contradictions of modern capitalism. They both recognized that a technological civilization accentuated the inequalities of social and economic power to "monstrous disproportions." The effect of these embedded structures of inequality clearly undermined the liberal dream of achieving liberty, equality, and fraternity, but they also threatened the security of those who lacked power and undercut the stability of society itself.[54]

Thus, he and Dewey both urgently sought to provide a defense of democracy against these new challenges, particularly the indifference to those left behind by the machinery of industrial capitalism and the interests of many of its exemplars. And Niebuhr, like Dewey, recognized that the central part of the task of renovation was to reframe the moral and cultural foundations of democracy. "If democracy is to survive," Niebuhr declared, "it must find a more adequate cultural basis than the philosophy which has informed the building of the bourgeois world."[55]

And yet for all that, Niebuhr savaged Dewey repeatedly in print for his naïveté, scorning Dewey's lack of realism, describing his elder's reconstituted democratic philosophy as bankrupt, impotent, and noxiously sentimental because it was rooted in a "romantic overestimate of human virtue." Niebuhr's broader targets were social gospel progressives and the secular rationalist progressives, of which Dewey was the archetype. At the heart of his critique was their moralizing idealism, their imagining that "the egoism of individuals is being progressively checked by the development of rationality or the growth of a religious inspired goodwill and that nothing but the continuance of this process is necessary to establish *social harmony* between all the human societies and collectives."[56] Dewey's view of solidarity, Niebuhr argued, was rooted in "faith in man; faith in his capacity to subdue nature, and faith that the subjection of nature achieves life's final good; faith in man's essential goodness, to be realized either when man ceases to be spiritual and returns to nature (romanticism), or when he ceases to be natural and becomes rational; and finally, faith in human history which is conceived as a movement upward by a force immanent within it."[57]

Niebuhr would have none of it. He accused Dewey and other moralists of the time of failing to see that there was a categorical difference between the morality of individuals and the morality of collective entities, such as social classes, corporations, or the state, which, he argued, "can never be brought completely under the dominion of reason or conscience. They do not recognize that when collective power, whether in the form of imperialism or class domination, exploits weakness, it can never be dislodged unless power is raised against it. If conscience and reason can be insinuated into the resulting struggle, they can only qualify but not abolish it."[58]

Niebuhr regarded Dewey's confidence in the expansion of scientific rationality and its comprehensive application to all social problems as a carryover of the excesses of the secular Enlightenment and thus dangerously misguided. In Niebuhr's view, Dewey mistakenly assumed that the methods of science could be seamlessly transferred from the realm of nature to the realm of social life. Such a view also played to "the prejudice of the intellectual, who is so much the rationalist, that he imagines the evils of government can be eliminated by the expert knowledge of specialists."[59] In turn, such assumptions fostered a vision of social engineering that featured unmistakably utopian ambitions that could never be achieved. In the end, the scientism implicit in Dewey's philosophy tended—and tragically so, in Niebuhr's view—to replace one dogma with another: the scientific in place of the religious.

It was a dogma that Niebuhr believed was impotent. A culture rooted in science and its rationalities could never provide the courage to stand against oppression, the will to resist injustice, or the affections that would build trust and loyalty. Nor could science explain or justify hope, the "confidence that life is good in spite of its evil."[60] Absent a deeper moral framework, Dewey's project of science, pragmatism, and experimentalism would invariably mutate into a cult of technique.[61]

For Niebuhr, it followed that scientific rationality was illusory as well in its misguided search for a unity and solidarity that could somehow transcend conflict. Dewey's efforts to achieve this were evident enough in *A Common Faith*, but they bordered on the fatuous in his earlier advocacy of the Outlawry of War campaign that culminated in the Kellogg-Briand Pact of 1928.[62] The consistency of his thought is what is significant here: Dewey believed that his instrumentalist and pragmatist ethics could be brought to bear on international as well as national problems. In his view, a successful effort to outlaw war began with and depended upon a campaign to educate the masses as to their moral responsibilities in world affairs.

Dewey's commitment to scientific reason as the source of a revitalized liberal democracy was profoundly flawed, from Niebuhr's vantage point. It operated with an inadequate anthropology and, as a consequence, failed to grasp the nature of the inherent particularities of lived morality—the ties to religious faith, social class, racial and ethnic ancestry, local associations, region and nationality, and all the other features of natural, organic solidarity. Dewey dismissed these organic ties as "backward," the source of all "outworn traditions, moth-eaten slogans and catchwords" and mouthed "platitudes." In his view, the sooner they were displaced by "knowledge," "skill," "intelligent thought," and "the planned scientific techniques" the better.[63] But despite the cosmopolitan pressures of the modern world, Niebuhr believed that these characteristics were intrinsic to life and identity and could not be effaced. Nor could the contradictory ethical character of human beings in their particularity be diminished. On the one hand, the "virtuous attitudes of natural man" and his "natural sympathies" found their sources in the common unities of family, neighborhood, class, and nation. At the same time, there was a danger in the ways these bonds could be used by authoritarian movements to mobilize people toward malevolent purposes as, in fact, happened in the Nazi cult of the Aryan race and in the "ecstatic sectarian cult" of Communism. In short, the particularities of human life and experience could generate as well as contradict and undermine humankind's highest moral ideals. They were sources of both virtue and "demonic fervor," and rationalistic systems like Dewey's simply failed to appreciate these fundamental human realities.[64]

It only followed, then, that Niebuhr would be highly dubious of Dewey's program of social and political redemption through educational reform—the idea, he scoffed, that "with a little more time, a little more adequate moral and social pedagogy and a generally higher development of human intelligence, our social problems will approach solution."[65] "It would be pleasant," he wrote, "to believe that the intelligence of the general community could be raised to such a height that the irrational injustices of society would be eliminated." But no such "general community" existed or would come to exist, and the idea that education would play a role in bringing it about was flawed on the face of it. For Niebuhr, such proposals were, once again, a "perfect and naïve expression of the modern illusion that human reason will be able to become the complete master of all the contingent, irrational, and illogical forces of the natural world which underlie and condition all human culture."[66]

In the end, the rationalist intelligence that Dewey celebrated, however softened by his humanistic claims of equality and justice, could never be exempt from the contradictions of particular self-interest and, in turn, the dynamics of competing bids for power. Naturalistic rationalism failed to take the measure of human beings in their rival lusts and ambitions, which could only mean that "the egoistic corruption of universal ideals is a much more persistent fact in human conduct than any moralistic creed is inclined to admit."[67] For Niebuhr, it came down to this: the "whole art of politics consists in directing rationally the irrationalities of men."[68]

Christian Realism

A far more compelling account, in Niebuhr's view, began with a recognition of the centrality of myth. Echoing the work of Georges Sorel, Niebuhr believed that only "myth" had the power to inspire effective political action by providing the grounds for "morale."

Contending factions in a social struggle require morale; and morale is created by the right dogmas, symbols and emotionally potent oversimplifications. . . . No class of industrial workers will ever win freedom from the dominant classes if they give themselves completely to the "experimental techniques" of the modern educators. They will have to believe rather more firmly in the justice and in the probable triumph of their cause, than any impartial science would give them the right to believe, if they are to have enough energy to contest the power of the strong. They may be very scientific in projecting their social goal and in choosing the most effective instruments for its attainment, but a motive force will be required to nerve them for their task which is not easily derived from the cool objectivity of science. . . . The world of history, particularly in man's collective behavior, will never be conquered by reason, unless reason uses tools, and is itself driven by forces which are not rational.[69]

Myth, for Niebuhr, was obviously not an illusion but rather a framing of history in the form of shared narratives of origins and future hope. Its appeal lay in part in its coherence but also in its emotional resonance, ethical appeal, and psychic demands. Most important, myth provided meaning. People could understand themselves and their lives within myth. Science, of course, had the power to explain human existence in its fragmented complexity, but myth had the power to illuminate "the source and end" toward which existence was oriented and to do so "without abstracting it from existence. In this sense myth alone was capable of picturing the world as a realm of coherence and meaning without defying the facts of incoherence."[70]

Thus, the extraordinary power and solidarity of National Socialism and Communism were not found in their industrial organization or even in their tyrannical zeal, but rather within the political myths that animated them. They were, in fact, secular political religions that provided a certain meaning to history and, in turn, to life within it. In these cases, however, the political myths were rooted in the will to power and the subjugation of others.

Against this stood the *prophetic* tradition in Judaism and Christianity. It too constituted a myth, but one that was life-giving. Its account of the Creation, Fall, God's judgment, and the redemption of history, in Niebuhr's view, provided a true account of the human condition.

As a churchman and theologian, Niebuhr could not see how the sentimental view of human persons guided by secular rationalism and its shallow optimism about human history could square with the hard nut of Original Sin. What Augustine called self-love and modern psychoanalytic theory called egocentricity was endemic to the human condition and inescapable. Sin, the source of evil, was manifest in the tendency of the self to make itself its own end, even to the point of making itself the false center of whatever community it inhabits.[71] By these terms, sin both corrupted the will and threatened the human community at every level. Against the inexorable reality of sin, the ruthless character of nature, and the sheer brevity and mortality of natural life, the more idealistic elements of Dewey's progressivism looked rather fatuous.

Since the sources of social and political conflict could not be eliminated, such conflict was "an inevitability of human history." Niebuhr put the matter lucidly: "If social cohesion is impossible without coercion, and coercion is impossible without the creation of social injustice, and the destruction of injustice is impossible without the use of further coercion, are we not in an endless cycle of social conflict?"[72] In this light, any justice was coerced; any solidarity was forcibly imposed.

What could break the endless cycle of injustice? The prophetic myth of Judaism and Christianity, both of which required "the spiritual discipline against resentment."[73] Such a discipline discriminated "between the evils of a social system . . . and the individuals who are involved in it." Niebuhr, for example, pointed to the ways in which the South had been galvanized against abolition when the abolitionist William Lloyd Garrison condemned slaveholders as sinners. "But individuals," Niebuhr argued, "are never as immoral as the social situations in which they are involved and which they symbolise." In making this distinction, we find profound and ultimate unities by recognizing the adversary's humanity. Solidarity can be found not in common interests but in an awakened sense of common human frailty. "The evil in the foe is also in the self." This, together with the concomitant "appreciation of all human life as possessing transcendent worth, creates attitudes which transcend social conflict and thus mitigate its cruelties. It binds human beings together by reminding them of the common roots and similar character of both their vices and their virtues."[74]

The spiritual discipline against resentment also entailed the counterintuitive renunciation of resentment on the part of the victim. Victims of injustice were entitled to resent their treatment but, lest it confer a claim of moral superiority that permitted them to seek revenge, they needed to repent every bit as much as their oppressors. None of this would bring an end to conflict, but it would "mitigate its cruelties."

Not least, the spiritual discipline against resentment required love through acts of contrition and forgiveness. "The religious ideal of forgiveness," Niebuhr wrote, "is more profound and more difficult than the rational virtue of tolerance."[75] Love, through contrition and forgiveness, made it possible for contending groups to fight without denying each other's humanity. Forgiveness, not tolerance, furnished the proper corrective to the egoism and self-righteousness of groups.[76]

A New Hegemony: Secular but Pregnable

By the mid-1920s, conservative Christianity, now fundamentalism, found itself on the margins of American public life. As I noted, in part it had been displaced from the centers of culture formation by elites weary of its regressive and repressive moral dogma. At the same time, fundamentalism had simply retreated to the margins because it had very little insight and wisdom to offer a more complex, changing, and pluralistic world. Still, it found compensation in the fact that most middle- and working-class Americans were still churchgoers, still hardworking, still bound to their families and neighborhoods, and still passionately and patriotically committed to the ideas of American democracy. They were willing to fight the nation's wars, work hard, and endure adversity in the belief that America's promise of freedom was the key to a better life for themselves, their families, and their neighbors. That promise was understood to be unique in human history and worth sacrificing for. And sacrifice they did. Valiantly. In World War II. In Korea. And however ill-conceived and controversial that war was, in Vietnam as well.

In this light, the intellectual work of a Dewey or Niebuhr and the debate between them was far removed from most Americans and, for that reason, was inconsequential. But often enough, the work of artists, poets, and scholars are a harbinger of things to come. Their works anticipate broader developments in the wider culture and may indeed provide intellectualizations of developments already underway that are very consequential to the average person. And so it would prove. But even in these decades, it was the gap in their respective worldviews—one secular, the other religious—and the tensions between them that is first noteworthy about the character of the Dewey/Niebuhr debate. Though Niebuhr was a rarified intellectual and a man of the political Left, he still credibly represented a religious imaginary that was dominant in the middle-brow culture of midcentury America. Although that gap didn't seem to be so wide to most people, it was to expand.

However deep the divisions were between Dewey and Niebuhr, they shared fundamental commitments to the ideals that liberal democracy in America stood for and shared understandings of the need to reconstitute the moral foundations of liberal democracy against the indifference of modern industrial capitalism to the vulnerable. In this, they also shared a rejection of the lazy Protestant pietism of the late nineteenth century and, in turn, a commitment to progressive political interventions into the social and economic dislocations of high industrialism. On the overarching project, then, they shared more in common than not. Where they did part company was in their views of the nature of the problem modern capitalism put forward and how the moral sources of democracy could be revivified to regenerate solidarity in the common project of liberal democracy.

Dewey's achievement was to provide a systematic secular rethinking of the foundations of liberal democracy and make it comprehensible and useful. Culturally, it was to carry the day, particularly among the intellectual and cultural highbrow but also among the leadership classes more broadly. Though a philosophical system is discernable in Niebuhr's extensive political and ethical writings, he was mainly known as a polemicist and critic. Some have said that he distorted the arguments of Dewey and his allies in order to score points, and it is true that there was more nuance in Dewey's thinking than Niebuhr allowed. In the end, Niebuhr's achievement was to be the uneasy conscience of early to mid-twentieth-century liberalism. His assumptions about the fallibility of humankind and the absurdity of human pretentions provided a powerful corrective to the increasingly dominant metaphysics, epistemology, anthropology, ethics, and teleology implicit within the secular turn of the hybrid-Enlightenment.

Not in spite of their differences, then, but because of them, Dewey and Niebuhr together represented a working through of America's hybrid-Enlightenment project in these decades *within* both its theological and naturalist sources.

In the end, it was Dewey's paradigm—his benign view of human nature, his sense of the inevitability of progress, his belief that the deficiencies of society could be cured by education—that defined the mainstream of American liberalism at midcentury, not least because it was embraced wholeheartedly within the expanding institution of public education. And yet, against the massive disruptions of the Great Depression, the incalculable bloodshed of two world wars, and the enslavement and annihilation of millions of Jews in the Holocaust, Niebuhr's skepticism about human nature and the power of social and political structures was proven to be shrewd. The sources and boundaries of solidarity had pivoted decisively in this moment of American political and cultural history. A confident secular liberal public philosophy had become hegemonic, particularly among elites, and yet as Niebuhr had revealed, there were weaknesses inherent in this cultural hegemony that would ultimately play out in unpredictable ways.

CHAPTER EIGHT

A Fragile Humanism

I N THE POSTWAR PERIOD, the puzzles articulated by Dewey and Niebuhr in their effort to work through America's hybrid-Enlightenment as a source of solidarity did not abate. To be sure, the secular turn toward sources of solidarity other than religion was no longer seriously contested within America's cultural establishment. Nor was the active hope for a humanistic alternative that would form the glue of a rapidly changing society in a nation acquiring a place of international power.

The Authoritarian Challenge

But circumstances had changed. Within the public at large, the cultural consensus around liberal democracy in America had remained fairly vibrant. That consensus had generated a strong enough solidarity to defeat fascism on the right and, for the time being, to contain Communism on the left. This was the "vital center" at the heart of liberal democracy that Arthur Schlesinger Jr. had championed four years after the end of World War II, in 1949.[1]

At the same time, the succession of these authoritarian movements brought home the epic failure of the Enlightenment project in the broader West to deliver on its promise to expand freedom, equality, justice, and peace. As Hannah Arendt observed, the moral and political authority of the Enlightenment project and the Western tradition more broadly was just too frail to prevent the challenge of totalitarianism in Italy, Germany, and later the Soviet Union. Instead of freedom, regimes constructed system-wide tyranny, persecution, and enslavement; instead of justice, they produced state-sponsored bigotry, cruelty, and prejudice. And instead of a source of truth and enlightenment, the workings of scientific reason became the organizational foundations of economic and political oppression. Led by the United States and Great Britain, the Western democracies had carried the day, but they also remained vulnerable to the external threat of authoritarianism, especially in the form of the totalitarian regimes of Communism.

These threats were hardly illusory. The succession of events that followed the Russian Revolution, with its overthrow of Emperor Nicholas II and the murder of the Romanov family toward the end of World War I, is nowadays too easily forgotten. The revolution took six years to complete, ending with the establishment of the Union of Soviet Socialist Republics by the Bolsheviks in 1922. It was clear from the start that Bolshevism was illiberal, violent in its means, and expansionist in its ambitions, colonizing more and more autonomous republics in eastern Europe, central Asia, Eurasia, and the Baltic region. In the United States, Communism was mainly known by its anarchist wing and its reputation for extremist propaganda and violent action, a reputation demonstrated by the spate of bombings targeting high-profile business and political leaders across the country in the spring and early summer of 1919. While never mainstream, Communist ideology did eventually develop a significant institutional and ideological influence in the American labor movement throughout the 1930s and 1940s. Its influence grew in part through the Communist Party, USA (or CPUSA), which received significant funding from the Soviet Union. No one was ever under any illusion about its designs: the party actively attempted to penetrate and manipulate trade unions and liberal organizations, set up front organizations, and provide intelligence to the Soviets. Globally, of course, Communism's footprint continued to expand. By the end of World War II, the Soviet Union had consolidated its power over Albania, Bulgaria, Yugoslavia, East Germany, Romania,

Poland, Hungary, and Czechoslovakia—all within three years—and it detonated its first atomic weapon a year later. A Communist North Korea—the Democratic People's Republic of Korea—was also founded in 1948, and just over a year later the People's Republic of China was established by Mao Zedong when his Communist forces sent Chiang Kai-shek's nationalist army packing to Taiwan. Cuba followed with a Communist revolution of its own that began in 1953. These successes made it clear that Communism presented an active threat *to*— and plausibly *within*—liberal democracies everywhere and America in particular.

Because the ideological differences were so obvious, a defensive posture against Communism by Americans, then, was certainly warranted. Hysteria and overreaction, however, were probably—and tragically—inevitable. Indeed, long before the McCarthy-era show trials of the 1950s, there was the controversial trial of Nicola Sacco and Bartolomeo Vanzetti in 1921—they were avowed anarchists, to be sure, but their trial for murder was scandalously prejudicial and their execution surely unjust. In the 1950s, as in the 1920s, the paranoia regarding anarchists, Communist infiltrators, and spies led to illegal search and seizure, entrapment, police brutality, violation of due process, illegal detention, and deportation. The reckless accusations of treason and subversion brought against those in government, the media, academia, and entertainment who were sympathetic to the ethical aspirations of Marxism but who were neither Communist spies nor infiltrators brought ruin to many. Once again, boundary work proved a messy business.

It was within this environment and the sense of existential threat to the nation that new pressures to work through the moral sources of liberal democracy emerged. Was there enough solidarity within liberal democracy to withstand the external threat of Communism? Was there enough solidarity to overcome the internal threat of fascism from the likes of Senator McCarthy or the Ku Klux Klan? Though authoritarian movements and regimes promise consensus and stability by means of coercion, they also undermine trust, comity, and goodwill. From what sources could liberal democratic solidarity be strengthened and sustained to meet the challenges facing regimes fundamentally committed to freedom?

Schlesinger's Hope for a Vital Center

Arthur Schlesinger Jr. had neither the philosophical chops nor the vocational interests of Dewey or Niebuhr, but as an exceptionally talented thirty-two-year-old historian, he had a clear fix on the ambivalence of the moment and how inadequate the moral resources of liberal democracy were at midcentury: "Our philosophical presuppositions were inadequate to the ghastly realities of the age in which we lived. My generation had been brought up to regard human nature as benign and human progress as inevitable. The existing deficiencies of society, it was supposed, could be cured by education and by the improvement of social arrangements. Sin and evil were theological superstitions irrelevant to political analysis."[2] In his most famous work, *The Vital Center,* published in 1949, he sought to work through the philosophical sources of liberal democracy.

Indeed, the context of any defense of democracy over tyranny was a good deal of fear. The conditions that gave root to the totalitarian impulse were, as we've seen, still very present. Schlesinger recognized that nothing had prepared Western democracies for Hitler or for Stalin. Even after its victory in World War II, America, Schlesinger argued, had found itself in "an age of transition; at worst, an age of catastrophe," "an age straining all the capacities of man." Neither a timid business class nor a sentimentally optimistic intellectual class was capable of leading through this crisis. For Western democracies to sustain their victories, the sources of liberalism needed, yet again, to be reconstituted and revivified and citizens needed to recommit to its ideals. "Our objective is clear," he wrote. "We must defend and strengthen free society . . . to restore the center" that mediates between collective purpose and individual interest.[3]

The "center," for Schlesinger, was not the ideological mean between the Right and the Left, but the liberal democratic commitment to freedom itself, and freedom against tyranny in particular. Its spirit was "the spirit of human decency, opposing the extremes of tyranny."[4] And at this moment in history, it was less an accomplishment than an aspiration, longing, or hope—a recognition of the need for a vital center of this nature if liberal democracy were to survive. For Schlesinger, the vital center was tenuous at best.

But upon what would these commitments to decency and freedom be justified? Like Dewey and so many other intellectuals, Schlesinger believed creedal religion was off the table; it was neither considered nor even mentioned. Traditional religion was simply passé in a scientific age. As for secular sources, he warned against looking for them within a naïve enthusiasm about human nature. Neither should one look for them in "the formalities of democracy" itself. Nor should anyone place any hope in a Whiggish millennialism—religious or secular—that would assure us that progress toward freedom was an inevitability. On this he was certain: "The belief in the millennium has dominated our social thinking too long," he argued. "The twentieth century," he wrote, "has at least relieved us of the illusion that progress is inevitable. . . . We must grow up now and forsake the millennial dream."[5]

Rather, the common ground of our commitment to freedom can be found in our shared humanity. As human beings, he argued, we have a natural moral disposition toward and a need of solidarity, freely chosen. "For all the magnificent triumphs of individualism, we survive only as we remain members of one another. The individual requires a social context, not one imposed by coercion, but one freely emerging in response to his own needs and initiatives." For this reason, "we require individualism which does not wall man off from community; we require community which sustains but does not suffocate the individual." The contradictions of the modern social order have "inflicted savage wounds on the human sensibility" that can be healed only "by a conviction of trust and solidarity with other human beings. *It is in these fundamental terms that we must reconstruct our democracy.*" Then, and only then, will democracy "be immune from the virus of totalitarianism."[6]

Schlesinger recognized that liberal democracy required a reworking of its philosophical sources in order to "recharge the deepest sources of moral energy," yet could offer only an affirmation of an opaque humanism.

Even so, Schlesinger was nothing if not earnest in his plea. "The center is vital; the center must hold," he concluded, and to that end, "we require . . . a rededication to concrete democratic ends; so that the exercise of democracy can bring about . . . a revival of the *élan* of democracy, and a resurgence of the democratic faith." Indeed, "we must commit ourselves to it with all our vigor in all its dimensions."

"Free society will survive, in the last resort, only if enough people believe in it deeply enough to die for it." Freedom, he wrote, quoting O. W. Holmes, must become a "fighting faith."[7]

Though determinedly secular and humanistic in its substance and underpinnings, his message was nevertheless entirely consonant with the civil-religious sensibilities emerging in the larger population in the postwar period. Even so, he understood that the case he was making was frail at best. This was, in part, because

> democracy, by its nature, dissipates rather than concentrates its internal moral force. . . . Its love of variety discourages dogmatism, and its love of skepticism discourages hero-worship. In place of theology and ritual, of hierarchy and demonology, it sets up a belief in intellectual freedom and unrestricted inquiry. The advocate of free society defines himself by telling what he is against. . . . *Democracy, however, has not worn too well as a philosophy of life* in an industrial age. . . . It has assumed, much too confidently, that the gnawing problems of doubt and anxiety would be banished by the advance of science or cured by a rise in the standard of living. The spectacular reopening of these problems in our time finds the democratic faith lacking in the profounder emotional resources. Democracy has no defense-in-depth against the neuroses of industrialism.[8]

And, as if this weren't enough, Schlesinger acknowledged that there were no higher ends toward which democracy could be oriented other than freedom itself—the freedom to solve problems in ways that advance security, social freedom, and individual fulfillment. And so, "when philosophies of blood and violence arise to take up the slack between democracy's thin optimism and the bitter agonies of experience, democracy by comparison appears pale and feeble."[9] Yet this was the challenge of recovering a vital center.

Lippmann's Quest for a Centering Authority

All Schlesinger's concerns were reaffirmed in 1955 by the progressive journalist and public intellectual Walter Lippmann with the publication of his book *The Public Philosophy*. Lippmann, now in his mid-sixties, had been writing seriously and steadily on the themes of freedom, democracy, truth, leadership, populism, and the role of journalism for forty years. His concerns had been nurtured early on at Harvard by teachers who included William James and George Santayana and classmates such as T. S. Eliot and John Reed, all against the backdrop of the yeasty intellectual environment of the early Progressive movement. And his productivity was prodigious: at the age of twenty-three, four years after his graduation from Harvard, he published *A Preface to Politics* (1913). This was followed by *Drift and Mastery* (1914), *Liberty and the News* (1920), *Public Opinion* (1922), *The Phantom Public* (1925), *A Preface to Morals* (1929), and *The Good Society* (1937). By midcentury, he came to believe that the circumstances facing liberal democracy were turning into "an historic catastrophe." Around the Western world, he wrote in 1955, "liberal democracies have been tried and found wanting—found wanting not only in their capacity to govern successfully in this period of wars and upheavals, but also in their ability to defend and maintain *the political philosophy that underlies the liberal way of life.*"[10]

Like Schlesinger, Lippmann recognized the instability of liberal democracy, an instability made more problematic by a general citizenry that had become, in effect, a mob with no capacity or even inclination for self-governance. Lippmann clearly had Senator McCarthy and his populist followers in mind. He found McCarthy's demagoguery and campaign of fear utterly repellent and McCarthy himself an ambitious and ruthless agitator set on cultivating his following to become "a mere horde of frightened, angry, suspicious and suspected separate egos."[11]

In this, Lippmann recognized the vulnerability of modern societies to the temptations of totalitarianism. For both Schlesinger and Lippmann, democratic politics as mainly the arena of competing power and interests—the Machiavellian view—was inadequate to the challenge. And while both men saw the need for working through democracy's cultural sources to achieve solidarity, Lippmann pushed toward a thicker account of those sources.

Ultimately, he traced the question of solidarity back to the problem of authority. As he put it, "With no authority above [democracy], without religious, political, or moral convictions which control its opinions, it is without coherence or purpose. Democracy of this kind cannot last long; it must, and inevitably it will, give way to some more settled [by which he meant authoritarian] social order."[12] Democracy, in short, required a standard that would resolve disputes; criteria that would establish the means, ends, and priorities of public action; and a compelling rationale that would motivate citizens to rally together to achieve common purposes.

In principle, of course, the authority of government lay in the sovereign will of its citizens. But in the wake of the dissolution of religion, "the people" had become erratic in temperament, fickle in their desires, and incapable of expressing a coherent and common will. Public opinion, as Lippmann argued, was now shaped by the techniques of mass communication and was therefore subject to manipulation through stereotypes, prejudices, and out-and-out propaganda. Ordinary citizens, then, had evolved into a mob because they had no "objective" understanding of their own interests and no capacity to act on them anyway. Worse still, no one could claim a privileged insight into or authoritative comprehension of the public good. The American public upon whose will democracy depended did not really exist. It was a fiction—in his own words, a "phantom."

As someone who came of age in the heyday of progressivism, he doubted that the church could reinvent itself into a viable public institution or that religion qua religion could ever again provide the necessary sources to address the modern problem of authority. There would have to be a substitute—new sources of moral and political authority to which Americans would give assent. But what were they? From what sources of authority could modern democracy draw legitimacy, vitality, coherence, and hope?

Before the outbreak of World War I, Lippmann thought, as did Dewey and many in the Progressive movement, that the discipline of science would fill the gap. In *Drift and Mastery*, he argued that only science offered "the escape from drift" for it held the promise of distinguishing fact from fancy, organizing and shaping the forces of change, and overcoming subjectivity—the "scattered anarchy of individual temperaments."[13] In a political order as complicated as modern American democracy, mastery over the forces of history required cooperation, which meant that "a great variety of people working in different ways must find some order in their specialties. . . .

The discipline of science is the only one which gives any assurance that from the same set of facts men will come approximately to the same conclusion. And as the modern world can be civilized only by the effort of innumerable people, we have a right to call science the discipline of democracy."[14]

By the end of the war, however, Lippmann began to have misgivings. He had witnessed how a supposedly objective, scientific intelligence had given way to the irrationality of hyper-patriotism and militarism. Science, he finally concluded, could neither address nor resolve problems that were fundamentally moral in nature.

He first laid out his case for the critical place of moral philosophy in liberal democracy in *A Preface to Morals* in 1929.[15] Across the range of particular theologies and philosophies that define a pluralistic society, he believed that one could still recognize a common affirmation of such virtues as courage, honor, faithfulness, truth-telling, justice, self-restraint, generosity, and love. In their totality, these virtues amounted to a humanism capable of absorbing the ethics of a wide range of creeds. Unlike the old religions, the authority of this humanism would not inhibit human nature as much as motivate and inspire citizens to do the right thing. The purpose of such authority, then, was not so much social control as it was knowledge of the good. The hope was that politics drawn from these sources could provide a moral regeneration through which the desires of ordinary citizens would be reeducated toward the public good. If liberal democracy were to remain vital, it was imperative that it be more explicit about identifying, calling out, and recommitting to the moral and humanistic foundations upon which he believed late twentieth-century democracy must rest.

By midcentury, Lippmann's reflections on the sources of solidarity had evolved into something he now called the "public philosophy." By this he meant the natural law tradition that posited a rational order to the universe and thus a universal system of positive principles and precepts "upon which all rational men of good will, when fully informed, will tend to agree." Natural laws "are the laws of a rational order of human society—in the sense that all men, when they are sincerely and lucidly rational, will regard them as self-evident. The rational order consists of the terms which must be met in order to fulfill men's capacity for the good life in this world."[16]

This is what Roman jurists called the *ius naturale:* the "law imposed on mankind by common human nature, that is, by reason in response to human needs and instincts."[17] It isn't a body of law per se, but rather a way of looking at the world, a "fabric of understanding," or what he also described as "a spirit of 'humane interpretation'" that framed the written law and reinforced it without being the law itself. A constitution, bill of rights, or charters, treaties, and contracts are simply the materializations of the natural law. And what makes it *natural* is that it "can be discovered by any rational mind." It doesn't have to be created or invented—it is simply known.[18]

In Lippmann's telling, the public philosophy had its roots in Greek antiquity and has been definitive for European civilization ever since. The tradition has been revived, most recently in the Enlightenment and the democratic revolutions it spawned. Indeed, it has been the "premise of the institutions of the Western society"; "liberal democracy," in particular, "is not an intelligible form of government and cannot be made to work except by men who possess the philosophy in which liberal democracy was conceived and founded."[19]

For Lippmann, the public philosophy delivered two very concrete benefits. First, it provided the foundations for citizenship. If self-government meant anything at all, he wrote, it must be exercised by citizens who by their second natures—formed by the public philosophy—preferred the higher law to the satisfaction of their own impulses, even to their own will to live. It was the ability to govern one's own appetites and impulses by the principles of the public philosophy that made one fully human and civilized. Unless citizens governed themselves by such internal authority, the Republic would be ungovernable.[20]

Second, the public philosophy provided the ground for "the widest consensus" in a fragmented society. "Except on the premises of this philosophy, it is impossible to reach intelligible and workable conceptions of popular elections, majority rule, representative assemblies, free speech, loyalty, property, corporations and voluntary associations." "All issues," he argued, "could be settled by scientific investigation and by free debate if—but only if—all of the investigators and the debaters adhered to the public philosophy; if, that is to say, they used the same criteria and rules of reason for arriving at the truth and for distinguishing good and evil." "Rational procedure is the ark of the covenant of the public philosophy." Its significance is fundamental: "When the adherence of the whole body of people to the public philosophy is firm, a true community exists; where there is division and dissent over the main principles the result is a condition of latent war." The very principle of toleration calls for the effort "to find agreement beneath the differences."[21]

In Lippmann's account, modern democracies had "abandoned the main concepts, principles, precepts, and the general manner of thinking" that characterize the public philosophy, and its cultural heritage had not been transmitted to recent generations. It was, then, essential to "revive," "renew," and "rework" the public philosophy for the modern age. The adaptation of its "common and binding principles was more necessary than it had ever been." If this was not accomplished, then "the free and democratic nations face the totalitarian challenge without a public philosophy which free men believe in and cherish, with no public faith beyond a mere official agnosticism, neutrality and indifference."[22]

Yet he also recognized that the difficulties in recovering the public philosophy were formidable. The masses, untrained in the traditions of civility, were therefore constitutively incapable of self-rule. As for the leadership class, "the public philosophy was in a large measure intellectually discredited among contemporary men." Certainly, it seemed to Lippmann, the drift of modern philosophy did not portend any hope of scholarly renewal. As a sign of what was to come among the intellectual classes, the French philosopher Jean-Paul Sartre did away not only "with God the Father, but with the recognition that beyond our private worlds there is a public world to which we belong. If what is good, what is right, what is true, is only what the individual 'chooses' to 'invent,' then we are outside the traditions of civility. We are back in the war of all men against all men." Lippmann found in his reading of Sartre "a proclamation of anarchy" that provides no framework of solidarity within a fragmented society, nor even a will to find any solidarity. The stripping away of any concept of a mind-independent truth creates a vacuum that is filled by "the intoxication of power," an intoxication that is "the greatest danger of our time." Indeed, he wrote, "any philosophy which, however unintentionally, contributes to it is increasing the danger of vast social disaster."[23]

Solidarity and the Burden of the Humanities

Doing the Work of Religion

In their worries about America's hybrid-Enlightenment and their efforts to rework it in the post–World War II period, Schlesinger and Lippmann were not alone. The burden of restoring and fortifying potent normative sources to democratic life within an affirmation of a vague conception of the human and the humane preoccupied public intellectuals everywhere and across the political spectrum. The burden was especially felt by the professional humanities and humanistic social sciences in Europe and the United States: figures such as Ernst Cassirer, Martin Buber, C. S. Lewis, R. G. Collingwood, and Erich Fromm. Among these scholars, there was a tangible awareness of the ongoing threat of totalitarianism, but also of the weaknesses and limitations of liberal democracy in the face of it. There was also a shared conviction that mass education was an essential part of the solution.

Lippmann's own views were very much in sympathy with the educational philosophy of Mortimer Adler; indeed, Adler was consulted on Lippmann's book. As an Aristotelean, Adler affirmed "the unchanging verities" of the Western tradition and championed the "great books" and the practices of *paideia* as the shared sources of human understanding in liberal democracy.[24]

Further to the right were figures such as Russell Kirk and John Courtney Murray who, in effect, were also working through the cultural logic of America's hybrid-Enlightenment, but as a rule, they simply affirmed its older formulations. For Kirk, it was the moral, political, and economic principles rooted in the Judeo-Christian tradition. "Christian morality is the cement of American life; and Christian concepts of natural law, natural rights, and necessary limitations to human ambitions all govern our politics and even our economic system."[25] In Murray's case, the task was reconciling the Catholic tradition and its current institutional authority with American pluralism, primarily through a commonly held though Catholic-inspired natural law tradition.[26]

It isn't as though the views of classicists like Adler or conservatives like Kirk, Murray, and William Buckley fell on deaf ears. They found large audiences in the general public for their reassertion of the older cultural logic of the hybrid-Enlightenment. Their efforts reignited conservatism as an intellectual force. But by 1960, intellectual conservatism was already on the margins of the mainstream of intellectual life. Even Lippmann's progressive peers, still smarting from McCarthyism, were unimpressed. His case for the retrieval of natural law was described in the *Saturday Review* as "eloquent, but unconvincing"; in the *New Republic* as the work of a "badly frightened man"; and worse yet, in the *Yale Review* as an argument that played into the hands of McCarthy and other authoritarians.[27]

The call to educate the masses into a broader humanism found fullest expression in a number of carefully crafted and broadly disseminated reports and manifestoes on the humanities written in the middle of the twentieth century. These include *General Education in a Free Society* (1945), also known as the Harvard "Red Book," *One Great Society: Humane Learning in the United States* (1959), and the *Report of the Commission on Humanities* (1964), the latter leading to the establishment of the National Endowment for the Humanities and the National Endowment for the Arts in 1965.

In the first of these, the 1945 Red Book, Harvard president James Bryant Conant convened a faculty committee to consider the state of American education for the broad American public.[28] The concern of education, Bryant charged the committee, was not "the development of the appreciation of the 'good life' in young gentlemen born to the purple. [Rather,] it is the infusion of the liberal and humane tradition into our entire educational system." The larger aspiration was "to cultivate in the largest possible number of our future citizens an appreciation of both the responsibilities and benefits which come to them because they are Americans and are free."[29]

The premise of the report was "that our society, like any society, rests on common beliefs and that a major task of education is to perpetuate them." The main problem the report sought to address, then, was the problem of generating "the necessary bonds and common ground" capable of uniting not only an increasingly fragmented society but a political system that seemed intrinsically inimical to commonality. As Conant wrote, "Some think it the Achilles' heel of democracy that, by its very nature, it cannot foster general agreement on ultimates, and perhaps must foster the contrary." So the question facing American education broadly—not just higher education—is "the question of common standards and common purposes" in a society characterized by "ever-growing complexity."[30]

To look for a common culture in religious faith would be a nonstarter, for "religion is not now for most colleges a practicable source of intellectual unity." Neither would the scientific outlook be promising for it has obvious limitations in addressing "the full horizon of life." The report was equally dismissive of a simple turn to the past or to innovation in the future as sources of commonality.[31] Rather, Conant and his colleagues posited "man" at the core of our common culture.

> Belief in the dignity and mutual obligation of man is the common ground between . . . contrasting but mutually necessary forces in our culture. . . . This belief is the fruit at once of religion, of the Western tradition, and of the American tradition. It equally inspires the faith in human reason which is the basis for trust in the future of democracy. And if it is not, strictly speaking, implied in all statements of the scientific method, there is no doubt that science has become its powerful instrument. . . . Just so, the tradition which has come down to us regarding the nature of man and the good society must inevitably provide our standard of good. Yet an axiom of that tradition itself is the belief that no current form of the received ideal is final but that every generation, indeed every individual, must discover it in a fresh form.[32]

In the process of understanding "man," of course, the humanities took pride of place. The purpose of the humanities was to enable "man to understand man in relation to himself, that is to say, in his inner aspirations and ideals." The main problem of the humanities and of education more broadly was to articulate these common "aspirations and ideals" that form the "necessary bonds and common ground" that join people together. By so doing, they both "help young persons fulfill the unique, particular functions in life which it is in them to fulfill, and fit them so far as it can for those common spheres which, as citizens and heirs of a joint culture, they will share with others." In this view, only the humanities recovered and maintained common assumptions and traditions central to civic trust, vibrant public debate, and strong democratic institutions.[33]

It isn't surprising that the Red Book emphatically affirmed the secular turn in the cultural logic of liberal democracy. It is interesting to note, however, its authors' sensitivity to the public they were attempting to persuade. "Given the American scene with its varieties of faith and even of unfaith, we did not feel justified in proposing religious instruction as a part of the curriculum. The love of God is tested by the love of neighbor; nevertheless, the love of God transcends merely human obligations. We must perforce speak in purely humanistic terms, confining ourselves to the obligations of man to himself and to society. But we have been careful so to delimit humanism as not to exclude the religious ideal."[34]

This meant that "religious education, education in the great books, and education in modern democracy may . . . work together to the same end, which is belief in the idea of man and society that we inherit, adapt, and pass on": namely, the idea of "the dignity of man . . . [and] the recognition of his duty to his fellow men." "The debt of these two ideas to the similarly interwoven commandments of the love of God and the love of neighbor is obvious."[35]

Clearly, the authors were struggling with the realities of an entrenched cultural pluralism and a growing secular public culture, but in acknowledging the religious sources of humanism and its contributions to liberalism, they were doing more than trying to bridge the growing gap between cultural elites and the general public. Even in the ways the report talked about the "human" in the humanities—speaking of the "dignity of Man," of "common duties," and a "common good"—they were, in important ways, framing a secular discourse religiously. Democracy, they argued, "by its very nature . . . cannot foster general agreement on ultimates," yet at the same time they were still asserting "ultimates" in the form of the "belief in the worth and meaning of the human spirit, *however one may understand it.*"[36] Their own working through of the cultural logic of America's hybrid-Enlightenment produced something new, but something that could still be inclusive of elites and the common person.

The arguments of the Red Book were reprised in slightly different ways over the next two decades, but all emphasized the "human" as central to the humanities and the humanities as central to democracy.[37] Notably, any discussion of the role of religion in the new humanities or as an older source of democracies' moral sources, even if only as a hat tip to the interests of ordinary folk, was absent.

Arguably the most important statement of the immediate postwar period was the 1964 *Report of the Commission on the Humanities*, co-sponsored by the American Council of Learned Societies, the Council of Graduate Schools, and the United Chapters of Phi Beta Kappa. The themes here were by now familiar: "The humanities are the study of that which is most human," the report states; "their subject is every man." Their importance is plain to see. "Over the centuries, the humanities have sustained mankind at the deepest level of being. . . . In the formative years of our own country, it was a group of statesmen steeped in the humanities who fused their own experience with that of the past to create the enduring Constitution of the Republic." But now, in the middle of the twentieth century, we face new problems, among them that "our social, moral and aesthetic development [has] lagged behind our material advance."[38] To remedy this dilemma, the Commission on the Humanities recommended the establishment, by an act of presidential and congressional authority, of a National Foundation for the Arts and Humanities.

The need for the humanities for the health of the nation was urgent. As the report argued, "All men require a vision be held before them, an ideal toward which they may strive. Americans need such a vision today as never before in their history. It is both the dignity and the duty of humanists to offer their fellow-country-men whatever understanding can be attained by fallible humanity of such enduring values as justice, freedom, virtue, beauty, and truth. Only thus do we join ourselves to the heritage of our nation and our humankind. [Moreover], 'democracy demands wisdom of the average man. Without the exercise of wisdom, free institutions and personal liberty are inevitably imperiled.'"[39]

And so through the National Foundation on the Arts and the Humanities Act of 1965, the National Endowment for the Arts and the National Endowment for the Humanities were founded. The centerpiece of the rationale behind the Act was that "democracy demands wisdom and vision in its citizens. It must therefore foster and support a form of education, and access to the arts and the humanities, designed to make people of all backgrounds and wherever located masters of their technology and not its unthinking servants." And further still, "to [foster] mutual respect for the diverse beliefs and values of all persons and groups."[40]

Middle America

The disjunction between the anxieties of intellectuals broadly defined and the hopeful dispositions of ordinary Americans observed at the start of the twentieth century did not lessen through the middle of the century and beyond. Despite the Depression and two world wars and then the Korean War, America was, for most, a hopeful country.

Enduring yet Evolving Dispositions

That hopefulness was reflected in a farewell address John F. Kennedy gave to his home state of Massachusetts a week before he assumed the presidency.[41] In it, he claims to have been "guided by the standard of John Winthrop set before his shipmates on the flagship Arbella . . . as they, too, faced the task of building a new government. . . . 'We must always consider, he [Winthrop] said, that we shall be as a city upon a hill.'" The biblical reference to Matthew 5:14 was well known both to Winthrop's audience 331 years before and to Kennedy's in 1961. In the same breath and in the spirit of the hybrid-Enlightenment, Kennedy quoted Pericles's speech to the Athenians: "We do not imitate—for we are a model." In that moment, American exceptionalism, rooted in sources of the hybrid-Enlightenment, did not seem diminished.

To be sure, the nation was still internally diminished by deeply ingrained racial and economic inequalities. Those ongoing contradictions to America's hybrid-Enlightenment ideals persisted in ways that were yet to be acknowledged. Yet the mood of the country emerging out of the hardships of the first half of the century was, by and large, upbeat. America was open for business again, becoming more productive by the day, and as a whole, the nation was getting wealthier. That prosperity was filtering into many segments of society. The middle class was growing, with more people than ever before graduating from high school and then going to college and getting white-collar jobs. To accommodate this wealth, the suburbs were being built and were expanding in every metropolitan area in the nation. And the country was also slowly—very slowly—becoming more inclusive. Identities rooted in national origin had diminished since the restrictive immigration laws earlier in the century. So too had working-class identities moderated due to the enlargement of the middle class. Perhaps most important at that time, denominational and creedal differences within and across the major faiths had also lessened. As a matter of public identity, it mattered less that one was a Baptist and more that one was a Protestant; likewise, being an Irish or Polish Catholic meant less than being just a Catholic. The distinctions among the three major faith traditions still mattered a great deal, but they mattered less.[42]

Literary figures of the mid-twentieth century liked to depict life in middle America in these decades through its pathologies—and pathologies there surely were. The cautious and complacent dullness, conformity, mediocrity, and boredom of Sinclair Lewis's *Main Street* were recognizable to many. Indeed, "the Main Street [in Gopher Prairie, Minnesota]," as Lewis put it, "is the continuation of Main Streets everywhere. The story would be the same in Ohio or Montana, in Kansas or Kentucky or Illinois, and not very different in Upstate New York or in the Carolina Hills."[43] So too was the loneliness, repressed sexual desire, ignorance, fear, prejudice, and melancholy found in Sherwood Anderson's *Winesburg, Ohio*. All these dark emotional pathologies were covered by a veneer of normalcy and harmony.

But that wasn't the whole picture either. As other commentators—from Tocqueville to Wendell Berry to playwrights and librettists too, such as Thornton Wilder and Rogers and Hammerstein—had highlighted, the rural towns and small cities that made up middle America have also long been and remain critical for the development of republican virtues—hard work, self-sacrifice, independence, volunteerism, and neighborly commitment. These have been places integral to human flourishing. In truth, the contradictory representations of peace, natural innocence, and simple virtue as opposed to backwardness, ignorance, bigotry, and limitation reflect realities that have long been simultaneously inwoven in middle America.

This ambivalence—particularly in the tension between elites and the larger public—was reflected in the public reception of artist and illustrator Norman Rockwell. On the one hand, art critics at the time disparaged the illustrations of Rockwell as sentimental and therefore irrelevant to twentieth-century art. On the other hand, in the 1940s *Time* magazine declared him the "best loved US artist alive" and the *New York Times* favorably compared his paintings to Mark Twain's novels. His corpus of paintings numbered in the thousands. For over fifty years, his works—over three hundred—graced the cover of perhaps America's most popular magazine, the *Saturday Evening Post*. These works and thousands of others were proudly middlebrow, celebrating the commonplace, all the while honoring the past and yet reveling in the inventiveness of the future. Rockwell once said, "I was showing the America I knew and observed to those who might not have noticed."[44] His paintings of everyday heroes, laborers, policemen, and roguish children; of homecomings, the dinner table, a first date, friendship, a woman at prayer, and so on, conveyed a world of safety, hard work, compassion, goodwill, charm, humor, and authenticity.

Yet Rockwell's paintings also conveyed the idealism of a nation that was working through its past in order to chart anew its future. FDR's 1941 "Four Freedoms" speech—freedom of speech, freedom of worship, freedom from want, and freedom from fear—inspired four paintings that the *Post* ran as a series of covers. The works became an overnight sensation, going on a tour of the country, ultimately used to raise over $130 million in war bonds through exhibition tickets and poster sales. Likewise, though controversial to some, his 1963 painting of Ruby Bridges being escorted to school by federal marshals inspired, for many, a vision of social justice. And his 1961 painting the *Golden Rule* depicted a group of people of different religions, races, and ethnicities standing together as the backdrop for the inscription "Do unto Others as You Would Have Them Do unto You," conveying the ethical obligations of respect and inclusion essential to solidarity in a liberal democracy.

Old-fashioned and sentimental, to be sure, but the mass appeal of Rockwell's art reflected the cultural and political dispositions of a large cross-section of the American public still very much committed to a shared mythos generated out of its hybrid-Enlightenment of American goodness and purpose.

The Transformations of Faith: Creedal, Civic, and Secularizing

Yet even for the broader public, how that mythos was understood was also changing. Religious faith remained pervasive and prominent, yet the character of that faith was evolving. Young people began their day in the public school with a recitation of the Pledge of Allegiance, a Bible reading, and a prayer, and politicians would earnestly invoke God's blessing on America. In 1955, President Eisenhower gave a speech to the American Legion that launched its "Back to God" campaign. "Recognition of the Supreme Being," he declared, "is the first, most basic expression of Americanism. Without God, there could be no American form of government nor an American way of life."[45]

Though unintended, his statement contained an important insight about a profound transformation in American religion. America was no longer a Christian nation but a Judeo-Christian nation. At midcentury, Protestantism, Catholicism, and Judaism had somehow melded in the national consciousness. This was the argument of the generation-defining book *Protestant, Catholic, Jew*, by Will Herberg, who concluded that "America today may be conceived, as it is indeed conceived by most Americans, as one great community divided into three sub-communities religiously defined, all equally American in their identification with 'the American Way of Life.'"[46] All three were Abrahamic faiths rooted in the Bible and thus all possessed in common a commitment to democracy through their shared "spiritual values: . . . the fatherhood of God and the brotherhood of man, [and] the dignity of the individual human being." Indeed, not to identify oneself and be identified as . . . a Protestant, a Catholic, or a Jew is somehow not to be an American." "To be a Protestant, a Catholic, or a Jew are today the alternative ways of being an American."[47]

Even the conservative wing of Protestantism participated in the cultural logics of this melding. In the 1940s, a group of conservative Protestant theologians and church leaders publicly repudiated the separatism of fundamentalism that, since the Scopes trial in 1926, had closed itself off to the world. It was marked by the founding of the National Association of Evangelicals in 1942, the publication of Carl F. H. Henry's *The Uneasy Conscience of Modern Fundamentalism* in 1947, the establishment of Fuller Theological Seminary in the same year, the emergence of Billy Graham's revivals in 1949, and Graham's founding of *Christianity Today* in 1956.[48] The motto of this movement: "Cooperation without Compromise." Without bargaining away any of its traditional theological commitments, it nevertheless sought to engage the larger world ethically and to find common cause with others of different faiths or no faith on a range of issues. In short, neo-evangelicalism also wanted to be an integral part of the ongoing and evolving American project.

At the same time that religion remained symbolically important to local and national civic life for the broad mass of Americans, it was, as it turned out, without a great deal of substance. It was a remarkable paradox. To take one example, Bible distribution increased 140 percent between 1949 and 1953. Moreover, eight of ten Americans believed that the Bible was not merely a great piece of literature but in fact the revealed word of God. Yet most Americans couldn't name the first four Gospels and more than half couldn't name one of them. Americans revered Scripture, but apparently didn't read it.[49]

Religious faith was losing the qualities of confidence, certainty, and inner compulsion within the laity. Thus, when the Supreme Court decisively eliminated prayer and Bible reading from schools in 1962 and 1963 (*Engel v. Vitale* and *Schempp v. Abingdon*, respectively), it was only religious conservatives who protested and by no means en masse. *Christianity Today*, the flagship publication of evangelicalism, for example, supported the prayer decision because its editors believed that the practice had become a mere pro forma exercise and was secularizing in its effects.[50]

For Herberg, the pervasive faith of middle America disguised what was, in fact, a growing secularity in the public—not everywhere, but for larger and larger numbers of (mostly white) middle-class Americans. This didn't mean that faith was hypocritical. Indeed, religious faith in its diversity was still, in practice, highly creedal. But rather than a way of orienting one's life to God, faith, for many, had become a way of belonging and of being seen as belonging. Solidarity was its net effect.

A Shallow Humanism

Boundary Work

Because these changes are so well established today, it might be easy to gloss over the significance of what unfolded in these religious and cultural developments. For one, the ancient boundaries of religious exclusion hadn't completely disappeared, but they did dissolve to a large extent, even as the boundaries of inclusion simultaneously widened. Anti-Semitism and anti-Catholicism had been fixtures of Western civilization for centuries and defining features of American social and political history through the nineteenth and early twentieth centuries. And while these bigotries didn't vanish overnight, they did permanently weaken in ways that both redefined American identity and worked through the sources of collective solidarity.

Much of the viability of the new tripartite faith was a function of "a good enemy"—"good" as in clearly defined and fundamentally oppositional. The enemy was no longer internal but external, no longer Catholicism or Judaism but totalitarianism. Thus, whatever differences religiously oriented Americans had with each other, what they shared was far greater than what they opposed, namely, "the godless Communism" of the expanding Soviet Union.

It was for this reason that atheists and agnostics in America remained so marginalized. Many regarded secularists as fundamentally un-American. A leading figure in Ethical Culture, cited by Herberg, declared, "There is a tendency to regard all people who are not committed to one of the three great faiths [Protestantism, Catholicism, and Judaism] as being disloyal to American principles and traditions."[51] This was not hyperbole. In 1958, the Gallup Organization found that only 18 percent of Americans would be willing to vote for an atheist for president even if fully qualified and nominated by their political party. Even as late as 1972, 58 percent of the American public favored the banning of atheists from teaching in colleges or universities.[52] As a marker of collective identity and solidarity, religious faith distinguished American society from all Communist societies.

Hybrid Sources

There is another point of significance. Though a cultural gap had continued to grow between elites and the larger population, there was nevertheless a mutually reinforcing relationship between the humanism promoted by elites and the civil religion embraced by the masses. In a cursory way, it was illustrated by Schlesinger's choice of language in *The Vital Center* to convey his passion for the humanism he proposed—the need for "a resurgence of the democratic faith" that would be a "fighting faith" for a freedom one would be willing "to die for." This not only illustrated the way in which civic humanism was consonant with civil religion but also recognized the ongoing importance of the religious element of the hybrid-Enlightenment. The framing language was significant. More substantively, civil religion and civic humanism shared a disposition—perhaps even a conviction—that affirmed the ideal of "the family of man" as the source of their common bond. Families may have disagreements but, as a rule, they don't annihilate each other.

This hybrid humanism represented yet another working through of the hybrid-Enlightenment, one forged by a nation confronting very real international challenges and anxieties in the war and postwar decades. It was a *universalizing humanism trying to do the cultural work of a universalizing religion without actually being religious in any particular sense.* What was at stake, as cultural critic Mark Greif put it, was the meaning of "Man" per se in the face of potential extinction.[53]

As in the past, its sources drew from the realm that melded religious faith and secular reason. Schlesinger, Lippmann, and the professional and institutional humanities gave voice to this humanism, as did many other scholars, writers, and novelists. The vast literature they produced articulated the range of urgent challenges facing humankind and an anthropology and ethics upon which national solidarity might be established. It was an aspirational solidarity, to be sure, but one that might bind and heal a broken, fragmented, conflicted world. It was powerfully reinforced within a popular religious culture that, in public anyway, was no longer exclusively Protestant but an amalgam now called "Judeo-Christian."

Even as its sources were worked through, the hybrid-Enlightenment continued to underwrite liberal democracy; the humanism it fashioned and leaned upon was viable in its time, strong enough to carry on the work of generating solidarity for a new moment.

Fragility

The language of this midcentury hybrid humanism, then, was often inspiring, comforting, warm, and reassuring, and the consensus it represented was stabilizing through the uncertainties of the postwar period. Yet, for several reasons, it had its points of weakness. Among the intellectual classes, for example, the polarities of the Cold War were not so straightforward. Liberals like Schlesinger and Lippmann sought to thread a needle. For them, liberalism and Communism had nothing in common, and for this reason, they were stridently anti-Communist. At the same time, they also deplored and fought McCarthyism. The Left was sharply critical of such liberals, believing that they not only intensified the confrontation between the United States and the Soviet Union, they also provided justification for the anti-Communist passions that led to McCarthyism. Conservative intellectuals, on the other hand, tended to regard the difference between liberalism and the Left as a meaningless distinction. Because liberalism tended to be rationalist, secularist, and hostile to tradition, and because its warm regard for the New Deal was seen as quasi-socialist, liberalism was viewed as incapable of opposing an adversary with which it shared so many underlying assumptions.

There was another source of fragility that had its roots in the anthropology it assumed and promoted. This was a hybrid humanism unencumbered by the complexity of the history of actual communities. "Man" was an abstraction, without grounding in time, geography, culture, or circumstance. As a source of solidarity in the postwar period, it sought to be inclusive but without fully recognizing those who had been excluded. Nor did it provide any practical way of addressing the ongoing contradictions of exclusion. The message was clear: African Americans and other minorities still didn't quite matter to the unfolding story of American exceptionalism and, in that particular moment, the phenomenon of America's rising prosperity and growing global prominence. To a great many at midcentury, being Black was still not quite being American; being a woman was not quite being a full citizen.

At the end of the day, the failure to fully acknowledge irreducible human differences within humanity—not least, of course, the particularities of race and gender and the histories that encumbered them—rendered the discourse of man mostly vacuous. But not entirely.

Resilience

While the working through of America's hybrid-Enlightenment in this midcentury humanism has been described as a failure, the true impact was more paradoxical. Its virtue was that, as in the past, the language and vision of this discourse were opaque enough for different communities and factions to read themselves and their own traditions and interests into it.

Yes, it failed in its time to address the concrete realities of race and gender, but it succeeded in providing a cultural logic for what would be successive waves of liberationist movements to come. Yes, the cultural logic of inclusion based on the universality of the "family of man" was mostly passive and empty, yet the appeal to this common anthropology became the foundation upon which concrete claims for equality could be made. The humanism of mid-twentieth century America, then, didn't *seek* to acknowledge, much less willingly confer, the rights of full citizenship to those who were excluded. But in the end, proponents of midcentury humanism were hard pressed to deny those who made such an appeal. The efficacy of midcentury humanism, then, was as a background imaginary—a structure of assumptions on which particular appeals could be made.

That appeal was first and most powerfully articulated in word and deed in the civil rights movement, a movement rooted in the historical and theological particularities of the Black church and, out of its rich resources, given powerful articulation by the Black clergy. This movement represented the continuation of the struggle to work through the ongoing and tragic contradictions of racial exclusion, and of course, it found its most compelling voice in the theologian and churchman Martin Luther King Jr.

Dissent and Solidarity: The Witness of MLK

The Reverend King's understanding of the nature of the "crisis of man" and what was at stake was entirely consonant with the views of twentieth-century humanism. As he put it in a sermon in 1958, "The question, What is man? Is one of the most important questions confronting any generation. The whole political, social, and economic structure of society is largely determined by its answer to this pressing question. Indeed, the conflict which we witness in the world today between totalitarianism and democracy is at bottom a conflict over the question, What is man?"[54]

His anthropology was also universalizing and in this was consonant with the ethical burden borne by midcentury humanism. Yet rather than opaque and rootless, King's anthropology was unapologetically grounded in the particularities of the Christian tradition. "All of God's children," he argued, "black men and white men, Jews and Gentiles, Protestants and Catholics" were made in God's image.[55] Over the course of his ministry, he relentlessly reminded his African American audiences that their dignity came not from the white man but from God: "During the years of slavery in America it is said that after a hard day's work the slaves would often hold secret religious meetings. All during the working day they were addressed with unnecessary vituperations and insulting epithets. But as they gathered in these meetings, they gained a renewed faith as the old unlettered minister would come to his triumphant climax saying, you—you are not niggers. You—you are not slaves. You are God's children. This established for them a true ground of personal dignity."[56]

The dignity that King wanted to bestow upon African Americans was a sense of inherent worth and ultimate significance—what King called "*somebodiness*."[57] That dignity would allow him and "my brother of blackest hue" to recognize "my rightful heritage and holding my head erect, may stand beside the Saxon—a Negro—and yet a man."[58] The resonances of continuity with David Walker's declaration 130 years before—"We are men"—and with the abolitionist movement of the late eighteenth century —"Am I not a man and a brother?"— are clear. King's emphasis on the inherent dignity of all human beings, African Americans among them, spawned the iconic placard for the Memphis sanitation workers' protest in 1968, "I am a Man," and thus became a rallying cry of the movement.

His theological anthropology, woven into the logic of the nation's Founding documents, provided the cornerstone of his ethics of protest. In this, he was very much aligned with the spirit of Reinhold Niebuhr and his emphasis on collective sin. "When the architects of our Republic wrote the magnificent words of the Constitution and the Declaration of Independence, they were signing a promissory note to which every American was to fall heir. This note was the promise that all men, yes, black men as well as white men, would be guaranteed the unalienable rights of life, liberty, and the pursuit of happiness. It is obvious today that America has defaulted on this promissory note insofar as her citizens of color are concerned. Instead of honoring this sacred obligation, America has given the Negro people a bad check; a check which has come back marked 'insufficient funds.'"[59]

The problem, of course, was that "one hundred years later, the Negro still is not free. One hundred years later, the life of the Negro is still sadly crippled by the manacles of segregation and the chains of discrimination. . . . One hundred years later, the Negro is still languished in the corners of American society and finds himself an exile in his own land."[60] King understood that as important as the legal changes after the Civil War were, they meant little if they were not embedded within the interpretive frame of the deep structures of cultural reality. "Today," he argued, "thirteen million black sons and daughters of our forefathers continue the fight for the translation of the 13th, 14th, and 15th amendments from writing on the printed page to an actuality. We believe with them that 'if freedom is good for any it is good for all.'"[61]

The problems were, like his humanism, anything but abstract. In his last book, *Where Do We Go from Here?*, he pointed to American education as a "system of exclusion" that had "not yet begun to approach the needs of the Negro and the poor."[62] Ten years after the *Brown v. Board of Education* decision, he protested, "Negroes lag one to three years behind whites [in elementary schools] . . . their schools receive substantially less money . . . one-twentieth as many Negroes as whites attend college, and half of these are in ill-equipped Southern institutions."[63] And the educational inequities were tied to the lack of economic opportunity. "Half of all Negroes live in substandard housing and , . . have half the income of whites." Moreover, "twice as many [are] unemployed," and of those who are employed, "75 percent hold menial jobs."[64] "One day we must ask the question, 'Why are there forty million poor people in America?' And when you begin to ask that question you are raising questions about the economic system. When you ask that question, you begin to question the capitalistic economy."[65] In his "Dream" speech in front of the Lincoln Memorial, he observed that "the Negro lives on a lonely island of poverty in the midst of a vast ocean of material prosperity."

> There are those who are asking the devotees of civil rights, "When will you be satisfied?" We can never be satisfied as long as the Negro is the victim of the unspeakable horrors of police brutality. We can never be satisfied as long as our bodies, heavy with the fatigue of travel, cannot gain lodging in the motels of the highways and the hotels of the cities. We cannot be satisfied as long as the Negro's basic mobility is from a smaller ghetto to a larger one. We can never be satisfied as long as our children are stripped of their self-hood and robbed of their dignity by signs stating: "For Whites Only." We cannot be satisfied as long as a Negro in Mississippi cannot vote and a Negro in New York believes he has nothing for which to vote. No, no, we are not satisfied.[66]

As Greg Thompson has pointed out, King labored to expose the imperfections of America not so that America would be humiliated, but so that America would be healed. Once again, his theological anthropology became the source of his vision of democratic inclusion and solidarity. "God," he preached, "is not interested merely in the freedom of black men and brown men and yellow men. But God is interested in the freedom of the whole human race and the creation of a society where all men will live together as brothers, where every man will respect the dignity and the worth of human personality."[67] As King said, "When you . . . look in the face of every man and see deep down within him what religion calls the 'image of God,' you begin to love him. . . . No matter what he does, you see God's image there. . . . Discover the element of good in your enemy. And as you seek to hate him, find the center of goodness and place your attention there and you will take a new attitude. . . . When you rise to love on this level, you begin to love men not because they are likable, but because God loves them. You look at every man and you love him because you know God loves him."[68]

Even their enemy—white people who hate, dominate, subjugate, and oppress Black people—are to be viewed with the eyes of Godly love.

This was the way that King imagined American democracy finally overcoming its most brutal and tragic contradiction; this was the telos that American democracy could help to achieve. "I still have a dream," he declared in his most famous speech. "It is a dream deeply rooted in the American dream. I have a dream that one day this nation will rise up and live out the true meaning of its creed: 'We hold these truths to be self-evident; that all men are created equal.'"[69] Elsewhere he asserted, "We have a great opportunity in America to build here a great nation, a nation where all men live together as brothers and respect the dignity and worth of all human personality. We must keep moving toward that goal."[70]

America was, for all of its faults, still a land of promise. "If America would come to herself," he declared, "one nation, indivisible, with liberty and justice for all, she would give the democratic creed a new authentic ring, enkindle the imagination of mankind, and fire the souls of men."[71] "Now is the time to make real the promises of democracy. Now is the time to rise from the dark and desolate valley of segregation to the sunlit path of racial justice. Now is the time to lift our nation from the quicksands of racial injustice to the solid rock of brotherhood. Now is the time to make justice a reality for all of God's children."[72]

A Fragile Solidarity

Even at its most effective, social reform is never anything but incomplete, and in the case of civil rights, it was incomplete for all of the reasons King pointed to. Thus, to say that the "age of the crisis of man" ended in failure is to belittle the massive achievements of the civil rights movement in particular, but also to fail to recognize how it provided a source for the realization of a wide array of liberationist movements to come. The inability to fully overcome the contradictions of exclusion, reflected, for example, in the race riots that followed the murder of King, portended a continuation, if not deepening, of social and political fragmentation, but in its moment, King's rhetoric of democratic promise, hope, concord, citizenship, and brotherhood had a profound and, arguably, unifying effect. His rhetoric served to generate greater solidarity than ever before on matters of race in large part because *his appeal drew upon underlying assumptions*—anthropological, ethical, and teleological—*embedded within America's hybrid-Enlightenment's surface and deep structures. King became a martyr to those assumptions.*

Though weakened, these assumptions continued to exist as viable sources of solidarity. They were even reflected in the testimony James Baldwin gave before Congress in 1968, eighteen days before King's assassination.[73] Though he had left both Christianity and America many years before, and though his rage at racial injustice had only intensified in the intervening years, he still affirmed the need to integrate Black history within American history. He understood that it would be difficult to teach, but it should not be hived off from the larger story of America and taught separately. "My history," he wrote, "contains the truth about America." Yet "it is our common history. My history is also yours." "I am flesh of your flesh and bone of your bone; I have been here as long as you have been here—longer—I paid for it as much as you have. It is my country, too. Do recognize that this is the whole question. My history and culture has got to be taught. *It is yours.*"[74]

That solidarity remained into the early 1970s as a framework of understanding that, despite growing anger and discontent from many quarters, still *contained* that discontent. This was the framework of broad agreement that formed the backdrop of outrage toward the Watergate scandal a few years later: a solidarity of collective indignation that united liberals and conservatives, Democrats and Republicans, in forcing the resignation of President Nixon.[75]

It was not to last.

CHAPTER NINE

The Evolving Culture War

O NE COULD PLAUSIBLY ARGUE that the life and death of Martin Luther King marked the end of a long phase of national solidarity, at least as reflected in the commitment to an ethical framework for working through difference. This is not to underplay just how controversial he was. In his day, King was as defiant of the American mainstream as anyone on the left—and not just against racism but against the war in Vietnam, sexism, and the excesses of capitalism. None of this sat well with conservatives.

And yet King never gave up the effort to realize a vision of national unity, calling America to heed its better angels. His arguments for freedom and justice, then, were not only constitutional but profoundly ethical, and not merely prophetic and critical but ameliorative and conciliatory, making every effort to generate solidarity across racial, social, religious, and political divides. As we know, his appeal wasn't at all perfunctory; it was ethically demanding, calling upon his people to love their enemies, something he demonstrated personally again and again. This was a theme he returned to many times in sermons over the course of his ministry. In this remarkable passage, King laid out the extraordinary ethical demands required.

We come to see that there is within every man, the image of God, and no matter how much it is scarred, it is still there.

And so, when we come to recognize that the evil act of our enemy neighbor is not the whole being of our enemy neighbor, we develop the capacity to love him in spite of his evil deed. *The other thing that we must do in order to love the enemy neighbor is this: we must seek at all times to win his friendship and understanding rather than to defeat him or humiliate him. There may come a time when it will be possible for you to humiliate your worst enemy or even to defeat him, but in order to love the enemy, you must not do it.* For in the final analysis, love means understanding goodwill for all men and a refusal to defeat any individual. . . . Love makes it possible for you to place your vision and to center your activity on the evil system and not the individual enemy who may be caught up in that system. And so, you set out to defeat segregation and not the segregationist.[1]

For King, there was nothing natural or easy about the work of building solidarity in a world so riven by conflict. He understood that a constructive and affirmative solidarity was, in large part, rooted in ethical encumbrances that were antecedent to choice, convenience, or expedience. Against the racism that constantly threatened his family and that eventually took his life, this lived ethical commitment was nothing less than heroic.

King, of course, was exemplary—a moral virtuoso. The burden he bore, the risks he took, the sacrifices he made were all rooted in a vision of national hope and a wellspring of commitment that were out of reach to mere mortals who could neither fathom nor share his special charisma. Even so, the reservoirs that fueled his moral commitment, drawn as they were from the hybrid-Enlightenment, were not only recognizable to most Americans, they resonated with most Americans as well. But it had been a bloody decade—JFK assassinated in 1963, Malcolm X in 1965, MLK and RFK in 1968, and the massive carnage of the war in Vietnam—and Americans were ready to move on, with little taste for sustaining the commitment necessary to reach for greater racial justice. Even within the civil rights movement, there was a widespread sense that King's strategy of binding dissent and solidarity together out of the resources of America's hybrid-Enlightenment was no longer sustainable or even effective.

A Waning of National Solidarity

The waning effectiveness of those cultural resources to generate and sustain solidarity was in large measure due to changing institutional conditions. Among the most important were new pressures within America's evolving political economy and new stresses due to a significant shift in the demographic landscape.

Neoliberalism

The changes within the American political economy were long in development. Their earliest roots can be traced back to the Progressive Era, taking form in the middle of the century but especially after World War II, and reaching a high point between the 1970s and the 1990s. I am referring, of course, to what has come to be called neoliberalism. It is a troubled concept, to be sure, one often used incoherently, but with hindsight, it can be seen as a coherent political philosophy, a functioning ideology, and eventually, a massively powerful cultural logic and set of practices.

Much has been written about neoliberalism, but in broad strokes, its centerpiece is a particular perspective on economic and political freedom in which liberalism takes an economistic turn.[2] Above all, neoliberalism valorized the free market to defend freedom and encourage economic prosperity. As Friedrich Hayek put it in his dire warning about the expansionist encroachments of socialist regimes toward the end of World War II, "Personal and political freedom has never existed in the past" without "freedom in economic affairs."[3] In the early 1960s, Milton Friedman restated the point, arguing that "history suggests . . . that capitalism is a necessary condition for political freedom."[4]

Freedom is one of those concepts that seems an unqualified good, self-evident in its meaning and transcending serious scrutiny. But quite a lot rides on how freedom is understood within neoliberalism. Two characteristics stand out. First, freedom is defined negatively, as in freedom from coercion.[5] Thus neoliberalism offered no substantive or positive account of freedom, rarely mentioning, for example, theories of natural rights. The freedom of neoliberalism was not "freedom for" but "freedom from." It was for this reason that its proponents have long been skeptical toward the state and its interventions. Beyond modest taxation, the provision of public goods (such as public safety, good roads, parks, and so on), the protection of civil order, and security from aggressive foreign powers, central planning and public ownership can lead to authoritarian rule and the renunciation of freedom. Collectivization in all its forms, in Hayek's phrase, takes a society down "the road to serfdom."[6]

There was another reason why freedom was disembedded from any historical or positive account: its main protagonists were "skeptical about the ability to acquire moral knowledge" in the first place, recognizing that there was "an epistemic barrier to knowing what is truly right and good."[7] Neoliberalism simply could not offer a vision of the common good. As Hayek put it, "It is at least doubtful whether at this stage a detailed blueprint of a desirable internal order of society would be of much use—or whether anyone is competent to furnish it."[8] "The real case for a free society and for freedom," Friedman argued, "is ignorance—we cannot be sure we are right." "All totalitarians," he wrote, "all people who have suppressed freedom, have done so because of the arrogance of their believing that they knew what sin was."[9] But in a free society, we recognize that there is no way to know what people ought to value or what conception of the good life people ought to have. People are free when they are free to answer these questions for themselves.

The second feature of the neoliberal view of freedom was its emphasis on individuality. The object of freedom, its "ultimate goal in judging social arrangements," as Friedman put it, is "the individual, or perhaps the family."[10] Individualism has always been a feature of American society, but as Robert Bellah and others have shown, biblical and republican forms of individualism became supplanted by the radical utilitarian and hedonic forms of individualism justified by the *Homo economicus* of neoliberalism.[11]

In questions of freedom, individuals are central. They are the only actors that matter, ontologically as well as methodologically—ontologically because "the delineation of property rights is, in effect, the instrument or means through which a person is initially defined"; methodologically because institutions, groups, communities, or any of the wide range of sodalities have no life or being or enduring substance of their own, but are simply aggregates of individuals, united voluntarily through an implicit or explicit contract. In the ideal world pictured within neoliberalism, then, the "world is peopled exclusively by persons who respect the minimal set of behavior norms dictated by mutual tolerance and respect. Individuals remain free to 'do their own things.'" Free exchange is facilitated by a commonly valued commodity—money—that allows for a comparison of values. The good, then, is whatever "tends to emerge from the free choices of the individuals who are involved," and "any outcome that emerges merits classification as 'good,' regardless of its precise descriptive content." In the end, "there is really no categorical distinction to be made between the set of rights normally referred to as 'human' and those referred to as 'property.'"[12]

Sociologically and historically, the public philosophy of neoliberalism had powerful effects that took form in governmental policies from the 1970s onward, but in time spilled out of the intellectual and policy worlds into everyday life as a deeply embedded cultural logic. The shorthand for this was "market totalization," and its effects were to shape, if not subordinate to the market, the concepts, metaphors, anthropology, and ethics of all spheres of social life, including philanthropy, education, and religion.

Its effects powerfully influenced liberal democracy as well. Rhetorically, democracy and capitalism were and are inseparable, for one promotes the other. But in the logics of neoliberalism, functioning competitive markets have priority over democratic institutions insofar as they are seen as creating an essential condition for the prevention of coercion and for the wide diffusion of power.[13] Friedman, among others, made this explicit. "Historical evidence speaks with a single voice on the relation between political freedom and a free market. I know of no example in time or place of a society that has been marked by a large measure of political freedom, and that has not also used something comparable to a free market to organize the bulk of economic activity." "Economic freedom was also an *indispensable means toward the achievement of political freedom.*"[14] In theory, but also in its net impact, democracy was understood to be subordinate to capitalism.

The net (arguably unintended) cultural effects of this largely amoral, materialist, secularizing, nonteleological, and reductive public philosophy were profoundly corrosive to the solidarity rooted in the cultural ideals and institutions of the hybrid-Enlightenment. The public sphere broadly was conceptualized as a competitive market, social and institutional authority was further undermined by its individualist and antinomian logics, the pre-political bonds of solidarity were further diminished to the alignment of identities and interests, and the practices of citizenship were reduced to mere voting.

These developments, of course, were contemporaneous with the rise and expansion of a managerial, technocratic, and professional class within the rapidly expanding corporate, governmental, scientific, educational, and philanthropic bureaucracies, a rise necessitated by the increased technical and organizational complexity of all modern institutions. These institutions ultimately became the carriers of the neoliberal ethos. Yet the managerial expansion had its own unintended consequences. The power of these unelected elites, especially within the governmental, scientific, and corporate spheres, represented a displacement of popular authority onto expert knowledge. Rationally "objective" or "neutral" expertise became one more substitute for the public good.

Immigration

The demographic changes were catalyzed by the Immigration and Nationality Act of 1965 signed during the Johnson administration. The policy abolished race and national origins policies that had been in place since 1921. Those policies had restricted immigration from southern and eastern Europe as well as Asia and Africa with the intent of promoting immigration from the Protestant countries of northern and western Europe. When still a senator, John F. Kennedy had called the prior immigration policy "the most blatant piece of discrimination in our nation's history."[15] This change brought about a shifting profile of the American population: between 1965 and 2015, new immigrants and their families accounted for 55 percent of the population growth. The actual number of the nation's foreign-born population increased from 9.6 million in 1965 to 44.8 million in 2018.

In this way, pluralism intensified considerably, and with it, waves of people for whom the hybrid-Enlightenment and the American mythos were, at the least, unfamiliar, strange, or perhaps incomprehensible. In turn, the assimilationist ethos that had been prevalent for generations became much more difficult to sustain. The demographic influx of non-European immigrants was parallel to and reinforced the decline of the mainline Protestant churches and the weakening of the WASP establishment and the regnant system of elite privilege, power, and class reproduction.

An Evolution of the Cultural Sources Themselves

The waning effectiveness of the hybrid-Enlightenment to generate and sustain solidarity was also due to the further evolution of those cultural resources themselves. But in what way? It should be obvious by now that the opacity that had long marked the hybrid-Enlightenment never implied neutrality or mere abstraction. The universal representation promised by liberal democracy as a matter of historical fact operated *within* a substantive frame that had always made comprehensive claims about the public good: what it meant to be a good American and what it meant for America to be a good and righteous nation. Partisanship and factionalism operated within that frame. But neither had that frame ever been static and unchanging. From the beginning, it evolved as it worked through the contradictions endemic to its own failed practice. Yet, through the last third of the twentieth century, the cultural resources provided by the hybrid-Enlightenment evolved in ways that demonstrably drained the meaning of those resources.

The Bond between Political Liberalism and Neoliberalism

In intellectual circles this could be seen in the assertions of what was to become the dominant school of political liberalism articulated by John Rawls in his *Theory of Justice*. A central element of his program was the belief that the state in a modern pluralistic society would aspire to be *neutral* with regard to different and competing conceptions of the good; that in practice, particular conceptions of the good should not be legislated at all. Reinforcing this approach was the moral duty that lawmakers, politicians, and citizens make political decisions according to principles of reasoning and rules of evidence that all people could reasonably endorse. Not only did this approach proscribe the public ethics of many different philosophical and religious traditions, but as many critics pointed out, it could not live up to its own billing of neutrality: from the outset, it was biased toward those conceptions of the good that privileged secular, atomizing, individualistic claims oriented toward personal fulfillment and the satisfactions of the sovereign self. In sum, though the purposes of the economic (neoliberal) and political (Rawlsian) views of justice and inequality were quite different, at a deeper level, these views were very much aligned. Rawls's conception of the moral agent, the mediating importance of contract, of freedom itself, and the technocratic nature of modern politics—its secularity, its individualism, and its valorization of expert knowledge—lined up with and was reinforced by the neoliberal conception of these matters. The nature of this complex of normative claims (from Rawls and the neoliberals) became apparent when set against a variety of alternatives, usually communitarian in character, that tended to privilege solidarity and mutual dependence.[16]

The Attenuations of Civil Religion

In populist terms, the draining of the meaning of the hybrid-Enlightenment could also be seen in the attenuations of civil religion. Through the 1960s, the mainline faith traditions had been influenced by and, in due course, participants in, the anti-Americanism of the Left. This hostility was generally rooted in the scandal of American hypocrisy—the failure of America to live up to its own ideals, particularly as they bore on the rights and treatment of Blacks and women. It was also rooted in the exploitation of people and the environment in America and around the world by the machinery of American capitalism. America, in short, had been and was still complicit in some of the worst evils in the history of humankind. Though these dispositions varied in tone and substance, the mainline denominations, especially their leadership, could no longer associate themselves with anything so ethically dubious as "love of country." Given America's legacy of oppression, what was there to love? There were some in the early 1970s who spoke of themselves and their project as "post-American."[17]

Among conservatives, especially evangelicals, the attenuations of civil religion came through the transformation of civil religion into a religious nationalism. As Philip Gorski noted, the transformation could be seen in the differences between Billy Graham in the 1960s and 1970s and Jerry Falwell in the 1980s and 1990s: both were evangelicals, but the former was a mainstream religious leader squarely within the liberal consensus and the latter was a sectarian movement activist outside of any social or political consensus. Where Graham avoided theological and political controversy, Falwell embraced it. Where Graham preached a simple message of grace in service of individual salvation from personal sin, Falwell prominently championed a Christian America whose very Constitution was divinely inspired against the threat posed by secular humanists—the "pagans, and the abortionists, and the feminists, and the gays . . . , all of them who have tried to secularize America."[18]

A Deepening Secularity

While the civil rights movement was as pragmatic as any of the other countercultural movements of the time, its moral energy—both in its protests and its efforts at conciliation under King—drew deeply and explicitly from an idealism rooted in the religious sources of Christian faith. Operating openly within the language and logic of the hybrid-Enlightenment, the civil rights movement grounded its appeal in a framework of understanding and interpretation that was native to ordinary Americans. But the successors to the civil rights movement largely abandoned those sources. There were certainly religious voices in the feminist, antiwar, and gay rights movements, but they were now in the minority. The successor movements themselves and the moral arguments they made reflected the hard secular turn presaged by Dewey earlier in the century.

The deepening of the secular turn among elites and the credentialed upper-middle class at this moment was probably inevitable, historically speaking. It took place amid the unprecedented expansion of higher education during the post–World War II period, an expansion necessitated by organizational and ideological changes well underway in the economic, political, educational, and technical spheres of the new American empire. The evidence amassed by Robert Wuthnow demonstrated that higher education, long a carrier of the secular Enlightenment, had a massive generational effect on both the secularization and liberalization of attitudes, beliefs, and commitments of the many young people who received it.[19]

The deepening of the secular turn among elites, along with the dissolution of American civil religion, meant that fault lines already well established between elites and the general public and between the Left and the Right became open cleavages by the 1980s.

A Center That Could No Longer Hold

And so it was that the "age of the crisis of man" came to an end against further fragmentation and division. For all the good it did achieve, the midcentury effort to work through America's hybrid-Enlightenment failed to respond to the fragmenting claims upon public life. It also failed to respond to the various threats to human existence posed by war and the instrumentalities of a world dominated by a technology untethered to ethical norms. It simply could not carry the weight of these contradictions. The institutional and cultural resources long relied upon to work through these contradictions had etiolated, drained of their vigor.

In the end, then, the center would not and could not hold.

On the surface of political life, there was much to occupy the attention of the public: campus protests against the war in Vietnam, the growing prominence and momentum of second-wave feminism, the Stonewall riots launching the gay rights movement, and the first Earth Day celebration initiating the environmental movement. Underneath these political roilings, though, the cultural center of midcentury humanism had collapsed due to a failure to recognize, much less address, its own inadequacies. The tragedy of this was not lost on Walter Lippmann. In 1969, nearly a decade and a half after publishing *The Public Philosophy*, Lippman, now eighty and in declining health, was asked by an interviewer if he thought the world was a better place than it had been when he was young. "Anything that makes the world more humane and rational is progress," he replied. "That's the only measuring stick we can apply to it." By this standard, however, he now thought that it was "a much less pleasant world to live in." Despite the advances in technology and human freedom, he sensed that the coming era, on balance, was "going to be a minor Dark Age."[20]

The Culture War: Early Years

The University of Chicago historian Martin Marty once described conservative Protestants in the decades following the Scopes trial of 1925 as a "cognitive minority" but a "socio-behavioral majority."[21] For precisely this reason, conservative Christianity, especially Protestant fundamentalism, withdrew from social and political affairs right through the 1960s.[22] Mainstream American values and norms related to sexuality, the nuclear family, and the role of men and women were overwhelmingly aligned with the legacy of traditional Jewish and Christian faith until the early 1960s. There were even prayer and Bible readings in the public schools. In the minds of most American Christians, including fundamentalists and evangelicals, there was no cause to engage politically. For them, the center was still holding.

But with the successes of second-wave feminism, the legalization of abortion, the growing rates of divorce, the increasing legitimacy of homosexuality and the success of the gay rights movement, along with the relaxation of sexual prohibitions generally in the late 1960s and early 1970s, conservative Christians believed that the complex of traditional values essential to a good life and an ethical social order was now under assault.

This, along with the continuing secularization of public institutions and what conservative Christians perceived as the weakening authority of the church through Supreme Court decisions surrounding the First Amendment religion clauses, meant that unless these trends were arrested, believers would become, to paraphrase Marty, *both* a socio-behavioral minority *and* a cognitive minority. So they reacted to defend a space of practice they had long assumed was safely preserved. And they did so with cultural logics that remained—at this point, anyway—well within traditional interpretations of the cultural logic of the hybrid-Enlightenment.

These were the provocations that set off the cultural conflicts that have come to be known as the culture wars. The cultural and structural roots of this conflict were, of course, as deep as the Western tradition itself, but what had played out mainly within elite culture from the late nineteenth century had percolated into mass society. Ordinary working-, middle-, and upper-middle-class Americans were now alert to the vast and comprehensive transformations within their civilization. They too saw that different ways of life were at stake.

The culture war that defined and animated political conflict in America through the closing decades of the twentieth century and the opening decades of the twenty-first played out both on the surface of political life as the "politics of culture" in multiple fields of conflict, and also in the "culture of politics," the deep structures that form the competing cultural logics of conflict.

Fields of Conflict

On the surface, the culture war presented itself in the media as a wide variety of discrete and seemingly unrelated political and policy conflicts over disparate and ostensibly unconnected cultural issues driven by mostly independent special-interest groups. At this level, the culture war was the aggregate of these disputes; it was a national conflict consisting of the sum of these discrete political and policy conflicts.[23]

The passion and conflict of the early decades of the culture war were mainly centered on the politics of the body. The dispute over gender and the personal and public rights of women, the contest over abortion, and the struggle over homosexuality were perennial and heated flashpoints of conflict. In all of this, it was easy to be distracted by the political atmospherics generated by particular legal battles or particular activists and imagine that these events were the main story. But underneath these issues and the specific events or people or behavior that made them "newsworthy" was a deeper contest over the nature and purpose of America's dominant institutions— family, education, the arts, the news media, politics, law, the military, medicine, and institutions of faith. All of these institutions evolved into fields of conflict in their own right.

THE FAMILY

The family was, in some ways, the center of the storm because of the long-held view that it is the "cornerstone of our society." If that is true or believed to be true, it is in the interest of everyone to foster healthy family life.

This, in fact, was the purpose of the White House Conference on the Family in 1980, sponsored by the Carter administration. In retrospect it is not surprising that even before the conference began, there was a dispute among organizers over what the American family was supposed to be in the first place. To solve the problem, they changed the name of the initiative to the White House Conference on *Families*. Statewide hearings and forums were held in all fifty states. But instead of generating ways in which public policy might strengthen American families, the initiative turned into a national fiasco. *Newsweek* called it "the biggest political battleground between conservatives and liberals since the National Women's Conference in 1977." The *Washington Post* described it as an "uproar [produced] by the 'pro-life' lobby, the abortion rights lobby, the gay rights lobby, the pro-family lobby and all the rest," noting that "these single-interest groups . . . approached the conference as a forum in which either to press their views or to defend them against assault from other quarters." The *Nashville Banner* wrote that in "the first three hours of the conference's forums, divorce, homosexuality, violence on television, sex education in public schools, welfare, and prayer came up, rose to debate, then fell into the boiling pot of controversy."[24]

Whatever particular policy issue was discussed, each raised the fundamental question "What is the family?" Is the structure of the traditional nuclear family and the roles assigned to men, women, and children divinely ordained and therefore good or were these a source of inequality and oppression? What constitutes healthy and legitimate sexual intimacy? Is the love and sexuality of persons of the same sex natural, or is it a perversion of the natural order? What are the obligations of family members—spouse to spouse, parents to children, and so on? Do individual members subordinate their interests to a family unit in mutual obligation, or do the rights of individual autonomy have priority? And are the reproductive rights of women shared with a spouse, or are they hers alone? Not least, what are the obligations of motherhood? Is the woman a mother at conception because she is carrying an unborn child, or does she only become a mother at the time of birth? As for childcare, is it the obligation of the government or a business to provide preschool care, or is it something couples bear on their own? As the National Organization for Women put it in their founding statement of purpose, "A true partnership between the sexes demands *a different concept of marriage*, an equitable sharing of the responsibilities of home and children and of the economic burdens of their support."[25] Progressives were not pressing just for an expanded idea of civil rights to include reproductive rights and equal opportunity for women, but for a fundamentally new conception of the family. Everything was up for grabs.

PUBLIC EDUCATION

Education, and especially public education, was a symbolically freighted field of conflict because its latent function, since the dawn of the modern nation-state, has been to reproduce national culture for succeeding generations. Among other things, a nation's mythos—its self-understanding—was at stake. Has America been an oasis of liberty—the "land of the free and home of the brave"—or has it been a place of hereditary oppression? Judgments about what knowledge is worth teaching bears not only on history but on literature, science, and health science. Which novels and poems (and which novelists and poets) are canonical and which are safely ignored? Can one teach evolution or climate science, knowing there will be dissenters? What responsibility do public schools have to weigh in on issues of sexuality?

On the ground, schools have performed this larger institutional role in partnership with parents. This naturally turns what can seem like abstract issues into profoundly personal ones. Parents on all sides project their own values and priorities onto their school, where these issues take concrete shape. It is no surprise that school board meetings have long been sites of cultural conflict.

AND HIGHER EDUCATION

All of these issues were contested as vigorously in higher education, an institution that has performed the same latent function as public primary and secondary education, but now for the nation's leadership classes. In the early years of the culture war, religious conservatives complained about the dominance of "secular humanism" among the professoriate in colleges and universities. Yet the threat to the conservative establishment was far more comprehensive.

The first was the often arcane reinterpretation of the Western philosophical, historical, and literary traditions in relationship to the economic, political, racial, and gender structures of Western modernity. Far from benign or liberatory, Western regimes and their cultural superstructures were seen as inherently oppressive to developing, colonial, and postcolonial societies. Against these regimes, various theories of resistance took form in colleges and universities around the country, through academic departments and through the wide range of professional guilds, to interrogate the ways in which the humanities and social sciences valorized oppression and to quietly reinstitutionalize academic fields in ways that recognized voices that had been suppressed. The challenge also took form in various spectacles of protest, such as the one staged by Jesse Jackson in 1987 at Stanford University. Five hundred protesters marched down Palm Drive chanting, "Hey hey, ho ho, Western Civ has got to go," in protest against the lack of diversity in Stanford's introductory humanities program and, by implication, the superiority of the Western canon it putatively embraced. The curriculum was soon replaced by "Culture, Ideas and Values," which gave priority to works on race, class, and gender by minority and women authors nationally and internationally.

But for all the attention it received, the Stanford protest was just one part of a sweeping reinstitutionalization of the humanities and social sciences away from the assumption of the natural superiority of the Western literary canon to a new multiculturalism focused upon a diverse representation of works and authors.

In its less controversial form, multiculturalism was simply a demand for recognition of the value and integrity of minority cultures. It allowed the full recognition and celebration of Black, Native American, and the wide range of ethnic cultures and their contributions to contemporary society but within a liberal political order. Consonant with the assumptions of the hybrid-Enlightenment, diversity was a public good to be embraced, not ignored. In this form, multiculturalism would promote tolerance and open-mindedness.

Multiculturalism also took a more radical expression, the premise of which was that assimilation was a form of violence and coercion against minority peoples and their cultures. In this light, the "canon" was simply part of the instrumentality of a white, male, Eurocentric, and Judeo-Christian power structure. Indeed, in the very concept of a "common good," liberal democracy suppressed difference and "otherness" and, at the same time, implicitly legitimated the presumed superiority of a white, Eurocentric, and Judeo-Christian social order.

A harbinger of this radical and separatist tendency could be seen as early as 1966. John Hope Franklin, one of the nation's most prominent Black historians, and two coauthors had published the junior high school textbook *Land of the Free: A History of the United States* that year, in part as a response to a call for history texts to "correctly portray the role and contributions of the American Negro and members of other ethnic groups" in American history. In sympathy with the mood set in the mid-1960s by King, the book maintained a patriotic tone by telling a nuanced yet integrated story of America in light of its ongoing struggle for freedom. Even so, its adoption in school districts was opposed by many conservatives. This was not a surprise. What was surprising was the opposition of Black nationalists. Indeed, just after the book's adoption in the Philadelphia school districts, thirty-five hundred African American students rallied in protest, asking instead for separate courses and texts taught by Black teachers.[26] In the coming decades, these tendencies would be more fully theorized and institutionalized in educational curricula, human resources agendas, and movement activism.

THE ARTS

The challenge to the ideals and values of the Western tradition was also the subtext of the arts. The avant-garde had long been disposed to shock the middle classes through transgressive art, but when the National Endowment for the Arts funded exhibitions in 1989 by Andrés Serrano and Robert Mapplethorpe, a national controversy erupted. Serrano's work often included photographs of corpses and used feces and bodily fluids as materials. The most controversial of all, though, was his award-winning photograph of a crucifix submerged in a glass container of his own urine. Mapplethorpe's photography ranged widely, but his 1989 exhibition—*The Perfect Moment*—

of the gay male BDMS (bondage, dominance, masochism, and sadism) subculture in New York City was, in the minds of many, beyond the pale. The dollar amounts of the NEA grants were insignificant—$15,000 for the Serrano exhibition and $30,000 for the Mapplethorpe exhibition—but the symbolic impact of the support of the American government for work that was regarded by many as blasphemous and obscene implicitly implied the government's approval. For conservatives, this was a bridge too far. These events were one more indication that the cultural elite was hostile to the conventions of middle America.

THE NEWS MEDIA

In democratic theory, the purpose of the press is to mediate knowledge and information without prejudice to the citizens of a nation. Though this has always been an elusive aspiration, in theory, the press's task is to remain independent of competing interests for the purposes of educating the public into knowledgeable participation in self-governance. But if journalism sought to achieve professional fairness and objectivity during the twentieth century, it never did—and never could. After all, by the very act of selecting stories to cover and the angle by which to interpret them, news organizations effectively determine what topics are important, what issues are relevant for public discussion, and what people and events are worthy of coverage. Even at its best and most impartial, the press has been a powerful filter through which citizens' perceptions of the world have been shaped.

Through the decades leading up to the turn of the century, communications technology was dominated by television, radio, magazines, newspapers, and newsmagazines. These media generally enjoyed the public trust right through the early 1970s.[27] By the 1980s, however, the leading news agencies had been pegged by conservatives as listing to port. As one celebrity pastor put it in 1988, "It's no secret to any of us how the liberal media manages the news and helps to set the national agenda on public debate. They report the news in such a way as to promote the political goals of the left. This censorship of Christian principles and ideas covers many more issues than abortion and the homosexual lifestyle. . . . The truth in all of these areas is being hidden."[28]

Traditionalists believed that they and their interests were being shut out of the national conversation. It was out of this frustration that conservatives dreamed of acquiring a large-circulation newspaper or television network. In 1985, they took action. A conservative group called Fairness in Media launched an initiative to buy out the television company CBS—the Columbia Broadcasting System. Under the authorship of Senator Jesse Helms, Fairness in Media sent out a missive to over a million conservatives asking each to purchase twenty shares of common stock in the company. While the bid ultimately failed, CBS had to bring in two law firms, an investment bank, and several public relations firms to defend itself. Its official response aligned itself with democratic principles. "CBS intends to take all appropriate steps to maintain the independence and integrity of its news organization." A spokeswoman added, "Our sole purpose is journalism, and our goal is objectivity."[29]

The initiative is long forgotten, but it is telling all the same. It marked a time when trust by the general public in the mainstream news media had begun to wane. Though the news media establishment embraced the idea of ideological independence and objectivity, it was in fact blind to its own biases. It also marks a time when conservatives recognized that to fight the culture war, they needed to control their own media. Just over a decade later, in 1996, the Fox News Channel was founded and, fairly quickly, became the most-watched network news channel in America.

ELECTORAL POLITICS

The politicization of social life in the United States is a complex phenomenon. And while its sources are many and varied, politicization intensified in the early decades of the culture war. Even in its early years, the culture war entailed a pivot from the tough haggling for compromise over different, though concrete, interests in matters of common concern to a symbolic politics defined by ideological purity. Not only electoral politics, but party mobilization and policy agenda became subordinate to the special interests of competing factions in the culture war itself. Politicians became symbols of competing cultural camps and were extolled or denigrated accordingly, all irrespective of the actual character, competence, or record of the politicians. Campaign debate was shaped by the issues and interests of special-purpose groups. Elections themselves became enactments of cultural struggle and rituals of factional solidarity. Through the culture war, party ideology, party platforms, party loyalty, and the categories of "Left" and "Right" themselves were redefined around its main cultural fault lines.

On the surface, then, it appeared as though candidates and political parties were using the symbols of the culture war in service to their own political ambitions. Certainly, this was the case. Yet a less obvious but equally plausible interpretation is that the politicians themselves were, in the main, interchangeable—that the culture war now provided the discursive and moral framework within which all politicians and their parties now had to operate. By this view, the instrumentalities of electoral politics became a device by which competing interests in the culture war would be advanced.

To the extent that politics became more polarized in these decades, then, it was largely because the culture that underwrote it had become more polarized.

LAW

The law, by definition, has been a field of conflict, and never less so than during the culture war of the late twentieth century. Whatever else it means, the law symbolically represents the patronage and power of the state and therefore the ultimate means of social control. When law is enacted, consensus is imposed—by force, if need be, through the presence and power of the police, national guard, and armed services. Every issue of the culture war quickly made its way to the courtroom to be litigated.

But as a field of conflict in its own right, one of the most visible ways in which the law became contested was through efforts to pack the courts with judges who were ideologically favorable to one side or another. Court packing had been a phenomenon since the Founding, but it mapped onto the divisions of the culture war beginning in 1987 with Ronald Reagan's nomination of Robert Bork as an associate justice on the Supreme Court. Senator Ted Kennedy took to the Senate floor immediately after the nomination to challenge it. "Robert Bork's America," he declared, "is a land in which women would be forced into back-alley abortions, blacks would sit at segregated lunch counters, rogue police could break down citizens' doors in midnight raids, schoolchildren could not be taught about evolution, writers and artists could be censored at the whim of the Government, and the doors of the Federal courts would be shut on the fingers of millions of citizens for whom the judiciary is—and is often the only—protector of the individual rights that are the heart of our democracy." Checking most of the boxes on the progressive side of the ledger, he went on to say, "Bork's rigid ideology will tip the scales of justice against the kind of country America is and ought to be."[30]

Four years later, in 1991, controversy erupted again with George H. W. Bush's nomination of Clarence Thomas to the Supreme Court. The confirmation of Thomas, a conservative, seemed to be a foregone conclusion until Anita Hill, a former aide to Thomas at the Department of Education and at the Equal Opportunity Employment Commission during the 1980s, accused him of sexual harassment. The allegations divided the Senate and the nation down the middle. Thomas and Hill became heroes among their respective supporters, villains to their opponents.

These appointments were portents of things to come. It wasn't that every nomination to the Supreme Court or to the federal bench in the coming years was equally controversial, but the respective parties in power consistently used their prerogatives to pack the courts with ideologically aligned judges.

The Question of Authority

The law is significant for yet other reasons, not least as a window into questions of authority. And yet underneath the contentious issues that would randomly but all too frequently crop up, and underneath the struggle over the meaning and purpose of broad institutional spheres of social life to which those issues pointed, and underneath the challenge to the ruling establishment that represented and defended the older order, there was yet a deeper conflict. This was the conflict over different and competing visions of America and the authority upon which the nation's major institutions, not least law and government, would be based. On what authority do claims to the ordering of public life and judgments about the rightness or wrongness of different and competing positions rest?

There were a few thoughtful and articulate voices that recognized this deeper level of conflict, Richard John Neuhaus's and Laurence Tribe's among them. For Neuhaus, the ultimate authority was a religiously informed natural law. For Tribe, it was the autonomous, rational self.

Neuhaus

At the time of his death in 2009, Neuhaus was arguably the most famous conservative Catholic in America. On the face of it, his profile was very similar to Niebuhr's, at least in his early years. Born during the Depression in 1936, Neuhaus was the son of a Lutheran pastor who cared for small parishes, first in Texas and then in Canada. Intellectually gifted, Neuhaus became a pastor himself in the theologically conservative Lutheran Church–Missouri Synod and, from 1961 to 1978, shepherded a mostly poor, largely Black parish in the inner-city Brooklyn neighborhoods of Bedford-Stuyvesant and Williamsburg. From this perch, he became a forceful critic of racial injustice, economic inequality, and the war in Vietnam. His credentials on the left were indisputable. He marched with Martin Luther King, was arrested at a protest march at the 1968 Democratic National Convention and, with Daniel Berrigan and Abraham Joshua Heschel, founded the antiwar organization Clergy and Laity Concerned about Vietnam. He famously declared that the Vietnamese people were "God's instruments for bringing the American empire to its knees." Like Niebuhr, then, he was a brilliant preacher and thinker, but also an activist and organizer. In one encounter, Niebuhr himself reportedly dubbed Neuhaus "the next Reinhold Niebuhr."[31]

Any similarities between the two receded against two "conversions" Neuhaus experienced, though these conversions were perhaps more superficial than substantive. The first was ecclesiastical: he converted to Roman Catholicism in 1990 and became a priest in the following year. In truth, Neuhaus never understood his Lutheranism as a separate denomination set against and in protest to Catholicism. Rather, he saw it as a reform movement within the Church, and when the issues that had historically separated Lutherans from Catholics were worked out, there would no longer be a need to stand by the formal distinctions. Neuhaus had always been very Catholic in his Lutheranism. He had now become a very ecumenically minded Catholic.[32]

The second conversion was political. Even as a man of the Left, Neuhaus never saw himself as anything other than a patriot. His biographer Randy Boyagoda began his account with a vignette set in 1967 at St. John the Evangelist, a thriving Lutheran parish in Brooklyn, where Neuhaus led "A Service of Conscience and Hope," an event that brought together prayer and protest over the injustice of America's war in Vietnam. As hundreds of antiwar activists gave away their draft cards, Neuhaus led them in a rendition of "America the Beautiful." Even then, it was odd if not utterly incongruous for left-wing activists to sing a paean to America—but for all, the song was not for what America was, but for what it could yet be.

Yet as the war de-escalated, he found that his allies on the left were more anti-American than antiwar. It was also about this time that abortion rights were secured through the Supreme Court decision in *Roe v. Wade*. Abortion on its own terms was morally unacceptable to Neuhaus, but it was even more galling for him to hear liberals suggest that some of his poor urban parishioners might have been better off never being born.[33] As Boyagoda put it, "This integration of rights for the poor and rights for the unborn placed him at a critical distance from a left in which private rights—made possible by and indeed protecting implicit race and class privileges—trumped responsibilities for others."[34] In Neuhaus's view, his allies on the left had lost sight of "first things"—not, incidentally, the title of the journal he was to eventually publish.

His move to the political right, then, emerged out of this recognition. But his commitment to the poor and to racial justice never changed. In part, then, his "conversion" to the right was a function of the median point of secular liberalism shifting further to the left on several matters—most importantly abortion. By the 1980s, Neuhaus had become the most forceful theological voice of the neoconservative movement in American politics.

As theologian, pastor, and reformer, Neuhaus believed that the American experiment needed to be understood theologically. In American history, he argued, this interpretive legacy was an unavoidable fact. From the start, it had been central to the nation's self-understanding: the Puritans, the Founders, and later Lincoln, representing the Republic's second founding, all, in various ways, understood America as part of a providential destiny. Against the backdrop of an increasingly secular political culture, Neuhaus's own theological working through of that mythos was a deliberate effort to recover this interpretive tradition and make it relevant again to foster the renewal of liberal democracy.

In his view, many in the past had understood America to be the place of the future *eschaton*, the "New Jerusalem." This was a grave error, for it would lead to nationalist idolatry. Against this view—following Niebuhr—he argued that it was always a mistake to confuse the real, though provisional, virtues of this world for the eternal virtues of the coming kingdom. America *is* Babylon, as are all nations of this world and, in Augustinian terms, the "City of Man" never can and never will become the "City of God."

But for Neuhaus, America was the Babylon we lived in and, for all of its problems and corruptions, it was arguably exceptional for all it had achieved and all it represented. It was therefore worthy of our commitment to make it better. American Christians especially, he contended, "have a responsibility for this country and its influence in the world."[35]

It might seem that a providentialist interpretation of liberal democracy would be peripheral at best and maybe entirely unnecessary to late twentieth-century conservativism, but it was a central pillar for Neuhaus. The reason was rooted in Neuhaus's foundationist political theory: liberal democracy depended upon the foundation provided by natural law. "Natural law is by definition not the property of any one religion or denomination, although it has been the providential task of the Catholic Church to guard and to propose again and again the truths of nature and nature's God that were assumed by the American Founders. 'From the beginning,' wrote the second-century St. Irenaeus, 'God had implanted in the heart of man the precepts of the natural law. Then He reminded him of them by giving the Decalogue.'"[36] Without exception, he argued, the Amer-

ican Founders agreed: "In rebelling against what claimed to be legitimate authority of the British crown, the Founders appealed to the
laws of nature and of nature's God, making the argument that they
were acting upon self-evident truths about inalienable rights with
which we are endowed by the Creator."[37]

Out of this, he argued, "was born what some call the American
civil religion, a religion that is intricately intertwined with the religion that most Americans call Christian."[38] Natural law, then, provided the underpinnings for truth and the ultimate protections for
life, liberty, and justice. This was why Madison pronounced in his
Memorial and Remonstrance, "Before any man can be considered as a
member of Civil Society, he must be considered as a subject of the
Governour of the Universe."[39] Citizens who claimed the rights of
self-governance had to be held to a higher standard. This was also
why, in the First Amendment to the Constitution—"Congress shall
pass no law respecting an establishment of religion, or prohibiting
the free exercise thereof"—the Founders prohibited the state from
controlling religious belief and practice. It not only secured religious
freedom, it also safeguarded the ultimate grounds of moral truth and
justice by which all human institutions would be held to account.

For Neuhaus, a critical turning point in the story occurred in
1947, with the Supreme Court's *Everson* decision. By his telling, the
Court "radically recast [the First Amendment] as the government's
'neutrality' between religion and irreligion, much to the benefit of
irreligion."[40] The consequence is what he famously described as "the
naked public square," by which he meant "the enforced privatization
of religion and religiously informed morality," the result of which
was to exclude all religious faiths that underwrite the natural law
upon which liberal democracy depended.[41]

Absent a religiously informed public life, there were no truths
that grounded the rights to life and liberty and, therefore, the state
could act arbitrarily to redefine or deny those rights altogether. This,
for Neuhaus, was precisely the reason why progressive abortion liberties enshrined in the Supreme Court's 1973 decision in *Roe v. Wade*
were so problematic and why abortion had become the central political concern of the religious Right. Nothing else dramatized more
poignantly for Neuhaus what John Paul II called the "culture of death."

If the lines of division weren't deep enough, Neuhaus antagonized his opponents further by arguing that while "atheists could be citizens" of the United States, it was impossible for an atheist to be "a good citizen." His argument was far more sophisticated than it might seem at first blush, and certainly more complex than his critics gave him credit for, but the net effect of the contention—its symbolic significance in public debate—pointed to the depth of the divisions between antagonists in the culture war. The cleavages separating secularists and orthodox religious believers now "went all the way down"; the differences between them were irreconcilable.

Tribe

Laurence Tribe was a towering figure of another kind and, in his world, every bit as influential. Tribe committed his life to understanding and interpreting a different kind of sacred text—the complex maze of constitutional law. Long before his retirement from Harvard Law School in 2020, he was among the most prominent constitutional scholars in America.

Tribe was born in Shanghai, China, in 1941 to Russian refugees. Because his father had become a U.S. citizen before coming to China, when the Japanese overtook Shanghai, his father was classified an enemy alien and was sent to a concentration camp until the American military liberated the camp in 1945.[42] Tribe, who waited in Shanghai with his mother through those years, developed into something of a *wunderkind*, matriculating at Harvard in 1958 at the age of sixteen, completing degrees in mathematics at twenty and then in law by twenty-four. He clerked for the California and U.S. Supreme Courts and received tenure at Harvard at thirty. Not only a prolific writer, he was an active practitioner of the law. Over the course of his career, he advised presidents, helped to write the constitutions of South Africa and the Czech Republic, and argued thirty-six cases before the U.S. Supreme Court.

As a constitutionalist, he was both personally and professionally committed to liberal democracy and the Enlightenment project that had long underwritten it. But the Constitution has always been contested in its interpretation, comprehensively so in the context of the culture wars. Throughout his career, Tribe was a lion of progressive jurisprudence.

Among all his expansive writing on the law, there is one work that stands out—at least in light of the arguments I am building here. What made *The Invisible Constitution* a significant book was that it offered a "code" for interpreting the Constitution in consistent and coherent ways.[43] It gestured toward the deep structures of culture.

"The visible Constitution," he argued, "necessarily floats in a vast and deep—and, crucially, invisible—ocean of ideas, propositions, recovered memories, and imagined experiences," "a swirling sea of assumptions and experiences"—"tacit postulates"—that not only include "the array of 'higher law' or 'natural law' ideas that many of the Constitution's framers took for granted but also the lessons drawn from thinking about the Constitution and its presuppositions and from the history of struggle to make it real." These were "the invisible, non-textual foundations and facets of [the] Constitution."[44]

The notion that "the 'true' Constitution contains nothing beyond what one can see in or readily infer from its written text" was, for Tribe, a mistaken premise. Both the Right and the Left deride each other when the other invokes it, arguing that it is simply "the disguised repository of the other side's political preferences." And yet both "the Right and the Left invoke that invisible Constitution when it suits their aims." Thus, on the one hand, the "unenumerated rights" tend to arise in arguments in support of the privacy rights of abortion, sexual choice, and medically assisted suicide while, on the other hand, "states' rights" tend to arise around federal statutes dealing with gun control. And yet certain principles found in the invisible Constitution are so "foundational to our legal and political order," so "indispensable to its legitimacy and . . . logically central to our governmental system's coherence" and "binding status" that they cannot be diminished even though they are not formally stated in any part of the written Constitution.[45]

The task of making visible what is invisible, however, is not entirely straightforward. For one, "the content of the Constitution," he argued, "cannot be captured by studying its visible surface." Rather, "we come to know this invisible Constitution only through reasoning to its contents": "constructing it through our reasoning," if you will. Tribe readily acknowledged that there was an "absence of consensus about the contents and application of these constitutional norms," but against Neuhaus's accusation, the invisible Constitution is neither "radically indeterminate" nor "arbitrary." As Tribe put it, "We cannot find in the invisible Constitution anything and everything we might wish."[46]

On the face of it, it sounds as though Tribe was just using a different vocabulary for what Neuhaus called "natural law." He acknowledged that most discussion about the unwritten Constitution over the last century and more "has focused on the degree to which the Constitution's framers and ratifiers viewed such a body of 'natural' law as real, objectively ascertainable, legally binding, and entitled to prevail over mere statutes and executive orders."[47]

Yet Tribe made it clear that he was coming from an entirely different epistemology. "My discussion," he stated emphatically, "proceeds without presupposing any imagined body of 'natural' law."[48] Quoting Christopher Tiedeman writing in 1890, Tribe agreed that "'there is no fixed, invariable list of natural rights'; that such 'rights vary and their characters change with the development of the ethical conceptions of the people,' and that 'the natural rights with which all men are proclaimed in the American Declaration of Independence to be endowed by their Creator, have been developed within the historical memory of man.'"[49] Building on the case, he continued, "Now, more than a century later and perhaps a bit wiser, we live in an era in which no system of beliefs in a universal, higher law could plausibly be regarded as a useful predicate for constitutional discourse and legal analysis. Most of the postulates and theorems that I see as constituting the invisible Constitution are far too historically contingent and institutionally specialized to count as serious candidates for 'natural law' canonization."[50]

And yet, while referencing neither a platonic ideal nor a carefully enumerated "natural law," he did offer eight "suggestive, not exhaustive," "amendable" but "bedrock" "constitutional principles and requirements . . . that go beyond anything that could reasonably be said to follow simply from what the Constitution expressly *says.*" These represent "the content of the invisible Constitution—regardless of *who* is interpreting it, or by what institutional process."[51]

Tribe insisted that his book was "not a selective brief in support of rights widely associated with the cultural and political Left."[52] Indeed, some of these principles, such as the prohibitions against states seceding from the union, are fixed and thus not subject to interpretation. But regarding two invisible principles that involve *substantive* human rights—prohibitions against torture and the limits to what government may control over each person's intimate private life— Tribe came down squarely in favor of the positions dear to the cultural and political Left.

What underwrote the substantive rights of privacy, for Tribe, and what may be the most fundamental value of the invisible Constitution, was the assumption of personal autonomy. For Tribe, autonomy was "indispensable to democracy." When you get down to it, "self-government writ large is the overarching theme of our Constitution," and "personal self-government," or autonomy, no less so. It is true, he acknowledged, that none of these rights—the right of reproductive autonomy, the right to die with dignity, or the right to sexual choice, among others—were "'enumerated' anywhere in the Constitution or its express amendments"—nor the right of autonomy itself—but all the same, he argued, the invisible Constitution included "crucial elements of respect for personal dignity and autonomy," the way, to take the example of abortion, "respect for the premises of self-government might entail embrace of substantive liberties such as reproductive freedom." In this instance, he argued, the "Constitution must at the very least treat with special concern a woman's liberty and equality interest in determining for herself whether to carry a pregnancy to term or to end it without giving birth to a child—whatever the countervailing interests in unborn life and whatever the authority of states to accommodate those interests." The virtual double helix of liberty and equality rooted in the almost sacred rights of individual autonomy also comprised the invisible constitutional facet that finally decriminalized homosexuality. The primacy of these core values can all be found "in the interstices of specific constitutional protections."[53]

Contested Sources of Authority

To the extent that Neuhaus and Tribe exemplified intelligent and thoughtful representatives of the opposing sides of the culture war— rare exceptions to the common incendiary sloganeering of the movement activists and their organizations—it is clear that more separated their views than different positions on public policy. Even their disciplinary areas of expertise—theology and law—pointed to different cosmologies.

Both figures demonstrated a strong commitment to the Enlightenment ideal of achieving truth through reason. Yet when seen against each other, they reveal the evolution of the long-standing tension between the transcendent and immanent foundations of reason and truth. Neuhaus and Tribe each follow their own beliefs to their logical ends in their different understandings of authority—of what is, finally, authoritative. For Neuhaus, it was God, known through Scripture and the traditions of the church, including its natural law traditions that are authoritative in public life. For Tribe, authority was embodied in the reason-bearing and autonomous subject-agent. Revealed religion versus autonomous rationality.[54]

These convictions were neither intellectual language-games nor flights into philosophical abstraction, but rather core principles that had tangible consequences for ordinary citizens. On what terms, after all, could claims be made to sovereignty over a woman's body, the unborn child's body, the bodies of straight people, gay and transgendered people, the bodies of minorities and immigrants, the bodies of the elderly and the disabled, and more abstractly, the "body politic"?

Thus, because of his conviction that all human beings are fashioned in the image and likeness of God, Neuhaus took it as a first principle that all human beings possess an inherent and equal dignity, a dignity that must be respected and protected equally under the law. This was not only true within the Christian tradition, in his view, but a foundational principle of the American constitutional order. To respect the equal dignity of all human beings meant liberating minorities from a system of racial oppression, providing for the poor and disadvantaged, not squandering the lives of young men and women in pointless wars, and protecting the unborn from slaughter.

But if God is not in the picture, at least in any tangible way, nor are the traditions that see God as sovereign over all of life—if, instead, the dignity of individuals is rooted in their capacity to choose for themselves how they will live, then it is incumbent upon the law to defend the rights of those people or groups from the coercive power of the state. This, for Tribe, was a fundamental principle of the American constitutional order, and following that principle meant, among other things, protecting the rights of women to choose to terminate a pregnancy, the rights of gay and transgendered people to live and love as they desire, the right to die with dignity, and so on.

It was due to these differences that the constitutional jurisprudence over church and state matters had long been a place of pitched battle. I've already gestured toward Neuhaus's view. For him, the metaphor of "the wall of separation" referred to by Thomas Jefferson in his letter to the Danbury Baptists should be low and porous, allowing institutions of faith to make legitimate claims on the ordering of public life. After all, he argued, the First Amendment religion clauses were in service to religious freedom. "There is really only one religion clause or provision, made up of two parts, each related to the other as the end is related to the means. The free exercise of religion is the end, and non-establishment of religion is an important means instrumental to that end."[55] There is, then, no inherent conflict between free exercise and no-establishment. For Tribe, by contrast, the wall of separation should be high and impermeable in ways that constrain or neuter the public claims of religion, especially as they undermine the autonomy of rational individual choice. The First Amendment religion clauses, in his view, give primacy to the no-establishment clause. For Tribe, there is a "zone which the free exercise clause carves out of the establishment clause for permissible accommodation of religious interests. This carved-out area might be characterized as the zone of permissible accommodation."[56]

Rooted in their competing assumptions, one read the First Amendment religion clauses as mainly about the freedom *of* religion and the other read it as mainly about the freedom *from* religion. In its net effect, the highly technical conflict over the proper meaning of the First Amendment religion clauses is fundamentally about authority. It was also widely read as the subtext of the controversy over abortion. As Tribe put it for his side, "The question [turns on] a decision as to what characteristics should be regarded as defining a human being." This decision "entails not an inference or demonstration from generally shared premises, whether factual or moral, but a statement of religious faith upon which people will invariably differ widely." Because preventing an alliance between church and state is "the 'first and most immediate purpose' [of] the establishment clause," the absence of a demonstrable secular purpose in a law makes "excessive entanglement" of church and state inevitable.[57]

Beyond the technical interpretation of constitutional jurisprudence, both Tribe and Neuhaus grounded the popular legitimacy of their positions on authority in rather sweeping appeals to the beliefs of "the vast majority of Americans."[58] Both asserted that the majority opinion of Americans rendered their position beyond dispute. But, needless to say, their positions remained endlessly disputed.

Incommensurable Differences and the Inevitable Hitler Trope

In the culture war, the polarization of public discourse was comprehensive in ways that made it difficult to imagine compromise, even if competing sides were willing to try to find it. This was true for Neuhaus and Tribe as well. After all, for both (and for each of the contending sides they represented), fundamental principles of justice were at stake. The opposing cosmologies, the utter intemperance of the rhetoric, and the complexity of legal-technical positions of actual legal and policy issues reinforced the depth of division.

In the broader public discourse, it had become a common tactic to deliver what is considered the coup de grâce for ending the public debate over one issue or another by associating the other side with the definitive evil of the twentieth century: Hitler, the Third Reich, and the Holocaust. Both sides have done so promiscuously in the hope of ending debate in their favor. Interestingly, it is because of their sophistication and not in spite of it that both Neuhaus and Tribe did the same.[59] Both are worth quoting at length.

For Neuhaus:

> One of the lawyers who prosecuted the Nazis in the war crimes trials explained how people could have acted so savagely: "There is only one step to take. . . . You have only to decide that one group of human beings have lost human rights." But, the objection is heard, such an observation is irrelevant to our discussion of bioethics and the Holocaust. In abortion, in fetal transplants, in embryo experimentation, in new methods of fertilization, in withdrawing food and water from the comatose . . . we are not dealing with "human beings." But we must ask whether such an objection is not touchingly naive. It assumes one favored outcome of the

debate that is still underway over who or what is a human
being.

"There is only one step to take," the prosecutor said. In
the case of the debates in which we are now embroiled, I
suspect that step was in the adoption of the idea of "quality
of life" as an indicator of who is and who is not to count as a
human being. Then they spoke of *lebensunwertes Leben*, life
that is unworthy of life. It is by no means clear to many
thoughtful people how we, in principle or in practice, distinguish *lebensunwertes Leben* from a "quality of life index." But,
we insist, it *should* be clear. After all, in the Holocaust they
were killing actual human beings, people who were undeniably, not just potentially or marginally, *real people with real
rights*. But, once again, it seems that we are found to be beg-
ging the question. It is exactly the point that they *did* deny
what we take to be undeniable. Similarly, . . . many today
deny what an earlier generation and, it would seem, most
Americans today take to be undeniable.[60]

For Tribe:

The abortion policies of Nazi Germany best exemplify the
potential evil of entrusting government with the power to
say which pregnancies are to be terminated and which are
not. Nazi social policy, like that of Romania, vigorously asserted the state's right to ensure population growth. But Nazi
policy went even further. Following the maxim that "Your
body does not belong to you," it proclaimed the utter absence
of any individual right in the matter and made clear that
abortion constituted a governmental tool for furthering Nazi
theories of "Aryan" supremacy and genetic purity.

Nazi propaganda constantly emphasized the duty of
"Aryans" to have large families. Family planning clinics were
shut down, often on the ground of alleged ties with communism. The Third Reich made every effort to control contra-
ception, ultimately banning the production and distribution
of contraceptives in 1941. The state, largely at the behest of
SS leader Heinrich Himmler, abandoned its commitment to

"bourgeois" marriage and undertook to promote the "voluntary" impregnation of "suitable women." Allowances were paid to women, married or not, for having children.

Abortion and even its facilitation were, in general, serious criminal offenses in Nazi Germany; a network of spies and secret police sought out abortionists, and prosecutions were frequent. By 1943 the penalty for performing an abortion on a "genetically fit" woman was death; those on whose premises abortions were performed risked prison sentences.[61]

Clearly more was involved in these two statements than rhetorical posturing. Both passages convey the deep suspicion that their opponents embrace an authoritarianism that can exist only at the cost of human liberty and, perhaps ultimately, human life.

At an Impasse

Neuhaus and Tribe were unusual in the depth and sophistication of their reflections on these important questions. But their reflections spoke to social and cultural developments that were much broader in scope and profound in historical significance. Against the backdrop of centuries of animosity and violence between Protestants and Catholics and between Christians and Jews, there has been a historically unprecedented realignment of these relationships grounded in the question of authority. As I discussed in *Culture Wars: The Struggle to Define America*, conservative Catholics, evangelical Protestants, and Orthodox and Conservative Jews discovered that they now had more in common with each other than they did with liberal and progressive members of their own tradition. In the same way, liberal Protestants, progressive Catholics, and Reform and secular Jews generally had more in common with one another than they did with the more orthodox members of their own tradition. What united the conservative and orthodox in these traditions was a belief in and commitment to a transcendent authority mediated through the authority of Scripture, the pope and the Catholic tradition, or the Talmud. In the same way, the liberal and progressive in these traditions were held together by their commitment to an immanent authority— whether science, history, personal experience, or subjective intuition.

Broad features of their world-picture related to policy positions on family values, sexuality, education, and the like, reflecting these different and competing sources of authority.

Neuhaus and Tribe, then, represented the intellectualizations of opposing sides of the culture war as each side grounded its visions of ordering public life in contrasting sources of authority. Both were thoughtful and principled actors operating within philosophical streams that, at this point, still remained recognizable within the liberal democratic tradition. Though diametrically opposed, rival sides were still recognizable to each other.[62] Each affirmed and operated within one strand of the hybrid-Enlightenment; each believed that there were more or less "objective" truths understandable through reason, not least of which was the Constitution itself. Both sides operated within "an account of language and the world that allowed each to characterize debate as about the truth of propositions of law and that there is a fact of the matter as to the resolution of the debate."[63]

But they also represented a deepening of the epistemological and metaphysical contradictions that were always present within the liberal tradition and within the hybrid-Enlightenment that underwrote it. Given their starting points, those contradictions predictably led to an impasse through which figures, even those as capable as Neuhaus and Tribe, were either unwilling or unable to find a way beyond. Neither side would seek to accommodate the other—nor could accommodate the other within their public philosophy. Neither side had the capacity to cast a vision that could be inclusive of the other's deepest commitments. They only could assert, as they often did against the other, "This is not what America is all about."

If the possibilities of any kind of organically generated solidarity yielded no compromise between Tribe and Neuhaus, then it was all the more difficult among the special-interest groups on each side of the cultural divide. Not only were competing factions divided philosophically, they were further divided by the polarizing rhetoric of social media and the interests that fueled them.

A Turning Point

Through the 1990s and the early years of the twenty-first century, key figures in the social science establishment had argued that there was no culture war to speak of beyond the ideological enthusiasms of a small number of activists.[64] Some even called it a myth.[65] In reality, through the last decade of the twentieth and the early decades of the twenty-first centuries, the culture war had evolved significantly. On or around 2008, it became apparent that a fundamentally new and different moment in the evolving culture wars was emerging. The conflict intensified, shifted its orientation, and in the process, transformed both the Left and the Right.

Intensification

There were several reasons why the culture war intensified. One factor had to do with the end of the Cold War in 1989. Lacking a common enemy around which the nation could find common resistance, the opposition against which national identity and solidarity is formed turned inward, from the external threat of the Soviet Union to the internal threat each side perceived coming from their antagonists on the other side of the cultural divide. The terrorist attack on the World Trade Center and the Pentagon on September 11, 2001, seemed, at the time, to bring a cessation to the conflict and a rare moment of national unity. The menace of Islamic radicalism to the West and America certainly fit the profile of a "useful" enemy. But as life returned to "normal" in the ensuing years, the specter of radical Islam receded and with it, the weakening of its galvanizing force. What followed was an expansion of the conflict to include other issues and accompanying rhetorical escalation. Symbolically, this was performed with ritual regularity as the conservative antipathy toward Clinton morphed into a progressive hatred of Bush, which turned into the conservative hostility toward Obama and then, of course, to the progressive loathing of Trump.

Yet another factor was the steady advance progressives enjoyed on several fronts, most conspicuously in the march toward gay rights, long the *bête noir* of Christian conservatives. What began as a small stream of victories for gay rights through the 1970s and 1980s became a surge through the 1990s and a minor tidal wave from the 2000s onward.[66] The legalization of gay marriage in 2015 in the United States was only the most visible triumph; there were many other less prominent successes in overcoming discrimination in employment, housing, and adoption; the legalization of gays serving in the military; the increasing prominence and legitimacy of transgender advocacy; and the recognition of nonbinary gender. These developments occurred in parallel with (and no doubt because of) the proliferation of local and national organizations in the United States and beyond that promoted gay, lesbian, and transexual rights—five before 1970, ten in the 1970s, nineteen in the 1980s, thirty-six in the 1990s, seventy-one between 2000 and 2009, and sixty-six from 2010 to 2020.[67] Through these legal and political successes, conservatives saw the ground they stood upon slipping away.

These factors generated factional pressure over the years, yet in the fallout of the Great Recession of 2008 and 2009, cultural conflict became even more intense. The cultural conflict that had defined so much of American politics leading up to this moment had been a conflict taking place *within* the broad middle class. Yes, there had always been class elements to this conflict, but they were mainly the shades of difference between the lower-middle and upper-middle classes in an economy that was expanding.

With the Great Recession, the objective conditions of middle-class life changed significantly. Members of the highly educated, professional upper-middle class were certainly surprised, even shaken, by the economic contraction. They experienced a paper loss in wealth from the drop in the markets, but relatively few were traumatized by its harshest effects—indeed, as the stock market reemerged and resumed its bullish ways in the subsequent decade, the prosperity of the professional and managerial class improved. Not so for those in the less well-educated, nonprofessional middle, lower middle, and working class who, through unemployment, foreclosure, and the loss of opportunity took the full impact of the economic collapse on the chin. As a social class, they never fully recovered.

What aggravated the social class divisions further was the fact that the financial crisis of 2008 had been engineered by large banking and finance companies and their technocrats. Yet virtually without exceptions, the managerial elite suffered no consequences for their recklessness; indeed, with massive bailouts given to the banking, finance, and insurance industries, they were fully compensated. In the end, it was ordinary Americans who paid the price of the financial collapse.

In short, the division in American public culture was now overlaid by a deepening division in social position and economic well-being. This meant that the culture war was not only over competing cosmologies but also over concrete life chances. A highly educated and progressive social and cultural elite had consolidated status, wealth, and influence; their less well-educated, poorer, and more conservative counterparts found themselves marginalized and disempowered, their horizons of opportunity shrinking.

Finally, and not least of the factors contributing to the intensification of the culture wars, was the candidacy and eventual election of Donald Trump to the presidency. Despite his extraordinary privilege, he understood both the class and cultural resentments of the Republican base and played to their anger with mischievous ease. Trump, for his base, was the norm-breaker who would challenge the smug presumptions of the progressive establishment in the media, technology, entertainment, higher education, and the government, often publicly saying outrageous things with an impunity that his supporters didn't enjoy. In this way, Trump effectively mobilized his base and galvanized his opposition.

Reorientation

Progressives found Trump and his presidency to be comprehensively objectionable. His repeated distortions of the truth, his mockery and bullying of political enemies, and his attacks on key governing institutions were all beyond the pale. Yet culturally, it was his statements and behavior denigrating women and minorities that generated the greatest offense and catalyzed the strongest, most enduring, and even global reaction: in the #MeToo movement in August 2017 and the Black Lives Matter movement in May 2020.

The point bears emphasis. It wasn't as though men behaved honorably toward women before 2017 or that there was no violent discrimination against Blacks before 2020. Obviously, there is a long history of repugnant attitudes and unethical and even criminal behavior well before this, even during the years of the Obama administration. There was even a prehistory of both the #MeToo and Black Lives Matter movements.[68] Yet it was during the Trump presidency that these countermovements captured the world's attention and fundamentally shifted the public debate.

Certainly, these movements marked a clear moment of reckoning over long-standing sexual harassment, assault, and abuse and the ongoing discrimination toward Black Americans, particularly in the realm of criminal justice. Given the video archive, there was no ethical ambiguity about the murder of George Floyd in 2020 at the hands of the police. But would the officers involved be exonerated as they had in the Trayvon Martin case in 2013, the Michael Brown case in 2014, the Eric Garner case in 2014 and again in 2019, and in endless others? And would men in positions of power who were well known for harassing and abusing women continue to get away with it? On the surface, questions of justice were very much in play.

Culturally, however, these movements were doing the boundary work of reaffirming the lines of an emerging progressive public ethics. For a man who for ample reason was perceived as racist and sexist to inhabit the highest office in the land symbolically gave implicit sanction to racial discrimination and sexual harassment. The violation of these ethical boundaries was regressive in the extreme and it would not stand. Many of the white men and white police officers who were actually implicated in these atrocities were called to account, but they were also symbolical substitutes for the person in the White House who was regarded as most culpable by virtue of the permission his office implicitly provided. Sociologically, a reaction was inevitable.

From the 1980s through the 2010s, the culture wars were fought mainly in the white middle class. Through these years, abortion and gay rights had been the flash points of conflict. Neither of these receded from public controversy. But the #MeToo movement breathed new life into the claims of feminism, and Black Lives Matter had moved race—how to think of racial difference, how to teach about the history of race in America, how to address ongoing racial discrimination—from the margins of national debate, where it had been since the civil rights movement, to the center.

And the Transformation

People commonly speak of the "Left" and the "Right" as though they were stable and mostly unchanging categories. That, of course, has never been true. It is not surprising, then, that the intensification and reorientation of the culture war have also been accompanied by fundamental transformations of the Left and the Right. These transformations were twofold. The first was positional, in terms of the constituencies and interests they addressed. The second was substantive, in terms of the message they crafted for their constituencies.

Of the Left

Through most of the twentieth century, politics in economically developed countries was defined primarily in economic terms in light of the inequalities of life chances generated by capitalism. For the Left, then, the focus of attention was on the condition of workers and the workplace, the solidarity and leverage of trade unions and organized labor against corporate interest, initiatives of social welfare for the impoverished and destitute, and various other calls to fairly redistribute the wealth of the nation in the name of general social welfare. The working class, in turn, supported those political parties that advocated these progressive policies. Political struggle reflected economic conflict. This was true of politics not only in Western Europe but in America as well.

And so it was that the American working class overwhelmingly supported the Democratic Party from the New Deal in the 1930s right through the Reagan administration in the 1980s. By contrast, the Republican Party had long been viewed as the party of the wealthy, the privileged, and the powerful, and thus the party of big money and corporate interests against labor.

But in the context of the culture war, this old configuration has been turned inside out. Much of the architecture for this transformation was laid out in the mid-1970s by a young, recently elected class of Democratic congressmen, the "Watergate Babies," who challenged the Democratic establishment. As Matt Stoller described it, the populist politics the Democratic Party had long championed was based on the idea that political and economic freedom were deeply entangled, that big business and democracy were, at root, rivals. And so among the critical changes they brought about were to the U.S. House Committee on Banking and Currency. For decades that committee had been focused on keeping financial power in check by waging a constant war on concentrations of economic power. They did this through "investigating corporate monopolies, high interest rates, the Federal Reserve, and big banks."[69] In the mid-1970s, the Watergate Babies abandoned this commitment under the assumption that concentrations of wealth were no longer a problem. The real question, they believed, was how to manage concentrations of wealth: either through the private sector, guided by libertarian principles (the conservative position of the Republican Party), or through the redistributionist priorities of a large state (the progressive position of the new Democratic Party). The consequences of these changes have been playing out ever since.

An accumulating body of evidence now shows that progressives have come to represent the privileged and the powerful. From the 1980s to the 2020s, the annual Forbes 400 list of the wealthiest Americans has shifted steadily to the left in terms of partisan contributions to progressive causes and the Democratic Party. And it isn't just the wealthiest donors who have shifted to the left in these ways but also highly educated professionals such as lawyers, physicians, software engineers, and technology executives. Likewise, from the Great Recession in 2008 to 2018, both gross domestic product and household income increased in Democratic districts and declined in Republican districts. Likewise, in educational attainment, the number of adults with a college degree grew significantly in Democratic districts compared to Republican districts, where it stayed roughly the same.[70] While conservatives and progressives have always spoken to different sectors of the American economy, their audiences reversed. Progressives now controlled the places most central to economic power and prosperity, and in the process, many progressives have grown distant from the day-to-day struggles of working-class Americans.[71]

Accompanying this shift was a transformation of progressive ideology from the interests of economic populism it historically represented to a social libertarianism and ultimately to the post-material and symbolic interests surrounding marginal identities—in short, identitarian politics.

These transformations began when the institutional carrier of progressive politics moved from labor unions to universities and its chief advocates shifted from working-class liberals and socialists to middle- and upper-middle-class college students, professors, and administrators. With these changes, the center of gravity within progressivism shifted to an orientation defined by the primacy of individual autonomy and self-determination, a distrust of all public authority, the abandonment of traditional religious, familial, and sexual norms, and an enthusiasm for social, sexual, bio-chemical, and religious experimentation. The agenda progressivism presented to the world was now an agenda of sexual freedom, feminism, gay rights, and environmentalism. By the 1980s, the critique of capitalism and advocacy on behalf of labor unions and the working class had largely receded from the docket. Not only had these new progressives become alienated from the old Left, they had become alienated from the values, beliefs, and habits of life of "middle America" as well.

By the late 1980s, the Left was to evolve further from its roots in political economy. The conditions for the emergence of a new sort of identity politics were coming into play. To be sure, identity politics has never been absent from democratic politics. It long predated the present, most importantly as it reflected the interests of women and Black Americans, but also Catholics, Jews, the Irish, and many others. Yet identity politics was never about identity as such, but rather identity as understood through the prism of economic fairness and political rights. Questions of recognition and respect were always assumed to follow from the right to work, a good job for a good wage, unfettered opportunity, and mobility unimpeded by bias and discrimination.

Identity politics, however, took a therapeutic turn and came to be centered on identity *as such*—as the politics of recognition and dignity, whether for women, people of color, gays, lesbians, transexuals, the disabled, and so on. Identity politics was *not only* therapeutic in character. Material injury, of course, persisted through economic discrimination, prejudice in criminal justice, police brutality, early death, enduring social stigma, and the like. And against these, policies were challenged and changed, voters were mobilized, new alliances were forged, and people were sent to jail. But a new element within the politics of recognition, psychological and emotional in character, had been introduced that went beyond these facts. The most prominent examples of this were the calls for safe spaces or trigger warnings and admonitions against microaggressions and the like.

The roots of this therapeutic turn can be traced to the radical expressions of multiculturalism. Even in the late 1980s, there was a conviction that the injury suffered by minorities was at least as much psychological as it was material. "Physical enslavement," one scholar had argued, has been succeeded by "psychological enslavement."[72] As a task force report on minorities in education put it in 1989, the "systematic bias toward European culture and its derivatives has had a terribly damaging effect on the psyche of young people of African, Asian, Latino, and Native American descent."[73] The self-esteem of young people of color had suffered under such conditions, and until the white monopoly on minority minds was broken, genuine liberation would be impossible.[74] The implication of this assessment was a belief in the need to highlight the group—or, in Schlesinger's terminology, "tribal"—identities, histories, and contributions of those formerly excluded.[75]

Progressives like Schlesinger worried that identitarian tendencies would have destructive consequences. In 1991, forty-two years after he had published *The Vital Center*, Schlesinger already could see a tragedy unfolding. "The vision of America," he wrote in *The Disuniting of America*, "as melted into one people prevailed through most of the two centuries of the history of the United States. But the twentieth century has brought forth a new and opposing vision." He recognized the good that came out of this. American culture "began at last to give shamefully overdue recognition to the achievements of minorities subordinated and spurned during the high noon of Anglo dominance. American education began at last to acknowledge the existence and significance of the great swirling world beyond Europe. All this is to the good." Yet Schlesinger recognized that something more profound had occurred as well. "Pressed too far," he wrote, the progressive idea of diversity "rejects the unifying vision of individuals from all nations melted into a new race." "Instead of a transformative nation with an identity all its own, America in this new light is seen as preservative of diverse alien identities. . . . The multiethnic dogma abandons historic purposes, replacing assimilation by fragmentation, integration by separatism. It belittles *unum* and glorifies *pluribus*."[76] His worries came to pass as the more extreme elements of multiculturalism had now spread beyond education into most institutions and within the Left were mainstreamed as an undisputed dogma.

In all of this, progressives were still concerned for the plight of those who suffered—victims of oppression near and far. This, of course, was the ideological link between progressivism past and progressivism present. But the primary source of oppression was no longer understood to be capitalism, but rather those *agents* who have possessed power and privilege within all oppressive systems: overwhelmingly, white people and males—and white males in particular.

I hasten to add that progressives had not lost sight of enduring injustice. It was plain to see in the patterns of policing and criminal justice, housing, banking, and employment. There was still much work to do. But the rhetorical and ideological center of gravity had shifted. The progressive claim to moral legitimacy was less the demand for economic equality or even economic fairness, and more the demand for racial, ethnic, gender, and sexual inclusion and the recognition it implied. Built on the gains generated by three generations of multicultural education, "diversity" defined by the demand for recognition and approval became the byword. The advantage of this ideological shift was that it created the artifice of concern for the marginalized while retaining the newly found economic, educational, and political advantages of elites. By shifting its focus from equality to diversity, progressives could now downplay, ignore, or otherwise dismiss the interests of struggling working-class people and their families—a demographic that would eventually include millions and millions of Trump voters.

The irony runs deeper still. Not only did the new progressives abandon the critique of capitalism and their defense of the interests of the working class and poor, they came to embrace bourgeois economic and cultural values. The injuries that had become more central to identity politics would now be evaluated against upper-middle-class norms of status, material comfort, mental health, and social independence, which meant that the measure of inclusion was now the income, lifestyles, and social respectability of the middle and upper-middle class.[77]

In these ways, progressives came to redefine America's meritocracy. *Unlike* the WASP meritocracy, the new meritocracy would be, in principle, multicultural (though the progressive activist demographic is overwhelmingly white).[78] But *like* the old meritocracy, wealth and privilege would be concentrated in ways that would be self-protective of its status, political power, and economic interest through such strategies as exclusionary zoning, legacy college admissions, favorable tax law, and barriers to economic and educational opportunities. And very much *like* the old meritocracy, perhaps even more so, upward mobility into the echelons of the elite would be accompanied by a corresponding elitism, the smug sense of being on the winning side of history.

The most obvious and also the most pervasive mechanism for protecting the power, privilege, and status of the new meritocrats, though, would be through the development of distinct linguistic innovations—ways of speaking (politically correct speech codes—words like *Latinx*, *whiteness*, *lgbtqia2s*, and *uterus-bearer*) and thinking (woke attitudes toward defunding the police and so on) that would distinguish "upper whites" from "lower whites," who is "in" and who is "out." These would be immediately recognizable status markers that would demonstrate what political faction one belonged to. And not just voters, but anyone who aspired to be upwardly mobile. In this respect, elite higher education—whatever else it might provide by way of specialized knowledge—had become a finishing school for those who aspired to advance within the leading institutions of the professional, managerial, and technocratic echelons of the social order. The young would not only have a credential or two at the end of their formal education, they would also know what to think, how to speak, and how to act in ways that were appropriate to membership in the class/cultural faction. It had become a central part of the process of admission into the dominant class.

While the tensions between the old rank-and-file progressives along with old-fashioned liberals and the new identitarian Left are deeply entrenched, momentum clearly shifted to the latter, the former now operating from a defensive posture. The ascendancy of the identitarian Left has not only enflamed conservatives but divided progressive organizations and alienated the Democratic base.[79] As one Democratic strategist put it, "Many working-class voters . . . believe that, unless they subscribe to this emerging worldview and are willing to speak its language, they will be condemned as reactionary, intolerant, and racist by those who purport to represent their interests."[80] The vanguard of the identitarian Left has pressed its advantage, demonstrating its ascendency through periodic rituals of social and moral purification (cancellation, scapegoating, doxing, and so on), even among their own. These purity fetishes and their ritual enactments are, in the end, nothing more than expressions of boundary work against any who manifest deviation from identitarian dogma.

Of the Right

While not understood sociologically by most on the right, the intent of these new speech codes and the cultural commitments they represented brought into relief both the cultural and economic alienation of working-class, small-town, and more often than not, religious people. This conservative half of the American electorate was now doubly estranged. The demographic from which most conservative voters came were looking very much like "losers" at this stage in the culture war and, thus, those whose views, values, or priorities were just not to be taken seriously. And they got the message. Infamous gestures of condescension highlighted for the working class just how progressives perceived them. In his 2008 presidential campaign, for example, Barack Obama described small-town voters in Pennsylvania and other states as "bitter" over lost jobs, which caused them to "cling to guns or religion or antipathy toward people who aren't like them." Eight years later, Hillary Clinton described a large swath of Trump supporters as "racist, sexist, homophobic, xenophobic, Islamophobic—you name it" and labeled them as "deplorable," "irredeemable" and "not America."[81] These were only the most prominent illustrations of a contempt that was pervasive. The sting, not surprisingly, did little to encourage social or electoral comity.[82]

The demographic and ideological heart of the conservative movement through the early decades of the culture war was a coalition between economic conservatives and religious and cultural conservatives. Money came from business interests, but the electoral power came from small-town, suburban, middle- and working-class white households in the Midwest and South.

But the coalition had changed. As to the interests of business, after the Great Recession, as we've seen, economic elites moved decisively to the left, as they accommodated the ethical agenda of Black Lives Matter, the #MeToo movement, and gay and trans rights through changes in hiring and HR policies, corporate donations, and corporate messaging and advertising. There was a wide range of reasons for this shift, but among them was certainly the brand-deflating vulgarity and populism of the Trump administration and the new Republican Party. As for rank-and-file conservatives, they may have remained religiously conservative through these years, but they were no longer leading with a religious message. Indeed, the Republican conventions continued to have the feel of a religious revival, but the cultural logics of the movement had changed fundamentally.

As a *public* philosophy, conservatism largely abandoned its *public* appeal to religious faith. Christian conservatives still made up the plurality of the conservative electorate, but the public appeal to religious ideals and the effort to ground conservatism in Christian theology had all but evaporated. A transition point occurred in the years immediately after the Great Recession. Activist conservatism regrouped into the Tea Party movement, a fiscally conservative movement mainly comprising libertarians and small-town and rural populists who were committed to lowering taxes, reducing the national debt, decreasing the federal budget deficit, and above all, opposing the Obama administration's efforts to universalize government-sponsored healthcare. The pragmatic and economic turn was also a largely secular turn.

There was one exception. Leading up to the election of Donald Trump, a very small number of fundamentalist pastors proposed that Trump was the modern-day equivalent of King Cyrus, the Persian king whose story is recounted in Isaiah 45.[83] Cyrus conquered Babylon in the sixth century BCE and ended the Babylonian captivity of the Israelites. Cyrus was a figure of deliverance. Though not a Jew and not one who worshipped the God of Israel, he nevertheless was an instrument—a "vessel," as proponents put it—of divine purpose to allow the people of God to return to their homeland. The new Cyrus, it was proposed, was Trump. No one, not even evangelicals, would deny that Trump was flawed by his narcissism, his crude philandering and misogyny, and his habitual lying, but the Cyrus story provided a way for Christians to reconcile his personal flaws with what they believed was his divinely ordained role in restoring a Christian America. Yet most Christians, including the mainstream evangelical institutions, regarded the Cyrus allegory as far-fetched at best.[84] To most everyone else, it was just kooky. Either way, its eccentricity only reinforced the absence of a thoughtful Christian cosmology as the grounds of its political vision.

The turn away from theology or any other biblical rationale for conservative activism constituted a fundamental shift for the Christian Right. This turn was bolstered by a generational shift. Most prominently, this was seen in the death of its founding leadership (including Ed McAteer in 2004, Jerry Falwell Sr. in 2007, D. James Kennedy in 2007, Paul Weyrich in 2008, Ed Dobson in 2015, Tim LaHaye in 2016, Phyllis Schlafly in 2016, and Pat Robertson in 2023) or their effective retirement from public life (such as James Dobson, Gary Bauer, and Beverly LaHaye). It was further bolstered either by the closing of key organizations in the movement (like the Moral Majority and the Religious Roundtable) or their decline and marginalization (for example, Christian Coalition, Christian Voice, Eagle Forum, Concerned Women of America, the Family Research Council) from mainstream politics. Finally, there were no new organizations to replace these. Apart from Franklin Graham (son of Billy Graham) and Jerry Falwell Jr.—two figures who were more extreme than their fathers—the generation that followed the founding generation of leaders had no taste for open conflict explicitly in the name of Christianity.

The historical significance of this shift is astonishing. In the middle of the nineteenth century, evangelical Christianity was the center of public culture. Its leadership was fully established in the elite colleges and universities, the most prominent urban pulpits, and the most vibrant social organizations. For good or ill, depending on one's perspective, its vision for the nation provided the cultural logics by which public life was ordered and solidarity established and sustained. A century and a half later, evangelical Christianity was an aging demographic, but still quite robust as a voting bloc. As a movement, however, it had been routed from the culture-forming centers of public life—now all but absent from the upper echelons of higher education, the arts, journalism, advertising, entertainment, fashion, and technology. This development was reinforced by the boundary work of the identitarian Left, whose linguistic codes, shaming, and ritual censuring had the effect of excluding conservatives—not least, Evangelical Christians—from the higher echelons of the culture industry. As a movement making claims on the public and political life of the nation, an explicit Christian faith and its ethics were absent, its most serious theologians and most thoughtful pastors silent. They found themselves outside the boundaries of the cultural mainstream for the first time.

The immensity of this shift was seen not only in the demographic's religious or theological silence, but also in its embrace of the cultural logic of its progressive opponents. Historically, conservative Christianity grounded its appeals in majoritarian terms—its interests squarely aligned with appeals to a "common morality." This was why conservative Christians could refer to themselves as the "silent majority," later the "moral majority." It was progressives who spoke for minorities by invoking the language of freedom and of rights.

It was through these years that lower-middle- and working-class white churchgoers came to see themselves as minorities whose way of life was being threatened. They were now victims of a secular, cosmopolitan elite. They cited as evidence a range of instances, including the Marine court-martialed for refusing to take down a Bible verse taped to her desk, a fire chief in Atlanta fired for self-publishing a book critical of LGBTQ sexuality, challenges to the accreditation of Christian schools, and people hurling epithets such as "hater" and "bigot" at Christians.[85] Books such as *Persecution: How Liberals Are Waging War Against Christians, Dangerous to Believe: Religious Freedom and Its Enemies,* and *God Less America: Real Stories from the Front Lines of the Attack on Traditional Values* reinforced the claim. In fact, the claim reflected a broad perception among evangelicals and conservative Catholics that they were the new targets of discrimination. Surveys found that "religious liberty is on the decline in America," that half of all Americans generally and 80 percent of white evangelicals believed that "discrimination against Christians is as big a problem as discrimination against other groups, including blacks and minorities," and that while two-thirds of religious leaders reported that they had *never* been "persecuted" for their Christian faith, over three-fourths said that they *expected* to face persecution for their faith in coming years.[86]

In this regard, conservative Christians viewed secular progressives as hypocritical. Why, they reasoned, was it possible to advocate on behalf of Black rights, immigrant rights, women's rights, gay and transgendered rights but not the rights of white Americans without being stigmatized as racist, sexist, or generally bigoted? Their recourse as a "cultural minority," "victims" of an oppressive cultural elite, was to invoke their own rights. As Andrew Lewis showed, this is precisely the logic now used to defend their interests in the culture war.[87]

In *Masterpiece Cakeshop v. Colorado Civil Rights Commission*, for example, the question was whether a baker could be compelled by nondiscrimination laws to bake a custom wedding cake for a same-sex couple. The conservative Christian legal advocacy organization defending the baker didn't argue that gay marriage was immoral or that the Colorado nondiscrimination policy was unconstitutional. Rather, it argued that the nondiscrimination policy represented the government attempting to force the baker to engage in "compelled speech" in violation of liberal free speech doctrines. Similarly, in *National Institute of Family Life Advocates v. Becerra*, the plaintiffs challenged the California Reproductive Freedom, Accountability, Comprehensive Care, and Transparency Act, which required pro-life "crisis pregnancy" centers to post notices about the availability of low-cost abortions. Legal representation for the crisis pregnancy centers sought to contest its enforcement, arguing that the act permitted the government to force citizens to engage in speech without weighty justification.

These cases were not merely illustrative of a tactical change or a shift in strategy; rather, they revealed an embrace of the cultural logic of identity politics long championed by progressives. Conservative Christians were now "victims of oppression" too, and they approached the defense of their interests *as* victims. The embrace of identitarian logics went further still. The framing of politics as identity rather than ideology brought into relief the racial character of the Christian Right. The new salience of "whiteness," "white masculinity," "white Christian nationalism," and so on was happily embraced by large swaths of the conservative rank and file and the extremes of the conservative media ecosystem.[88]

The embrace of the cultural logics of identity politics by the Right also subtly revealed a public profile defined far less by faith than by the economic and cultural resentments of those whose world was not only openly disparaged but seemingly disappearing. In this light, the turn to "Christian nationalism" was not a return to the serious nineteenth-century millennialist theology that—for all of its problems—placed America in hopeful providential history. It was, rather, a defensive trope that confirmed that politically conservative Christians could no longer offer an imaginative and constructive vision for the future of the nation *as a whole*.

Boundary Work and the Shifting Lines of Solidarity

The culture war that dominated American public life in the last decades of the twentieth and the early years of the twenty-first centuries can be seen as a new but also different iteration in the long and evolving ordeal of working through the meaning of America and the cultural sources that have sustained it as a nation. Through the perspectives of our exemplars, one can see resonances in the tension between Dewey and Niebuhr earlier in the twentieth century and in the tension between Tribe and Neuhaus at the end of the twentieth century. In each, the antagonists understood explicitly that cultural authority was at stake in their disagreements—that is, the sources by which claims to the ethical ordering of society could be legitimately made. By the end of the twentieth century, however, the differences of cultural tradition and voice within America's hybrid-Enlightenment had been radicalized. While each side's position was still recognizable to the other, the positions they took had become incommensurable, neither side willing or able to accommodate the other to find some pragmatic place to work for common goods.

On the surface, the issues of cultural conflict evolved to include ongoing racial inequalities, gender and LGBTQ concerns, and immigration. At the same time, there was a transformation and radicalization of the ideological profiles of the Left and the Right. None of these developments—indeed, nothing about the culture war itself—seemed too alarming for liberal democracy so long as it played out in a context of general prosperity. All of that changed with the Great Recession of 2008. The economic downturn brought the stakes of the conflict into relief. Not least, it heightened the differences in power between the Right and the Left: the Left consolidating its dominance across the range of cultural institutions and, increasingly, economic institutions as well; the Right feeling the full social and financial effects of the stagnating economy, with political office as the *only* real instrument it possessed to challenge the Left. As power and privilege were more openly at stake, the conflict created the sense of existential peril.

Sociologically, the evolving culture war continued to arbitrate the contested boundaries of legitimate and tolerable difference (the pluribus) contained within the boundaries of national solidarity (the unum). The conflict sought to mediate the line between inclusion and exclusion and the terms by which it was justified. Who is part of the unum, with all the rights, protections, and opportunities that inclusion implies, and who is not? Gays? Women? Immigrants? Blacks? Evangelicals, Catholics, and other conservative religious believers? The urban working class? The white, rural poor? Should a modern America tolerate what the Left perceives as racism, misogyny, xenophobia? Or what the Right perceive as bigotry toward religion, sexual perversion, the killing of the unborn? Progressives of the highly educated upper-middle class continued to press the case for the greater inclusion of Blacks, immigrants, the LGBTQ communities, and women. Conservatives whose base was grounded in the mostly white lower middle and working classes, many of whom were evangelical and fundamentalist Christians, found themselves ostracized by these progressives, their traditional values and beliefs disparaged—simply beyond the boundaries of good taste, ethical propriety, and sound thinking as progressives defined them. After centuries of enjoying the social, political, and economic benefits of cultural dominance, traditionalists now saw themselves as a persecuted minority, at risk of being "replaced" by a multicultural multitude.[89]

Importantly, both sides could claim to be inclusive in their own way, but not with each other. Even when there was diversity of opinion *within* their respective camps, they shared the same "enemy." The solidarities of the past were a fond but distant memory for some, a continuing nightmare of repression and cruelty for others. Actors on each side had begun to abandon the idea of civic persuasion and, with it, the idea that democratic processes could organically generate any kind of solidarity. For all practical purposes, such possibilities were no longer imaginable, much less achievable, precisely because the disagreements on the surface of public life were underwritten by fundamentally different assumptions about what it meant to be human and a full member of the body politic, what is valued, what constitutes flourishing, how we should treat those who are different from ourselves, and not least, how we know what we claim to know—that is, the authority upon which claims upon public life are justified. The claims of competing factions and the cultural authority upon which they were made were no longer recognizable by the other side.

The evolution of the culture war in these ways would signal still more troubling changes to come.

CHAPTER TEN

Exhaustion

F OUR DECADES OF POLITICAL and cultural conflict left adversaries weary of fighting, with no end in sight and each side thinking it had little to show for the effort. Their exhaustion marked the beginning of a new and different turn in the ongoing story of the effort to work through the contradictions in America's hybrid-Enlightenment.

But the exhaustion was more than an expression of the mental and emotional fatigue, frustration, and seeming futility experienced by activists and citizens more generally. More important, we see exhaustion in the cultural sense—as an expression of depletion. Peering through the fog of cultural warfare, it was becoming clear that the cultural ideals of liberal democracy were losing their normative grip. Its ethical ideals were no longer as compelling as they had been. These developments signaled something deeper. It was not just that the cultural logic of America's hybrid-Enlightenment did not provide the sources necessary to achieve national solidarity or to lead to a workable vision of justice and the public good or to discover terms by which the interests of private factions could be reconciled with the public good. Rather, these sources were, in some respects, making matters worse.

Put differently, there were distinct ways in which America's hybrid-Enlightenment lost standing (in the sense of status and credibility) as an animating source for collective self-understanding and purpose.

Some actors came to see the hybrid-Enlightenment as itself the problem; others would invoke it but, for all practical purposes, treat it as unhelpful; while still others simply treated it as irrelevant. Whether in theory (for the Left), in practice (for the Right), or as a matter of conceptual framing (for an emerging technocratic class), there were indications of a distancing from the hybrid-Enlightenment and, in turn, the task of working through the ever-evolving contradictions of *E Pluribus Unum*. This abandonment was by no means universal, but it was certainly evinced by the most intellectually serious figures within the contending camps in the culture war. Yet the paths by which they reached that conclusion were very different.

Exhaustion within the Left

By the later decades of the twentieth century, criticizing the Enlightenment had become almost obligatory on the intellectual Left. Graduate students in literature departments were thunderstruck by the mystifying proclamations of a Michel Foucault, a Jacques Derrida, or a Paul de Man. But the roots of the critique were much broader and deeper, particularly in political theory, where criticism ranged across an ideational spectrum that included postmodernists, progressives, communitarians, pluralists, and conservatives.[1] Nearly all of this work, however, was inaccessible to the broader liberal public.

Richard Rorty and the Abandonment of Metaphysics

Part of the greatness of Richard Rorty lay in his ability to bring this deconstructive project down from the theoretical heights and place it in conversation with the political concerns of ordinary progressives. As Rorty himself often complained, most devotees of postmodern theory despised not only the Enlightenment but everything to which it had given birth as well—liberal political theory, the idea of human rights, America. They saw the very existence of the United States as an outrage against humanity and devoted themselves to repudiating Americanism in every aspect. Rorty, however, was never capable of such a wholesale repudiation. It is his iconoclastic philosophical position combined with his ongoing commitment to the American project that makes him such a compelling figure.

Movement progressivism ran in Rorty's family. For one thing, he was the grandson of the progressive Baptist theologian Walter Rauschenbusch, who had rejected traditional Christianity in favor of a "social" interpretation of the Gospel that stressed structural wrongs and social and political reform over individual sin and redemption.

A more immediate influence were Rorty's Trotskyist parents. The young Rorty read socialist literature and ran errands for the Workers Defense League and the Socialist Party. "I grew up knowing that all decent people were, if not Trotskyites, at least socialists," he would later write of his childhood opinions. "I knew that poor people would always be oppressed until capitalism was overcome."[2] Like many others who were Trotskyists in the first half of the twentieth century, Rorty would soften his attitude toward capitalism in the second. But his commitment to social progressivism and the uplift of the oppressed persisted.

Yet Rorty was also a sophisticate and an aesthete who chafed at his fellow progressives' insistence on politicizing everything. He found that he was as incapable of uncritically embracing socialist dogma as he was of honestly reciting the Nicene Creed. As a result of this inward struggle, Rorty ended up placing his progressivism on a new foundation—or rather, as he put it, on no foundation at all.

The great animating thesis of Rorty's political theory was that the just cause could not be defended through rational argument. This was not, as he insisted, a concession that his adversaries had a point or were equally right. Rorty professed fervent belief in the causes he espoused. Where he differed from his grandfather Rauschenbusch and from the Trotskyists of his parents' generation was in his denial that there could be any sure rational basis for his commitments. Reasoned argument could never decisively settle an argument between Rorty and a conservative. It could not even settle an argument between Rorty and a Nazi.

For another philosopher this might have been a shameful or sorrowful admission. Rorty, however, did not agonize over the demise of shared rationality. Anti-foundationalism fit his aesthetic and skeptical disposition, his passionate attachment to the perishable and the fleeting. Indeed, Rorty believed that some of the greatest minds of the nineteenth and twentieth centuries, including the postmodern

and deconstructionist philosophers who were so beloved by the doc-
trinaire leftists of the universities, had shown a way to reconcile
anti-foundationalism with a vibrant and active progressivism. Of these
great minds, the one Rorty cited most often and professed the greatest admiration for was the pragmatist John Dewey.

Dewey, of course, has already played a part in this narrative as
one of the leading figures in an effort to work through the hybrid-
Enlightenment along secular lines in the face of the contradictions of
early twentieth-century industrial capitalism. Rorty admired Dewey's
unapologetic Americanism, his secularism, and his commitment to
progressive social change. Dewey had played a part in the socialist
circles to which Rorty's parents were adjacent, having, for example,
chaired the 1937 commission of inquiry that issued a report exoner-
ating Trotsky after he had been condemned by Stalin's government.
In his maturity as a philosopher, Rorty came to feel that Dewey
represented the best of a dynamic and distinctively American tradition of thought that rejected the calcified dogmas of European philosophy and embraced flux and impermanence. This tradition was
American pragmatism, and although Rorty was plausibly accused
of playing fast and loose with the term, there is no doubt about his
personal admiration for Dewey and the pragmatists.

Rorty was right that Dewey shared his attraction to flux and
historical change. Dewey certainly believed in human progress. He
sought to free Americans from what he saw as the dead coils of tradition, and he did indeed deny that politics should be grounded in
an unchanging concept of human nature. All of this had been radical
at the beginning of the twentieth century but seemed somewhat less
so as it drew to an end. However, Rorty's reworking of Dewey moved
beyond these claims to realign Dewey with his own anti-metaphysical
views.[3]

This was no easy task. Rorty failed to understand that even as
Dewey developed his own radically new version of the hybrid-
Enlightenment framework, he remained indebted to the form and
content of the same vision of public reason that had animated political life in the early Republic. Dewey saw that a political culture had
to be grounded in something other than pure will, and he looked to
the history of the hybrid-Enlightenment and its confidence in the
power of free reason as a basis for new stages in American intellec-

tual and political development. In purposefully forgetting that debt to the Enlightenment vision, Rorty would make a break far more radical than anything the radical Dewey had dreamed of.

If Rorty was aware of the discrepancies between his understanding of Dewey and the genuine article, his conscience was probably untroubled by them. He could justify his appropriation of Dewey's name and thought as having been undertaken in defense of valuable aesthetic and political ideals. More important than the real content of Dewey's thought was his status as a kind of mythic progenitor of Rorty's narrative about the emergence of an indigenously American school of truth-indifferent thought. Although Rorty was, as a matter of principle, unconcerned about historical *accuracy*, historical *consciousness* was critically important for his project. It was dead, controlling tradition that he feared. A flexible, open-minded, and manipulable tradition gave his ideals depth and substance by association. As he wrote in *Achieving Our Country*, "We raise questions about our individual or national identity as part of the process of deciding what we will do next, what we will try to become."[4]

Rorty, like the other figures I have examined in this book, was seeking a new system of binding agreements adapted to the changing conditions of his moment. Yet his anti-metaphysical bent led him to a decisively different approach to the problem. Rorty's politics were simple. He believed with all his heart in what he saw as the seamless garment of the progressive project—alleviating material want while increasing opportunities for personal freedom of action and expression, using government power when necessary. His justification for this political program was also simple: it amounted to a resounding *just because*. In *Contingency, Irony, and Solidarity*, Rorty explained in bracingly forthright language how his method of political argument differed from more familiar procedures: "On my account of intellectual progress as the literalization of selected metaphors, rebutting objections to one's redescriptions of things will be largely a matter of redescribing other things, trying to outflank the objections by enlarging the scope of one's favorite metaphors. So my strategy will be to try to make the vocabulary in which these descriptions are phrased look bad, thereby changing the subject, rather than granting the objector his choice of weapons and terrain by meeting his criticisms head-on."[5]

This was certainly an unusual approach to political argument, but Rorty believed it was the only one that could be more than wishful metaphysical thinking. Instead of admitting the possibility of a shared language for debate with his opponents, Rorty simply proposed to muscle them out of the way. Indeed, he claimed that this approach was not only necessary but also impeccably liberal: "It is central to the idea of a liberal society that, in respect to words as opposed to deeds, persuasion as opposed to force, anything goes."

For Rorty himself, that slightly ominous-sounding "anything goes" did not mean that insults and accusations could be deployed without restraint. He had something more civil and, he hoped, more effective in mind: what he called *joshing*, the attempt to nudge stubborn opponents out of their beliefs through gentle ridicule and respectful intolerance. "Moral commitment, after all, does not require taking seriously all the matters that are, for moral reasons, taken seriously by one's fellow citizens," he wrote. "It may require trying to josh them out of the habit of taking those topics so seriously. There may be serious reasons for so joshing them."[6]

Rorty's certainty that this approach would have the desired effect shows just how confident he was in the absolute hegemony of his preferred brand of progressivism. His use of the first-person plural in certain crucial passages betrays his utter certainty that his own views were in the ascendant and those of his enemies were in decline. Take, for example, this discussion of the proper attitude toward opponents of liberal democracy:

> To say that there is no place for the questions that Nietzsche or Loyola would raise is not to say that the views of either are unintelligible (in the sense of "logically incoherent" or "conceptually confused"). Nor is it to say that they are based on an incorrect theory of the self. Nor is it *just* to say that our preferences conflict with theirs. It is to say that the conflict between these men and us is so great that "preferences" is the wrong word. . . . We heirs of the Enlightenment think of enemies of liberal democracy like Nietzsche or Loyola as, to use Rawls's word, "mad." We do so because there is no way to see them as fellow citizens of our constitutional democracy, people whose life plans might, given ingenuity and

good will, be fitted in with those of other citizens. They are not crazy because they have mistaken the ahistorical nature of human beings. They are crazy because the limits of sanity are set by what *we* can take seriously. This, in turn, is determined by our upbringing, our historical situation.[7]

Presumably Rorty's confident talk about a unified progressive "we" was partly the consequence of his spending his life safely ensconced in uniformly progressive university humanities departments. He was well aware that many Americans did not share his political views. But he felt able to repudiate such people without apology. "I feel no need to be judicious and balanced in my attitude toward the two sides [of the] culture war," he wrote in 1992. "I see the 'orthodox' (the people who think that hounding gays out of the military promotes traditional family values) as the same honest, decent, blinkered disastrous people who voted for Hitler in 1933. I see the 'progressivists' as defining the only America I care about."[8] Not only Nietzsche and Loyola but the Moral Majority were "mad," at least by what Rorty saw as his own true-blue American standards.

Rorty's 1989 book *Contingency, Irony, and Solidarity* offered the clearest and most comprehensive account of his political theory. It is a beautifully written and sparklingly allusive book, but its principal argument is straightforward. Rorty's thesis, which he reframes several times with the help of various literary and philosophical sources, is that no politics can be justified metaphysically, universalistically, or rationally. All we have are contingently held beliefs whose appeal to us is just that we, born in this time and place, happen to *approve of* or *identify with* them. The liberal is thus necessarily an *ironist* who holds passionately to her beliefs while understanding perfectly well that there is nothing transcendent behind them.

In the American context, this meant that "we heirs of the Enlightenment," with a long history of struggle for toleration at our backs, happen to believe what Rorty believes about gays in the military, the goodness of relatively free markets with certain humanitarian correctives, and many other things besides.

And if it happens that anyone, despite sharing a time and place with "us," somehow fails to share those beliefs, "we" can rightly regard that person as alien to our political community. We cannot hope to engage with such a person on a rational level, because neither his beliefs nor ours are grounded in anything that could be argued about coherently. The only solution to this problem that Rorty has available involves using rhetorical tricks to induce him to abandon his outdated views: making his vocabulary "look bad," or "joshing" him into embarrassed submission.

The philosophers' quarrel over Rorty's interpretation of Dewey's pragmatism is thus highly significant. Rorty, consciously or unconsciously, invoked Dewey in support of a condition that Dewey himself had warned would emerge as a result of the abandonment of a common standard for discourse: "the subjection of some persons to the personal opinion of other persons."[9] Dewey believed in the progress of human opinion, but he also believed that this progress took place within a shared horizon of experience. Rorty, by contrast, saw himself and his political enemies as living in entirely separate worlds, with a gulf between them that could be bridged only by a kind of ironical or aesthetic leap of faith.

The dream of a hybrid-Enlightenment solidarity worked through amid conflict and contradiction was dead in Rorty's work. For all his personal insouciance, gentility, and abundant good humor, his rejection of a common standard of judgment was a symptom of a profound exhaustion setting in on America's cultural battlefields. Although the jocularly coercive methods Rorty proposed were supremely mild—no one ever died from being joshed—his utterly unapologetic resort to something like a coercive cajolement was a severe blow to the old American hope of finding solidarity amid contradiction.

Curiously, however, Rorty not only shrank back from but actively resisted the more militant elements in the progressivism of his own time. "There is a problem with this left: it is unpatriotic. In the name of 'the politics of difference,' it refuses to rejoice in the country it inhabits. It repudiates the idea of a national identity, and the emotion of national pride."[10] *Achieving Our Country*, its somewhat dubious interpretations of Deweyan epistemology aside, was primarily a brief against the left-wing anti-Americanism that was then in vogue among elite humanists. Rorty thought that the Left was in the grip of a metaphysical politics and that abandoning high theory would make leftists both more patriotic and more effective in achieving their own stated goals. For someone who was perfectly happy to attack

his political enemies as un-American, Rorty was surprisingly preoccupied with ensuring that progressive politics remain accessible to a
broad base of supporters. Commenting on identity politics, for example, he wrote, "To take pride in being black or gay is an entirely
reasonable response to the sadistic humiliation to which one has
been subjected. But insofar as this pride prevents someone from also
taking pride in being an American citizen, from thinking of his or
her country as capable of reform, or from being able to join with
straights or whites in reformist initiatives, it is a political disaster."[11]

In a strangely prophetic passage that suddenly began to be quoted
widely in 2016, Rorty even predicted that a hyper-moralized leftist
politics indifferent to material conditions would eventually drive
"members of labor unions, and unorganized unskilled workers" into
the arms of "a strongman . . . someone willing to assure them that,
once he is elected, the smug bureaucrats, tricky lawyers, overpaid
bond salesmen, and postmodernist professors will no longer be calling the shots."[12]

To avoid this fate, Rorty argued, "the Left should put a morato-
rium on theory. It should try to kick its philosophy habit." And it
should "try to mobilize what remains of our pride in being Americans."[13] In short, Rorty thought that the abandonment of political
metaphysics could actually open space for new binding agreements
to flower. What he forgot, perhaps by choice, were the vast socially
conservative masses whom he could so cheerfully dismiss as "the
same honest, decent, blinkered disastrous people who voted for Hitler in 1933" who lay outside "the only America I care about." Somehow, Rorty thought it would be possible to build a political community without paying any mind to such people. Perhaps he imagined
joshing them or their children into the fold little by little.

Rorty turned away from the democratic process of *durcharbeiten*
as a means for achieving solidarity because he believed that the progressive world-picture had triumphed—triumphed so thoroughly
that he and his allies would be able to sweep their reactionary foes
from the field through social opprobrium alone, with no ideal dis-
courses or reasoned arguments required. The progressive cultural
hegemony that inspired him with such confidence would continue
to transform American society long after he had passed from the
scene in 2007. Support for causes that had ranged from unthinkable

to merely implausible when Rorty published *Contingency, Irony, and Solidarity*—gay marriage, transgender recognition, reparations for slavery, nonenforcement of petty crime laws, the replacement of policing with mental health services—rapidly became widespread or even mandatory in progressive circles. The revolution of the 1960s had changed form and found new objects to pursue, but its force seemed to have continued unabated through the first decades of the new century.

Exhaustion within the Right

Because the conservative base was attached to the hybrid-Enlightenment and the ideals of the Founding by bonds of affection as well as utility, conservatives had more to lose by openly rejecting the ideas and sources of public reason. Confronted with the threat of a sweeping progressive triumph in the culture wars, however, they showed themselves perfectly capable of doing so in deed, if not in word.

An early sign that the Right was ready for war came with the rise of Newt Gingrich in the 1990s. Reputed to be ruthless and profoundly unprincipled, Gingrich saw politics as a brutal game that had to be won by any means necessary. His aggressive tactics in Congress helped to inaugurate a new era of no-holds-barred legislative politics, but perhaps even more telling was a now-notorious memo that Gingrich's GOPAC group sent to Republican statehouse candidates in 1990. Bluntly entitled "Language: A Key Mechanism of Control," the memo gave these candidates—the equivalent of Republican minor leaguers—two lists of words, one that their campaigns should use to describe themselves and another that they should use to describe their opponents. The second category included *traitors, destructive, sick, pathetic, coercion, threaten, devour, disgrace, cheat*, and *steal*. "These words and phrases are powerful," Gingrich explained in an accompanying letter. "Read them. Memorize as many as possible. And remember that like any tool, these words will not help if they are not used."[14] Rorty, with his understanding of disparaging language as a tool superior to rational argument, might have written the pamphlet himself—though he would certainly not have distributed it to Republicans.

The GOPAC memo was hardly the most significant moment in

Gingrich's career-long assault on the old ideals of civil discourse and civic harmony. But it captured the imagination of the chroniclers of that era because it showed how intent Gingrich was on depicting his adversaries not just as rivals with contrasting views but as dangerous enemies of humanity. Gingrich himself did not seem to have seen things that way: he fondly recalls the late nights he spent in the White House working out budget compromises with Bill Clinton.[15] What mattered more, however, was the apocalyptic morality play he put on for the voting public. To hear Gingrich and his acolytes talk about the Democrats, you would never have imagined that negotiating with such a pack of nihilistic liberal villains was possible.

Yet however much Gingrich might have wanted to release conservatives from the old norms, he never quite finished the job. That, at least, was an increasingly popular view among Republicans as the Obama presidency neared its end. The Left's advantage in the culture wars had only increased since Gingrich's heyday in the '90s. The most influential discourse institutions—the places where public reason was supposed to be conducted—were thoroughly dominated by the Left. Rorty doubted that a truly neutral discourse was possible on philosophical grounds. Conservatives came to doubt it on practical grounds. They looked around them and saw universities, news organizations, and even the new social media websites—all the proud inheritors of the liberal discourse tradition—cheerfully employing every tool at their disposal to restrict the range of acceptable opinion.

These failures did not result from any lack of effort in the political arena. In fact, an energetic and well-funded political Right had been playing the liberal game for decades, with considerable success. The Republican apparatus for getting the right people into high office was performing well. Republican appointees still held a majority of seats on the Supreme Court, and lower courts were full of Federalist Society–approved judges. The GOP was especially successful at the state level, maintaining control over a majority of governorships and state legislatures even after Barack Obama's commanding victory in the 2012 presidential election. Well-funded conservative think tanks hosted posh fundraisers, and right-wing super PACs flooded the airwaves with advertising. All Republicans needed was to win the presidency back in 2016—surely no difficult task, with inevitable backlash to the incumbent party to count on, along with the immensely unpopular Hillary Clinton, the long-presumed Democratic nominee.

And yet American *conservatism* had strangely little to show for all that winning. The fight over abortion, the great conservative cause of the late twentieth century, had, at that time, apparently stalled, and single-issue voters were growing tired of trooping to the polls year after year with little to show for their efforts. As for same-sex marriage, it was clear by 2014 that most Americans either supported it or were reconciled to it. A series of federal court rulings were striking down state-level bans even as substantial and growing majorities of Americans expressed support for the issue in opinion polls.[16] The Affordable Care Act, which inspired another great battle of the Obama era, had survived its first and strongest Supreme Court challenge and gradually became an established part of the social entitlement landscape. Conservatives would continue to mutter about repeal and replacement, but no serious plans to that effect would ever emerge. None of that Republican electoral success had been able to mitigate the inescapable fact that progressives controlled every important cultural and intellectual institution and appeared to be capable of winning any cultural fight they chose.

Finding themselves in such dire straits, it was only natural that conservatives would start questioning the canonical political methods favored by the institutional Republican Party. After Mitt Romney's crushing defeat in the 2012 presidential election, a GOP commission released a hundred-page report, popularly known as "The Autopsy," that advised the party to make more of an effort to reach out and show "care" for diverse voters.[17] And yet the Republican Party would take a very different turn in 2016. That year's pugnacious nominee embodied the conservative base's disdain not only for the Democrats but also for the more conciliatory Republicans who, they felt, had handed culture war victory to the Left.

In 2016, most of the conservative movement's intellectual firepower was concentrated at neoconservative-tending institutions like the Heritage Foundation, the American Enterprise Institute, or the *National Review*, with a few libertarian allies in economics departments and at the Cato Institute. None of these outfits was especially attuned to the Trumpist message—or the emergent strains of a Trumpist cult—that first emerged during that year's campaign. Yet although Trump himself operated more on instinct than on big ideas, there was an intellectual basis for his pugnacious and frequently apocalyptic brand of conservatism. Its most able exponents were found not in the reputable Washington think tanks but at far smaller and lower-profile institutions. Of these, the best prepared to seize the Trumpist moment, and the most energetic in doing so, was the Claremont Institute.

The Claremont Institute: Populist Revolt and the Forsaking of Democratic Deliberation

Claremont is not exactly situated at the center of things. The institute's home is a nondescript concrete office cube in the vast suburban expanse surrounding Los Angeles. It is a small operation, reporting $5.5 million in revenue in the 2015–16 fiscal year.[18] (The Heritage Foundation took in $85 million in 2016.)[19] And while other conservative institutes publish papers laden with charts, graphs, and complex plans for reshaping incentive structures, Claremont is not strictly a policy shop. Most of the institute's scholars are students of political philosophy, more interested in Machiavelli and Montesquieu than in marginal tax rates or marriage penalties. Theirs is not a politics of incremental adjustment. They believe the American way of life is threatened by bad ideas about the very nature of politics and human life, and they want to see those ideas defeated before it is too late.

Although it sits well to the right of the mainstream academy, Claremont maintains a serious intellectual reputation. Its scholars produce difficult, closely argued interpretations of classic texts, and the institute offers a number of fellowship seminars that are intended to give conservative writers and activists a stronger intellectual grounding in the tradition of political thought. Claremont has had an enduring influence on many prominent figures, including Supreme Court justice Clarence Thomas, and its fellows serve as faculty at high-ranking institutions like Notre Dame, Amherst, Washington & Lee, and nearby Claremont McKenna College (which has no formal relationship with the institute). Consequently, some observers were surprised by how quickly and wholeheartedly the Claremont group embraced Donald Trump.

The surprise was unwarranted, however, because the distinctive school of thought favored at Claremont was strikingly well adapted to the Trumpist moment. First, as the writer Jon Baskin explained in a Trump-era profile of the institute, Claremont's shared tendency has always been anti-technocratic, and Trump's disdain for bureaucrats and experts of all kinds endeared him to political philosophers yearning for a statesman to triumph over the wonks.[20] But there was also a simpler explanation laid out by institute doyen Charles Kesler in a 2021 book called *Crisis of the Two Constitutions:* Claremont believed that the American idea was in deadly peril, and Trump, unlike his Republican colleagues, was willing to fight hard in its defense.

Kesler's writings would go a long way toward explaining how an urbane group of PhD-holding scholars of classical political thought and the American Founding came to support the presidential campaign of a coarse, anti-intellectual self-promoter. *Crisis* begins with a summary of Claremont's somewhat unusual interpretation of the Founding. First developed by Claremont's founding sage Harry Jaffa, the doctrine that holds that the American Founders were not, as is generally claimed, a group of Enlightenment modernists who believed that a perfectly rational political science could channel man's wicked passions and create an unvirtuous but livable political order. Rather, they were inheritors of the tradition of classical political thought and therefore believed that government existed to secure "public happiness" in accordance with the objective and universal dictates of natural right. Kesler distinguished, for example, between the natural right theory of Locke, who had an important influence on Jefferson, and that of Rousseau, who received relatively little attention from the Founders. Locke, Kesler argued, believed that man was by nature disposed to obey the natural law, while Rousseau believed that man was naturally solitary and amoral.[21] Kesler also offered an unconventional natural right interpretation of the *Federalist Papers*, arguing that Publius's famous embrace of factional politics concealed a deeper commitment to fundamental consensus on the ends of government:

There must be a uniformity of opinion underlying the multiplicity of interests and sects otherwise the result would not be pluralism but civil war or anarchy, not America but Lebanon. Pluralism, then, is not enough; before men can be divided by interests and sects they must be united by citizenship. Far from "turn[ing] away almost in horror from the human 'zeal for different opinions,'" Publius himself inculcates an opinion; far from eschewing zealous politics, Publius concludes [Federalist] Number 10 by declaring, "And according to the degree of pleasure and pride we feel in being republicans, ought to be our zeal in cherishing the spirit and supporting the character of federalists."[22]

In the same vein, Kesler insisted that American freedom of religion was intended not to drive piety from public life but to strengthen its hold on the American mind: "Separation was intended not to divorce but to unite civic morality and the moral teaching of religion: disestablishment was meant to establish common standards of morality to guide political life."[23]

In other words, Kesler and his Claremont colleagues rejected the familiar interpretation of American liberalism as a non-metaphysical attempt to build a "low but solid" modus vivendi among adherents of radically opposed philosophies and creeds. Equally, they rejected the common view of the American idea as a radically new product of the Age of Enlightenment, a turn away from classical prudence and toward rationalist humanism. Instead, they claimed that the Founders were seeking a new institutional framework for an ancient and permanent idea of human and political excellence.

These fundamental truths, according to Kesler, make up the soul of the American Constitution, and they are true absolutely—not just for us, in our time and place, but permanently and without qualification. This is not to say that the Founders' institutional framework should be copied by every nation on earth; Kesler devoted some space in *Crisis* to explaining that the Bush-era project of nation-building failed because the right political institutions vary with local conditions. Nevertheless, the ends of political life are constant and eternal. Abraham Lincoln, according to the influential interpretation advanced in Jaffa's *Crisis of the House Divided*, helped to rescue these permanent ideals from Confederate identitarianism.

However, the Claremont scholars believe that Woodrow Wilson, the president who brought the ideals of progressivism into main-stream American politics, inaugurated a radically new political order, the "second Constitution" referenced in Kesler's title. Wilson established the first rudiments of the administrative state with his regulatory program, and his foreign policy marked the beginning of the idealistic internationalism that has predominated in the U.S. State Department ever since. In Wilson, Kesler saw not only a new set of policy priorities but a new cosmology, anthropology, and political metaphysics opposed to the classically inflected ideas of the Founding. According to Kesler's interpretation, Wilson was the enemy of all permanent ideas about the human and political good. Instead, he was committed to a Darwinian concept of politics as continual adaptation to changing conditions. "Natural law, which he regards as the most unalterable of laws, is inconsistent with human liberty and especially with the freedom of action of statesmen," Kesler explained. "To open the American regime to progress therefore requires of Wilson a critique of the Declaration that severs the connection between the ends ordained there by natural law or right, and the means adopted to secure these rights in the Constitution."[24] In other words, the Claremont political theorists saw a link between Wilson's historical relativism and his defense of consolidated, bureaucratized federal government. In their view, Wilson favored a powerful, technocratic central authority because he believed that only a consolidated state could evolve quickly and effectively in a dynamic environment. Several times Kesler quoted Wilson's evocative declaration that "no living thing can have its organs offset each other as checks, and live. . . . Living political constitutions must be Darwinian in structure and practice."[25] This preoccupation with the evolutionary fitness of the government led Wilson to reject the prudence of the Founders in favor of an imperial model of political power in which experts would hold absolute dominion. In Wilson's foolish repudiation of the classical ideals of virtue, the Claremont thinkers argued, lay the roots of today's progressive excesses.

Kesler's tone was generally cautious and intellectual rather than aggressive. He favored high-minded theorizing about American politics and culture over Gingrichian or Trumpian attacks on his political enemies. Nevertheless, his interpretation of the American crisis offered plenty of justification for those inclined to a more openly conflictual approach. Kesler explained in the introduction of *Crisis of the Two Constitutions* that "America may be leaving the world of normal politics and entering the dangerous world of regime politics— in which our political loyalties diverge more and more, as they did in the 1850s, between two contrary visions of what constitutes the country." *Regime politics,* by the way, "is about who rules and for the sake of what ends or principles. It unsettles any existing political order, as well as its limits. It raises anew the basic questions of who counts as a citizen, what are the goals of the political community, and what do we honor or revere together as a people."[26] In other words, we are fighting over philosophy, not policy—over the basic orientation of our political institutions. Kesler's invocation of the 1850s was a blunt reminder that compromise under such circumstances is at best difficult to imagine.

Indeed, Kesler regarded the enemies of the first American Constitution not just as mistaken but as dangerously blind to the "self-evident truths" of the Declaration. Because these truths are present in nature and readily accessible to the human intellect, Kesler suggests that they cannot be rationally proven. They are instead, to use a remark of Lincoln's that the Claremont scholars love to quote, "the principles and axioms of a free society."[27] Those who deny these axioms have made themselves inaccessible to rational argument. Thus in a crucial passage Kesler wrote, "The conditions of all demonstration cannot themselves be demonstrated. But self-evident propositions are not necessarily self-evident to everyone. If their terms are not understood or recognized, then their truth will not be grasped."[28] Because progressives have failed to grasp "the conditions of all demonstration," they cannot be argued with. This, the Claremont scholars believe, was the situation in the 1850s, when the quarrel over principles and axioms was settled on the battlefield. It is also, in this view, the situation today.

Despite Kesler's loathing of nihilism, his political theory thus has a hidden nihilistic side—not in theory but in practice. In theory, Kesler was battling for the restoration of a natural right anthropology, one grounded on the self-evident truth that all men are created equal and endowed with the right to pursue the good life. In practice, he and his colleagues at Claremont found themselves engaged in a cataclysmic battle against a great mass of enemies who inexplicably failed to grasp these simple truths of nature. The Claremont scholars' belief in this great, unbridgeable divide is the second, unarticulated part of their anthropology. They see the world, or at least the United States, as divided between good people who grasp the "principles and axioms of a free society" and wicked people who are blind to those principles. The Enlightenment aspiration to mediate political disagreements through rational persuasion has disappeared from their thinking, since they believe that the wicked cannot be persuaded. What remains is struggle.

FLIGHT 93

Less restrained than Kesler is his friend and former student Michael Anton, who studied at Claremont Graduate University (CGU) with Kesler as "his principal teacher and mentor," according to the acknowledgments in Anton's book *The Stakes*.[29] Anton, who evidently started out in CGU's PhD program, seems to have left after earning his master's to work as a speechwriter for Rudy Giuliani. Other gigs in and out of conservative politics followed, and in September 2016 he was a managing director at the investment management company BlackRock, his name unknown to the public.[30] That month, however, with an epochal presidential election fast approaching, Anton published a pseudonymous article in the *Claremont Review of Books*, a publication edited by his old teacher Kesler. "The Flight 93 Election" summoned the Right in the most urgent terms to rally behind Trump. The stakes, Anton argued, were nothing less than existential: like the hijacked Flight 93's doomed passengers on September 11, Republicans must "charge the cockpit or . . . die."

In the end, Anton's analysis was simple: the Left, he argued, was instituting policies that would lead inexorably to its final triumph. The mainstream conservative movement—"Conservatism, Inc."— seemed content to respond with policy alternatives when the moment in fact demanded big institutional and structural changes. Immigration, which was hollowing out the American middle class and increasing the Democrats' vote share to unbeatable levels, had to be stopped. The universities and media, chief propagandists for the Left, had to be tamed. Trump might or might not do this effectively, but with Hillary Clinton, the avatar of technocratic progressivism, on the other side, the choice for conservatives was crystal clear.

Kesler's analysis of Wilsonian progressivism and the administrative state gave Anton a theoretical basis for these dramatic claims, but the substance of "The Flight 93 Election" was sufficiently standard right-wing fare that Rush Limbaugh devoted an entire segment to reading as much of it as he could on air. In that moment, with the unlikely but somehow also inevitable marriage of Claremont's theory and Limbaugh's pugilistic praxis, a new phase of the Trump movement had begun.

Anton would go on to a position on Trump's National Security Council and then, after an amicable resignation, to a lectureship at Claremont-influenced Hillsdale College.[31] There he wrote a book-length follow-up to "The Flight 93 Election," 2020's *The Stakes*.

Much has been made of the Trump movement's departures or failures to depart from the conventional policy positions of the American center-right. Anton, however, makes it clear in both "Flight 93" and *The Stakes* that his quarrel with the Never Trump conservatives had little to do with policy detail. He and Trump certainly departed from many of the standard Republican approaches to trade, war, and immigration, but he freely admitted that many conservative intellectuals hold what he regards as the correct views on these issues. The conservative movement's problem was not a lack of good ideas. It was a lack of fighting spirit—and, though Anton did not quite put it this way, a lack of appropriate terror at the prospect of single-party Democratic rule for the foreseeable future.[32]

To put it another way, the crucial difference between Anton and the old-style Republicans whom he savaged was not a set of political opinions but a *way of seeing*. The Never Trumpers continued to see classically conservative principles and America's governing philosophy as worth preserving and therefore saw their political opponents essentially as persuadable fellow citizens capable of hearing sound arguments about the policies required to secure the common good. Anton was all in favor of conservative principles, but his frustration with the process of achieving them was palpable. Against an immovable bloc of enemies in a life-and-death struggle, "what can they [classical conservatives] do against a tidal wave of dysfunction, immorality, and corruption? 'Civic renewal' would do a lot of course, but that's like saying health will save a cancer patient. A step has been skipped in there somewhere. How are we going to achieve 'civic renewal'? Wishing for a tautology to enact itself is not a strategy."[33] The position of traditional conservatism represented the "typical combination of the useless and inapt with the utopian and the unrealizable."[34]

The 2012 GOP autopsy stressed the need to persuade immigrants to embrace the conservative message. Anton, however, thought erroneously that immigrants have "no tradition of, taste for, or experience in liberty" and will thus remain deep-blue Democrats until the day they die.[35] But even immigrants are merely foot soldiers in the Left's long assault on American order. In *The Stakes*, Anton offered an extended taxonomy of the defenders of the progressive order. Immigrants would come last, functioning primarily as electoral muscle. Ranged alongside them in the order of battle are three more classes of progressive "Minions": "Freeloaders"; "the Wokerati," or "true believers"; and the "Avengers." All of these are permanent constituencies. Anton was more sympathetic to the "Freeloaders" than many conservatives are; he conceded that stagnant wages and rising prices have made it so that "for those aspiring to a 'middle-class' standard of living . . . redistribution or debt or both are necessary, not to live but to enjoy what prior generations could easily afford on one income."[36] What this meant in practice, however, was that "the free-stuff constituency is large and growing," and that is bad news for the traditional American constitutionalism that preached the virtues of self-reliance.[37] As for the Wokerati, Anton discussed their curious beliefs with an anthropologist's bemused detachment, shaking his head at their fervent pursuit of an underspecified idea of justice. He never even gestured at the possibility that this confused multitude might be educated or persuaded out of their delusions. They are "they," a dangerous mob of utopians who are willing to destroy anything in pursuit of their hazy vision. Finally, the Avengers were driven by furious hatred of a country they believe is irredeemably racist. "If reaping benefits turns out to be too difficult, they'll happily settle for seeing their enemies suffer," Anton explained. "They're all for making everything worse so long as doing so punishes the objects of their hate."[38]

The real power, however, lay with the "ruling class": the investment bankers, tech executives, upper-level bureaucrats, and newspaper editors who have nothing to fear from middle-class collapse and cultural decay. As Anton puts it, the ruling class "protect . . . their power by making you inert."[39] The elites tolerate and even encourage the Wokerati and the Avengers because anti-American narratives "demoralize" the public, and "a demoralized population is unlikely to rise in its own defense, to assert its right, to insist on a say in how it is governed, or to demand a share of the future."[40] The Freeloaders and the immigrants are useful as well, since the rulers prefer a lower class that passively accepts handouts in return for votes to one that asserts its dignity and political power.

Anton did not exactly believe in a cloak-and-dagger conspiracy; he acknowledged persistent tensions among his left-wing blocs. Nevertheless, his taxonomy of progressives gave the overriding impression that a vast, interlocking political apparatus was working in relative harmony to advance a dangerous agenda. Some members of the blue tribe—the ruling class, the Freeloaders, and the immigrants—are motivated by simple self-interest. Others—the Wokerati and the Avengers—are motivated by religious zeal. None, however, seem to be reachable through the ordinary work of reasoned political persuasion and democratic deliberation. Instead, "A top priority must be to attack, relentlessly, the legitimacy of the ruling class—to deprive them of any pretense of legitimacy. They are unpatriotic, hostile to the common good, ignorant and uneducated (despite their endless list of credentials), selfish and venal, corrupt, seditious, foreign-influenced, hypocritical, racist (but the 'good' kind), above the law, moralistic and hectoring, anti-constitutional and anti-democratic. Ridicule them. Constantly expose their corruption and hypocrisy. The fake-news media—the ruling class's Praetorian Guard—must also be attacked, mocked, and discredited every bit as relentlessly." In fact, our cultural rift is so deep that there is no point in even trying to bridge it:

> The merest shred of cultural unity would seem so far out of reach as to be scarcely worth trying to attain, at least for the foreseeable future. I don't believe the country can continue indefinitely without any semblance of a common culture, but focusing right now on a near- and medium-term impos-

sibility would be folly. . . . One side needs to achieve and keep—electorally!—the upper hand for a while: specifically, the side that has been getting the short end of the stick for the last generation. Should that happen, its leaders will, of course, and of necessity, use their power to benefit their side— their base—but they must also use it to right the ship, to rebalance and benefit the whole.[41]

Anton needed to specify that he had electoral power in mind because some of the later passages in *The Stakes* warn ambiguously that violence might become unavoidable if the situation continues to worsen. For example, he speculated that red states might become like Paris's *banlieues*, "no-go zones" where "it might (say) become inconvenient for an FBI or ATF or BLM agent to buy gas, or get table service in truck stops, or friendly smiles from motel clerks in the hinterlands." If red staters were to underscore the message by "taking full advantage of their states' and counties' open carry laws," they might be able to intimidate the feds into a "pullback."[42] Then, of course, there is the possibility of secession; Anton gamed out several possible scenarios, some peaceable and some violent.

There was no reason not to take Anton at his word when he said that such prospects horrify him. The crucial point is that he thought the chasm between Left and Right was so deep, and the Left's commitment to its self-contradictory and destructive political philosophy so firm, that conflict was a real and immediate possibility. For the Claremont scholars, everything tended to come back to Lincoln, the subject of Jaffa's opus. Lincoln famously warned that a house divided against itself could not stand, and Claremont was intent on showing that our house is once again so divided. And like Lincoln, the Claremont scholars are not shy about taking a side in the coming struggle; they are not hand-wringing analysts of American division but partisans zealous for the victory of what they are certain is the just cause.

It is not entirely surprising, then, that in the months surrounding the contentious 2020 presidential election, Claremont affiliates went to troubling lengths to discredit Joe Biden's victory.[43] In September 2020, Anton wrote an article called "The Coming Coup" for the institute's Web-only publication *American Mind*. The piece warned that the Democrats would stop at nothing to get Trump out of office, no matter the election results. On the most charitable reading, Anton was simply arguing, not unreasonably, that Republicans should be prepared for Democrats to resist the election results in the event of a Trump victory. In light of what actually happened, however, a more cynical interpretation of the article offered itself: Anton was preparing his readers to see any news of a Biden victory as the result of a massive conspiracy involving "harvested ballots" and the aggressive deployment of "the ruling class's massive propaganda operation."[44] This, in fact, seems to be how a large number of Americans came to see what was in fact a Biden victory, and while relatively few of them had read Anton's article, its broad strokes are discernible in a great deal of more popular conservative conspiracy-theorizing about the election.

Sure enough, as absentee ballots started tipping the balance decisively toward Biden, Anton and his Claremont colleagues saw his prophecies being fulfilled. "The Democratic Party's rule changes allow them to tamper with the election," explained four institute executives in a November 5 *American Mind* statement. "The Right must now make a show of support that says: *enough*," they continued.[45] Meanwhile, Claremont Graduate University PhD and institute fellow John Eastman, a former clerk for Justice Clarence Thomas, was becoming one of the principal figures in Donald Trump's absurd campaign to overturn the election results, working on Trump's legal case and telling a crowd at the now-notorious January 6 rally that election officials "were unloading the ballots from that secret folder, matching them to the unvoted voter, and voila, we have enough votes to barely get over the finish line."[46] Eastman also advised Vice President Mike Pence that he had the legal authority to invalidate the election results.[47]

In the end, most of the Claremont scholars, including Anton and Kesler, admitted the obvious: that no convincing evidence of *decisive* election fraud had been presented by Trump's team.[48] But their post-inauguration writings, along with the writings of fellow travelers, suggested that the turbulent election of 2020 had only deepened their conviction that the Democratic Party was determined to destroy conservatism and the American constitutional order and must somehow be stopped.

One interesting application of the emerging Claremont sensibility was a project called New Founding, based in Dallas and led by *American Mind* founding editor (and CGU PhD) Matthew Peterson. Declaring, "Our most vocal elites hate America's virtues and undermine America's promise," New Founding promised to "cultivate a new market—including networks, job boards, conferences, and more—so our members can connect and transact within the alliance."[49] In other words, the mission was to provide conservatives with a parallel commercial universe and allow them to avoid doing business with corporations whose leaders belong to the hated liberal ruling class. An ideologically motivated commercial alliance is perhaps only a small step toward separatism, but it may prove to be a symbolic one, especially if the conservative public continues to share Claremont's view that there is no longer any point in negotiating with the Left.

The most significant function of the Claremont project was to provide elite legitimation and intellectual coherence to the impulses of Trump's white working-class base of supporters. White evangelicals, rural voters, whites without college degrees—the overlapping demographic blocs that drove Trump's support in 2016 and 2020—felt doubly alienated: first by a globalizing, post-industrial economy that was rapidly leaving them behind, and second by a wave of cultural change that was rendering cherished forms of belief and practice unacceptable in polite society. The 2008 mortgage crisis deepened this sense of alienation. Multinational corporations recovered beautifully and carried on with their program of offshoring and automation while simultaneously embracing the symbolic vocabulary of cultural progressivism. Meanwhile, middle- and working-class families that had pursued the American dream of homeownership as a pathway to prosperity found themselves reduced to the peasantry, with only undignified service-sector jobs on offer even as the nation's upper class consolidated its wealth.

Trump's future support base was caught in an awkward middle. These people had traditionally supported the American conservative movement, which spoke the language of values they favored and stood for personal responsibility and self-reliance. But elite conservatism had little to say about the economic forces that were hollowing out the middle classes, or the economic winners who were profiting from their downfall. Progressives, who saw the future Trumpists as culturally reactionary enemies, could not spare much sympathy for them either. Few outside Claremont and associated institutions perceived that the crisis of the middle class was, in fact, a crisis of American conservatism—a challenge to the Lockean idea of the proudly self-sufficient smallholder capable of assuming virtuous responsibility for himself and his family. It was a culturally conservative vision, a bourgeois vision, perhaps even a patriarchal vision. But it was also the vision of the good life shared by millions upon millions of ordinary Americans. People of many races shared this vision, but Trump was able to concentrate his support by appealing to the added sense of grievance felt by whites who had been disfavored by affirmative action policies.

The Claremont scholars argued that the ideal of the virtuous smallholder had been the ideal of the Founders, and that the new progressive constitution was responsible for its demise. That is why Anton devoted the first part of *The Stakes* to an extended lament for the middle-class California of his childhood, a time and place where an ordinary father could buy a home in paradise for his wife and children and support them on a single decent income. Now, Anton says, coastal California is the preserve of the fantastically wealthy, whose extravagant lifestyles are maintained by a desperately poor immigrant underclass. The proud American middle had been destroyed, and Anton asserted that it will soon be destroyed across the country.

How do you rein in a self-serving aristocracy and restore a decent life for the bourgeoisie? Anton allowed himself some ambiguous remarks about the possibility of an American "Caesar," though he stopped well short of endorsing the idea. What was clear was that Trump's support base was perfectly happy to see a strongman in the White House if that was the best way for them to defeat their enemies. And many of the Claremont scholars, whatever their convictions about Caesarism, were perfectly happy to play along with Trump's post-election attempts to defy the written Constitution and preserve himself in power. Claremont's apocalyptic picture of a struggle between natural right and pure blind perversity legitimated this nihilistic abandonment of the procedural ideals that had long held the country together.

The Technocratic Alternative

Between Claremont on the right and the heirs of Rorty and Rawls on the left, the idea of public reason took a beating in the Trump era. Pained meditations on the confusions of populism, like Tom Nichols's bluntly titled book *The Death of Expertise*, were written and gravely passed around among the educated classes. The COVID-19 pandemic and the official experts' long struggle to convince Americans to comply with public health measures only deepened the sense that the country was gripped by a crisis of authority.

Sunstein, Vermeule, and the Rejection of Popular Sovereignty

Where could perplexed Americans turn for an enlightened, rational discourse about government and politics? As it turns out, an elite group of academics and officials had dedicated themselves to keep the flickering flame of expertise alive amid the gales of the early twenty-first century. Their insistence on the value of rational thought, sensible deliberation, and methodologically sound inquiry might have seemed like a desperately needed defense against bipartisan irrationalism. Yet underneath all their protestations about the importance of a sure and certain basis for public policy, these technocrats were, in a strange way, also skeptics of public reason. Reason itself they certainly believed in; they had boundless confidence in the capacity of new theories and methodologies to uncover hidden truths about human nature and action. But they were not so certain about the capacity of the democratic public to grasp those truths. The pursuit of the common good, they felt, might not be altogether compatible with the old ideals of popular sovereignty or democratic self-determination. Navigating the complex challenges of the new millennium might require a little less talk and a slightly firmer hand.

The undisputed figurehead of the technocratic alternative, the man whose life and thought most perfectly embodied their ideals, was the law professor Cass Sunstein. Although Sunstein was no WASP—his grandfather was a German Jewish immigrant who landed at Ellis Island—he became a class A exhibit of the late twentieth-century American aristocrat, attending the elite Middlesex School in Concord, Massachusetts, and then Harvard for a bachelor's and a law degree. After clerking for Supreme Court justice Thurgood Marshall, Sunstein took a professorship at the University of Chicago's law school, where he would stay until he moved back to Harvard in 2008.

The utilitarian, calculating, hyper-analytical style that would characterize Sunstein's work seems to have been in the water at Chicago as he was beginning to build his career. A 2010 *New York Times Magazine* profile of Sunstein opened with a discussion of the university's unique intellectual culture: "The professors in Hyde Park believe in something called the University of Chicago mind. It runs cold and analytical when the rest of the culture runs hot. Chicago scholars tend to be social scientists at heart, contrarian but empirical, following evidence to logical extremes. They are centrally interested not in what it is like to be an individual within society but in how society washes over individuals, making and remaking them."[50]

Sunstein, the profile went on to explain, made a perfect exemplar of the Chicago mind. And as the *Times* profile suggested, he found plenty of like-minded scholars in Hyde Park. One of these was Richard Thaler, a behavioral economist at Chicago's Booth School of Business with whom Sunstein coauthored a hugely influential book called *Nudge: Improving Decisions about Health, Wealth, and Happiness.*[51] The book's theses emerged from a synthesis of Thaler's advanced behavioral science—the study of patterns in human irrationality— and Sunstein's political and legal work. The result of this interesting collaboration was the theory of "choice architecture": the idea that our decisions are shaped not only by our intentions but also by the external conditions under which we decide. Choice architecture, Sunstein and Thaler rightly argued, was an inevitable part of life, however much we might long to make our decisions as autonomous, rational agents. Instead of trying to escape it, then, we should try to exploit it for public benefit. "Nudging," or "libertarian paternalism," was the method Sunstein and Thaler proposed for bringing choice architecture under rational control.

To "nudge" someone was to shape the relevant choice architecture in such a way as to guide people toward wise and rational decisions while leaving the final choice up to them. Sunstein and Thaler saw nudging as liberal because it seemingly avoided coercion. A person with a strong preference will have enough force to resist the promptings of the choice architects; only a person who does not much care one way or the other will tend to go where she is nudged. But as Sunstein has frequently emphasized in his writings, enormous numbers of people have no special preferences on a whole range of issues. Letting them choose at random when they would be just as happy with a wise decision guided by clever choice architecture seemed to Sunstein and Thaler to be a tragically wasted opportunity to improve society.

Sunstein and Thaler saw little conflict between their program of progressive paternalism and the American liberal tradition. They believed that nudging operations could be carried out in a constrained and democratic way. Their favorite examples of nudging were not hidden defaults or subliminal messages—in fact, they suggested that the latter should be prohibited on principle—but explicit messaging addressed directly to rational agents. Signs reminding concertgoers to drink water and ATMs that returned users' cards before dispensing cash counted as nudges. Of course, more complex problems might require more complex nudges: for example, workers enrolling in a pension plan might be advised to choose an expertly selected default option before being allowed to choose from the full range of available possibilities, or homeowners might be furnished with a special meter that tells them how their energy usage compares to that of their neighbors. Sunstein and Thaler were especially fond of nudges that helped people commit themselves to difficult decisions ahead of time, like retirement programs that would automatically raise participants' savings rates over time or lists of problem gamblers who had chosen to be banned from casinos.

Many of Sunstein's nudges, then, are intended to help people move through the complicated and impersonal bureaucratic procedures they need to secure retirement funds, medical care, access to political participation, and various social supports. Others are intended to combat the perverse influence of self-interested corporations that use nudges of their own to market products that damage their users' health and well-being. Few of the nudges favored by Sunstein and Thaler seemed especially objectionable in themselves. Many simply amounted to good pieces of advice presented to captive audiences at opportune moments, while others offered people structured means of controlling their own impulses. Moreover, Sunstein and Thaler insisted that nudges must remain transparent and consensual. Nudgers should serve interests that their targets would, on reflection, be able to identify with on their own. People should not be nudged toward different political opinions or life plans; they should be helped to realize aims they already believe in.[52]

Yet Sunstein and Thaler's theories also reflected deep suspicions about the viability of popular judgment. Their practical ideas were grounded in the new field of behavioral economics, which Thaler had helped to pioneer in research that would win him the Nobel Prize in Economics in 2017. Thaler and his colleagues in the field had grown dissatisfied with the tendency in conventional economics to treat human agents as perfectly rational deliberators. They argued not only that human beings often failed to live up to this standard of judgment but also that their foibles or innate "cognitive biases" conformed to predictable patterns and could be shaped and mitigated through intelligent policy design. For example, they cited research showing that most people are more averse to loss than desirous of gain, then suggested ways in which intelligent rhetoric might make use of this tendency by framing good choices as loss-avoidant. Critics might have seen these appeals to deeply rooted human cognitive tendencies as forms of emotional manipulation, but Sunstein and Thaler argued that they were simply logical ways to help ordinary, not entirely rational people live longer, safer, and healthier lives.

Sunstein and Thaler did not exempt themselves from their own assessment of flawed human nature; in fact, *Nudge* is full of humorous anecdotes about the two University of Chicago professors falling prey to the same cognitive biases they are analyzing in the text.[53]

Sunstein's plans for improving Americans' lives may be open to legitimate disagreement, but he certainly meant well: he has wanted to help us save more money for retirement, misplace fewer personal items, maintain better physical health, and consume less energy. However, his dim view of individual responsibility, his confidence in new techniques of behavioral control, and his faith in the capacity of experts to determine what is right for us sum to a vision of political life that leaves little room for shared rational democratic deliberation. Sunstein often praised democratic deliberation in the abstract, but a truly restive public, like the one that elected Donald Trump president, might seem to be incompatible with the expert rule that he thinks would best secure peace and prosperity.

In his own unusual way, then, Sunstein is as much a child of our exhausted era as Richard Rorty, Michael Anton, or Charles Kesler. Sunstein saw himself building on the tradition of one of his heroes, Walter Lippmann, whom Sunstein identified as one of the great figures in the history of technocratic political theory. He stressed Lippmann's pessimism about the character of the general citizenry that, in his view, had become a mob, incapable of self-governance. In this light, he also shared Lippmann's concerns about the mismatch between the complexity of contemporary problems and the difficulty of productive public discourse. "In Lippmann's view," Sunstein explained,

> the last thing we need are earnest platitudes about governance by We the People. Of course, the public is ultimately sovereign. But it needs to empower "a system of analysis and record"—that is, a government structure that makes space for statisticians, scientists, and other experts, who will acquire reliable information and make it accessible to both public officials and the public. Lippmann insists on a large role for technocrats, who are subject to representative government but who can disregard people's beliefs in various "pseudo-environments" and help public officials to deal with the world as it actually is. "The real sequence should be one where the disinterested expert first finds and formulates the facts for the man of action," with pride of place for the "experimental method in social science."[54]

Here Sunstein used Lippmann as a cudgel against other, more populist radicals whose approach to politics he believed is inadequate to the complexity of our moment.

Sunstein justified his technocratic ideas in liberal terms by insisting that administrative institutions can and must be subjected to constitutional control. Yet it is impossible to read his work without sensing an anthropology that differs substantially from the hybrid-Enlightenment's world-picture. Sunstein seemed to look down on humanity as a whole (including, in fairness, himself) from a great distance, as if he were watching slow-moving ants take wrong turns in a vast maze. He would want to reach down and guide us in the right direction, and he would feel quite confident that the right kind of expertise can tell him and his colleagues where we should go and how he can get us there. Whatever Sunstein would say about democratic deliberation in theory, such a vision would leave little room for democratic deliberation in practice—except, perhaps, an up-or-down vote on a technocratically minded presidential administration that will, on securing approval from a majority, then feel free to set about enacting its vision of the good life using the vast array of tools available to the executive bureaucracy. It was not a vision that placed a very high value on popular understanding or discussion.

Other believers in the new behavioral science have seen more clearly than Sunstein the difficulty of reconciling technocracy and liberal democracy. One of Sunstein's friends and colleagues during his Chicago years was a young law professor named Adrian Vermeule, who, like Sunstein, had grown up near Boston, attended Harvard for undergrad and law school, clerked for a Supreme Court justice, and then taken a professorship in Hyde Park. (He also wound up returning to teach at Harvard, just two years before Sunstein did the same, and the two remain colleagues to this day.) Vermeule leaned in a different political direction than Sunstein—he had clerked for Antonin Scalia and received support from the conservative John M. Olin Foundation—but he too possessed an outstanding specimen of the coldly rational University of Chicago mind, and he shared Sunstein's fascination with behavioral science. He and Sunstein coauthored four papers during their time together at Chicago, and he is thanked in Sunstein and Thaler's acknowledgments for *Nudge*. Unlike Sunstein, however, Vermeule never seemed to have felt any special need to justify his program in the old language of liberal democracy. His productive scholarly career has been largely devoted to a comprehensive defense of executive branch power, as exercised by both the president and the federal bureaucracy.

As a matter of fact, this was a surprising direction for a former Scalia clerk with Federalist Society connections to take. Since the Reagan administration, American legal conservatives had largely placed their hopes in the judicial philosophy of *originalism* or *textualism*. Originalism purported to offer a neutral and apolitical standard for constitutional judgment: rather than deciding legal questions on the basis of their own views about justice or morality, judges are supposed to defer to the intent of the authors of the original constitutional text—and thus, indirectly, to the American people, whose will is theoretically embodied in the Constitution and its amendments. In practice, originalism has been indelibly associated with the settled policy positions of the Republican Party; the most prominent originalists, like Antonin Scalia, Samuel Alito, and Clarence Thomas, side almost invariably with the political Right on controversial questions.[55] This did not make originalism a sham, however. American conservatives are by definition more willing to accept the framers of the Constitution as possessing some form of binding authority, while American liberals, who are more likely to believe in moral progress over time, naturally see that claim to authority as contingent and arbitrary.

Originalism and political conservatism have thus shaped one another reciprocally. Legal conservatives have sometimes had to contort themselves and their arguments to justify their preferred outcomes in originalist terms. At the same time, however, the reverent originalist attitude toward the Constitution and the Founding has profoundly influenced the priorities of the conservative movement. American conservatives are almost unique in the West in their deep emotional attachment to civil liberties and principles like due process. While the conservative movement is not always perfectly consistent in its adherence to these ideals, the eighteenth-century liberal dream of a noninvasive, rights-respecting government still plays a substantial role in conservative rhetoric and practice. It famously moved Scalia to join the Supreme Court majority defending flag burning in *Texas v. Johnson*, and it has sometimes provided a counterweight to the more standard conservative concern with law and order.[56] It would also comport well with the American Right's general concern for preserving individual liberty against an activist state bureaucracy.

Vermeule's defense of executive power amounted to a direct challenge to this originalist orthodoxy. Practically speaking, the originalists had traditionally sought to rein in the administrative state and restore the supremacy of the people's elected representatives in Congress, whereas Vermeule argued that unelected expert bureaucrats were better suited than legislatures to dealing with the complex realities of modern governance.[57] The originalists saw the political theory of the American Founding as a kind of permanent bedrock, while Vermeule held that "there is no constitutional structure or institutional allocation of power that just is generally and systematically best, regardless of the economic, social, and political environment, and regardless of the nature of the second-order risks that constitutional rulemakers will confront."[58] And where the originalists tended to share James Madison's horror of abuse of power by the executive, Vermeule argued that such overreach should be understood as merely one risk among many, to be optimized and managed rather than stamped out at any cost.[59] He and his colleague Eric Posner, another sterling exemplar of the University of Chicago mind, referred to the Madisonian aversion to executive power as "tyrannophobia."[60]

Yet while Sunstein advanced his defenses of the administrative state in the vaguely utopian language of Clinton-Obama centrist liberalism, Vermeule gave his arguments a slightly transgressive reactionary cast. In his defenses of executive branch discretion and constitutional flexibility, he liked to invoke the work of Carl Schmitt, a controversial German jurist who worked in the Nazi legal apparatus in the early 1930s.[61] Along with Posner, Vermeule took a stand for presidential emergency powers during a moment—the Bush-era War on Terror—when polite liberal opinion in the legal academy was decidedly opposed to flexible executive power.[62] And in 2016, Vermeule, whose academic work had never evinced any particular theological concerns, converted to Catholicism and suddenly began a parallel career as a public intellectual of the religious Right, publishing in conservative organs like *First Things* and *American Affairs* and maintaining a hyperactive and rather impish Twitter presence. Vermeule quickly became the leading American exponent of what he and his allies called "Catholic Integralism," a school of political thought that advocated for the subjection of temporal to spiritual power. This provocative refusal of one of the fundamental principles of American liberalism—the separation of church and state—won Vermeule notoriety in the press, a sizeable contingent of young admirers online, and enough friends in the conservative movement's high places to get him appointed to the Administrative Conference of the United States, an executive branch advisory body, during the Trump administration.

As is often the case, Vermeule's religious conversion was not so much a radical transformation as the extension of a logic that already animated his thought and work. In fact, his belief in the priority of personal authority to codified authority seems to have been a major motive for his passage over the Tiber: as he explained to *First Things*,

"Raised a Protestant, despite all my thrashing and twisting I eventually couldn't help but believe that the apostolic succession, through Peter as the designated leader and *primus inter pares*, is in some logical or theological sense prior to everything else—including even Scripture, whose formation was guided and completed by the apostles and their successors, themselves inspired by the Holy Spirit."[63]

With his reverence for expertise and his unapologetic embrace of hierarchy, Vermeule was naturally drawn to a severe Catholic political theology that stressed the authority of an elite priesthood over the passing whims of the laity. Integralists claim, albeit controversially, that their politics of spiritual authority is in line with the perennial teaching of the Church, and it is not a coincidence that anti-Catholicism played a central role in the political rhetoric of the early American Republic. In a 2019 talk at George Mason University's Center for the Study of the Administrative State, founded and funded by mainstream conservatives who favor the reduction of bureaucratic power, Vermeule argued that bureaucracy might easily further religious interests and hinted at a deeper connection, remarking that "one might say that the genius of Catholicism is precisely the marriage of bureaucracy with mystery."[64] The key for Christians, as he argued in that talk and elsewhere, lay in turning the administrative state toward appropriate ends rather than quixotically seeking to destroy it.[65] As he explained in an article for the integralist site *The Josias*, "The ideal-type principles of hierarchy and unity of top-level command that animate bureaucracy, especially but not only military and security bureaucracies, are not obviously the sort of principles that threaten to inscribe liberalism within the hearts and minds of participants. Hence my own version of *ralliement*, which hopes for eventual integration effected from within institutions currently extant in liberal-democratic orders, focuses on executive-type bureaucracies rather than on parliamentary-democratic institutions *per se*."[66] More specifically, Vermeule suggested elsewhere that his vision of a creedally Catholic politics might be achieved as "nonliberal actors strategically locate themselves within liberal institutions and work to undo the liberalism of the state from within. These actors possess a substantive comprehensive theory of the good, and seize opportunities to bring about its fulfillment through and by means of the very institutional machinery that the liberal state has providentially created."[67] The administrative state, deplored for so long by conservatives as a covert vehicle for progressive ideological takeover, is reimagined by Vermeule as a "providentially created" covert vehicle for conservative ideological takeover.

From a practical standpoint, Vermeule's dream of a gradual conversion of the federal bureaucracy seems so unrealistic as to be positively dangerous for any conservatives who might try to put it into practice. The Right tends to oppose the administrative state not only on principled grounds but also because it is largely staffed by their opponents. Of twelve thousand federal government employees who donated to a major-party nominee in the 2020 election, for example, 84 percent gave their money to Joe Biden.[68] While Vermeule's perch at Harvard Law School gave him access to top young legal talent, efforts of immense scale and discipline would be required to turn the administrative state in a conservative direction.

In a sense, however, that objection misses the point. Vermeule may not have a workable strategy to offer his friends on the right, but he put forward something that might be more significant in the long run: a paradigm shift in their political theory. The ultimate goal of his politics was not the persuasion of friends but the capture of powerful institutions from his enemies. And those institutions themselves, once captured, are singularly unconcerned with public argument. Vermeule's embrace of what he calls "integration from within"—*the realization of theocratic political ends through bureaucratic capture*—amounted to a tacit admission that the public cannot be persuaded through ordinary, noncoercive means to accept his and his church's views about the common good.[69]

As an empirical matter, Vermeule was likely correct on this point. Political Catholicism of the kind he favored, which is very different from the more accommodating, less stridently orthodox variety practiced by the likes of Joe Biden or Nancy Pelosi, is deeply alien to mainstream American political sensibilities, and in any case Catholics make up only one-fifth of the U.S. population. Even if the Catholic integralists were able to enlist America's more conservative Protestant factions as allies—which is unlikely, since the most conservative Protestants are typically also the most hostile to Catholicism—what appears to be an inexorable secularizing trend in public life would render such an alliance toothless over time. The integralist turn toward the administrative state thus looks like a desperate gamble born out of despair at the exhaustion of all other options.

That overriding sense of the inadequacy of democratic means was, in fact, precisely what Vermeule had in common with more conventional technocrats. Vermeule and Sunstein, with their profoundly different views of the common good, could nevertheless collaborate on intellectual defenses of the administrative state because both believe that the public was incapable of apprehending what was necessary for its own well-being. Even his language was telling: speaking of "rulers" and "subjects" rather than "leaders" and "citizens."[70]

Vermeule's recognition of the failure of popular sovereignty was reinforced by the observations of the Nazi legal theorist Carl Schmitt. In *The Crisis of Parliamentary Democracy* (1923), Schmitt dismissed the old republican ideals as simply unworkable amid the realities of an industrial age:

> Great political and economic decisions on which the fate of mankind rests no longer result today (if they ever did) from balancing opinions in public debate and counter-debate. . . . As things stand today, it is of course practically impossible not to work with committees, and increasingly smaller committees; in this way the parliamentary plenum gradually drifts away from its purpose (that is, from its public), and as a result it necessarily becomes a mere façade. It may be that there is no other practical alternative. But one must then at least have enough awareness of the historical situation to see that parliamentarism thus abandons its intellectual foundation and that the whole system of freedom of speech, assembly, and the press, of public meetings, parliamentary immunities and privileges, is losing its rationale. . . . How harmless and idyllic are the objects of cabinet politics in the seventeenth and eighteenth centuries compared with the fate that is at stake today and which is the subject of all manner of secrets. In the face of this reality, the belief in a discussing public must suffer a terrible disillusionment.[71]

For Schmitt, the collapse of the parliamentary ideal in the face of the proliferation and growing scale of "great political and economic decisions" was inextricably linked to the turn toward more forthright and open forms of political conflict. That seems to be the way Vermeule sees it as well. "The hunger for a real politics must, in some way or another, be sated," he has written. "Better that it be sated through a sacramental feast."[72] The administrative state, governed by its distant experts, is not the kind of thing that can be deliberated over by an immense and incurably ignorant public. It—Sunstein's imperial "we," endowed with the power to make the members of that public safer, freer, and longer-lived—must simply act, and the way it acts will be determined by whoever can control it. That is why Vermeule's dream of a reenchanted federal bureaucracy is, though certainly implausible, perhaps the best of all the bad options facing orthodox Catholics who believe it is their duty to realize their vision of the common good in a profoundly hostile social order. It is also why Sunstein, however much beaming optimism he may express about the future of American democracy, was just as much a figure of exhaustion as the openly Schmittian Vermeule.

Politics on the Ground

Though often abstruse, these arguments were all, in distinct and often deliberate ways, drifting away from the cultural logics of the hybrid-Enlightenment. Yet neither were they floating above the political fray; they found traction in the partisan clashes of the early twenty-first century.

Most serious commentators understood that Trump's electoral victory in 2016 was more a consequence than a cause of America's political crisis. The foregoing account reinforces the point. Not only the seeds but the shoots of America's apocalyptic politics appeared long before 2016: Rorty's blithe dismissal of absolute right and his endorsement of purely expressive forms of political rhetoric; Claremont's despairing assertion that the builders and defenders of the administrative state had abandoned the plain natural truths understood by the Founders; and the technocrats' rejection of public reasoning in favor of utilitarian multitude management.

Yet there is also no doubt that the rise of Trump and Trumpism accelerated the decay of the hybrid-Enlightenment ideal. The fiery controversy that Trump generated with such insolent ease gave both his supporters and his detractors implicit permission to throw off the appearance of mutual respect. For conservatives, this was simple: they needed only to follow their leader, who made his disdain for his political enemies as open as he could. Famously, of course, he broke with protocol and basic courtesy by calling his adversaries creatively insulting names—"Sleepy Joe," "Crooked Hillary," "Crazy Nancy" (Pelosi), (Senator) "Jeff the Flake" Flake, "Do Nothing Democrats," "the failing *New York Times*"—but more fundamentally important was his tendency to depict them not as misguided fellow patriots but as deadly enemies. The press, long criticized in more moderate terms by Republicans, became "the enemy of the people," while opponents in Washington became "bad and evil people."[73] As countless observers noticed, Trump played expertly on his supporters' sense that the country's elite belonged to a different tribe with whom compromise was impossible.

In the competition for invective, Trump walked away with the biscuit, yet this hostility was not altogether unique to Trump or the new Republican Party. In fact, polling in 2019 found that Democrats were somewhat more likely than Republicans to admit thinking "on occasion" that "we'd be better off as a country if large numbers of the opposing party in the public today just died."[74] Democrats were also more likely than Republicans to agree that violence would be justified if the other party won the 2020 election. Similarly, Democrats were more likely than Republicans to describe their opponents as "un-American" (by eight points), "un-Christian" (by thirteen points), "dangerous" (by twenty-two points), and "evil" (by nine points).[75]

Poll results must always be handled with care, and something like the well-known "shy Republican" effect might be keeping some conservative poll respondents from revealing how they feel about the other side. Still, the curious fact remains that despite Democrats' efforts to occupy the moral high ground opposite the Trumpian mud pit, substantial numbers of progressives feel genuine rage and hatred toward the other side.

Trump, in fact, granted Democrats the same license to open hatred that he granted Republicans. So outlandish and disgraceful was his demeanor that progressives felt justified in treating him and his supporters as outsiders to the American political community. For example, a number of liberal intellectuals, including senior Yale professors Timothy Snyder and Jason Stanley and former secretary of state Madeleine Albright, wrote books arguing that Trump was a fascist.[76] To an outsider ignorant of the way academic discourse works, the vital question of Trump's goodness or badness might have seemed conceptually distinct from the more abstract question of his resemblance to the leaders of a particular early twentieth-century political movement. However, the real text of Snyder, Stanley, and Albright's fascism books was their subtext: since fascism is broadly acknowledged by Americans of many political persuasions as a serious evil, *Trump and his supporters are fascists* simply meant that *Trump and his supporters are enemies.* If you are fighting a fascist, you are defending humanity itself, and you should go at it with no holds barred. The charge of fascism was intended to shake up the old consensus order in which conservatives were tolerated as the loyal opposition.

It was not a coincidence, then, that the four years of the Trump administration also saw both progressive and conservative institutions grow increasingly intolerant of dissenting speech and argument. In conservative circles—not just the new Republican Party but many evangelical and Roman Catholic churches as well—anything other than total personal loyalty to Donald Trump and his version of the facts became a career liability. Meanwhile, in predominantly progressive institutions, including most major universities and media organizations, a parallel kind of censoriousness, widely referred to as "cancel culture," took hold. The term was imprecise and covered a disparate set of phenomena, from student activists demanding the cancellation of controversial figures' speaking gigs to organizations investigating or firing employees for questioning diversity protocols. All these events, however, followed from the same larger crisis of discourse afflicting the country. Conservatives and progressives alike had spent decades laying the intellectual groundwork for their retreat from the practices and conventions of liberal democracy. They had long told stories depicting their adversaries as beyond the reach of rational argument. The logic of that position entailed that those adversaries should be excluded from civilized institutions. In the end, the mutual fear and hyperpolarization of the Trump years merely gave partisans on both sides the excuse they needed to make the exclusion of the other complete.

The new forms of oppositional partisan discourse still contained vestigial appeals to the aims of the hybrid-Enlightenment. Restrictions on speech were defended as essential for protecting public safety. Progressives painted Trumpism as a threat to democracy itself; conservatives did the same for "critical race theory," "queer theory," and other new ideas from the Left. The old ideas and old ideals were still present, but the cultural agreements they referred to were fading fast.

The 2020 election and its aftermath both illuminated and advanced the crisis. Trump, of course, refused to accept the result—how could he do otherwise, with his own ego and, in his own rhetoric, the fate of the nation in the balance? Many Claremont scholars and others on the insurgent Right cheered him on, as did a majority of Republican voters; by late December 2021, 70 percent still said they believed Trump had won the election, and 50 percent said there was solid evidence that he had done so.[77] The most ardent supporters of this view, of course, had forced their way into the U.S. Capitol on January 6, 2021, in an apparent attempt to stop Congress from certifying the election results. In the end, top Republican officials upheld Joe Biden's claim to the presidency and no civil war–ready right-wing militias materialized, but Trump never formally conceded the election, and fears about future transfers of power persisted. For their part, progressives took the post-election crisis as reason to adopt more hardline measures against the Right. Social media sites started assigning warning labels to what they deemed "extremist content," while PayPal announced plans to prevent extremist organizations—as identified by progressive nonprofit groups—from moving money.[78]

The long, slow COVID-19 crisis of 2020–22 tragically revealed that polarization extended even to matters of basic public health. Not even a global pandemic could generate the negative solidarity of coming together to defeat the disease. More significant, the pandemic put the collapse of public reason on further display. For half of all Americans, the scientific and medical establishment did not speak with credible authority. It didn't help that the technocrats charged with managing the American response to the pandemic showed little respect for the public's capacity to think for itself. In several notorious cases, Dr. Anthony Fauci and other top public health officials told outright lies about scientific findings in an effort to promote what they saw as the most effective collective response to the pandemic.[79] Social media platforms also took a heavy-handed approach to censoring what "expert fact-checkers" determined to be "misinformation" about the pandemic, applying warning labels and suspending offending accounts. While these moves did slow the spread of a number of dangerous falsehoods, they also overreached, stifling reasonable and highly important debates, including, most famously, the discussion over the virus's possible origins in a research laboratory. Facebook removed posts defending the so-called "lab leak hypothesis" for months—right up until mainstream media outlets and government agencies suddenly began to argue that the idea was worth taking seriously.[80]

Thus, what might have been an occasion for national unity quickly turned into yet another bitter field of conflict in the corrosive culture war, with each partisan faction interpreting events in light of its fear of the other. Conservatives saw a progressive monolith taking advantage of the crisis to undermine their freedoms; progressives saw a conservative mob clinging selfishly to individual prerogatives at the expense of the social whole. The contempt of the progressive and technocratic knowledge class toward these "populist know-nothings" was matched by the contempt of middle- and working-class people toward the "socialist wokerati" and their fellow travelers. On such grounds, little real persuasion was possible, and little occurred.

Exhaustion as Depletion

In sum, what had occurred in the discourse among the most thoughtful actors in this drama was also playing out on the ground in real time by key institutional partisans. Combined, we see not only indications of a retreat from established democratic practices, but also a weakening of liberal democracy's cultural infrastructure.

For all of America's extraordinary wealth, talent, innovation, and goodwill, none of the key actors in this drama could provide an authoritative account of current events, much less the arc of American history. None would even try to articulate a vision for the future capable of acknowledging the legitimate concerns or claims of their opponents. Neither could any of these actors inspire a plurality of citizens to constructive action in the face of dire national and global challenges. Indeed, all the key institutional actors had given up on persuasion and the arduous task of working through the present contradictions in pursuit of an unum large enough and capacious enough to hold an expanding and ever more contentious pluribus together.

Rather, for the partisans in this conflict, their opponents had become the "repugnant cultural other." Persuasion and compromise, they concluded, were futile. The only option left was to do an end-run around the opposition—for the technocrats, an end-run around popular sovereignty itself. Most profoundly of all, the cultural sources that had long underwritten liberal democracy—albeit repeatedly worked through at this point—seemed spent.

To be sure, the hope for a renewal of democracy has remained in the breasts of many if not most American citizens, but such a renewal depends upon at least a partially shared ethical vision of the world as the world could yet be. Such a vision and the larger cosmology that could make it real and compelling are now nowhere to be found. In their absence the possibilities of achieving national solidarity anytime in the foreseeable future appear bleak indeed.

PART IV

Late-Stage Democracy

CHAPTER ELEVEN

A Great Unraveling

The Solidarity That Remains

In the personal relationships of friendship and family that constitute private life and in the quotidian routines of day-to-day life—work, shopping, preparing meals, going to restaurants or to the gym—one can find a kind of ritual solidarity rooted in interdependence but also in mutual care, kindness, and generosity. The affective bonds of solidarity in these places are not ubiquitous but they are surely authentic, and they remain in abundance. Likewise, in the ordinary work that constitutes local governance, one can find a solidarity grounded in a commitment to address common problems that affect the citizens in these institutions' reach. In these settings, things still get done. Not everything is reduced to ideology; all is not condensed to political warfare.

In a way, this picture aligns with an important argument advanced by Jeffrey Stout in the 1980s contending that the kind of moral complexity ubiquitous today did not, or at least *did not necessarily*, lead to a Babel-like chaos.[1] Of course, he acknowledged, there are important and deeply divisive questions surrounding warfare, abortion, and all the particular issues that touch on freedom and equality that seem to be unending. Yet, he contended, this wasn't the whole picture. Indeed, any contention that liberal society lacks any shared conception of the good was simply false.[2] Stout argued instead that even if we can't agree on any particular theory of human nature or some ultimate telos or even on the rules by which rational disagreement could take place, one can find a relatively limited, but nonetheless real and significant, agreement on the good. Our disagreements don't go "all the way down." There remains much that Americans agree upon. Those agreements take form in moral platitudes that represent vague agreements, of which there are "far too many to mention."[3] Together, they form a "moral bricolage" derived from a "selective retrieval and eclectic reconfiguration" of inherited moral fragments that are somewhat coherent but, most important, prove useful in addressing real problems that naturally crop up in daily life.

Published in 1988, Stout's *Ethics After Babel* was both appealing and persuasive at the time. His liberal pragmatist account remains persuasive, perhaps especially so, as I noted above, in local and more intimate settings. *But, it would seem, less so now.* The argument has become less persuasive as a description of relationships within families and among neighbors, demonstratively less persuasive as a description of the workings of local governance, whether in city councils or in neighborhood associations, school boards, PTAs, and other local organizations. And it seems utterly *un*persuasive as a description of the dynamics of national politics and the *most national and public* of our public discourse. Even essential platitudes about an abhorrence to violence are no longer taken for granted by citizens as they once were (though more on this in chapter 13).

Myriad Local Initiatives

Yet ordinary citizens and local leaders are not giving up without a fight. It is in this context that we can understand the proliferation of initiatives launched in the early decades of the twenty-first century, all seeking to build on this goodwill. These organizations and initiatives number in the hundreds. Their names signal their purpose: Search for Common Ground, AllSides, Unite, Bridge, USA, Bridge Alliance, Bridging Divides Initiative, Bridge the Divide, Younify, Stand Together, CommonAlly, Search for Common Ground, Unify America, In This Together, #NationBuilder, Purple America, American Public Square, Crossing Party Lines, Unity, More in Common, The Reunited States, Center for Deliberative Democracy, Let's Talk

Democracy, Sacred Discourse, Living Room Conversations, the National Institute for Civil Discourse, and America Indivisible. All of these initiatives are driven by an acute awareness of what is at stake, and all speak to the desire to deepen the level of mutual understanding and to build trust among citizens of various backgrounds as a way of rediscovering the bonds of solidarity. Their participants are local leaders and citizens motivated by ethical convictions often rooted in faith and reason and the hope of a better world, and to this end, they are keen to continue the task of working through the evolving contradictions still present in national life.

These initiatives are often inspiring. Weave: The Social Fabric Project, the brainchild of *New York Times* columnist David Brooks and supported by the Aspen Institute, believes that "relationships can transform our lives and our communities . . . and ultimately mend our deeply divided nation. We work in our neighborhoods and towns to create connections and lead with love." Another example is Re-united States, an organization built around a film of the same name that features the #HealAmericaPledge that individuals and organizations can sign.

> I commit to the mission of healing America.
> I will resist demonizing those I disagree with
> and instead listen to understand their concerns.
> I embrace my responsibility to reduce hostility,
> because I believe our shared future depends on it.[4]

Still another is Braver Angels, a national citizens' movement that seeks to bring liberals, conservatives, and others together at the grassroots level, "not to find centrist compromise, but to find one another as citizens." Through workshops, debates, and campus engagement, "Braver Angels helps Americans understand each other beyond stereotypes, form community alliances, and reduce the vitriol that poisons our civic culture."[5]

Surely all those involved in such efforts would agree with Stout that "wisdom begins in a refusal to let over-simplified, excessively abstract contrasts define our options."[6] Their efforts are predicated upon that wisdom. But one cannot help but wonder why they haven't yet been scaled up to a level that would displace the more caustic, hyperpolarized, and destructive norms of civic and political engagement. If such ameliorative efforts can happen locally, why can't they happen nationally?

The Vast Chasm between the National and the Local

Intuitively, the difficulty reflects the same reasons that parents who wish to protect their children from the corrosive effects of the internet or popular culture struggle as they do. The family is a weak institution compared to the popular culture industry. Parents may have limited success, but the institutional power of the entertainment industry and of the internet more broadly ensure that any success is, at best, temporary.

The reasons are sociological and obvious. Public discourse at the national level operates in an entirely different institutional context than discourse at a more local level. The former operate primarily within the new and ever-evolving communications technologies (beginning with radio, television, and mass print media and evolving to the range of social media platforms: Facebook, Twitter [now X], YouTube, and the like). The latter operate more or less face-to-face. The new communications technologies have created the conditions that require a short form of discourse in which exchange is rapid, facile, unnuanced, impersonal, titillating, and mostly anonymous, with little or no accountability to truth, nuance, and subtlety—a form that very easily allows communication to take on a life of its own. This highly manipulable mode of discourse and its extraordinary autonomy from accountability is reinforced by popularity-based algorithms that concentrate messaging to different segments of the population. They also maximize user engagement through sharing, liking, and retweeting: a practice bolstered by the powerful economic incentives of modern advertising. And the advertising industry itself ties messaging to the baser interests, fears, status anxieties, and desires of segmented demographics. In sum, while these technologies don't cause polarization, they do intensify it.[7] Local, face-to-face discourse is in every way the opposite of this mode of civic exchange. It is a long, difficult, processual, and intensely interpersonal form of public discourse that requires attentiveness, nuance, and accountability.

To state the obvious, these are different species of public discourse, each governed by its own very different cultural logic. The cultural logics that characterize and govern the new communications technologies are embedded within the most powerful institutions of late modern America, and as such, those cultural logics set the backdrop for the more local and interpersonal forms of public discourse. There is no end to good intentions among ordinary citizens, but good intentions are no match for the kind of institutional power wielded by Facebook, Twitter, YouTube, and their kind. Precisely because of their institutional setting and power, these shallower forms of public discourse mediated through the new communications technologies invariably seep into the ways in which we think and speak in everyday life. Seepage is everywhere in its form and in its effects. Both the technology and its cultural logics seep into interpersonal discourse and local organizations. In their wake, we see not only exaggerated forms of disagreement spilling into personal life and local organizations but anger, bitterness, and animosity. In instances too numerous to count, this seepage has contributed to the destruction of bonds of local affection and disrupted the effective functioning of local politics and life. At times, reputations and livelihoods have been destroyed in the process. Instances of such dysfunction and brokenness are not ubiquitous, but in the intervening years since Stout published *Ethics After Babel*, they do seem to be more and more common. Nearly everyone has a story to tell.

The Solidarity of the "Procedural Republic"

Indeed, as one moves from the local to the national level, the conduct of politics has become defined by a consistent—arguably increasing—brutalizing symbolic and institutional environment. In the last decades of the twentieth and early decades of the twenty-first centuries, affirmative solidarity has, at best, rested upon a thin proceduralism that through bitter contestation has only become thinner.

Though the preconditions for this weakening had been developing long before the emergence of Donald Trump, his presidency surely marked a turning point. It was neither Trump's astonishing ignorance of the institutions and protocols of governance nor his lack of experience that were the defining characteristics of his influence. Rather, it was his flawed character and the way his character became manifest in how he rose to power and the ways he wielded it that were so destabilizing. His penchant for exaggeration, lying, and bullying, his provocative flaunting of the conventions of his office, his assault on what are supposed to be the truth-telling institutions of government (from the Justice Department and intelligence agencies to the Office of Management and Budget) and the media, his disregard for the established rules of international diplomacy, and his leadership in transforming the Republican Party from an institution grounded in the ideals of classical conservatism to something closer to a personality cult animating a settler-nativist populism and nationalism—all revealed how fragile that proceduralism was.

Importantly, that weakened proceduralism was still resilient enough to ensure an effective (if ugly) transfer of power in 2020, but not strong enough to be peaceful, as the violent protests at the Capitol on January 6, 2021, demonstrated. It was robust enough to restore stable governance in the years following Trump's term of office, but not stable enough for the Biden presidency to be seen as legitimate by large segments of the American population.

Trump's presidency was surely a defining moment, but as I've noted, there was history behind it. Accusations and counteraccusations of election-rigging, voter fraud, and theft have been common among partisans on both sides for quite some time. The 2000 contest between George W. Bush and Albert Gore was the first since 1888 in which a candidate won the Electoral College vote but lost the popular vote. Yet what made his election particularly controversial was the margin by which Bush won the state of Florida (officially, 537 votes) and with it, Florida's Electoral College votes, and the intervention of the U.S. Supreme Court (in a split, partisan decision) in halting any recount. Each side accused the other of trying to enact a "legal *coup d'etat.*"[8] The chair of the Democratic National Committee at the time, Terry McAuliffe, stated that Gore had "actually won the last [2000] presidential election . . . [but Republicans] STOLE" it.[9] In 2004, Democratic members of the House and Senate objected to Ohio's electoral votes going to Bush, though he won the state by more than 118,000 votes. A lawsuit was filed seeking an injunction against certifying the state's election, accusing the Bush-Cheney campaign of "high-tech vote stealing," and asserting that there was sufficient evidence of fraud to halt the electoral process until a thorough investigation could be completed.[10] Likewise, in 2008 and 2012, Republican activists argued that Barack Obama would not have been elected without the registration of ineligible or nonexistent voters in the inner cities and without the scores of Mexicans bussed over the southern border using aliases to vote. John McCain declared in a presidential debate that the group committing this swindle was "on the verge of perpetrating one of the greatest frauds in voter history in this country, maybe destroying the fabric of democracy."[11] Again in 2016, Hillary Clinton won the popular vote over Trump by nearly 3 million votes but lost the Electoral College count. Trump claimed that he would have won the popular vote had it not been for millions of illegal votes. Democrats responded in kind, charging Trump and his allies of voter intimidation. In protests around the country, rank-and-file Democrats chanted "Not my president."[12] And after evidence emerged of Russian meddling in the election, Clinton herself declared Trump an "illegitimate president," suggesting, "He knows that he stole the 2016 presidential election."[13]

Though not comprehensive by a long stretch, this account of the challenges to the legitimacy of presidential elections in the early twenty-first century is illustrative of a suspicion and a practice of protest that has come to infuse electoral politics generally. There is an observable symmetry between the two parties in this account of electoral challenge and counter-challenge—a symmetry that extends to each party denying voting irregularities when they win. Yet my point is not to argue for some kind of political equivalence between the two parties. Clearly the protest of January 6, 2021, and Trump's culpability in encouraging it brought the phenomenon to an entirely new level. Rather, my thesis is that American electoral policies already reflected a thin proceduralism by virtue of those policies being determined at the state level where, from the beginning, there has been no uniformity regarding the regulations surrounding voter registration, early voting, absentee voting, voter ID requirements, what votes count, and how electoral districts are formed. These inconsistencies have created conditions that have been easy to contest and exploit. And as they have been, it has only further diminished any procedural solidarity that has remained in our national politics, rendering much of the system simply—and at times catastrophically—dysfunctional. It is difficult to imagine how circumstances might constructively change.

A Great Unraveling

That difficulty is made worse when considering dynamics within the deep structures of culture—the habitus—upon which even the thinnest of proceduralism rests. We see this in the working metaphysics, epistemology, anthropology, ethics, and teleology latent in public life.

Reality Deconstructed

That our views of reality and the means by which we know it are no longer those of the late eighteenth and early nineteenth centuries goes without saying. The cosmic imaginary of the early Republic was suffused by religious meaning even, as I've noted, among the Enlightenment skeptics and materialists who dissented from religious doctrine.[14] It was still, as Charles Taylor put it, a society in which it was "nearly impossible not to believe in God," and even those who dissented, dissented religiously.[15] Today, of course, epistemologies rooted in a high view of the natural law or in the revelations of Scripture may still be embraced as authoritative by considerable numbers of people, but *as the prevailing logics of public culture*—not least in law, policy, government, academia, industry, finance, and the corporate world—their plausibility has dissolved, and where not dissolved, they have been discredited as either anachronistic or as the foundations of bigotry.

Our views of reality and the means by which we know it are no longer those of the early twentieth century either. The kind of robust and confident secularist commitment to reason and science represented by John Dewey, to take one case, has also been challenged and mostly discredited. Thus, the early and high modern hope that reason as a universal and autonomous faculty would bring about progress, emancipation, and the fullness of human potential has buckled under its own weight. By the mid-twentieth century, even Dewey had recognized this.[16] The very achievements of instrumental rationality in the application of science and technology have carried, along with benefits, pernicious, even if unintended, consequences. Indeed, two world wars, the proliferation of nuclear weaponry, the industrial de-spoiling of the environment, the reckless using up of the earth's re-sources, the creation of perverse financial instruments, and the like have eroded any confidence that "reason" as such or "science" as such were unalloyed goods. Beyond this, of course, the hope of emanci-pation through reason, technology, and science had created new forms of domination.

It is true that science could be pragmatically successful as a method, but it has also become clear that it could not be "true" in any privileged sense. Indeed, "rationality" has given way to multiple and competing rationalities, none of which is privileged. Sociologi-cally, there is no single truth, only multiple truths, each with its own public. Underwriting all of this was an "incredulity" not just toward metanarratives, as Jean-François Lyotard noted, but toward virtually everything that does not align with a person's (or a faction's) own well-formed predispositions.[17]

All of this is a quick distillation of what became commonplace among so-called postmodern intellectuals who were all too happy to expose the cultural logic of the secular Enlightenment and its aspi-rations as hollow. These intellectuals arrived at a "post-truth" mo-ment long before anyone else did.

Among philosophers, of course, the relativism they discovered or declared remains contested, but historically and sociologically it is an apt description of the world we now live in. The evolving cul-ture war is a testament to its bitter consequences.

Yet it would be facile and wrong to conclude, as many conserva-tives have, that this is all the fault of postmodernists.[18] That is not how culture works. Postmodernists were, however, a harbinger. The ability of those theorists and philosophers to interrogate, doubt, and highlight the imperfections and hypocrisies of the social and politi-cal order was a luxury that they could enjoy only so long as the rest of the citizenry did not. As long as the majority of Americans—even if some of them were "deplorable" or "clinging to their guns or reli-gion"—continued to operate within the hybrid-Enlightenment and commit to the American project (including fighting its wars), there could be relative political stability. But now the skepticism of intellectuals has percolated into the general public. Now nearly everyone is a skeptic, nearly everyone sees the hypocrisy, nearly everyone doubts the goodwill of their leaders—and that, it turns out, is one of the keys to understanding the comprehensive epistemic crisis that is distinctive about our political moment.[19]

But the source of the epistemic crisis was not due to the soft nihilism of postmodern scholars. There were, in fact, multiple sources, but among the more important ones were those built into the new technologies of communication themselves.

The techno-utopians at the dawn of social media and the internet more broadly, of course, imagined it differently. They believed that the new information technologies would prove a singular benefit to democracy by giving a voice to all. With no one controlling access, there would be no censorship. No one would be sidelined; all would be recognized. As a marketplace of ideas and information, it would be impossible for even the most powerful to foist a distortion or lie upon a credulous public. But as it turned out, the new social media created the perfect conditions for what has become something akin to epistemic anarchy—and with it, the proliferation of misinformation and worse.

The root of the problem begins from the nearly infinite multiplication of sources of information—the so-called "marketplace of ideas"—and the bewildering number of choices it imposes upon all of us. Information, no less than numeric data, is not self-interpreting. "Raw information," as Stanley Fish observed, "cannot distinguish between benign and malign appropriations of itself."[20] So people must choose. From psychology, we know that when confronted with a range of information sources, people as a rule do not choose rationally according to some independent criteria, but rather act out of their preconceptions, biases, and feelings: choosing the information that validates their prejudices and avoiding what does not.[21] It is also easier to accept what you already believe and significantly more difficult to resist falsehoods, particularly when beliefs are vested with emotional commitment. The tendencies toward confirmation bias are well known: they work to predispose people to sift the evidence that supports their views from anything that challenges it.

It is not clear that anything is capable of penetrating these echo chambers. Fact-checking has been shown to be ineffective, especially in polarized contexts.[22] Documentary evidence carries a presumption of veracity, but machine-learning algorithms can produce images and sound recordings that are fabrications.[23] Satire seems to only deepen the cynicism toward the very idea of fact-based truth.

Protests notwithstanding, the social media industry itself seems mostly indifferent to the loss it has contributed to. A large part of this change in disposition was due to the business model upon which the industry was established. Profitability was driven almost entirely by advertising revenue rather than subscription income. The industry's ecosystem, now permeating older mainstream news and information sources, has become dependent upon the income generated through clicks on thinly sourced stories or sensational headlines. What matters is not the quality of the information, of course, but the number of people who see the story and the advertisements accompanying it. The greater the number, the greater the revenue.[24] Perverse incentives indeed! Nor are the algorithms for "likes" or "recommends" or "retweets" optimizing what is accurate or fair. Fake accounts on Facebook, trolls who purposely inflame and antagonize, bots on Twitter that artificially and anonymously magnify disinformation—these techniques are ubiquitous on the internet and their omnipresence only cultivates doubt about everything that is communicated online.

The entire informational ecosystem spawned by the new communications technologies and the market dynamics by which they proliferate, then, render truth and reality beside the point. It is not that public officials lost the capacity to distinguish truth from falsehood, but rather they became indifferent to the distinction under the pretext that effectiveness mattered more. As the former Senate Majority Leader Harry Reid put it after having been criticized for making up a lie that a Republican presidential candidate (Mitt Romney) had not paid taxes for a decade, "Well, they can call it whatever they want. Romney didn't win, did he?"[25] In an equally revealing moment, in the 2016 election, Newt Gingrich dismissed FBI crime statistics showing that crime of all sorts was in decline, saying, "As a political candidate, I'll go with what people feel and . . . let you [the CNN interviewer] go with the theoreticians."[26] Hyperbole, spin, fearmongering, and the like have been and remain commonplace among political actors. The difference is that they are amplified many times over by contemporary communications technologies rendering the epistemic context chaotic.

On the receiving side, it is not that ordinary citizens have become more stupid or more gullible than in times past but rather, as Christopher Lasch put it, that they have no real institutional alternative to the consumption of hyperbole, spin, distortion, and lies.[27] For the average person navigating this baffling symbolic landscape, what gets filtered tends to be information that reinforces their own understanding of the world, an understanding shared with anonymous others in a simulated community.

For political actors, the incentive is simply to generate momentum around stories irrespective of the quality of information, thoughtfulness of opinion, or subtlety and balance of argument. These qualities are all but absent. What ultimately matters, as Lasch observed, is "the particular version of unreality the American public could be induced to accept."[28]

This is an arena in which manipulation, duplicity, and bigotry face little to no obstruction. Indeed, a large study of Twitter users showed that false stories circulated at a rate much faster and more widely than true stories.[29] For progressives, the problem of "fake news" can be laid at the feet of conservatives, and indeed, the manipulation of truth claims or claims to facticity in part break along partisan lines.[30] In the end, though, *this is a systemic problem* in which all sides are implicated, and because of this, the line between truth and falsehood, fact and fiction, real and unreal has become nebulous at best. That between one-half and two-thirds of adults in America now regularly get their news through social media means that this problem will remain entrenched for as long as this media environment exists.[31]

Myth and Misinformation

The systemic deconstruction of epistemic authority built into the new communications technology and their markets generates conditions for mass credulity. Georges Sorel and Karl Mannheim each witnessed this in the early part of the twentieth century: for Sorel in the lead-up to World War I and for Mannheim at the end of the Weimar Republic.[32] In the face of mass confusion and anxiety, average citizens look for simplistic, often monocausal accounts to make some sense of the uncertainties in the world and their place within it. Rumors, urban legends, myths, and conspiracy theories, typically distilled through simple metaphors and aphorisms, offer some degree of existentially satisfying coherence and plans of action to the people who embrace them.

Most of the time, of course, these legends and myths are understood by observers through the lens of psychology or logic. These ideas are either evidence of mental illness (such as paranoia, hysteria, irrational phobias) or just deficient logic (where there is a lack of evidence). In short, people who hold such madcap ideas as a stolen election or the COVID-19 hoax or the existence of the QAnon conspiracy are either crazy or stupid, but in either case, irrational. Against these fabrications, cottage industries have emerged among opponents and the media that offer conclusive counterevidence of the irrationalities of these ideas and fallacies of their logic.

Yet all of this effort misses the point. Debunking is an important democratic task, but in a late modern context where there is very little agreement as to what constitutes facts or truth or how to arrive at them consensually, these strategies will never fully gain traction with those operating in a different epistemic register. In fact, such beliefs are mostly impervious to counterevidence, fact-checking, or empirically grounded logic because the fabrication and propagation of these ideas and beliefs are finally exercises in meaning-making in a world that lacks stability or coherence or the means of rendering the world meaningful. However flawed or irrational, these ideas function to make sense of the world, and they work because they resonate with the life circumstances and experiences of the people who hold them.[33]

Incommensurable Public Ethics

The deconstruction of public knowledge and its sources is problem enough. Yet it extends to the realm of moral knowledge and understanding. Here, though, it has its own peculiar history, dynamic, and effect.

The history of this conundrum begins with the catastrophic failure of religion in Western modernity to provide a shared and stable background and foundation for a universal understanding of the good and, in the wake of that failure, the tragic inadequacy of secular philosophies to fill that vacuum.[34] Despite repeated and often heroic efforts, these failures have occurred in the rarified discourse of the academic guilds as well as within the broader public philosophies of nation-states. The brief history I have provided in these pages has been an attempt to show historically the complex ways in which this has unfolded in the unique circumstances of American public life.

What is familiar to many scholars who study these things is now obvious to most Americans: any "background consensus" (Habermas) of morals or "settled convictions" (Rawls) of ethical practice upon which the dominant public institutions have operated have largely unraveled. In the early 1980s, it would have been plausible to dispute Alasdair MacIntyre's dark description of moral discourse in his seminal work, *After Virtue*, as a "greatly exaggerated account of our predicament."[35] As I have suggested, his thesis is more difficult to dispute now, particularly in the ways that political and media institutions drive public discourse around the myriad ethical issues that define our times.

And what public issue today is not infused with moral evaluation? Abortion, sexuality, gender roles, race, the police, criminal justice, immigration, climate change, COVID-19 and public health, the composition of the courts, education, the economy, relations with foreign powers, the strictly procedural matters of electoral politics and governance (such as the filibuster)—all are inescapably imbued with ethical significance, and "debate" over each can be fairly described as interminable. Even if these truncated debates could be expanded to be made logically coherent, they would still find no mutually agreeable compromise or resolution because they trace back to premises that are, in the end, incommensurable. MacIntyre's elegant summary applies even more today than in the early 1980s when he wrote it: "From our rival conclusions we can argue back to our rival premises; but when we do arrive at our premises argument ceases and the invocation of one premise against another becomes a matter of pure assertion and counter-assertion."[36] This is true for the leadership classes and the literate public. Professional philosophers do no better than anyone else.

It isn't just the arguments that are incommensurable and thus interminable, so are the key moral concepts invoked in those arguments. Concepts such as justice, fairness, freedom, rights, equality, equity, tolerance, inclusion, hate, and the like are themselves contested and manipulable because they too are lifted out of the context of larger conceptual frameworks or traditions from which those concepts derived their significance. They become, as MacIntyre put it, "an unharmonious mélange of ill-suited [ethical] fragments."[37]

This may be why public and political discourse tends to be characterized by an aggressive exchange of slogans and clichés, insults, denunciations, and invective.[38] This was a trade that Trump did not invent—indeed, this vastly truncated and combative form of discourse had been institutionalized for decades before he became president— but it was a form of discourse at which he excelled and which he used his office to promote.

If these challenges to public ethics and moral discourse aren't difficult enough, compounding the problem is that there are "no rational ways of securing moral agreement" in our public culture and no established way to decide between rival claims or the rival premises upon which those claims are based. What criteria or authority could be invoked that would be more or less agreed upon by a healthy majority to settle any particular dispute? God? "Right Reason"? The Bible? Human nature? No longer. Human rights? Science? Democracy itself? Less and less. In his *A Short History of Ethics*, MacIntyre wrote, "Between the adherents of rival moralities and between the adherents of one morality and the adherents of none there exists no court of appeal, no impersonal neutral standard."[39]

His description is an expression of what professional philosophers call emotivism, a doctrine that holds that all moral judgments are nothing more than an expression of personal or subjective feeling, preference, or attitude. As such, moral evaluation is the expression of standard-less, criterion-less choice, "the kind of choice for which no rational justification can be given."[40] And precisely because it is subjective and without an authoritative standard by which to make its claims, its moral judgments are arbitrary. Within emotivism, then, all rational disagreements are never-ending.

As a school of academic moral philosophy, emotivism failed.[41] However, it has succeeded beyond measure, even if unintentionally, as a central element of the latent cultural logic of late modern public philosophy in America. It has done so for two reasons. First, emotivism as an ethics is entirely sympathetic to the antinomian ethos that has grown like kudzu in American history and culture—its hyper-individualism and its general hostility toward established authority.[42] Second, emotivism operates in ways that are in sympathy with and, in turn, reinforced by the institutional influence of a pluralist polity and consumerist market economy.

What is especially important about emotivism as a latent public philosophy is its functional approach to moral language. Even as an academic school of moral philosophy, emotivism was concerned not only with the subjective expression of moral feelings and attitudes, but with the desire to produce the same feelings and attitudes in others. The significance of moral utterance, then, was less about an expression of truth because, even if truth was intended, there was no way it could be established. Rather, its public significance was in its usefulness in influencing others. Moral language, then, is highly and often intentionally manipulable. Within emotivism, winning arguments is, crudely, about using moral language to incite emotional responses in others.

In the end, one can justifiably conclude with MacIntyre that "there is nothing to such contemporary [public, and increasingly private] disagreements but a clash of antagonistic wills, each will determined by some set of arbitrary choices of its own."[43] His observation tightly aligns with Nietzsche's conclusion about moral philosophy in the late nineteenth century, that the claims to objective moral truth, in the end, only mask the subjectively based and thus arbitrary will to power. "What?" Nietzsche prodded in *The Gay Science*, "You admire the categorical imperative within you? This firmness of your so-called judgement? This absoluteness of the feeling, 'here everyone must judge as I do'? Rather admire your selfishness here! And the blindness, pettiness, and simplicity of your selfishness! For it is selfish to consider one's own judgement a universal law, and this selfishness is blind, petty and simple because it shows you haven't discovered yourself."[44]

Nietzsche went too far in generalizing this *reductio ad potentiam* to all morality, but he was spot on in describing the net effect of the dominant emotivist moral ethos that prevails today in American political culture.

A great deal of our ethically laden political discourse may not be so much about establishing truth or fact—even if it is intended to be—but rather, at least in its net effect, about eliciting an emotional solidarity among the like-minded and a shaming of those who dissent. On the right . . . freedom, family values, tradition, virtue, morality, patriot, as well as un-American, unpatriotic, reverse racism, perversion, and the like. On the left . . . justice, tolerance, inclusion, diversity, equity, as well as racism, white supremacy, bigot, homophobe, hater, and so on. In an emotivist ethos, moral discourse, whatever else it might be or intend, is a tool—a means to rally allies and a weapon of social control to limit, harm, and discredit opponents. *Moral language, then, fails as a means to truth but succeeds as a means to power and boundary creation and maintenance.* It would be interesting if these dynamics were safe within the world of speculative philosophy and social theory, but because they are often institutionalized within universities, the media, social media, popular entertainment, political parties, state legislatures, federal departments, social movements, philanthropies, the HR departments of major corporations, and not least, many churches and other institutions of faith, they are rightly alarming.

In its totality, public discourse in America over the most important and often the most trivial issues of the day is not discourse at all. Under the conditions of late modernity, public discourse as a rational exchange of competing positions is difficult and perhaps impossible in our public culture. Surely if it isn't possible within colleges and universities, as it seems to be, it is not likely anywhere else, least of all among movement activists, policy makers, party officials, and politicians. What we have, rather, is a simulacrum of public moral debate that has come to conceal a raw and brutalizing competing will to power.

A Shrinking Telos

Among the fragments that remain of our collective moral culture is a common desire to improve ourselves and the world around us. This is, after all, basic to the nature of ethics, both theoretically and practically. Indeed, the language of change, improvement, reform, transformation, and even revolution is common. But toward what?

As it bears on individuals, there are ideals of health, fitness, weight, and beauty that are common enough. So too are desires for financial stability and even prosperity and the comforts they provide. Following from this are matters of lifestyle: the kinds of material goods we own, where we live, and how we spend our leisure time if we have it. All of these desires can be experienced as ideals that carry in varying degrees the weight of a moral imperative. Multibillion-dollar industries understand the range of these desires, refine them, amplify them, and leverage them for profit. This ecosystem constitutes a significant part of mass culture. But such desires are appropriated almost entirely as personalized ideals, as motivations to achieve individual and personal happiness. They are not experienced as a common hope for which we all work together. If these are goods that we share in common, they are mainly "common" in a statistical sense, not in the sense of a common project. Questions of ends are relevant, but they have been mostly privatized.

But what of the common weal?

As we've seen, for much of American history, the telos was defined by a secular and biblical millennialism that, though drawing from different sources, was united in its understanding of America as exceptional—exceptional in its resources, its Founding ideals, its achievements, and its promise. This understanding was shared across different religious traditions, racial and ethnic groups, and ideological factions, and it was a powerful means by which Americans in their differences were able to work through the contradictions of the hybrid-Enlightenment and their common life. However misbegotten, secular and biblical millennialism signified that American history had meaning, and participation in civic life by its citizens meant that their part in nation-building also had significance.

By the early twentieth century, millennialism had been replaced by secular notions of progress. In Europe, fascists and communists embraced utopian forms of historical finality for an imagined time when justice and peace would be fully realized. But by the end of World War I, British and American intellectuals had concluded that progress as a utopian possibility was nothing more than a superstition—"the one notion," Lewis Mumford wrote in 1932, "that has been thoroughly blasted by the facts of twentieth-century experience." A few years earlier, Christopher Dawson had called it the "deadest of dead ideas."[45]

In its more quotidian expressions, progress as the assumption of steady improvement into the future held sway through most of the twentieth century. Yet as the century drew to a close, even this had lost credulity except in the realm of technological innovation.

As to the political ideals of "freedom," "equality," "justice," and "tolerance," public opinion surveys have continued to show broad agreement about their importance, but these agreements have also been mainly statistical in character. There is no common meaning to these words in the abstract or in particular circumstances where the realization of these ideals might be hoped for. Any notion of justice, then, requires a conception of what justice would look like if achieved. And any notion of equality requires at least a vague conception of what equality would look like if it were realized. Freedom, tolerance . . . the same. It is precisely these conceptions that we no longer have. Absent a fuller picture of what a free, equal, just, and tolerant society would look like, it is difficult to see how they could achieve common meaning and give rise to a common purpose.

These puzzles are complicated by the fact that it is not clear how any of these moral ideals come together or relate to one another coherently. What, for example, is the relationship between religious freedom and the rights of nondiscrimination? Can equality be achieved without diminishing or limiting the freedom of others or without diminishing standards of excellence? For conservatives, how does a commitment to the sacredness of life and of unborn life in particular square with the freedom to own and use semi-automatic weapons? For progressives, how does a commitment to the inclusion of the weak and vulnerable align, as it often does, with support for euthanasia or physician-assisted suicide? And why are advocates for family values so often opposed to a higher minimum wage for the poor? There is an obvious incoherence in the way positions on various issues are packaged that creates genuine tension.[46] As MacIntyre put it, "Unless there is a *telos* which transcends the limited goods of practices by constituting the good of a whole human life, the good of a human life conceived as a unity, it will *both* be the case that a certain subversive arbitrariness will invade the moral life *and* that we shall be unable to specify the context of certain virtues adequately."[47]

This puzzle is magnified at the societal level, where it is difficult to imagine the good of "the world" conceived as a unity. A common good, then, depends upon common purposes: or, at the least, common intentions. The absence of moral cohesion in American public culture is, then, in large measure due to an absence of a shared telos or end to which social institutions and the majority of people are committed and toward which they work.

What has replaced these once powerful but deeply flawed teleological visions? Millennialism, of course, has been abandoned by all but the most conservative Americans, the remnants of whom have twisted the old millennialism into a crude Christian nationalism—at this point, a collective fantasy of power by those who individually have been marginalized and experience self-worth to the extent that they attach themselves to such a fantasy. Utopian aspirations are also implicit in the purity rituals of activists, political parties, special-interest organizations, and professional organizations on all sides that purge any who depart from ideological dogma. Finally, remnants of these teleologies show up in slogans conjured by political marketers to Make America Great Again or to Save America's Soul. Like all emotivist gestures, political slogans like these create an appealing emotion that resonates with different demographics, but the phrases themselves have no intelligible meaning.

Against our capacity to speak of, much less pursue, a common telos, even provisionally, is a boundless capacity to speak its negation, especially in politics. This is manifest in the rhetoric of change "from" rather than "to." And "change from" is nearly always a means to denigrate the character or competence of the opposition.

A telos is important because within it is the possibility of realizing its ends. Both meaning and hope rest upon it. Without ideal images of a better world, collective life has no animating direction. But an overarching and comprehensive telos is unimaginable in a world like ours. Wendy Brown put it this way: "History becomes that which has weight but no trajectory, mass but no coherence, force but no direction; it is war without ends or end. Thus, the extent to which 'dead generations weigh like a nightmare on the brains of the living' is today unparalleled even as history itself disintegrates as a coherent category or practice."[48]

Against the background of political parties interminably deadlocked, even a conception of short-term and conditional social purposes aiming for specific pragmatic ends seems out of reach. Like our ethics, teleology becomes subjectivized into personal desire, or else politicized by various factions as the will to annihilate.

Personhood Diminished

If the question of a *common* conception of human personhood hinged on the abortion issue, the answer would, of course, be that it doesn't exist. But only in a limited sense. The disagreement here, while deep and interminable in the ways I've described earlier, is limited to the idea of personhood at a particular stage in gestation, naught else. In this respect, the abortion issue is an outlier. Apart from this instance, very few would dispute who is a human in a biological sense. *Rather, what has long been in dispute, and has continued to be so, is our conception of the moral worth of the person*—who is welcomed into the human community, who is esteemed and valued and, among those who are disadvantaged or vulnerable, who is protected and cared for—and who is not. The moral worth we confer is expressed not only in our response to basic human need but in our rendering to others recognition, regard, and significance.

The question of the moral worth of the human person, as I have posed it, is *the fundamental question* for any society that imagines itself to be—or aspires to become—genuinely humane. It is definitional and yet it is also a moving target. In the years marking the turn to the twenty-first century, the question of the moral worth of persons took a therapeutic turn in which the *feeling* of esteem, or respect or welcome or safety, became of paramount importance to large portions of the American public. Across the ever-increasing number of demographic or identity groups, it was clear that no one was getting enough.

Needless to say, in the contemporary environment, the sense of the lack of respect or esteem or welcome by so many has been politicized. While politicization may have some merit, it mainly distracts attention away from the broader conditions of the modern and late modern world that form a backdrop of institutional realities that in their nature challenge the moral worth of everyone living under these conditions. This backdrop is overwhelmingly—possibly essentially, even if not *comprehensively*—dehumanizing. And its reality is tangible, experienced by most people in the course of everyday life. That backdrop is so well established at this point and now so pervasive and commonplace that it is hardly noticed.

It is constituted by several interwoven elements, most of which are well known. One of these is the ubiquity of bureaucratization, a feature of every major institutional sphere—from markets, business, commerce, and entertainment to government, law, public policy, communication, healthcare, and the military. Its culture of instrumental rationality oriented toward maximum productivity and efficiency operates, as Max Weber put it, "without regard for persons."[49] The featureless character of bureaucratic structures and procedures renders relationships impersonal, work alienating, ethics instrumentalizing, and insofar as agency and authority are tethered to the holders or clients of offices rather than to specific individuals, personal identity merely functional.[50]

There is, of course, considerable variation in the alienating and anomic experience of modern life. The alienation a high school–educated working-class pipefitter experiences on the factory floor is of a different species from the alienation a Yale-educated associate at Goldman Sachs experiences on the trading floor, but they are of the same genus.[51] Recognizing these variations qualifies the case, but it doesn't fundamentally alter it.

All of these effects are reinforced within symbolic and expressive spheres of culture in modern and late modern societies, where knowledge and information are mass-produced. Whether it is the news media, entertainment media, social media, advertising, or public education and higher education, this powerful and interrelated culture industry fosters a "mass culture" that standardizes, homogenizes, and commercializes images, symbols, characters, narratives, news, and information and, in the process, washes out the inherited and communal distinctives rooted in religious, ethnic, racial, and regional identities and practices. Local cultures that are the wellspring of particular customs, habits of life, and identities are, if not destroyed, certainly leveled, absorbed, or colonized into a featureless homogeneity.[52]

Yet another element is what Peter Berger called "the pluralization of life-worlds." By this he meant the fragmentation of consciousness, grounded in the historical and sociological fact of an escalating transience, mobility, and pluralism, that undermines the stability and integration of life experience. These dynamics tend to leave modern people metaphysically rootless, a condition he called "homelessness."[53]

Intensifying these effects is the general desacralization of the modern world. Whatever advantages it may have provided, "disenchantment" has left modern and late modern persons without a framework of ultimate and transcendent meaning to order life and to provide a sustaining account of suffering and death. Disenchantment, as a rule, has rendered the individual alone in the cosmos, unbuffered by the terrifying and unknown contingencies of history and circumstance.

These massive historical and sociological pressures simultaneously generate and presuppose a weakening of the ties that once bound individuals to the personal face-to-face relationships and associations of families, neighborhoods, charities, clubs, unions, and places of worship that long functioned to integrate them into social life, foster belonging and trust, and insulate and mediate between the isolated individual and the megastructures of the public sphere, thus insulating them from the alienating effects of modern life. Without doubt, the severing of these organic ties has had liberating effects for many in releasing them from a variety of social constraints, and yet it has also come with a cost of disintegrating organic association and tradition and atomizing social life. For the scholars on the left, that cost has been powerlessness; for those on the right, it has been the absence of belonging. For both, the want of strong intermediate associations has generated conditions that foster meaninglessness. Surveying modern life in 1956, C. Wright Mills wrote, "Life in a society of masses . . . isolates the individual from the solid group; it destroys firm group standards. Acting without goals, the man in the mass just feels pointless."[54] What was true in the mid-twentieth century is even more accurate today.

Through inventiveness, willpower, and a measure of affluence, some people can improvise and find barriers and buffers to these effects. Localism is one of those ways. Yet within the leading institutions of modern life, there are few resources.

Indeed, the undermining of the moral worth of persons in late modern societies is highlighted within contemporary American democracy through the emergence and proliferation of identity groups—

those groups around which contemporary identity politics are built. Identity groups are, in effect, compensatory. Against the backdrop I have described, such groups represent a *means to power and influence* in a world that has rendered average citizens powerless over the conditions of their existence, an assertion of *distinctiveness* in a world that tends to flatten or level all meaningful differences, the possibility for *meaningful belief* and purpose in a world that denies ultimate meaning and renders most beliefs a matter of mere taste, an anchor of certainty in a world of contingency, a way of *belonging* in a world that atomizes our existence even as it weakens the ties of local and organic community, a heartfelt plea for *recognition and the dignity it confers* in a world that cares very little for the individual personally and cares for you publicly only insofar as you perform the role that you play, and *the hope of living a meaningful and significant life*, a life that matters, in a world that makes most of us feel our lives are insignificant and inconsequential. In sum, identity groups are compensatory networks that emerge in response to the dehumanization endemic to the modern and late modern world.

Critics on both the left and the right have argued these compensations are, at best, spurious—that, at most, they provide an artificial community, simulated agency, faux recognition, and a counterfeit belonging, none of which can ever satisfy the heart's deepest longings. They are spurious because the meaning, belonging, influence, recognition, and community they seem to provide are organized around nothing deeper than political interest.[55] Those consolations may be better than nothing, and in the end, they may be the only consolations available to many, many people.

Because identity groups define themselves around their political interests, such groups have become both a cause and a reflection of the hyper-politicization of public life. In such a regime, the state (its laws, policies, and procedures) becomes the predominant framework by which we understand collective life, its members, its leading organizations, its problems, and its issues.[56] Practically, this has come to mean that we regard others less as fellow citizens committed to the common project of self-governance, instead viewing them narrowly and reductively in terms of their alignment with or opposition to particular political interests. In other words, in such a regime, the moral worth of others (and others' views of our own moral worth) is determined in large measure by how we line up politically and ideologically with various political identities. This represents a sea change for the role of partisanship in political life.[57] Just as bureaucratization reduces people to their role and performance in that role, identity politics reduces citizens to their ideological commitments and tribal allegiances—or at least our perceptions of those allegiances.

These dehumanizing tendencies latent within the institutional structures and practices of late modern democracy find little resistance among the intellectual classes. Among a certain vanguard, there are declarations of the "erasure of man" and the death of humanism.[58] In the broader academy, the defense of "the humane" or some new reworking of "humanism" through which the moral worth of human beings could be affirmed has not been a priority for quite some time.

Authority and Legitimacy

A democracy without a humane view of all its citizens and without a working telos that can rally those citizens toward common goods would not be healthy, and what's more, it might be impossible to sustain. But a post-truth democracy is a contradiction in terms. It would mean that a nation is ungovernable. The dissolution of any agreement over what constitutes moral truth or factual truth is now a given, and there would seem to be no authority or logic or shared premises, or "neutral observational language," as Thomas Kuhn put it, by which we could arrive collectively at agreement.[59] And, as we've seen, the institutional carriers of information and communication today only render the possibility of agreement less likely.

The conditions for an enduring if not permanent post-truth politics are even further entrenched by a significant loss of authority within the ecosystem of "truth-telling" institutions. There are always ups and downs, but the credibility of all of these institutions has been trending downward in the eyes of ordinary citizens since the mid-twentieth century.[60]

This is most obviously true for the institutions of the federal government, less so in local governments. Disaffection and cynicism are deeply ingrained across the ideological divide. Reams of data collected over nearly six decades have demonstrated beyond doubt that a disaffection between the electorate and the political establishment—what scholars have called the legitimation crisis—continues to expand through the population and to harden in the collective political consciousness. The number of Americans who have little to no confidence that "the government in Washington" will actually solve the problems it purportedly sets out to solve has grown to two-thirds of the public. To the same degree, the majority also believes that "the current two-party system isn't working."[61] The ire of the American public is especially directed toward the political leaders in the power centers of government. For decades, vast majorities believed that "most politicians are more interested in winning elections than in doing what is right"; that while the "system of government is good . . . the people running it are incompetent." Add to this, two-thirds of the public have little to no confidence at all "in the people who run our government to tell the truth to the public."

Such disaffection and cynicism have extended to other institutions: most obviously the leading outlets for print, television, and electronic journalism, publishing, and academia. All of these are seen as solidly progressive enclaves that make no pretense to political or ideological neutrality. In academia, whether in the professional associations or in colleges and universities themselves, the ideal of free intellectual inquiry untainted by ideological partisanship and pressure has significantly diminished. Especially in the humanities and social sciences, higher education has become a reliable institutional base for progressive political interests, ideology, and activism. In journalism, highly publicized scandals and increasingly visible ideological division between the conservative and progressive media ecosystems rendered the claim of journalistic impartiality less and less plausible.[62] In science, the crisis of replication and the periodic but highly publicized cases of scientific misconduct promoted the impression that science itself was highly manipulable.[63] In spite of its great achievements during the COVID-19 pandemic, the scientific establishment has become viewed as suspect; many believe that what it represents publicly as factual is not necessarily true. On the ground, of course, the majority of scientists, scholars, editors, and journalists remain committed to the virtues of their professional methods—careful research, modest and nuanced claims, and high standards of excellence in the pursuit of incremental gains in knowledge. But as institutions, all have lost significant credibility in the eyes of the broader public that they could be fair-minded or even-handed.

Against this backdrop, the presidency of Donald Trump marked something new. Progressives made much of the sheer volume of his distortions, misrepresentations, and fabrications—which were remarkable by any measure. Key media outlets kept track of his lies and were astonished by their quantity and brazenness.[64] This was certainly justified, but what was novel about Trump and the Republican Party leading up to and after the 2016 election were their open and unremitting attacks on the authority of what is supposed to be the truth-telling infrastructure of American democracy. This included attacks on the media and journalists, on the FBI and law enforcement, on the Department of Justice and the rule of law, and on the CIA and the intelligence community.

Other presidents have lied and had difficult relationships with these institutions, but their lies were, in some respects, a tribute that vice paid to virtue insofar as they honored the authority of those institutions that held them to account. Even Richard Nixon, whom Barry Goldwater called "the most dishonest individual I ever met in my life," said in his resignation address that "the constitutional purpose [of his presidency had] been served," that "the interest of the Nation must always come before any personal considerations," and that he "must put the interest of America first"; he then asked for "the understanding, the patience, the cooperation [that his successor, Gerald Ford] will need from all Americans."[65] A liar he may have been, but in the end, Nixon honored the authority of the government he served and that had ousted him. Though he never acknowledged wrongdoing, he accepted the verdict of his impeachment and left without a fight.

Trump, by contrast, showed nothing but contempt for these institutions and regularly articulated that contempt from the office of the president. He carried this contempt through to the very end, announcing in advance that he would never accept an election outcome that showed him losing. Even against those in his inner circle who told him that he had lost the 2020 presidential election and that any attempt to overturn the election would be illegal and unconstitutional, he sought to undermine the transfer of power to his successor by intimidation and threats of violence.[66] In these ways, he gave permission to his followers to share his contempt and put it into action, as they did on January 6, 2021.

The loss of confidence in the leading institutions of liberal democracy, though long in the making, hit an inflection point with the presidency of Donald Trump. His aggressive hostility to these institutions further undermined their credibility and authority, rendering them suspect as arbiters of democratic fairness, truth, or justice. In the process, he undercut the legitimacy of liberal democracy as a whole, which is likely his most enduring legacy.

Withered from Its Roots

It is not an exaggeration to say that American public life is divided not only in its opinions but in its vocabularies, and not only in its vocabularies but in its premises about what is real and true and how we know these things, about what is right and just, and about what the nation is and what it should be. In the midst of it all, the moral worth of citizenship has been reductively indexed to different political or ideological positions.

We have, in the process, become unable to tell a common story about ourselves except the story that ours is now a fragmented and polarized society. Everyone does seem to agree on this. Even the long-standing idea that America is "an exceptional nation," which remained uncontroversial through the mid- to late twentieth century, is now, as Steve Lagerfeld put it, "just a club wielded by combatants unaware that the fight [over the idea] has ended. The term has so many meanings that it has no meaning."[67] Even a more generic understanding of "American exceptionalism"—the idea that the nation has a role as a standard-bearer of freedom and democracy—has lost plausibility, both for Americans themselves and for the country's allies.[68]

As we've seen, this unraveling is not only symbolic and ideational but institutional and systemic, entrenched as it is in the practices of the most powerful culture-defining organizations. The confusion and dysfunction that follow are clearly on the surface of what we witness in our politics week to week and year to year, but they are ultimately also apparent in the dissolution of the sources that have underwritten liberal democracy. A battered proceduralism remains functional, but it is fragile and contested. Apart from this, there is no credible ethical, institutional, or political authority that would lead Americans democratically on a path beyond fragmentation and polarization.

A broad and shared legitimacy of the political order, then, is no longer possible because the preconditions for its legitimacy on the surface and within the deeper structures of culture are no longer present. Broad public trust is absent because the cultural prerequisites of trust are absent. And political solidarity has dissolved because the cultural substructure of political solidarity has dissolved. Absent viable cultural sources, on what possible terms could any kind of common mythos be reforged?

The hybrid-Enlightenment, as it has been reworked over the centuries, still resonates with many Americans, and among these are many with a desire to continue the hard work of working through the contradictions that remain in American public life. Weave: The Social Fabric Project and the myriad other local and regional initiatives mentioned earlier in the chapter are proof enough of this. But the cultural resources for doing that hard work have dwindled to naught, and more pointedly, the leading institutional actors that are in a position to foster the effort show little interest or resolve in doing so. American democracy, flawed as it was from the very beginning, is now largely dysfunctional in significant measure because the culture that has long underwritten it has unraveled. What is more, the cultural logics that have replaced the nation's underpinning sources of unity present challenges that render the renewal of democracy even more daunting.

It is to this that I now turn.

CHAPTER TWELVE

Nihilism and Its Cultural Logics

D ESPITE WHAT APPEARS TO be a fairly comprehensive unraveling of the endlessly reworked hybrid-Enlightenment,
we don't end up with a gaping void. That might leave
the impression for some that all that is needed to remedy this problem would be a renewal of the cultural logics of the
hybrid-Enlightenment through, say, revived civics education in primary and secondary schools. That might be a good idea if teachers,
parents, and the schools of education could agree on what that would
look like. The problem, of course, is deeper and more historical and
sociological in nature than a reflection of neglect or even malevolent intention. There is indeed a void generated by the unraveling of
America's hybrid-Enlightenment, but it is a void now filled with a very
different cultural logic, a cultural logic that owes more to Friedrich
Nietzsche than to Thomas Jefferson. Filling that void, at least much
of it, in our public culture are the cultural logics of nihilism.

Thinking about Nihilism

The concept of nihilism has a history. Though used throughout the
nineteenth century, it was Nietzsche who understood that nihilism
was not simply an abstract concept of academic philosophy but a
phenomenon that thoroughly permeated human culture. He also un-

derstood earlier than anyone the gravity of its implications. For many following him, nihilism was often used as an abstract denunciation of decadence or a verdict of civilizational decline. Oswald Spengler's monumental treatment of the subject in *The Decline of the West*, written just after the end of World War I, was a case in point. The polemical uses of the concept can be powerful. But against this tendency, I prefer to use the term sociologically and thus descriptively as an ideal type that is more or less useful as an empirical description of our current situation.

The first thing one must know about nihilism as a philosophical and cultural reality is that it is not one thing. Rather, it is a cluster of themes that follow from the "death of God"—or, more accurately, the death of all "god-terms"—that for most of human history established within the cosmology and culture of societies certain ultimate, transcendent, and universal conceptions of truth, value, and purpose.

The first theme is *epistemological failure:* the recognition that there are now no objective, knowable truths; that all claims to authoritative knowledge are without foundation; that "reason" as an autonomous capacity independent of presuppositions or free from any vested interests is a fiction. "Every belief," Nietzsche wrote, "every considering something-true, is necessarily false because there is simply no *true world*." In this sense, nihilism is "a denial of a truthful world, a denial of being."[1]

A second theme is *ethical incoherence:* the recognition that we are at "the end of the moral interpretation of the world"; that there are no absolute moral or ethical values, but rather, that right and wrong, good and evil are, in the end, nothing more than vague constructs tied to social circumstances and emotional states. In our experience, moral truth may seem obvious, natural, or objective, but in the end, it is arbitrary and without warrant. As Nietzsche famously put it, "The highest values devalue [or invalidate] themselves. The aim is lacking, and 'Why' finds no answer."[2]

A third theme is *existential despair,* which denies any intrinsic meaning or ultimate value or purpose to individual or social life. The world and life within it are void of significance or purpose and therefore all that we do, all that we achieve, and all that we endure in suffering is pointless. We struggle throughout our lives for something that never happens and that wouldn't matter even if it did. There is, then, a cosmic purposelessness in which "everything lacks meaning." As Nietzsche put it, "Existence has no goal or end."[3]

Deriving from these others, one might add the theme of *political annihilation*, which manifests itself in a will to obliterate all that obstructs the will to power, a will to bring enemies to nothing, to destroy completely. "There is nothing to life that has value," Nietzsche wrote, "except the degree of power—assuming that life itself is the will to power." Emanating from this is the "will to destruction as the will of a still deeper instinct . . . the will for nothingness."[4]

At the end of the day, these distinctions are analytically clarifying, but in experience, they bleed together and build upon each other. And all are present in the public culture of contemporary America. Nihilism, as I have described it here, is certainly *not* the whole of public culture. It does, however, define a prominent and persistent element within it. And tragically, it seeps into the private lives and personal experiences of many Americans as well.

The Paradox of Nihilism without Nihilists

However prominent nihilism may be, a genuine nihilist is a rarity. He or she would believe in nothing, value no one and no thing, nor have any purpose beyond personal pleasure or the desire to rule indiscriminately over others. If such people exist, they are relatively few in number, fewer still in academic philosophy, and they would probably be viewed by most as mentally and emotionally deranged. If there are so few nihilists, then how is it that nihilism comes to be so pervasive in American political culture?

The answer lies in the nature of culture itself: culture, as I have insisted throughout this book, has a life of its own more or less independent of people's intentions or will, and it is most powerful when the meanings or rules by which people live are taken for granted. The relative autonomy of culture has been well established in the social sciences for over a century.[5] An obvious illustration: even in the early twenty-first century, most Americans still believe in God or a higher power, yet our *public* culture is overwhelmingly and aggressively secular in character. If a culture were simply the composite of beliefs and values of its citizens, this would not be the case. But the rules by which people operate in most work settings are completely devoid of transcendent meaning. So it is with the entire system of symbols and rules that constitute a culture. They are objectified as social realities over which individual actors have little control. In this way, nihilism operates as a reality of contemporary public life more often than not independent of the sincerity or goodwill of the individual and institutional actors involved.

Passive Nihilism

In the contemporary world, it is important to make the distinction between passive and active nihilism.[6] For my purposes, passive nihilism is the *net effect* of large, institutional dynamics intrinsic to the modern world—its technology, its bureaucracy, its markets, its pluralism, its entertainment—unfolding in the public sphere. It is intensified under the conditions of late modernity. Nihilism presents itself in the ways described in the previous chapter: the profound confusion that derives from the sense of multiple realities and multiple ways of knowing, the relativization of value through pluralism and choice, the absence of authority and with it the sense of meaninglessness in life and history, the diminution of the moral worth of all human beings (though some more than others) through their instrumentalization, and the absence of clear, coherent, and common purposes to which individual and collective life might be directed. These vary widely in human experience—even today—but they have become more or less commonplace in the modern and late modern world. In this sense, nihilism is not so much a carefully developed system of thought as it is a condition of exhaustion, "the recognition of the long waste of strength." It reveals itself in that terrible moment when "a deep feeling of standing" succumbs to "the feeling of valuelessness." Nihilism of this passive kind has become so quotidian that it seems to be the ordinary state of affairs, "a normal condition" as Nietzsche put it.[7] Karen Carr took it further and simply called it "banal," though no less insidious because of its banality.[8]

But there is an active form of nihilism that plays out politically. Nietzsche pointed in this direction when he wrote that "nihilism is

. . . not only the belief that everything deserves to perish; but one actually puts one's shoulder to the plough; *one destroys.*"[9]

How does this bear on the matter of solidarity?

Active Nihilism and the Cultural Logic of Ressentiment

The Solidarity of Counterpublics

To say that there is no common story we can tell about ourselves as Americans—that we have no shared mythos—is not to say that there are no stories at all. To say that there is little political solidarity that binds us together is not to say that solidarity is entirely absent from our politics. There *are*, in fact, stories and there *is*, in fact, solidarity, but the stories and the solidarity they produce are found within what Nancy Fraser called "counter-publics" generated out of the identity groups that have proliferated in the late modern context.[10]

The concept of counterpublics comes to life against the backdrop of the classical liberal idea and ideal of "the public sphere." The public sphere—or, as some prefer, the civil sphere—was long theorized as a realm of social life and discourse in modern liberal societies around which citizens would talk about issues of common concern on behalf of a common good. As a space of public engagement, it would be open and accessible to all, a space where the issues addressed would be of concern to everyone and where inequalities of power and position would be set aside, allowing individuals and groups to engage one another as peers. In its net effect, this civic space would, in a rough-and-tumble way, generate a consensus around a common good that would inform political decision-making but also hold political and economic power to account.

In reality, the public sphere was more of an ethical aspiration than a political reality. In practice, it never made good on its claims to openness and accessibility, and inequalities of power were never fully offset through the ethical or legal imperatives of "equality under the law." Moreover, those who advocated on behalf of the civil sphere often spoke of an all-encompassing "we" without recognizing how their position masked their own interests or acknowledging the ways the "public" they spoke for and defended actually excluded others from participation through various strategies of containment. The obvious cases come to mind of Black children, for example, barred from public education in the nineteenth century or of women barred from voting until 1920 or of Native Americans barred from citizenship until 1924. There are important ways in which "we" was a strategic fiction.[11]

In this light, the civil or public sphere never emerged as a single, comprehensive, and integrated space of discourse. The playing field was always tilted toward those groups that had disproportionate financial or political or demographic influence.

Yet marginalized groups rarely suffered in silence. To the extent that they were able and with whatever resources available to them, they created "counter-publics," or parallel discursive arenas—by means of local meeting places, churches and synagogues, associations, colleges, literature, poetry, music, scholarship, lectures—"where members of subordinated social groups could invent and circulate counter-discourses, which in turn permitted them to formulate oppositional interpretations of their identities, interests, and needs."[12] This helps to explain how, in the nineteenth century, feminism grew in influence, how Mormons, Catholics, and Jews achieved (some) legitimacy, and why the Black church was so central to the life and vitality of African Americans. These various counterpublics were, in short, a civic response to the exclusions of the dominant public sphere, and as such, they provided spaces in which marginalized people could meet to regroup, crystallize their interests and collective identities, coordinate strategy, and develop new concepts and modes of argument, which they then could carry into the mainstream public sphere in defense of their shared interests.

Here is where we see the difference between the counterpublics of the past and those of the present. Historically, the counterpublics of various religious, ethnic, racial, and gender minorities were forged out of their disenfranchisement from the mainstream of *political* and *economic* life. That was the primary source of their grievance. Their interests, then, were defined by their quest to be enfranchised on these terms. But it isn't clear that that is the case anymore, not least because the legal apparatus for political and economic equality and its protections, while far, far from perfect, is fairly well established. When discrimination occurs, there are courts of appeal, and the law is on the side of those discriminated against.

Yet as Max Weber taught, power is not found only in economic and political position (what he called "class and party"). It is also found in *status*, or social esteem. What contemporary identity groups press for, then, is a therapeutic compensation for grievances rooted in the felt absence of recognition and the disrespect it implies. This is why the counterpublics generated by aggrieved identity groups frame opposition as an existential threat. The words and arguments of an adversary—and very often its very presence—are interpreted as a threat to the right of the aggrieved to exist.

This means, of course, that solidarity outside of one's own identity group (or those adjacent to it) is impossible. However, within one's identity group (and those adjacent), solidarity is both possible and a significant part of what makes them attractive. The solidarity of these counterpublics is generated from the cultural logics of *ressentiment*.

Ressentiment

Ressentiment is a species of resentment, of the indignation one experiences if treated unfairly. Nietzsche couldn't find a word in his native German that was adequate to the reality he was trying to describe. The English word *resentment* didn't make the cut either. He insisted on the French word *ressentiment* as a term of art that may lack a concise definition but can be usefully described.

The more common-variety "resentment" is a personal experience of anger and even bitter outrage at having been treated unfairly. Of course, others can experience the same emotion and for the same reasons, but the emotion isn't dependent upon the group or its collective psychology. Resentment, in this sense, is not a pathology that should be hastily severed from experience. To bury memories of atrocity through repression or to quickly and uncritically forgive injustice can be equally harmful to the psychological and emotional well-being of the victim. In the same way, resentment is not necessarily immoral, particularly insofar as the memory of an injustice can be the means by which its perpetrators are brought to account. Among those attributes that distinguish resentment from ressentiment is that the former comes to be contained in life experience without it becoming all-consuming. Resentment tends to lead toward an "off-point" or perhaps an end where the feeling is, in one way or another, resolved through acts of justice, remediation, or reconciliation.[13]

Narratives of Injury

Ressentiment is of a different character.[14] It is a psychology as well and, as an experience, it can be deeply felt. It too can be the root of an authentic plea for justice. But simultaneously and more importantly, *ressentiment* is *a cultural logic that is encoded within institutional life*. It begins as a shared narrative of injury, a story of woundedness that can be real or imagined or even anticipated. Importantly, ressentiment emanates not from specific harm or injury to specific individuals, or if it does, the event-causing injury may be seen as representative or symbolic of other, more diffuse harm. More often than not, then, the injury arises from what are seen as the general conditions of existence.

In ressentiment, the injury is lived and relived, felt and refelt again and again and again in ways that get etched onto individual and collective consciousness, against what Nietzsche saw as a more natural propensity to ultimately forget. The memory of injury and the rage it fosters become obsessive. The inability to put the injury aside is in large part what fuels ressentiment. Its memory may be contested, but for those who see themselves as victims, it is a paramount reality and it festers into malice, hatred, and vindictiveness. Max Scheler, a generation after Nietzsche, called it a *self*-poisoning of the mind, but it is doubtful that the subject intends this so much as they succumb to it.[15] Nietzsche described that obsessiveness this way: "The sufferers, one and all, are frighteningly willing and inventive in their pretexts for painful emotions; they even enjoy being mistrustful and dwelling on wrongs and imagined slights: they rummage through the bowels of their past and present for obscure, questionable stories that will allow them to wallow in tortured suspicion and intoxicate themselves with their own poisonous wickedness."[16]

Negation and the Ethics of Revenge

As Nietzsche argued, it is only natural that every victim, every sufferer "instinctively seeks a cause for his suffering," a culprit or an offender "upon whom he can release his emotions, actually or in effigy, on some pretext or other."[17] But just as the injury or harm is typically unspecified, its cause can also be an abstraction: perhaps a person or movement or change or set of ideas that symbolizes the source of injury. The demonizations fostered by conservative Christians and secular progressives functioned in these ways in the early decades of the culture war. For many years in the late twentieth century, all that was wrong with the world for evangelical Christians could be traced back to "secular humanism," just as all that impeded development toward justice for progressives could be laid at the feet of capitalism, capitalists, and their fellow travelers (among them, evangelicals). These abstractions may be personified in this or that leader, this or that organization, or this or that movement, but even then, the harm and its cause remain radical yet opaque simplifications of all that is wrong with the world.

By identifying a perpetrator, there is now an object for revenge, for hate always evolves into a thirst for retaliation. Of course, it isn't thought of as retaliation by victims, for that would seem ethically sordid. So, revenge is construed as a righteous punishment, as something owed to the perpetrator as just deserts. Nietzsche, of course, would have none of it. In his view, it was nothing more than the effort to "sanctify *revenge* with the term, *justice*."[18] "Punishment," he observed, "is what revenge calls itself; with a hypocritical lie, it creates a good conscience for itself."[19]

And yet this inversion of moral status is one of the hallmarks of ressentiment and, again, part of its appeal. It is those who suffer who are virtuous and those who oppress (or are viewed as such) who are evil. Thus, negating or devaluing the existence of the other and all related to them is essential for victims to feel moral superiority. It is the contempt nurtured that is part of the intoxication they enjoy. Negating the oppressor (real or imagined) is a precondition of one's own affirmation and elevated moral status.

Scheler saw ressentiment and the rage and revenge that flowed from it manifested chiefly as "indiscriminate criticism without any positive aim." This kind of unremitting negation can never be mollified, for it is characterized "by the fact that improvements in the conditions criticized cause no satisfaction—they merely cause discontent, for they destroy the growing pleasure afforded by invective and negation. Many modern political parties will be extremely annoyed by a partial satisfaction of their demands or by the constructive participation of their representatives in public life, for such participation mars the delight of the oppositionism. It is peculiar to 'ressentiment criticism' that it does not seriously desire that its demands be fulfilled. It does not want to cure the evil: the evil is merely a pretext for criticism."[20]

The indiscriminate nature of negation means that critique and blame are totalizing. Nuance and complexity are minimized or obscured, for to qualify critique and judgment can be regarded as offering aid and comfort to the enemy: something that cannot be allowed. Ressentiment cultivates a negation of all the ideas that victims oppose—indeed, the very existence of those who espouse them.

The Ubiquity of Negational Discourse

The ubiquity of negational discourse in contemporary public and political life is in plain sight. Virtually all political discourse has become a discourse of negation in which every party, group, or interest aims to undermine the credibility and legitimacy of opponents. The conditions for its metastasizing growth have become more conducive over recent decades. In part, this is simply due to the dynamics of negative solidarity run amok: in times of profound social change, a group or a class or political party will be drawn together through acts of opposition to what represents that change. These are the basics of boundary work. And so, in the fluid and fragmented world we live in today, every identity group defines itself against some other group, the net effect of which is the destruction of common life.

But the ubiquity of the negational discourse is also a function of changes in the technological landscape, not least in the media of communication. These have unfolded slowly enough to seem unexceptional. We notice only that public discourse is hotter than it used to be, not the reasons why.

But along with these broader historical changes have been active developments in the strategies of resource mobilization, strategies that have remarkable symmetry across political and cultural divisions.[21] In short, the negations at the heart of ressentiment have become deliberate and methodical strategies of a powerful and professional class of political and media consultants who have perfected the use of new communications technologies within public discourse.

Since the end of the twentieth century, the techniques of negation have developed into something of a science, especially as they bear on elections. Consultants advise clients to go negative and to do so according to carefully developed guidelines. "Clean campaigns are nice, but they lose. If you don't play by the [negative] rules of the game, you lose." To this end, they advise, it is essential to follow "key points . . . when going negative," such as hire a "professional opposition research firm," "keep it graphic," "be visual," "don't be shrill," "keep it smart and factual—without sacrificing the emotion." The emotional element is especially important. "Excite the emotions," one consultant said. "It's much easier and more effective to persuade with the heart than with the head alone. Fear, anger, envy, indignation, and shame are powerful emotions in the political arena." In this line of work, one must be prepared to "go the distance" and to always "remember, you're playing to win." As another put it, you'll never win with kindness. "You never see the week's kindness award. . . . If you throw enough mud on your candidate, you look cleaner."

The industry that has developed these techniques is quick to justify the methods and practices of its trade, saying these techniques "open up the process: they draw contrasts between competing candidates or dueling interests . . . and . . . provide citizens with the mother's milk of political decision-making: information . . . information that is relevant, timely, and well-researched."[22] But a political opponent's qualities also constitute important information. So too does information that complicates an issue or that presents the valid points of the other side's position.

The fact is that in the symbolic economies of the late modern world, moral rage becomes a form of capital. It is the means by which political parties and special-interest groups mobilize their supporters. It also becomes the primary means by which special-interest groups raise money in support of their cause. And precisely because it entertains and enrages, it also becomes the substantive means by which social media and the mainstream media generate revenue. Politicians, media celebrities, movement leaders, and even ordinary citizens on social media have become "rage-traders" in a political culture that, as Peter Sloterdijk put it, stores inscriptions of injury in "rage banks" of collective memory.[23] The financial interests in provoking and amplifying outrage and the fear and ressentiment that issue from it are substantial.[24] It is a fuel upon which the dominant parts of American political culture now run.

Outrage as Authority

But the greater significance of rage is its tacit cultural function. Rage against injury and its perpetrators emerges as a source of moral authority. More accurately, rage is a proxy for older forms of authority and, by itself, a demonstration of their regress. Absent any shared notion of reason, revelation, human nature, republicanism, or "revolution" as the grounds to establish claims or to resolve disputed claims—absent any more or less fixed cosmology within which the world could be ordered—authority becomes rooted in subjectivity. This is not news. It is one of the hallmarks of modernity.[25] In the late modern age, however, this culminates *politically* in a subjective and intersubjective rage that, in turn, becomes the source from which any claims to grievance are made legitimate, from which any claims to redress are justified and made compelling, and from which solidarity *within* identity groups is formed.

Injury and Identity

One of the critical functions of this negational discourse and perhaps the key psychological reason for its doggedness is, according to Nietzsche, that it acts as a "narcotic" against this hurt, "a longing for an anesthetic against this pain." The revenge, to clarify, is oriented not toward avoiding further suffering, but used "to deaden a tormenting, secret pain which has become unendurable" by means of a more violent hatred.[26] At best, its relief is temporary, and so the negations must be reenacted again and again.

Given its psychological benefits, it is probably inevitable that the most significant marker of ressentiment is the way in which injury becomes internalized as a source of personal and collective identity.

Even through the early modern period, it was believed that a person possessed a "soul" that was understood to be part of an order that God, nature, nature's God, or the gods—the sacred by any other name—had established and sustained. The world in its entirety and in its parts had a place and purpose. But in a world that has no innate definition, the self is merely "will." It becomes what it becomes only in opposition to others. Outrage against a grievance caused by others, then, becomes the source of authentic identity and authentic action. In this strange calculus, the more rage the better.

In turn, rage, hatred, and the desire for revenge that emanate from injury become the source of meaning and purpose for those who see themselves as victims. Injury, then, is definitional. Identity—formed negationally—depends upon an active and hostile enemy to exist at all. As Wendy Brown put it, "Politicized identity emerges and obtains its unifying coherence through the politicization of [and protest against] exclusion."[27] And so it is that on the left, ressentiment depends upon the existence and ubiquity of such abstractions as the "radical Right," "toxic masculinity," "white supremacy" or just "whiteness," "Christian nationalism," and the like. On the right, ressentiment depends upon the existence and universalization of such abstractions as the "radical Left," "socialism," "woke elitism," the "deep state," "secular humanism," and "snowflakes." These are tactical but useful inventions. Without these antagonists, Brown observed, identity groups would have to give up much of their claim to injury and exclusion, thus weakening their claims to the political significance of the difference they represent.[28] This is why various identity groups look for, repeat, and often exaggerate atrocity stories to exemplify the evil that must be repudiated.

Unintended Consequences

The cultural logic of ressentiment unintentionally leads to the very opposite of what it ostensibly hopes to accomplish. Brown argued that politicized identity is so heavily invested in and dependent upon its own woundedness, impotence, marginalization, and subordination that it cannot give them up without giving up its identity. This is why she memorably describes ressentiment as the moralizing revenge of the powerless: the triumph of the weak as the weak.[29]

Identity groups become so deeply attached to their own impotence, exclusion, and subordination because they provide the premises upon which the group's existence depends. So even while the group seeks to avenge injury, it reaffirms injury as the foundation of its existence; even while it seeks to resist its subordination, it reinforces its subordination as the basis of its identity. Absent a transcending telos—for none are available in the late modern age—and absent the moral logic for forgiveness, the group lacks the capacity to imagine a future either for itself or for others that overcomes the injury. In this way, ressentiment becomes a perverse ontology, a mode of being, dependent for its existence on the very thing it loathes and opposes. Take away the injury, take away its cause, take away the revenge it seeks, and both meaning and identity for the aggrieved dissolve.

This, of course, raises the question of whether the dependencies of the aggrieved upon their injury, subordination, and powerlessness actually subvert the aim to transcend them, leading them, for all practical purposes, to *reproach equality* rather than live constructively into it, to *reprove empowerment* rather than work toward it, to *disdain freedom* rather than practice it and enjoy its benefits.[30]

A New Common Culture?

On the surface of public and political life, America remains profoundly polarized on every conceivable cultural issue. But polarization is also, and more significantly, reflected within the deep structures that underwrite public and political life: in different and competing premises, in basic perceptions of reality and how reality is apprehended, in moral languages and ethical commitments, in the ends to which national life is oriented, and in the stories that we tell about ourselves as Americans. This is why the culture war has been so enduring and why national solidarity and, increasingly, local solidarity are so elusive. It is also why these features of American public and political life will not likely change anytime soon.

Yet there is another story unfolding here as well, a story playing out simultaneously within the deep structures of American political culture. One could describe it as an emerging "common" culture, *the form of which* is manifest within and across every faction and division in American public life. Its shared cultural logic is defined by a moral authority rooted in rage, anger, and often hatred. Its *mythoi* or collective self-understandings revolve around narratives of injury and woundedness. Its ethical dispositions are defined by the desire for revenge through a predilection to negate. Its anthropology effectively reduces fellow citizens to enemies whose very presence represents an existential threat. And its *teloi* are power oriented toward domination.

It is important to emphasize that not everything in public and political life is reducible to ressentiment and its cultural logics. And yet all of these elements are more or less present within every major and even minor faction in American politics today—and not least within faith traditions.[31]

So, ironically, this constellation of presuppositions does, *in effect*, constitute a common culture—with a common language and a shared framework of understanding and action—and yet one that has turned in on itself. Despite the deep cultural continuities across every political faction, party, and movement, these continuities cannot and never will lead to collective solidarity, only a solidarity within the counterpublics generated across the range of identity groups.

Woven through this common political culture is yet another element: fear. While people can be fearful of different and often opposing things, fear is a common thread.[32] It transcends race, age, gender, and political ideology as well as religious belief or nonbelief. Because fear and its twin, anger, are such powerful incentives, they are tested by focus groups, refined, slickly packaged, monetized, and repeated through every conduit of contemporary social media, instrumentalized to mobilize the faithful but also to further dehumanize the opposition. And with fear comes a deepening distrust, once again shared by all sides and all factions, the young being the most distrustful of all.

All these developments play out on the surface and depth of American public culture. As we've seen, they are, in part, built into the fabric of late modernity, but they are also actively cultivated as strategies of mobilization and counter-mobilization. If, then, our politics possess a nihilistic character, it is because they rest on a public culture that is itself significantly, even if not comprehensively, nihilistic. And if the cultural logics of nihilism are more or less present within the governing institutions of public life, how could their effects not seep into local communities and institutions, families, and personal lives?

The Will to Power: Annihilation Is the Point

When politicization is oriented toward furthering the specific interests of the group without an appeal to the common weal, when motives are grounded in revenge, when political mobilizing is accomplished through a cultivation of fear via strategies of negation, power is stripped down to its most basic form. Political action may still operate within the bounds of legitimate democratic participation, yet what drives it is a will to power whose end is simple domination.

There are theorists, of course, who would say that this is unexceptional. All social life comes down to power and domination, and the justifications we offer are of no real account. But historically and phenomenologically, this view discounts the meaning that infuses social and political life, layers of meaning that make vast differences in whether life flourishes or withers under oppression. Even so, current circumstances in political life have come increasingly to imitate this Nietzschean view.

The cultural logic of ressentiment can bring about symbolic victories, but they tend to be self-defeating. They deplete and exhaust rather than renew and refresh public life and democratic politics. A culture and politics of ressentiment simply cannot heal wounds and it cannot bring about a just reckoning. Against what could very well be legitimate claims against injustice, ressentiment ultimately denies the possibility of a public life as a shared project, for there is nothing in this that requires or even encourages a person or group or organization to seek the consent of others.

Just the opposite. Ultimately the cultural logic of ressentiment is a cultural logic of annihilation. Annihilation, in other words, is not an accidental feature of political life in late modernity—it is foundational to its nature. It is not incidental to our cultural politics—it is its essence. Within the cultural logics of ressentiment, "cancellation," whether from the Left or the Right, is the point.

For Nietzsche, the advent of nihilism in these overlapping ways would prove to be a most destructive force in history, and thus the crisis it would present for humanity would prove catastrophic and worse, inevitable. "I describe what is coming," he wrote, "what can no longer come differently. . . . This future speaks even now in a hundred signs, this destiny announces itself everywhere; for this music of the future all ears are cocked even now." "Necessity itself is at work here." Nihilism grows "from decade to decade: restlessly, violently, headlong, like a river that wants to reach the end."[33]

As I wrote at the beginning of this chapter, nihilism in political life is neither ubiquitous nor inevitable. What is more, history is full of contingency. There is ample room for human agency. Even so, the cultural logics of nihilism are well established and institutionally invasive, and the challenge they present to liberal democracy is formidable.

CHAPTER THIRTEEN

The Authoritarian Impulse

I N 1920, OLIVER WENDELL HOLMES observed, "Between two groups of people who want to make inconsistent kinds of worlds, I see no remedy but force."[1] Holmes was prescient about our current circumstances. When few if any of the fundamental premises concerning truth, reality, human nature, public ethics, and the shared purposes of a culture are held in common, when there is no common story a people can tell about themselves, and no common means by which a people might sort these things out, what else is there to order collective life?[2] Indeed, the unraveling of our political culture, the political fragmentation and polarization that have followed in its wake, and the deep culture of ressentiment that has filled the void are all too profound and too well established to be addressed by anything other than coercion. And coercion is not a democratic option.

Authority and the Authoritarian

It only follows: the *absence* of credible, recognized, and legitimate authority—whether established, circumstantial, or provisional—fosters the conditions for authoritarian rule, in which coercion is the principal tool. Whatever else it might be, authoritarianism is a solution to the problem of—the absence of—solidarity. Authoritarianism (of which fascism, tyranny, and totalitarianism are versions) is a non-democratic surrogate for authority. Yet qualifications matter.

The Transformation of Authority

The model of European authoritarianism circa 1930s and '40s would seem to be a remote possibility at this point in American political history. As Hannah Arendt experienced it, authoritarianism required a rigidly hierarchical and well-integrated bureaucracy "whose seat of power resides at the top."[3] While there are family resemblances between the past and present, this older authoritarian form is unlikely today because neither the cultural ethos nor the legal apparatus of government is suited to sustain it over any length of time. The political culture is too fragmented and any particular polity is far too contested to reestablish 1930s-style authoritarianism.

But although this older authoritarian form is unlikely, there are clear indications that an authoritarian impulse is not only present but expanding. As Umberto Eco put it, "Behind a regime and its ideology there is always a way of thinking and feeling, a group of cultural habits, of obscure instincts and unfathomable drives."[4] In this historical moment, this constellation of thoughts, feelings, desires, and habits increasingly lists toward the authoritarian.

Authoritarianism, as I say, is an attempt to solve two related problems at once. It attempts to address the absence of solidarity in a divided society through nondemocratic means. If solidarity cannot be generated organically, it will be imposed nondemocratically. The authoritarian regime does this through an end run around the messiness of democratic deliberation and the difficult processes of working through the enduring contradictions of the nation's past or new contradictions that emerge from the reconfigurations of power. What is most obviously at play is a conflict over the boundaries of legality and illegality on a wide range of policy issues: perhaps less obviously, a contest over the boundaries of acceptability and unacceptability on an array of social norms.

What is at stake—and the critical difference between authority and the authoritarian, as Arendt pointed out—is legitimacy.[5] But legitimacy has two faces: legitimacy *claimed* by those who rule or seek to rule, and legitimacy *conferred* by those who are or would be governed (the "consent of the people"). All power sees itself as legitimate, as having a rightful claim to rule or to exercise power over others. That doesn't mean that legitimacy will be conferred by those subjected to its influence. Legitimacy is conferred when the ideals and interests of the populace are aligned with the vision and agenda of their leaders and when the leadership is accountable to those they govern. There is confidence and trust that leaders and the institutions they oversee operate within the boundaries of the public interest. Legitimacy, then, is strongest when the legitimacy *claimed* and the legitimacy *conferred* are aligned.

It is, of course, the lack of such an alignment that lies at the heart of the deepening legitimation crisis and the decline of effective governance. The turn toward extra-democratic means to establish and maintain the boundaries of social and political solidarity appears to be the only option to a growing number of prominent partisans. Voices across the political spectrum can now be heard gesturing toward this conclusion.

Portents of the Authoritarian

From the Left

On the left, the grounds for an authoritarian turn were inadvertently laid by Richard Rorty. Specifically, his rejection of the possibility of a common space for argument and compromise opened the way for harsher and higher-stakes forms of cultural conflict.

As the culture war evolved in the early decades of the twenty-first century, political battles came to be fought without a trace of Rorty's genial self-restraint. Rorty might have failed to see what was coming because he had too much faith in his own implicit anthropology, which was grounded in a profound aversion to cruelty. From his Trotskyist upbringing he had preserved a deep desire to protect the small, the overlooked, the oppressed. In the final section of *Contingency, Irony, and Solidarity*, the work that laid out his great doctrine of fluidity and deconstruction, he made a last attempt to square the circle and assert a firm moral principle that might outlast his own contingent and perishable preferences. In Nabokov and Orwell he found examples of "how a loathing for cruelty—a sense that it is the worst thing we do—[could] be combined . . . with a sense of the contingency of selfhood and of history."[6] Rorty thought the hatred for oppression that he himself felt so strongly, that he had learned from his parents and all those illustrious American leftists around his dinner table as a child, could be transmitted not dogmatically but poetically, not as a formal interdiction but as a shared *loathing*, a certain *sense* of wrong.

His notion of "joshing" spoke to a desire to be gentle and generous to his adversaries. One joshes a friend who has momentarily taken leave of his senses, not an enemy who lacks any sense at all. In his prophetic calls for the Left to abandon its dogmatic metaphysics, we can recognize a deep and humane aversion to the cruelties and counter-cruelties that always result from a clash of cosmologies. Rorty thought that his insistence on geniality would preserve the humanity and decency that he admired.

The problem was contingency. Rorty made everything contingent and then chose to be a nice guy on a purely contingent basis. His successors followed him in reducing politics to will, but they did not follow him in choosing to be nice. How could they, when their willed desires were threatened by what they regarded as implacably wicked and powerful forces on the right?

Moreover, the younger generation's contingent ethical upbringing had been quite different from Rorty's. He had grown up in a leftist political movement that saw all people as brethren, united in the search for a good life and divided only by misunderstanding and the machinations of the ruling class. Politics for the socialists of the early twentieth century was not a zero-sum game; it was an ennobling struggle for the betterment of everyone, whether everyone knew it or not.

Today's Left, by contrast, is largely made up of people educated in the identitarian tendencies that Rorty feared. At their most extreme, these tendencies treat political life as a death struggle for scarce resources rather than as shared progress toward common goods. No wonder, then, that verbal and sometimes physical bludgeoning has taken the place of joshing. The union of Rorty's anti-metaphysics and identitarianism's adversarial politics turns out to be far more oppositional than either was alone.

If the practical consequence of Rorty's personal mythos had been a hopeful program of gradual reform, the practical consequence of the new reality was an unremitting opposition to a vast array of enemies and a relentless attack on what a new woke Left saw as an irredeemably racist, sexist, and homophobic status quo. Rorty had done his part in dissolving the hybrid-Enlightenment, but his hoped-for contingent replacement had dissolved in turn, and far more quickly than the original.

From the Right

On the right, a telling portent of the authoritarian turn was evident as early as 1996 in a symposium entitled "The End of Democracy?" the proceedings of which were published in the November 1996 issue of *First Things*.[7] The symposium addressed what Richard Neuhaus saw as the "troubling judicial actions that add up to an entrenched pattern of government by judges that is nothing less than the usurpation of politics." Have "we reached . . . the point where conscientious citizens can no longer give moral assent to the existing regime"?

In the symposium, Judge Robert Bork argued that by a "judicial oligarchy," "the most important moral, political, and cultural decisions affecting our lives are steadily being removed from democratic control." "The last term," he asserted, was "rich in examples. The Court moved a long way toward making homosexual conduct a constitutional right, adopted the radical feminist view that men and women are essentially identical, continued to view the First Amendment as a protection of self-gratification rather than of the free articulation of ideas."

In its net effect, "what is happening now," Neuhaus argued, "is a growing alienation of millions of Americans from a government they do not recognize as theirs; what is happening now is an erosion of moral adherence to this political system." As the law professor Russell Hittinger put it, the country now operated "under an altered constitutional regime" whose laws were "unworthy of loyalty." "What used to be the most loyal citizens—religious believers—[have become] enemies of the common good whenever their convictions touch upon public things."

Neuhaus himself spoke of "the prospect" or "some might say the present reality—of despotism" in America, precisely because the constitutional order had been displaced "by a regime that does not have, will not obtain, and cannot command the consent of the people." The options that remained ranged, he claimed, "from noncompliance to resistance to civil disobedience to morally justified revolution." Finally, Charles Colson argued that America may soon be coming to the place where "the only political action religious believers can take is some kind of direct, extra-political confrontation" with the "judicially-controlled regime."

A regime "not worthy of loyalty"? "Morally justified revolution"? "Extra-political confrontation"? These are fighting words. Ironically, the Supreme Court would shift to a decidedly conservative majority a quarter century later, but no matter. Their message in 1996 gave voice to a brewing sentiment very much taken to heart on January 6, 2021.

But by this time, that sentiment had been intellectualized far beyond the consternations of the *First Things* symposium. A new movement of "national conservatism" (or "common good conservatism") had emerged that formalized a debate over the future of conservatism itself.[8] There was a great deal of intramural scholasticism around questions of natural rights, natural law, Edmund Burke, and the like, but what was at stake was whether to defend the classical liberal order or to aim for a counterrevolution and a refounding of the American Republic. At this point, all of the moral energy of this debate was for a "counterrevolution."

The character of this counterrevolution was rooted in the idea that liberal democracy and its sources had been depleted and had now ripened into a despairing anger. The influential Claremont intellectuals and their fellow travelers (many of whom became players in the Trump administration) shared the belief that "the U.S. Constitution no longer works," that "our norms are hopelessly corrupt," that "there is almost nothing left to conserve," and that "the original America is more or less gone." Indeed, "most people living in the United States today—certainly more than half—are not Americans in any meaningful sense of the term."[9] What was more, the rationalism of democratic procedure could no longer be trusted to deliver anything resembling conservative outcomes. As Josh Hammer put it in an essay in the *Harvard Journal of Law and Public Policy*, "Conservatism in the Anglo-American tradition is preeminently concerned with the societal health and intergenerational cohesion of the nation-state, with the structural integrity and formative capability to inculcate sound republican habits of mind in the intermediary communitarian institutions that exist between citizen and state, and with the flourishing of individual citizens in a way that serves God and nation and comports with the great Western religions' conceptions of the teleological ends of man."[10]

In this signature essay of the national conservative movement, Hammer effectively redefined conservatism *against* the conservatism of the classical liberal tradition. By doing so, he laid the groundwork for a conservatism "open to wielding state power, when need be, to 'enforce our order,' or even to 'reward friends and punish enemies (within the confines of the rule of law).'"[11]

For the national or common good conservatives, the "common good" is a substantive vision of the good "which soberly resists the illusion of a 'values-neutral' public square or a 'values-neutral' constitutional interpretive methodology."[12] Rather than an evolving universalizing understanding of the common good, the "substantive vision of the good" that national conservatives have proposed owes more to an early modern Christian life-world than anything resembling present-day conditions. In other words, it asserts a particular conception of the common good and is willing to use state power to enforce it against the other half of the nation that would find it objectionable. The solution to the puzzle of E Pluribus Unum would be to impose an unum, by force if need be.

From the Technocratic Elite

Among the apologists of the technocracy, the authoritarian impulse looks different still, not least because its enactments are subtle. The starting point is, on the one hand, the condescension that the technocracy has toward popular sovereignty, the legislature, and the courts and, on the other, the high regard it has for those experts who decide what is best for the public weal and the executive branch that would enact it. The reality for those who think technocratically is that a great deal of political power must belong to the "choice architects" who shape decision-making conditions. This power should be entrusted wherever possible to appropriately qualified experts and those experts should not be afraid to use it.

Sunstein understood that the theory of nudging raised difficult questions about human freedom, and he tried to address some of these questions in a short book, *On Freedom*, that he published several years after he had published *Nudge*. There he continued to insist on his commitment to maximizing choice, but he also admitted forthrightly that he thought experts might be justified in shaping ordinary people's preferences under the right circumstances. In general, he argued, nudges should be governed by the "as-judged-by-themselves" standard. People's actions should be shaped in directions they would choose for themselves. In some cases, however, "preferences are an artifact of nudging." People have no special preference prior to being nudged but acquire one as a result of the nudging. In those cases, he argues, "there is no escaping an inquiry into well-being. . . . We need to ask what kind of approach makes people's lives go better."[13] Moreover, as he explained in the last paragraph of his last chapter, there are times when even people's considered judgments after the fact do not make an adequate basis for determining where and how to nudge:

> People's judgments, *before the fact*, are [not] always authoritative. . . . People might not welcome a nudge or a mandate even though it is very much in their interests. If the question is whether people's judgments, *after the fact*, might not be authoritative, the answer is less simple. If we are concerned about people's well-being, it is surely relevant, and not at all a good sign, that people reject a mandate or a ban. In a free society, the presumption should be that they are right. But presumptions can be rebutted. If the issue involves serious harm and if the evidence is very clear, we will have to abandon the "as judged by themselves" standard. Reluctantly, but still.[14]

On one level, Sunstein was simply reinventing the traditional and largely uncontroversial claim that governments should be allowed to restrict individual action in the service of public well-being. In the context of his theory of nudging and the deeply contested view of what constitutes public well-being, however, these remarks indicated a less canonically liberal attitude toward political life. Sunstein seemed to be suggesting that in cases where "very clear" evidence of the threat of "serious harm" points to the need for restriction but "people reject a mandate or a ban," their refusal to accept what is good for them gives "us" license to nudge them in accordance with a truer understanding of what they really need.

Vermeule shares all of this distrust toward popular sovereignty as well as the high regard for expert-informed executive power, but he takes it quite a few steps further in a marriage between technocratic rule and national conservatism. As with national conservatism, the "common good constitutionalism" he has proposed sounds fairly innocuous. It is "based on the principles that government helps direct persons, associations, and society generally toward the common good, and that strong rule in the interest of attaining the common good is entirely legitimate." The COVID-19 pandemic was a case in point.

All legislation, he rightly noted, is "founded upon some substantive conception of morality" and thus the state should embrace a "candid willingness to 'legislate morality.'" This and a list of other conservative principles very much aligned with the Christian Right "promote the common good and make for a just and well-ordered society."[15] That a restive citizenry might find his particular vision of the common good problematic doesn't trouble him.

Those in power should not be "ashamed of strong rule" and therefore should not shrink in "horror" from "political domination and hierarchy, because it sees that law is parental, a wise teacher and an inculcator of good habits." "Just authority in rulers can be exercised for the good of subjects, if necessary, even against the subjects' own perceptions of what is best for them—perceptions that may change over time anyway, as the law teaches, habituates, and reforms them. Subjects will come to thank the ruler whose legal strictures, possibly experienced at first as coercive, encourage subjects to form more authentic desires for the individual and common goods, better habits, and beliefs that better track and promote communal well-being."[16]

This, as I noted in chapter 10, is a world of "rulers" and "subjects," not elected leaders and citizens. It "is legitimate for rulers to

pursue the common good" . . . giving "broad scope for rulers to promote . . . *peace, justice,* and *abundance.* Today, we may add health and
safety to that list, in very much the same spirit."[17]

In a more contemporary vein, "common good constitutionalism
will favor a powerful presidency ruling over a powerful bureaucracy,
the latter acting through principles of administrative law's inner
morality with a view to promoting solidarity and subsidiarity. The
bureaucracy will be seen not as an enemy, but as the strong hand of
legitimate rule."[18]

Legitimacy claimed is not the same as legitimacy conferred, and
in a democracy, both have to be present for the legitimacy to be
authentic. Claiming it is not enough. Any tin-pot dictator can do that.
But this is, in effect, what Vermeule has proposed. In a world as fragmented and politically polarized as ours, his vision of common good
constitutionalism will bring delight to some. For those millions not
aligned with it, it would be an authoritarian nightmare. Vermeule is
unconcerned about authoritarian excess in large part because he believes that rulers, as rational actors, will moderate their actions under
the pressures of public opinion and the need to mobilize votes in an
election.[19] As with the movement of national conservatism, Vermeule's
vision of governance is an overtly illiberal and authoritarian vision,
one madly out of touch with the realities of the moment even as it
simultaneously seeks to respond to the realities of the moment.

The authoritarian impulse within technocracy takes a more fore-
boding turn in late modern America as one broadens the definitions
of both *governmentality* and *nudging.* On the former, Matthew Crawford has argued that Silicon Valley represents "a locus of quasi-
governmental power untouched by either the democratic process or
by those hard-won procedural liberties that are meant to secure us
against abuses by the (actual, elected) government."[20] Mark Zuckerberg himself has said that "Facebook [now Meta Platforms] is more
like a government than a traditional company" in the way it sets social
and political policies for its nearly 3 billion users. "What has emerged
is a new form of monopoly power made possible by the 'network
effect' of those platforms through which everyone must pass to conduct the business of life." It is not only a source of profit for these
platforms but, collectively, "a metastasizing grid of surveillance and
social control."[21]

As for nudging, it has expanded into algorithms for which decision-making is neither explainable (even by those who wrote the algorithms) nor possessed of actual human accountability. The technology is mystifying in the way magic is mystifying. As Crawford put it, "Mechanized judgment resembles liberal proceduralism, . . . but its effect is to erode precisely those procedural liberties that are the great accomplishment of the liberal tradition [by placing] authority beyond scrutiny."

From Political Theory: The Emergence of Agonism

Newer developments in political theory also, albeit unintentionally, reflect the authoritarian turn.

In chapter 3, I argued that in Western modernity, the nature of solidarity in liberal democracies had long been theorized within three different camps: the foundationalist, the proceduralist, and the communitarian. Though often abstract and esoteric, the debate among proponents of each was not only a language game for those in the ivory tower. In rough terms, these disagreements reflected historical tensions in American public opinion. Even within our weakened "procedural Republic" today, a vast number of ordinary Americans operate out of foundationalist and communitarian commitments. But the main point I'm driving at is that these tensions have resided securely within the liberal tradition—the primary issue of disagreement being just how thick or thin the sources of solidarity need to be.

But in the early twenty-first century, a novel camp has emerged around the banner of "agonism." Against its own best intentions, it ends up operating outside of the liberal tradition. As such, it provides justifications for authoritarian tendencies already well established in the broader political culture. How so?

Agonism (*agon:* struggle), in short, is a political theory that emphasizes the inherent reality and centrality of conflict in political life. The long-standing idea that political consensus can be achieved through a rational, neutral, and universal framework of deliberation is not only untenable on its face, proponents argue, but it unwittingly neutralizes dissent by requiring it to fit a particular definition of "reasonableness." Agonism, by contrast, discards that fiction, recognizing that power and plurality are pervasive fixtures of the late modern world and that together they create the conditions for dissensus and unending contestation.

The most comprehensive account of agonism in political theory has been developed by the Belgian political theorist Chantal Mouffe.[22] Like Vermeule, Mouffe draws upon the work of the Nazi political theorist Carl Schmitt for her understanding of the centrality of conflict to politics, in particular his famous work *The Concept of the Political*.[23] For Schmitt, the defining binary of politics is the distinction between friends and enemies and the conflict that naturally and inevitably ensues between them. As Mouffe has rendered it, "In an agonistic politics . . . the antagonistic dimension is always present, since what is at stake is the struggle between opposing hegemonic projects which can never be reconciled rationally, one of them needing to be defeated."[24]

Though a theorist of the Left, she is also a woman of her times. And so it isn't surprising that the focus of her conflict model is not on the classic concerns with unequal class relations but rather the power dynamics of identity groups. In her words, "The political is from the outset concerned with collective forms of identification, since in this field we are always dealing with the formation of 'us' as opposed to 'them.'" For her, the heart of politics is not contested ideas or contested class interests but "the centrality of collective identities and the crucial role played by affects in their constitution."[25]

It is important to highlight that Mouffe is not a disciple of Schmitt. Rather, she sees his work as a challenge to overcome. Ultimately, she seeks "to use his insights in order to strengthen liberal democracy against his critiques."[26] Indeed, she passionately argues that "liberal democracy is not the enemy to be destroyed."[27] In fact, she argues that it isn't possible to find more radical principles for organizing society than the ideals of liberty and equality.[28] Her objective is to reform and radicalize liberal democracy along agonistic terms.

Radicalizing democracy, she argues, begins with the recognition that the resolution of differences rooted in identity and essential to identity will never come about through discussion and deliberation. Nor should they. Compromise toward some pseudo-consensus is dishonest and deceptive. Agonistic democracy values these identitarian differences and depends on them. Her aim, then, is to mobilize power in a democratic way and, by so doing, mobilize a broad diversity of voices in the struggle for hegemony. In the end, as Mouffe puts it, "we have to accept that every consensus exists as a temporary result of a provisional hegemony, as a stabilization of power, and that it *always entails some form of exclusion.*"[29]

The agonistic democracy that she advocates, then, is one that defuses or tames the severe Schmittian insight into the friend/enemy nature of the political. To accomplish this, she aspires to turn antagonism between *enemies* into an agonism between *adversaries.*[30] The difference is key: with the former, both sides seek to destroy the other; with the latter, they do not. The taming is made possible by citizens swearing "a common allegiance to the democratic principles of 'liberty and equality for all,' even while disagreeing about their interpretation." Because of these shared allegiances, adversaries "do not put into question the legitimacy of their opponent's right to fight for the victory of their position."[31] The taming is also aided by "fostering allegiance to our democratic institutions . . . by creating strong forms of identification with them," that is, by forming a strong citizenship identity.[32] In sum, the competition between "opposing hegemonic projects" is "played out under conditions *regulated by a set of democratic procedures accepted by the adversaries.*"[33]

Whether appealing or not, there is no question that the agonistic account of politics as an ineradicable conflict over hegemonic power is a better reflection of contemporary American political culture than the picture provided by the other theoretical schools. Agonism is a theory tailor-made for the culture war. Within American democracy today, politics has devolved into a competing will to power, and within the work of Chantal Mouffe, we find its intellectual justification.

But for all that, the efforts by Mouffe and other agonistic theorists to rescue liberal democracy from the worst excesses of the Schmittian nightmare still depend upon a "center" defined by the democratic principles of liberty and equality, a commitment to proceduralist mechanisms for realizing those principles, and a broad popular allegiance to them. These things together, for her, form the basis of a constructive solidarity and the terms by which liberal democracy maintains its popular legitimacy. Agonistic democracy, in other words, requires a procedural and ethical commitment by *all* factions *prior* to the work of political contestation to keep it from descending into a Hobbesian war of all against all.

But where do the ethics of democratic "respect" come from and what are their sources? Likewise, from where does "a common allegiance to the democratic principles of 'liberty and equality for all'" derive, and on what terms can it be made plausible and legitimate? Similarly, why should anyone have a strong allegiance to democratic institutions, especially if those institutions are viewed as "rigged"? And, not least, why should adversaries in a life-and-death struggle for hegemony prefer democracy over dictatorship in the first place? As George Crowder put it, "Antagonism may be natural and inevitable, but agonism is not: a case needs to be made."[34]

Mouffe would probably respond that a case doesn't need to be made, that there is no need to respond to these objections. After all, "allegiance to democracy and belief in the value of its institutions," she has written, "do not depend on giving them an intellectual foundation." Rather, she argues, "It is more in the nature of what Wittgenstein likens to 'a passionate commitment to a system of reference.' Hence, although it's belief, it is really a way of living or of assessing one's life."[35]

In Wittgenstein's terms, "a passionate commitment to a system of reference" is an allusion to his idea of "the forms of life" that underwrite any possible agreement in belief or commitment. But it is precisely these "forms of life"—what I have called the deep structures of culture—that have disintegrated in our public culture. Moreover, the "giving of reasons" is a democratic imperative.

In the end, Mouffe offers no credible answers to these questions. Here too, "Why?" has no answer. That makes the normative aspirations of the agonism she proposes merely arbitrary: assertions of personal hopefulness but detached from any actual existing institutional framework or practices that might render those ethical aspirations concrete. There are, then, no compelling reasons why agonism should not descend into antagonism—or why, in Stephen White's helpful distinction, a "tempered agonism" should not quickly transform into an "imperializing agonism" whose chief aim is to subdue one's opponents.[36] The cultural logic of mutual annihilation has primacy and nothing in Mouffe's framework would impede political actors from following that logic to its natural Schmittian conclusion.

Ironically, though her work is in service to progressive identitarian politics, there is nothing that prohibits the theoretical logic of agonism from being enacted by adherents of reactionary identitarian politics as well—which, of course, they have done with great relish and damaging effectiveness. In this respect, agonism as a political theory isn't radical after all. It simply, even if unintentionally, serves to legitimate the status quo of brutalizing polarization in American politics and the nihilistic competition of power politics with no plausible way beyond it.

From America's Deep Structure

Yet a final portent of the authoritarian impulse I'll note is prior to all the others. It can be found deeply embedded in America's historical mythos, especially its story of origins and destiny: *the idea of Puritan perfectionism*. Utopian dreams of moral purity are common enough in global history. Yet the idea of America as a nation "exceptional" among all nations—a "citty upon a hill," as John Winthrop memorably put it in 1630—and its people chosen by God to pursue a mission to be a model of moral and spiritual purity found fertile soil here. Winthrop's sermon was remarkable for the detail he laid out about the nature and texture of the community the Puritans were called to build, the reasons for building it, and the stakes involved in getting it right.[37] Their community was to reflect the kingdom of God as "a modell of Christian charity," and the judgment of history ("the eies of all people") and of God rest with their obedience in building it.[38]

A century ago, George Santayana observed that the passion that drove the Puritans to these shores was "metaphysical"; they came to this land "in the hope of living more perfectly in the spirit."[39] That passion "to live more perfectly" has been replicated and reconfigured through the length of American history. Both within local communities and in the nation as a whole, Americans have sought to create righteous communities. Puritan perfectionism has, in fact, survived its pluralization into faiths other than Calvinism, and it has survived its secularization into movements that are self-consciously nonreligious.

That ethos endures and proliferates today within identity groups, both on the left and on the right. Here too, morality merges with ontology, producing competing factions that are animated by a vision of moral purity. They too have sought to establish their own righteous communities organized around fundamentally different versions of reality and fundamentally different visions of justice. And, of course, these righteous communities insist that their own is the only correct one. In these worlds, a sharp line is drawn between the righteous and unrighteous, the saved and the damned, those included and those excluded. It only follows that their votaries are not bashful about doing the boundary work necessary, in Winthrop's delicate words, to "moderate and restrain the wicked"—though in our day, such boundary work is called cancellation, doxing, scapegoating, and negation. These performative acts of purification often betray a moral certainty that can be as severe, cruel, unforgiving, *and* authoritarian as any of the caricatures of the gray, gaunt, and graceless Puritan divines.

This does, parenthetically, raise a paradox: if, in the strictest sense, nihilism represents the giving up of moral valuation, how then do we account for the intensity of moral valuation within factions of the Left and Right?

An answer is that the nihilism that emanates from the death of God is passive, institutionalized within the broad fabric of society. The hyper-moralism of various social and political factions reflects the active nihilism of those in the thick of the competing will to power. Their negations presuppose the existence in their minds of an ideal world far beyond and above what is attainable in the present world. For the Left, that ideal world is defined by opaque notions of justice; for the Right, it is defined by an equally opaque nostalgia for the past. Perhaps the assumption of an ideal world, however defined, is a lingering echo of a moral vocabulary not entirely past, or an effect of some fundamental anthropological need for meaning.[40] Either way, the more remote and utopian the ideals of justice or of a former way of life, the closer their negations lead to nihilism, for reaching beyond meant negating what was already here.[41] And the intensity of the longing for an ideal world, then, is redirected into fury against the present, a fury channeled into the demand to purge, dismantle, deconstruct, and negate. This is why, in Nietzsche's formulary, "moral value judgments are ways of passing sentence."[42] Moralism, whether in a reactionary or revolutionary bearing, is not a way of life but a weapon of coercion.

Coercion, Violence, and the State

All of these are merely portents or signs rather than full-throated justifications for coercion. They are alarming enough on their own terms because they implicitly recognize the logic of O. W. Holmes's observation about force noted at the beginning of the chapter.

They are alarming as well because hovering in the background is the state. Though in recent times the state has sought to present itself as neutral on questions of the public good, neutrality is a fiction, and even fairness is a standard that often seems honored only in the breach. When it formulates law, sets policy, and makes judicial decisions, the state cannot help but take sides on matters of the public good.[43] Through law (the language of the state), the state makes binding decisions affecting the whole of society in the name of society itself. What puts an edge on this reality is that the state, as Max Weber established long ago, is founded upon and maintained by coercion. In enforcing compliance to the law, it claims the sole legitimate use of violence. The problem is that the coercive power of the state today tends to be seen as illegitimate in the view of those out of power.

In the larger struggle for hegemony, then, much of contemporary political conflict takes shape over the patronage of the state and its power to coerce compliance. This is why competing sides depend upon executive order, the courts, and the federal bureaucracy to establish law and policy that would likely fail to achieve broad popular backing had they actually been subject to public debate.

These dynamics play out most obviously at the federal level, but they also take place within states that have strong conservative or progressive majorities. In these settings too, laws are used to punish companies or nonprofits (including religious organizations) that fail to conform to the ideological interests of the dominant party.[44]

The practice of using the power of the state to coerce solidarity, then, is well established. But now the coercive element, already present in the state, has been intellectualized and justified by partisans on the left, on the right, and by the technocratic and managerial elite toward hegemonic purposes. And they are reinforced by developments in political theory. What had been unthinkable is now imaginable—and therefore implicitly permissible. The ground for such a turn has been softened.

Clearly, the authoritarian impulse emerging today is not the same across the ideological spectrum. The tone, substance, and credibility of the arguments vary according to their place within various economic and status hierarchies. And so does the potential threat. Because of their hegemonic position within cultural institutions, progressives and their technocratic counterparts tend to be blind to their own authoritarian tendencies. Moreover, they have the linguistic skills and institutional capacities to quickly justify efforts to muffle or marginalize dissent. By the same token, because conservatives are on the defensive and because the main tools available to them are political, their authoritarian tendencies often incline more toward the aggressive and bare-knuckled. Thus the frequent allusions to a revivified fascism.[45] But what is common to all is the impulse to sidestep democratic process and impose their own particular conception of social and political solidarity upon those who would dissent.

Clearly the broader situation is highly volatile, but could coercion escalate from here?

Indeed it could.

Civil War?

In the December 2019 issue of *The Atlantic*, the editors tackled the issue "how to stop a civil war." The idea that the current political polarization could devolve into a violent conflagration is disquieting, to say the least. The editors quickly dismissed the idea that the conditions in contemporary America resemble those of the 1850s, but they still "worry that the ties that bind us are fraying at alarming speed—we are becoming contemptuous of each other in ways that are both dire and possibly irreversible."[46]

To be sure, the idea of a civil war conducted through the mobilization of standing armies against each other is more than a bit farfetched, for the simple reason that opponents in America's culture wars are not divided regionally or by states. There has been a sorting and clustering that create concentrations of conservatives and progressives within regions and within institutions, but "red and blue" America are intermingled in many ways, not least in a system of economic interdependence.

This does not mean, however, that the conditions in the nation are not ripe for violence. They are. Anger and hatred, it would seem, can be sustained only for so long before they become violent. But in the late modern age, the preferred forms of violence are acts of terror or guerilla warfare—fast-moving, small-scale violence against a person or group or an institution that symbolizes the "enemy" or promotes the "enemy's" agenda. And while it tends to be episodic rather than systematic, this kind of violence can escalate into something more frequent and better organized.

Violence of this nature is already present, particularly among those who perceive themselves out of power with democratic options closed down.[47] There is no simple parity here. The most significant domestic terrorism threats since 1994 have come from the extreme Right, by those motivated by racial and ethnic superiority, opposition to government authority, and conspiracy theories. Of the nearly 900 acts of domestic terror between 1994 and 2020, 411 were carried out by right-wing individuals or groups, and of these, 329 resulted in fatalities. Among these were the attack against Latinos at a Walmart in El Paso, Texas, in 2019, in which the perpetrator claimed he was reacting to a "Hispanic invasion of Texas," and the attack on the Tree of Life Synagogue in Pittsburgh in 2018 that killed eleven and wounded six others. In this same period, there were 219 left-wing attacks by those motivated by anarchist, anti-capitalist, and Black nationalist ideologies, and of these, there were twenty-one fatalities. These famously included the shooting attack on congressional Republicans practicing baseball in Alexandria, Virginia, seriously injuring six.

Between 2020 and 2022, the number of domestic terrorist threats and acts increased. The majority still came from far-right groups and individuals (49 percent), though the number of far-left attacks grew significantly (to 40 percent).

Over nearly two decades, the targets have changed, but increasingly they have focused on government, military, and police locations and personnel. The attack on the FBI offices in Cincinnati, Ohio, in August 2022 is one just case. More egregious was the storming of the Capitol on January 6, 2021, in the effort to prohibit the certification of President Biden's election. These numbers do not include the number of threats made against members of Congress, which rose from 902 in 2016 to 3,939 in 2017 and to 9,600 in 2021.[48] As researchers noted, the threats came from a mishmash of ideological directions: conservatives threatening progressives (about one-third of those indicted), progressives threatening conservatives (about one-quarter of those indicted), conservatives threatening other conservatives who were deemed not conservative enough.

These tendencies toward violence have been aggravated by the incitements of conservative political leaders. President Trump's own incitements of the armed protesters on January 6, 2021, represent only the most obvious case, but there are others as well—Marjorie Taylor Greene's infamous statement "The only way you get your freedoms back is it's earned with the price of blood" or Arizona congressman Paul Gosar's tweet of an anime-style video that showed a character that looked like him killing another character that looked like New York congresswoman Alexandria Ocasio-Cortez.[49]

All of this is especially concerning in light of changes in the public's general disposition toward political violence. According to research conducted at Stanford in 2020, one-third of all Americans who identify as Democrats or Republicans believe that violence could be justified to advance their party's political goals. This was about 20 percent of the total population.[50] Another poll found that one-third of all Americans say that violent action against the government is justified.[51] Those justifying violence are especially concentrated among the most ideologically partisan, those who are either "very liberal" or "very conservative." Indeed, most Americans expect violence from the losing side after future presidential elections.[52]

Culture Wars and Shooting Wars

Reading of these developments, one cannot but hope that they are a passing phenomenon. But there are no indications that the cultural conditions for ideologically motivated violence are diminishing. Indeed, culture wars always precede "shooting wars." Violent conflict doesn't necessarily follow, but the violence will not occur without the ground having been softened up for many years by deep cultural antagonism. Otherwise, violence is merely arbitrary. Culture, then, provides the justifications as well as the targets for violence.[53]

CHAPTER FOURTEEN

Whither Liberal Democracy?

Liberal Democracy and the Dream of America

The dream of America is a dream many times betrayed, but it has been, nonetheless, strong enough to unite Americans in a solidarity that not only has endured through most of its history but has also been an inspiration far beyond America itself to other lands and other peoples.[1] This dream derived from an ethical vision for the re-formation of public life, a vision for the fostering of freedom and flourishing of individuals and communities, built on the hope that the world and the lot of ordinary people could be made better. It was a powerful and compelling vision, one imbued with a certain "sacred" quality that made it worth sacrificing for—and at many times and in many circumstances, worth dying for. Liberal democracy was not identical with that vision of the public good, but its rituals, practices, and institutions served and supported it all the same. At its best, liberal democracy gave political expression to that vision.

Problems, nevertheless, were present from the beginning: the promise of freedom for all but the denial of freedom for vast portions of the American people; the guarantee of legal equality to every person but the withholding of that pledge for broad segments of the nation; the commitment to justice for all yet the practice of systemic injustice to millions; and the assurance of toleration for a multiplicity of communal beliefs and practices but an often strident intolerance for those whose beliefs were and are outside the boundaries of acceptable opinion. And layered through these contradictions was the conundrum of how to reconcile private and factional interests with the common good. These were the problems that have many times betrayed the effort to realize the dream of America. Yet against these contradictions and new ones still emerging, real progress has been made, although not without the long, difficult, frustrating, seemingly interminable, and conflict-laden process of working through those contradictions.

E Pluribus Unum and Its Contradictions

For the Founders, *E Pluribus Unum* was less an accomplishment than it was a puzzle to figure out. It was, as it turned out, a puzzle that would require solving anew with every successive generation. Even at the Founding, the architects of the new Republic wondered what would happen when the laws of nature and the will of God became unclear or contested. On what authority would disputes be resolved when individuals and groups pursued competing notions of the social good? And what hope was there for national unity when individual citizens failed to act within the dictates of reason, pursued nothing but their own interest, and abandoned concern for the common good?

E Pluribus Unum, the national motto on the Great Seal of the United States, was proposed by John Adams, Benjamin Franklin, and Thomas Jefferson in 1776. By the time Hamilton wrote Federalist 9 and Madison wrote Federalist 10 in 1787, the destructive force of factionalism (one face of the pluribus) was already a worry. In their wildest reveries, neither of them could have imagined how broad and how deep the ideological, demographic, and economic factionalism would become in our late modern era. They could never have anticipated how this evolving factionalism would challenge the frameworks of solidarity and the deeply entrenched boundaries of tolerable difference along the way. In short, they never could have imagined how infinitely more complex the puzzle of E Pluribus Unum would become.

Over the course of two and a half centuries, the contradictions internal to the hybrid-Enlightenment and the factionalism and conflict they ignited have been repeatedly and imperfectly worked through to widen the boundaries, to render the nation more inclusive, just, and equitable, even while still sustaining solidarity. Where progress was made for the descendants of African slaves, Native Americans, Catholics, Mormons, Jews, the Irish, Chinese, women, and others, it has very often come at the cost of generations of humiliation, discrimination, and violence, some still continuing. Most, however, believed that the cost was worth it. Born enslaved in Tennessee in 1854 and rising to become a physician and a bishop in the African Methodist Episcopal Church, Dr. Evans Tyree captured that ambivalence for many African Americans and other marginalized people when he wrote, "America has put herself on the defensive more than once for the sake of others far away, but here black sons have suffered and died by the hundreds within her own dominion, and none have come to their rescue. These are things we see with much sorrow, but we shall live and die loyal to the stars and stripes, in obedience to law and order."[2]

Even against the high price that has been paid, the fidelity to the American project shown by the Black community and so many others on the fringes of the social order has been a measure of the mythic power of the American ideal.

To be sure, that ideal has evolved over time. As the sources of solidarity were worked through over many generations, the older ideals retained their ethical force even while the ideals themselves came to mean something different. As the composition of the pluribus expanded, the meaning of the unum enlarged. The story Americans could tell about themselves became more capacious, but it retained sufficient opacity to allow different factions to read their own particular creeds, history, national culture, and interests into it. In this way, the past, with all its tragedies and its triumphs, was made intelligible in light of the present. At the same time, the challenges of the present were made comprehensible in historically recognizable ways. To be sure, the adhesive power of this solidarity was weakening due to the solvents of demographic change and expanding pluralism, the proliferation of neoliberal economic thought and practice, and the slow discrediting of the WASP establishment. Even so, the "One" continued to contain the "Many," making possible a workable solidarity within which compromises could be worked out. Even in their differences, then, Americans could see a line of continuity. Their lives were still part of a common project, a project fueled by the hope of betterment.

Warring Hegemonic Projects

The line of continuity would now seem broken. We have ended up in a place of warring hegemonic projects visible in the substance of most public issues but rooted in the irresolvable differences of normative assumptions underwriting competing points of view and ways of life. In the effort to predetermine the outcome, the conflict extends to the rules, practices, and procedures of governance through which conflict gets sorted out. While many worry about fragmentation, polarization, and the potential for violence, among leading political actors, the idea of a common good sought through common hopes is nowhere invoked, much less pursued. The ethical boundaries that define solidarity are erected and maintained by one side in direct opposition to the boundaries constructed by the other, neither side willing or able to come alongside the other to democratically work through their differences to achieve a *medium terram*. The very idea of seeking the common ground of mutual affection or mutual responsibility represents a betrayal. Even the politically indifferent are accused of being complicit in perpetuating the greatest evils afflicting the world. At the end of the day, a center of solidarity, it is believed, will come about only through the triumphant imposition of one side's conception upon the other, and to the exclusion of the other.

Tragically, all actors involved understand the situation in existential terms. The other side is the enemy of all that is or could be right and good about America. And it is to be treated accordingly. For the other side to win is to be stigmatized, excluded, dominated, and oppressed. For those involved, it feels like a life-and-death conflict.

They may be right—if not literally, then culturally.

The centrifugal forces that threatened to unravel the hybrid-Enlightenment from the earliest days of the Republic have evolved, to be sure, and in some ways intensified. Along with the slow deconstruction of the hybrid-Enlightenment has been a loss of resonance among many Americans for the world the hybrid-Enlightenment attempted to idealize. Given the seemingly infinite expansion of pluralism, including moral pluralism, where now will the limits to tolerance be drawn? From what sources could any civic and political authority capable of adjudicating what is just from unjust, fair from unfair, be established? Upon what common affections, sensibilities, or political creeds could any solidarity be found in a political culture defined by the cultural logics of revenge? And on what basis can private interests, often incorporated within influential, highly factional special-interest organizations and powerful corporations, be reconciled with the public good?

On all sides, key public intellectuals, activists, politicians, and the various institutions they represent have, for all practical purposes, given up trying to work through their differences. Few, it would seem, have the appetite for it. What, they might plausibly ask, would be the point?

Making matters more challenging, of course, is the depletion of the deep cultural reservoirs from which Americans had long drawn to sustain the liberal democratic order through its many trials. There is now *no* authority by which questions of truth or reality or public ethics could be settled definitively. Even more perplexing, the emotivism that has come to dominate public ethics on all sides obviates the possibility that they ever will be settled definitively. Likewise, any bold vision of national purpose has been abandoned, replaced by a stripped-down pursuit of partisan power. Not least, the concept of "citizen" has been reduced to a range of politicized identity markers and the rights demanded by those who claim them. Rarely if ever is the question of corresponding civic responsibilities addressed. In all of these ways and others, the cultural logic of the hybrid-Enlightenment that underwrote the liberal democratic regime has dissolved as a working logic of the public sphere.

In his version of a liberal utopia, Richard Rorty believed that "democracies [were] now in a position to throw away some of the ladders used in their own construction," ladders such as "reason" and "moral obligation."[3] He wrote this in 1989. It is fair to say that he got his wish.

Filling the void is a very different cosmology that fosters a new and very different kind of common culture, one characterized by deeply entrenched nihilistic elements. Many of these elements have become institutionalized within the background of late modern civ-

ilization. These would include the dissolution of a shared reality or
even the means by which to determine a shared reality (the problem
of epistemological failure), the absence of any fixed and shared moral
knowledge (the problem of moral incoherence), and the loss of any
intrinsic meaning or value or purpose to individual and social life (the
preconditions for existential despair). Still other elements—notably
the cultural logics of ressentiment that spawn an ethics of revenge—
are actively cultivated in the hegemonic politics of mutual annihilation. In identity politics, a social and political development that aims
for genuine human goods (genuine recognition, genuine toleration,
genuine justice)—and sometimes achieves them—has also, by the cultural logics of ressentiment, become both dehumanizing and, in large
measure, self-defeating.

Democratic Renewal?

In her failed bid for the governorship of Massachusetts in 2022, the
Harvard political theorist Danielle Allen reflected on what she had
learned from the process. "In the 200-some communities we visited,
we encountered an appetite and readiness to build . . . partnerships
[across communities and among the public sector, nonprofits, and
business]. Everywhere across our Commonwealth, people were ready
to come together and face pressing challenges—the opioid epidemic,
the housing crisis, the threat of rising sea levels. People were hungry
to come together." Here, in the moral compasses of ordinary citizens, we find seeds of democratic renewal. Yet Allen invariably came
up against institutional hurdles in the party system that made it impossible for her even to make it onto the ballot for the state primary.
"We the people are healthy," she wrote, "but our vehicles of political
participation need attention."[4]

Allen's experience maps onto the pattern observed earlier. Surveys of American public opinion continue to show that Americans,
on the whole, love their country. Vast majorities continue to believe
that "America is the greatest country in the world" or at least "a great
country" along with others and that America is even an "exceptional
nation." Most Americans describe themselves as "moderately" or
"very patriotic."[5] Out of this comes an abundance of goodwill among
ordinary citizens who are willing to do the difficult work of coming

together to find democratic solutions to the problems they face. Yet the myriad initiatives that seek to overcome partisan polarization in local communities run up against entrenched and powerful institutional forces in the interconnected cultural economies of technology, media and social media, the party system, and the like.[6] One wants to believe that if there were just more people willing to do this work, and if they all just worked harder, democratic renewal would follow. Yet these larger institutional forces playing out in the national and global realms tend to render all such grassroots efforts ineffective at changing the framework in democratic directions.

Solidarity and the Instrumentalities of the Law

The only tools left to forge solidarity would seem to be the instruments of law and the coercive power of the state. Defenders of this strategy of change often speak of the law as a teacher. Adrian Vermeule, it will be recalled, was one of those who justified "strong rule" (by my reading, authoritarian rule) by appealing to the "parental" and pedagogic functions of the law. Perhaps laws, regulations, and procedures are effective in reinforcing or clarifying rules that are already informally known and embraced but are ambiguous or ill defined. But such instruments are far less effective in teaching new lessons. Law is an administrative tool. Its pedagogic properties are at best secondary, and thus seriously limited. If a people are not already predisposed culturally to the substance of the law, if their moral intuitions and imaginations are not already formed by the deep structures of their culture in ways that are consonant with the law, they will likely reject the lessons it has to teach. The law would have only limited legitimacy. Citizens will abide by it only out of fear of the coercive instrumentalities of the state. Eluding such coercion, they will do as they please, the law be damned. They will find workarounds.

The Supreme Court, in the *Dred Scott v. Sanford* decision, attempted to impose solidarity on the matter of race for a country that had not worked through the deep cultural realities of unequal humanity. Though the North's triumph in the Civil War followed by the passage of the Thirteenth, Fourteenth, and Fifteenth Amendments to the Constitution were great and necessary achievements, the laws could do only so much work. A new solidarity was imposed on a nation that had not worked through the contradiction of unequal humanity nor the economic and political interests tied to slavery. Consequently, many of the worst features of slavery were effectively reconstituted after Reconstruction. The workarounds had names such as Jim Crow, the Ku Klux Klan, lynching, and red-lining. The deeply embedded racism of the Confederacy found a workaround.

In the same way and closer to our time, the Supreme Court decision in *Roe v. Wade* in 1973 was an attempt to impose solidarity on the question of abortion without having settled the dispute between the freedom of women to choose versus the humanity of the unborn. The overturning of *Roe* in the Supreme Court decision *Dobbs v. Jackson Women's Health Organization* changed the setting for the dispute, but it did nothing to resolve it. The nation was as divided under one Supreme Court decision as it had been under the other. Prior to *Dobbs*, conservatives found workarounds. In the wake of the *Dobbs* decision, progressives have already started to find their own.

Other well-known cases in the past, such as the Eighteenth Amendment and the Volstead Act creating Prohibition or Bryan's pyrrhic victory in *Scopes v. Dayton, Tennessee* favoring creationism, illustrate the same point. There is an attempt to have the law do the work of culture, forcing a consensus where none exists. The effort to use the law as a proxy for solidarity becomes a shortcut for avoiding the difficult task of working through fundamental differences. This, of course, explains why the first recourse of various actors in the range of disputes of the present culture war is litigation. The reliance upon the courts, or at times the legal power of executive order, implicitly recognizes that neither the Right nor the Left has an agenda that will generate popular support if it were openly deliberated. Evading the hard work through legal and political shortcuts seems like the only practical way to achieve resolution.

The point here is not so much to ruminate on the past but to highlight the dilemma of the present: the same flawed cultural logic is now at work within the authoritarian tendencies pervasive today and among those—Left and Right—who are tempted by them. Every effort to impose an artificial solidarity regarding this issue or that through the instrumentalities of the state on a restive citizenry will aggravate more than mollify, inflame more than assuage. The law may be a teacher, but it is a lousy one.[7]

The Present Crisis

A democratic politics underwritten by warring hegemonic projects is not sustainable. As disruptive as it is, the problem is not far-reaching polarization as such. Rather, the problem is with the resources by which polarization is worked through. Those cultural resources in public and political life, as I have argued from the start, have been depleted. This can only mean that polarization will not end any time soon. Indeed, just as the "Great Recession" of 2008 radicalized much of the conservative base and consolidated power and privilege among progressives, further economic contractions will only aggravate the social, cultural, and economic resentments.

That does not mean that democracy in America is dead. It is not. But it is far from healthy, and prospects for its vitality are not at all bright. In all likelihood, it will endure in form, but its substance will continue to be hollowed out. In its wake, the legitimation crisis will continue to harden: confidence in the range of governing institutions will continue to weaken, cynicism toward the leadership class will deepen, and the alienation of ordinary citizens from their nation will worsen. What is there to impede or reverse this course? And so the stability of the regime will undulate. At times it will seem better and at other times it will seem worse. But until the underlying conditions are addressed, liberal democracy will still be vulnerable to the kind of instability that followed the 2020 election.

That vulnerability of liberal democracy in America is only amplified by the decline in liberal internationalism. The international environment, as my colleague John Owen has demonstrated, can either "buttress or undermine constitutional self-government."[8] The growing power of populist authoritarian parties on the right and the left around the globe not only creates an inhospitable environment for American democracy (and democracies generally), it renders the United States more exposed to outside threat.[9] The concerns Arthur Schlesinger Jr. had in the 1950s, then, may be more poignant now than in his day. "Free society," he wrote, "will survive . . . only if enough people believe in it deeply enough to die for. However reluctant peace-loving people are to recognize that fact, history's warning is clear and cold; civilizations which cannot man their walls in times of alarm are doomed to destruction by the barbarians."[10]

The questions posed at the start of this book, then, come into sharper focus. How does liberal democracy—an Enlightenment-era political institution—continue to survive, thrive, and constructively evolve in a *post*-Enlightenment culture? Is there anything that remains of the hybrid-Enlightenment that might be salvageable or renewable? What, if anything, can be reconstructed from this deconstructed culture? Or, if salvaging the hybrid-Enlightenment is neither possible sociologically nor desirable politically or ethically, then what encompassing ethical vision could underwrite liberal democracy going forward? What credible authority could establish the factual or moral truth of matters or could command the respect and assent of the majority of citizens? What telos could bind Americans together in common hope? What mythos or common story could reunite Americans in all their differences? And given that the culture war has riven all the institutions of civil society—institutions of faith, education at all levels, philanthropy, the news and entertainment media, the law, professional associations in every field, and now even corporations—what institutions could be the carriers of this vision, this story, this hope?

More troubling still, what, at the end of the day, is the reply to nihilism in American public and political culture, that "whole tremulous realm of subterranean revenge"?[11] Is there a reply? None of the major contenders in public and political life seem to have one, apart from saying nihilism in American political culture is only a problem of the other side.

So, we are left with a very simple but daunting question: is the end of the American experiment in liberal democracy all but assured?

It doesn't have to be. And yet it likely will be if we fail to take the full measure of the challenges we face.

Coda

Imaginaries of Hope

THERE ARE MANY WHO say, "I know that things are bad, but I remain optimistic about the future."

As a response to our troubled world, the words come out almost involuntarily, like a reflex. But I suspect that the thought signifies more—perhaps an unconscious defiance against uncertainty and fear, like a mother comforting her child—"There, there, it will be okay." Such a reaction strikes me as profoundly human, entirely understandable, and on the face of it, admirable.

But then silence follows. "Why?" has no answer.

Defiance it may be, but it may also be an assurance tinged by denial.

A Long Road Ahead

So, what would it mean to take the full measure of the present crisis in American democracy?

At the very least, it would lead to a sober realization that there are no quick fixes, foremost because the cultural resources that would underwrite democratic renewal have been so depleted. Neither will the course of history naturally and organically make things right. This, of course, is a message no one wants to hear, especially within the political class. There are policies and proposals that might miti-

gate effects of the nihilism that pervades America's political and public culture, and certainly it is easy to be sympathetic to many of
them.[1] But by themselves, they are inadequate to address the deepest
parts of the crisis.

The Poverty of Radical Pessimism

Many who intuit the darker possibilities of the moment are drawn
toward imaginaries of the past. Though it can be comforting, nostalgia for a world that has slipped away is, in fact, a manifestation of
radical pessimism. I certainly am not saying that we should ignore
the past or the wisdom it offers. Quite the opposite. I am only questioning the tendency to fetishize the past. The past can never be recovered or re-created, and thus romantic reconstructions of the past
become blinders for those who are unable or unwilling to face the
challenges of the present and a salve to those who have given up on
the future.

Others who intuit the same dark possibilities are drawn to imaginaries of apocalypse. Here too, I'm not saying that we should ignore the very real possibilities of catastrophe in this fragile planet on
which we live. Unending global health crises, environmental devas-
tation, renewed conflicts among superpowers with nuclear weapons,
worldwide economic instability, not to mention epidemics of loneliness, social isolation, opioid use, and deaths of despair are all too real.
Rather, I refer to visions of the apocalyptic so pervasive today in
literature and film, in the inflections of our political rhetoric, and in
the attitude of many voices on all sides that imply that the only real
solution to the problems of the world is to just "burn it all down."
These too are manifestations of radical pessimism. It is a dream of a
clean slate, made possible by the complete and utter destruction of
the ruling powers of evil from which the righteous will arise.[2] Here
too, the apocalyptic is a concession to despair about the future.

Closer to home . . . it would be easy to lump the argument I have
laid out here as yet another example of radical pessimism. My argument does paint a dark picture—no denying that—but it is not radically pessimistic. Nor is it despairing. One does not tell a person
with a life-threatening disease that they have a bad cold. If the argu-

ment is right, then it becomes the starting point for genuinely beneficial interventions.

And, truth be told, I myself am very hopeful—not because I don't see the seriousness of the problem and its dangerous implications, but because I believe that the times are full of real opportunity if one has the eyes to see them. Sadly, my eyesight is not very good. I can only gesture toward a path I dimly see, a path that begins within the imaginaries of hope.

On Hope

By hope, I do not mean optimism. Though often conflated, hope and optimism are not the same. Optimism, in its modern usage, is a corollary to ideologies of progress. It is "a kind of cheerful fatalism," as Christopher Lasch put it, that assumes that the present is better than the past and that the future will invariably deliver yet better things than we now enjoy, as we are "carried along on an irresistible flood of innovation."[3] Optimism, as an element of an ideology of progress, is reinforced by technological innovation and modern marketing which, by definition, always sells "the new and improved."

The field of professional psychology not only conflates optimism and hope but reinforces their ideological character by framing them as highly valued personality traits. Optimism/hope, for the psychologist, is a belief that "good things will happen, and one's wishes or aims will ultimately be fulfilled."[4] Psychologists push the ideological turn further by instrumentalizing optimism as a manipulable therapeutic tool for the purposes of attaining better mental and physical health as well as high levels of personal achievement.[5] Positive, optimistic people, they say, are healthier, happier, and go further in life. Lasch was right when he described optimism as an opiate because the point of optimism or "positivity" is to keep people focused on their own subjective well-being and happiness regardless of the social, historical, or political circumstances people find themselves in.[6] It lulls us "into a false sense of security." Optimists have little need for authentic hope because they have a future of limitless progress on their side. Optimism, then, is not a requisite of change but a strategy of adaptation.

Hope, by contrast, operates on a different plane.[7] It does not require a belief in progress or improvement but is formed out of a reckoning with truth and justice. It builds out of a source of value that transcends the transient and utilitarian realities of everyday life. It draws on or is oriented toward a sense of the underlying order of things that will not be violated with impunity. As Martin Luther King Jr. put it, hope is a conviction that "something in the very structure of the cosmos . . . will ultimately bring about the fulfillment and the triumph of that which is right."[8] The sources of hope can be many— in metaphysical commitments or religious belief or a more modest but firm commitment to the goodness that is in the world. They can be found in an ideal of the "good" in the Platonic sense or a vision of the New Jerusalem or the Kingdom of God found in biblical faiths, or in the "Way" found in many Asian traditions.

King himself and his followers in the Black community had suffered too long and too much to believe in progress. Hope, then, operates with a tragic sensibility that recognizes that the future holds further disappointments. "Shattered dreams! Blasted hopes! This is life," he declared. "Of course, some of us will die having not received the promise of freedom," King admitted. "But we must continue to move on. On the one hand we must accept the finite disappointment, but in spite of this we must maintain the infinite hope. This is the only way that we will be able to live without the fatigue of bitterness and the drain of resentment."[9]

As Eugene Genovese, Lasch, and many historians have noted, this "conviction kept alive the hope of emancipation among slaves in the old South. . . . It would be absurd to attribute to the slaves a belief in progress on the grounds that they hoped for the promised land of freedom." Christianity "gave them a firm yardstick with which to measure the behavior of their masters, to judge them," and to articulate a "promise of deliverance as a people in this world as well as the next."[10]

The Problems and Possibilities of Idealism

There are those who worry that the idealism upon which hope rests is either "useless or dangerous," that it "lacks practical import" and therefore it "ultimately leads to an evasion of real politics."[11] More-over, the ideals to which hope points can easily mutate into a utopi-anism that, like nostalgia, can represent a turning away from the dif-ficulties and discomforts of real politics. Idealism qua utopianism, as Nietzsche observed, can be yet another source of nihilism.[12]

These dangers are real, and yet to leave it there is to disregard the historical place of idealism in the formation of democracy in the early modern period and in what has sustained it over generations. Without underplaying the importance of the material and institu-tional dynamics in history, liberal democracy took form in large part through an ethical vision for the re-formation of public life, an ideal that imagined and sought to realize the more capacious possibilities of human flourishing. Liberal democracy, as I have repeatedly noted, was not that ideal, but it served it. In Masaryk's terms, it was and—if it is to be renewed—will be "the political form of the humane ideal."

The ideals to which hope points and the idealism upon which hope rests are, then, fundamental. A vision of a transcendent future rooted in the capacious possibilities of human flourishing provides both the vantage point to critically assess the present and the moral energy to work toward, build upon, and sacrifice constructively on its behalf.

Let me be clear: idealism must be tempered by an awareness of the real dangers inherent within it. It must be chastened by the tragic realization that—people being who they are—our ideals will never be fully realized in history. It is, then, anti-utopian. It must also be pragmatic. To leave idealism in the realm of abstractions renders it vulnerable to the corrosions we see in a politics driven by symbolic gestures; rather, idealism needs to be employed in the service of solv-ing concrete problems incrementally. It must also be chastened by the obligations of care for the world being critiqued, including care for those people (the "enemy") implicated in that critique. Other-wise, critique is a negation that can only lead to annihilation and not beyond it. But within a chastened idealism, we both see our present circumstances more clearly and we possess a realistic picture toward which individual effort, collective action, and institutional life can be oriented.

Conditions, Not Policies

As fundamentally pragmatic people, Americans want a plan. But in light of the argument of this book, it becomes clear that to enumerate the "ten policies that will revive the culture of democracy," however sincerely intended, misses the mark. The impasse of the contemporary culture war has only become more entrenched, further damaging the public trust. What is more, for all the time, money, and effort put into it by all sides, the conflict has produced no ideas for how to move forward.

The starting point for this kind of reflection is not talk of a "revolution" that seeks a clean sweep but rather a paradigm shift *within* liberal democracy itself that entails new ways to imagine and articulate public life. Its aim would be to move beyond the burlesque of democratic politics we now have to a democratic politics worthy of its name. To get there, one must imagine the conditions without which the renewal of democracy would likely be impossible.

So, what are they?[13]

The most obvious of these conditions has just been noted (yet again), but it may also be among the most difficult to achieve because the current framing of public and political life is so deeply entrenched within the practices of America's leading institutions. As it was at the time of the Founding, so it is now: liberal democracy in the late modern world will not find renewal without the moral imagination to envision a public life that transcends the present warring binaries, and with it, a fresh vocabulary with which to talk about and pragmatically address the genuine problems the nation and the world face. It would be a *re*newed ethical vision for the *re*-formation of public life, for the institutions that sustain it, and for the citizens who put it into practice. This vision would be embedded in a mythos that doesn't deny the story of America, but reframes it toward what it could yet be. Democratic politics would not be that vision, as I say, but it would serve it all the same. To imagine it and to give it voice would require poets more than power brokers.

A central premise of this ethical vision would be a realism that recognizes, following Niebuhr, that the sources of social conflict can never be eliminated, that force is inescapable in politics, that social cohesion itself entails an element of coercion and thus injustice, and that no regime will ever be perfect. Even so, it would recognize that the cruelties that follow the struggle for power can be mitigated by a range of practices oriented toward de-escalating animosity.

There are, undoubtedly, many such practices, some of which resonate with practical proposals recommended by others and touched upon earlier in the book. Among these would certainly be an absolute and universal condemnation of political violence. A fundamental premise of democracy is that one does not kill another over differences; rather, one talks through those differences—seriously and substantively.

Against the pervasive politics of ressentiment, Niebuhr's proposals are as good a starting point as any. Among them is the discipline of distinguishing between the morality of citizens and the morality of systems, recognizing that it is possible to condemn a system in the strongest terms without imputing the worst motives to everyone in the system.[14] Another fundamental concept is the retrieval of the idea of forgiveness, a practice that allows opposing factions to fight tooth and claw without denying the humanity of the other. The importance of this was driven home by Arendt, for whom forgiveness was one of the faculties necessary for political life. "Without being forgiven," she wrote, "released from the consequences of what we have done, our capacity to act would, as it were, be confined to one single deed from which we could never recover; we would remain the victims of its consequences forever."[15] (And if forgiveness is too high a bar, then perhaps we could learn to somehow let go and pass by.)[16] On the other side of the coin, forgiveness would also require abandoning the moral conceit of self-righteousness, even when it is justified, for "the evil in the foe is also in the self."[17]

Underwriting a new ethical vision for the re-formation of public life would be the cultural resources of a reconstituted humanism. It is critical that we rediscover human beings underneath the abstractions of our inflammatory symbolic politics. This, it seems to me, will be a project of retrieval, addition, and re-formulation. Unlike the humanism of the mid-twentieth century, the universal affirmation of human persons would not be a flat, generic, and thus contentless humanism incapable of seeing, much less affirming, difference. The world today is vastly more pluralistic, and thus there are cultural resources available to us beyond those of the older hybrid-

Enlightenment. King himself signaled this direction by drawing on the Hindu teachings of Mohandas Gandhi and the Buddhist teachings of Thích Nhât Hanh. And so a reconstituted humanism would be something like a "meta-humanism," the premise of which would be the incontrovertible plurality of the late modern world and its irreducible particularity. As such, it would acknowledge and draw upon the multiplicity of particular and thicker humanistic traditions—classical, Jewish, Christian, Islamic, secular, Native American, Hindu, Buddhist, Confucian, and Africanist, among others—bound together in part by a common affirmation of human frailty, need, proneness to error, and suffering, but also in part by the universal questions human beings have posed for millennia about the nature and purposes of life, the meaning of suffering, the ethics of care and compassion, especially toward strangers, the character of the good society, the problem of evil, and so on. Out of this would emerge an unqualified affirmation of the supreme and equal dignity and value of all human beings. Quite apart from any benefits a reconstituted humanism would provide to our political culture, it would be a source of ethical resistance to the life-denying depredations built into late modern civilization.

An ethical vision for the re-formation of public life rooted in realism would also recognize the limits of politics—that politics is an administrative apparatus and is thus severely limited in what it can accomplish. However florid the rhetoric of politicians can be, politics can never be redemptive or salvific. Part of the paradigm shift within liberal democracy, then, would be to depoliticize the vast civic space that has been colonized by ideological and partisan interests. As it stands, public and private education at every level, the news media, the judiciary, and philanthropy have all been politicized, and such politicization is the corrupting virus within those institutional spheres. The point is that liberal democratic politics operates at its best within an ecosystem of civic but nonpartisan institutions, and it will have a greater chance of thriving if the ecosystem within which it is embedded is thriving.

At the same time, the renewal of democracy will not be possible without a serious reconsideration of civic formation. We tend to think of civic formation as a matter of acquiring civic knowledge and skills in the formal setting of primary and secondary schooling. Certainly

this is needed, and on this count, the record of the educational establishment in recent generations has been abysmal. But even if it
could be renewed, this approach is far too narrow. One becomes
a citizen by doing the work of citizenship. For all the emphasis on
voting, casting a ballot is only the smallest part of civic duty. Formation into citizenship is a process of learning to care about and to
contribute to the public good in many different ways, few of which
are actually political or partisan in nature, and it occurs through the
wide range of civic institutions over the course of life. While civic
knowledge and civic skills are fine as far as they go, the formation of
citizens is surely more about cultivating the love of a place and a
community and a commitment to addressing the needs of that community precisely because in that place, people share a common fate.

By my lights, the most difficult condition of all to bring about
concerns the matter of leadership. A leadership capable of enacting
a renewal of democracy would require qualities not commonly found.
Rather than a leadership generated and sustained by publicity ma-
chines, or an insular leadership guided by narrow technocratic imperatives, the leadership required would be one that is learned, principled, courageous, and humble, embodied in lives lived sacrificially
toward the realization of that vision. This kind of leadership would
have to be prepared to be ignored, then dismissed as naïve, and then
despised by the main partisans who would ultimately see its exemplars as a threat to their interests. Such is the progression in any important paradigm shift. Invariably, reputation and livelihood would
be at risk, but without putting such things at risk, leadership would
lack credibility or authority. Vision and courage are essential, but
they are the qualities most missing from our leadership class.

The need for this quality of leadership is not only for the political class but for leaders in every other sphere as well—business and
the corporate world, civil service, academia, philanthropy, the special interests, professional associations, and institutions of faith not
least. Achieving this requires a commitment to mobilizing the resources available to these leaders to instantiate this vision within the
organizations they lead, but also in service to concrete public goods
more broadly. In this respect, leaders would understand that their
institutions are civic actors with civic responsibilities. In the end, ideas
don't change the world unless they are embedded within the institu-

tions of social life and the structure of rewards and deprivations that define their boundaries. Yet institutional change of this kind and magnitude cannot happen without a different kind of leadership than we commonly see today.

Finally, the renewal of democracy would be impossible if citizens and leaders alike give up on the processes of durcharbeiten, of "working through" difference, contradiction, past and present injustice, and the fears that attend them. These are serious matters that require serious thought and hard work by serious people. Yet the manner in which contemporary politics is conducted is noteworthy for its lack of seriousness—its many bad-faith misrepresentations and its penchant for artificially contrived moral panic. What has been normalized as democratic politics today is, at best, a parody of the real thing.

In sum, what we need is a paradigm shift *within* liberal democracy rooted in an ethical vision for the re-formation of public life, a courageous and visionary leadership capable of enacting it as practices within the entire range of major institutions, a well-formed citizenry that would support it and participate in it, a healthy civic ecosystem within which the *non*political elements of politics would develop and thicken, all drawing on the affirmations of a renewed humanism that would affirm the humanity of all human beings in their particularity and repudiate any and all political violence toward them. It would define a new, vital, principled, capacious, and defiant center, the conditions of which would encourage the insight to see the nihilisms that undermine human flourishing, would arouse the resolve to renounce them, but then would inspire the wisdom and ingenuity to imagine ways of seeing and ways of living that move beyond them. *It would recognize that the most serious culture war we face at present is not against the "other side," but against the nihilism that insinuates itself in the symbolic, institutional, and practical patterns of the late modern world, not least its politics.*

A Hope against Hope

Again, to be clear, these are not proposals, and together they do not constitute a plan. Rather, they are just one way to envision conditions in late modern America that could, over time, foster a democratic politics worthy of its name.

Against the background of the argument in this book, though, all of this sounds outrageously . . . idealistic. It is. But that's the point: without ideal images of a better world, without myths of a completion of the past in the future, without a world ordered toward goodness, truth, and beauty—in short, without imaginaries of an inclusive, encompassing, even if tragic hope, we become creatures of mere impulse with few ambitions other than personal safety or pleasure or, perhaps beyond that, public power. We become something like Nietzsche's "last men."

Only a hope against hope can bridge the chasm between our present world and its disappointments and the world for which we long. It is to that end that we must continue to work and contend together through those disappointments . . . in hope and toward hope. Through it, what might seem like the imminent end of the story of liberal democracy may yet presage a new beginning.

Notes

Epigraph 1: Reinhold Niebuhr, *The Children of Light and the Children of Darkness* (New York: Charles Scribner, 1944), xi.

Epigraph 2: Abraham Lincoln, "The Dred Scott Decision and the Declaration of Independence," in *Little Masterpieces* (New York: Doubleday, Page, 1907), https://ia800502.us.archive.org/3/items/abrahamlincol2396linc/abrahamlincol2396linc.pdf.

Epigraph 3: Frederick Douglass, "Oration," delivered in Corinthian Hall, July 5, 1852, https://archive.org/details/Douglass_July_Oration/page/16/mode/2up.

Preface

1. Kernels of this argument were published in *The Hedgehog Review: Critical Reflections on Contemporary Culture*. See J. D. Hunter, "A Discourse of Negation and the Ironies of Common Culture," *The Hedgehog Review* (Winter 2004): 24–38; J. D. Hunter, "Liberal Democracy and the Unravelling of the Enlightenment Project," *The Hedgehog Review* 19, no. 3 (Fall 2017): 22–37; and J. D. Hunter, "Dissent and Solidarity," *The Hedgehog Review* 22, no. 3 (Fall 2020): 20–30.

2. Arguably, the question of solidarity is the fundamental question of sociology. Generation after generation of social theorists pose the question anew: what holds society together? No one posed this question more insistently than Émile Durkheim in his magisterial works *The Division of Labor in Society* (New York: Free Press, 1933), *Suicide* (New York: Free Press, 1951), *The Elementary Forms of the Religious Life* (New York: Free Press, 1995), and *Sociology and Philosophy* (New York: Free Press, 1974). Against the arguments of Thomas Hobbes and John Locke, who argued that modern societies were held together through contract (in, say, the market exchange or in law), Durkheim contended that there were shared "pre-contractual"

understandings and obligations that bound people together. These were found in a shared moral code, often oriented around the sacred, the shared rituals that enacted those shared beliefs, and the trust that all of these interactions generated. Every contract, then, depends upon an implicit trust that those involved in an agreement will abide by its rules. Solidarity, in short, was an expression of the *conscience collective* or collective consciousness of a society or social group.

3. Daniel Walker Howe, "The Evangelical Movement and Political Culture in the North during the Second Party System," *Journal of American History* 77, no. 4 (March 1991): 1216–39.

4. J. D. Hunter, *Culture Wars: The Struggle to Define America* (New York: Basic Books, 1991).

5. Hannah Arendt, *The Human Condition* (Chicago: University of Chicago Press, 1998), 5.

6. Reinhold Niebuhr, *The Nature and Destiny of Man*, vol. 2, *Human Destiny* (London: Nisbet, 1964), 278, https://archive.org/details/in.ernet.dli.2015 .203877/page/n267/mode/2up?q=.

Chapter One. The Cultural Crisis of Liberal Democracy

1. An archetype of this line of thinking can be found in an op-ed by John Kerry, former senator and secretary of state under Obama. See John Kerry, "Saving Our Future," *New York Times*, September 23, 2018. Even the political scientist Morris Fiorina frames the problem in these facile ways. In a YouTube series entitled "Policy Stories" published by the Hoover Institution at Stanford University, he summarizes his solution to the "Crisis of Confidence in Democracy" by stating that in the past, "decisive elections set democracies on new paths." "Today, we're waiting for a modern-day Reagan or Mitterrand to construct an enduring electoral majority, a majority that unites the distinct and myriad interests of a wide swath of the public. Until then, I'm afraid, today's problems of democratic governance will persist." https://www.policyed.org/policy-stories/overcoming-our-crisis -confidence-democracy/video.

2. The means for achieving this are policies that embrace the specialized economy and that protect and rebuild the cultural institutions. Yuval Levin's conclusion essentially consists of asking people to make a new commitment to mediating institutions, and this is probably where his bootstrapping tendencies really become evident: "To achieve that formation in a free society—where we do not want the state to direct or compel it—requires that we commit ourselves to more than our own will and whim. It requires a commitment precisely to the formative social and cultural institutions that we have seen pulled apart from above and below in our age of fracture." See Yuval Levin, *The Fractured Republic* (New York: Basic Books, 2017), 203.

3. Robert Putnam's analysis of the decline of social capital in all areas of social life contrasts with his singular optimism that citizens today can be as civically creative as were those who lived in the Progressive Era. The solution, he says, lies in an assertion of individual and collective will. He writes: "So I set before America's parents, educators, and, above all, America's young adults the following challenge: Let us find ways to ensure that by 2010 the level of civic engagement among Americans then coming of age in all parts of our society will match that of their grandparents when they were that same age, and that at the same time bridging social capital will be substantially greater than it was in their grandparents' era." See Robert Putnam, *Bowling Alone*, rev. ed. (New York: Simon & Schuster, 2020), 404. Alan Ryan was right when he asked, "Why then does [Putnam] expect anyone to listen when he presents them with a task they do not know how to perform?" Alan Ryan, "My Way," *New York Review of Books*, August 10, 2000.

4. These would include a national year of paid service, revived civics education, massive worker retraining, a "contract for American social responsibility" to be signed by corporations, and redistricting reform, among other things. See E. J. Dionne, Thomas Mann, and Norman Ornstein, *One Nation after Trump* (New York: St. Martin's, 2017). As the authors put it, "By reviving a sense of shared identity based in mutual interest, communities can begin to counteract the mistrust and sense of hopelessness."

5. Distilled from the thoughts of Pete Wehner, who is quoted in Conor Friedersdorf, "A Call to Police Comity among Political Allies, Not Opponents," *Atlantic*, June 30, 2017, http://www.theatlantic.com/politics/archive/2017/06/a-call-to-police-comity-among-allies-not-opponents/532314/. Benjamin Barber took a like-minded position, arguing that it is essential to recommit ourselves to the virtues that make civil public discourse possible—a commitment to commonality, deliberation, inclusiveness, provisionality, listening, learning, lateral communication, imagination, and empowerment. "We have to decide whether we want bread, circuses, and horse races from our politics, or the conditions—not always so entertaining—that make possible civil self-government and long-term democracy." Benjamin Barber, *A Place for Us* (New York: Hill & Wang, 1998), 122–23.

6. Cass R. Sunstein argues in *#Republic* (Princeton, NJ: Princeton University Press, 2014) that a combination of government nudging and voluntary self-regulation by media and social media organizations would restore the (virtual) spaces in which citizens can benefit from serendipitous encounters with one another, and in particular from views opposing their own, in accordance with the two discourse principles he outlines: that "people should be exposed to materials that they would not have chosen in advance" and that "many or most citizens should have a wide range of common experiences" (6–7). He counts on a combination of dutifulness

and self-interest to induce media organizations to pursue these ends. Recent trends in social media are not encouraging in this regard.

7. Michael J. Sandel, *Democracy's Discontent: America in Search of a Public Philosophy* (Cambridge, MA: Harvard University Press, 1996).

8. Mark Lilla, *The Once and Future Liberal* (New York: HarperCollins, 2017). Lilla's aim in *Once and Future* is to defend a properly political (as opposed to expressive-individualist) disposition that could take the place of identity politics on the left. "Elections are not prayer meetings, and no one is interested in your personal testimony. They are not therapy sessions or occasions to obtain recognition. They are not seminars or 'teaching moments'" (115). "The only way out of this conundrum is to appeal to something that as Americans we all share but which has nothing to do with our identities, without denying the existence and importance of the latter. And there is something, if only liberals would again begin to speak of it: citizenship" (120–21).

9. No one has been more eloquent and inspiring on this subject than Jean Bethke Elshtain in her book *Democracy on Trial* (New York: Basic Books, 1995).

10. Os Guinness called for Christian revival in America on the basis that Christianity remains America's leading faith. See Os Guinness, *The American Hour* (New York: Free Press, 1993). He writes that a "massive revitalization of American public life, including both its ideals and institutions, [can occur] through a movement of decisive spiritual renewal and reformation. If sufficiently powerful and penetrating, such a renewal could restore the spiritual vitality to America's social and political order and resolve the crisis of cultural authority" (385–86). Guinness further writes that this revival would have to begin in the hearts of individual Americans. "The integrity and effectiveness of America's future in the world depend ultimately on the integrity and effectiveness of the faith in the hearts and lives of Americans. And this generation of Americans will be answerable for that decision" (399).

11. Among these I would highlight Elshtain's, Sandel's, and Lilla's work as well as William Galston, *Anti-Pluralism* (New Haven, CT: Yale University Press, 2018).

12. An interesting illustration of this is found in Marc Dunkelman, *The Vanishing Neighbor* (New York: Norton, 2014). Dunkelman gives an extended analysis of the disappearance of what he calls the "middle rings"—a concept of civil society with clear counterparts in Tocqueville as well as figures like Sunstein and Levin. He offers a few positive policy prescriptions meant to restore the middle rings, but in the last chapter addressing the solutions to our crisis of community is an extraordinary profession of faith in sheer effort. Citing Walter Mischel's immortal marshmallow study and Angela Duckworth's work on grit, Dunkelman argues that "success, in essence, is born from the ability to maintain the types of relationships

that once suffused the middle rings, and those sorts of ties are predicated on self-control" (218). "A grittier America would, at least, make it more likely that we'd each connect with a wider range of neighbors" (219). In short, Dunkelman puts a social-scientific gloss on the old claim that the crisis of American community is the result of the decline of a universally agreed-upon set of virtues. Although he shies away from claiming that grit is a sufficient condition for a recovery of neighborliness, he hangs much of his hope for the future on the Protestant ethic in its updated Mischel-Duckworth version.

13. David Moss, quoted in Conor Friedersdorf, "Finding Faith in Democracy at Moments of National Conflict," *Atlantic*, June 26, 2017, https://www.theatlantic.com/politics/archive/2017/06/have-faith-in-democracy-at-moments-of-national-conflict/531564/.

14. As Arthur Mann observed in the last quarter of the twentieth century, the people of the United States have always believed that American know-how could convert problems into opportunities. "The idea that some problems might be insoluble was foreign to the national spirit. They would yield, as they had in the past, to ingenuity, will, good-will, money, and concerted effort." See Arthur Mann, *The One and the Many* (Chicago: University of Chicago Press, 1979), 3. There is a history behind this. Tocqueville observed the trait in the nineteenth century in *Democracy in America*, ed. Harvey Mansfield and Delba Winthrop (Chicago: University of Chicago Press, 2002), as well as Mark Twain in his entertaining novel *A Connecticut Yankee in King Arthur's Court* (New York: Charles Webster, 1889).

15. And let me be clear: I believe many of these solutions to be genuinely constructive. Yet I also believe that they fall short of addressing the fundamental problem I outline in this volume.

16. Against the broad range of sociological approaches to culture, mine has overlapping places of alignment with Jeffrey Alexander's "strong program" of cultural sociology. Most important, it shares the view that "no matter how impersonal or technocratic, [institutions] have an ideal foundation that fundamentally shapes their organization and goals and provides the structured context for debate over their legitimation." This not only ascribes a certain relative autonomy to culture, it allows one to see what Alexander and Smith (quoting Wilhelm Dilthey) describe as the "inner meaning of social structures." See Jeffrey C. Alexander and Philip Smith, "The Strong Program in Cultural Sociology," https://ccs.yale.edu/strong-program. This commits the scholar to the hermeneutically and semiotically rich methods of description and interpretation. Much more could be layered onto my argument by way of thick description, but because of its historical sweep, I was constrained by space as to what I could do here. Weaving the thought of various "intellectuals" into the narrative was one of the ways I sought to incorporate at least a thicker description.

17.   I draw from an argument I developed in "On the Priority of Culture," in *The Hedgehog Review Reader: Two Decades of Critical Reflections on Contemporary Culture*, ed. Jay Tolson (Charlottesville: University of Virginia Press, 2020), 9–11.

18.   And prior to economics and prior to everything else as well. Which means that the news media, much of academia, and most social movements get it backwards. The qualification here is that while these distinctions are analytically important, phenomenologically, the distinctions largely disappear: the cultural (symbolic and expressive) and the material (the institutional) are mutually constituted. This point would seem obvious, but it is important to state if only because mainstream social science ignores the inextricably central role of culture, treating it as a mere epiphenomenon. Arguably the most compelling theoretical explication of these dynamics can be found in the work of my mentor Peter Berger in his classic work (with Thomas Luckmann), *The Social Construction of Reality* (New York: Doubleday, 1966).

19.   This insight is well established in social theory, most forcefully by Émile Durkheim's idea of a conscience collective, a solidarity rooted in a shared moral code and a shared orientation toward the sacred. A wide range of other social scientists have gestured toward this implicit level of culture including Claude Lévi-Strauss, Edward Sapir, Ludwig Wittgenstein, Thomas Kuhn, Norbert Elias, Richard Weaver, Jean Piaget, Michael Polanyi, Kenneth Burke, Arnold Gehlen, Alfred Schutz, Jacques Lacan, Louis Althusser, Michel Foucault, Erving Goffman, Pierre Bourdieu, Peter L. Berger, and Charles Taylor. Over more than a century, the idea had remained unspecified. A greater specification is something I am pursuing in a presently unfinished manuscript, "The Deep Structures of Culture," for which the present inquiry is a case study. This section draws heavily from this work.

20.   This raises a question about "the differentiation of value spheres," one of the hallmarks of modernity and late modernity. It is a concept developed by Max Weber in his essay "Religious Rejections of the World and Their Directions," in *Max Weber: Essays in Sociology*, ed. H. H. Gerth and C. Wright Mills (New York: Oxford University Press, 1946), chapter 13.

     The concept points to an institutional theory of value differentiation as a form of comparative religion. Weber saw this differentiation, the increasingly irreconcilable conflict among values, as a mark of the "polytheism" of modernity. The variation of spheres of action is often conflated with secularization and privatization, but what he describes is more of a pluralization of competing value systems among different institutions. I would argue that in early modernity, the implicit cosmology of the deep structures continued to underwrite these increasingly differentiating value spheres even if various institutions appropriated them differently. There was, in short, overlap. The opacity of America's hybrid-Enlightenment functioned in this way. In the story I tell here, the increasing fragmentation and polarization of American political culture in the late twentieth and early twenty-first centuries reflect how the underwriting and adhesive functions of the hybrid-Enlightenment gave way to its own differentiations. The hybrid-Enlightenment itself became polarized in even more extreme forms into what Weber called a "war of the gods."

21. Richard Weaver, *Ideas Have Consequences* (Chicago: University of Chicago Press, 1949) alluded to culture in this way. More recently and more evocatively, Charles Taylor did so with his concept of the "social imaginary." By social imaginary, Taylor is referring to the ways in which people "imagine their social existence, how they fit together with others, how things go on between them and their fellows, the expectations that are normally met and the deeper normative notions and images that underlie all of these expectations." See Charles Taylor, *Modern Social Imaginaries* (Durham, NC: Duke University Press, 2004), 23. My concept of the "deep structures" is very much aligned with his, though I would suggest it is less vague than Taylor implies: culture at this level has more structure by virtue of it being organized around fundamental, albeit implicit, philosophical questions.

22. The concept of cultural logic is closely related to the concept of institutional logics introduced by Robert R. Alford and Roger Friedland in *Powers of Theory* (Cambridge: Cambridge University Press, 1985). The basic argument is that different institutional orders possess a central logic that guides their organizational principles and provides individuals within them vocabularies of motive and identity. Interests, identities, values, and assumptions of various groups and individuals are embedded within these institutional logics. Actors within these institutions are both enabled and constrained by these logics in pursuit of their own advantage. In this way, decisions and outcomes are a result of the interplay between individual agency and institutional structure. A useful summary of the entire literature on institutional logics can be found in Patricia Thornton and William Ocasio, "Institutional Logics," in *The Sage Handbook of Organizational Institutionalism* (London: Sage, 2008). In its time, the institutional logics approach was a vast improvement over rational choice theory. In my view, though, the concept was misnamed. The constitutive elements of any institutional logic are, in fact, symbolic—or *cultural*—in nature. Institutional logics, then, are cultural logics. While the approach represented an important breakthrough in understanding the surface of institutional life, it failed to specify and emphasize the premises or assumptions by which institutional logics work. These premises constitute the innermost parts of any institutional structure.

23. Very few have understood or intuited this difference, but two who did were John H. Evans and Lisa M. Nunn in "The Deeper 'Culture Wars' Question," *Forum* 3, no. 2 (2005), https://doi.org/10.2202/1540-8884.1078.

24. Michael Oakeshott, *Religion, Politics, and the Moral Life*, ed. Timothy Fuller (New Haven, CT: Yale University Press, 1993), 93 (emphasis added).
25. This is derived from my aforementioned manuscript, "The Deep Structures of Culture."
26. Alasdair MacIntyre, *Whose Justice? Which Rationality?* (South Bend, IN: University of Notre Dame Press, 1988), 176.
27. A version of this dilemma was articulated by Ernst-Wolfgang Böckenförde, a professor of law and judge in the Federal Constitutional Court in Germany. He stated the dilemma this way: "The free, secularized state lives on conditions that it cannot guarantee itself. . . . On the one hand, it can only exist as a liberal state if the freedom it grants its citizens is regulated from within, from the moral substance of the individual and homogeneity of society. On the other hand, it cannot by itself procure these interior forces of regulation, that is not with its own means such as legal compulsion and authoritative decree. Doing so, it would surrender its liberal character (*freiheitlichkeit*) and fall back, in a secular manner, into the claim of totality it once led the way out of, back then in the confessional civil wars." Ernst-Wolfgang Böckenförde, *Staat, Gesellschaft, Freiheit* (Frankfurt: Suhrkamp, 1976), 60. Early criticisms of the "Böckenförde Dilemma" claimed that he had made too much of the role of religion, but he clarified his argument in 2010. "To conceive of such a state, the liberal order needs a unifying ethos, a 'sense of community' among those who live in this state. The question then becomes: what is creating this ethos, which can neither be enforced by the state nor compelled by a sovereign? One can say: first, the common culture. But what are the elements and factors of that culture? Then indeed we are dealing with its sources such as Christianity, Enlightenment, and humanism. But not automatically any religion." Quoted in Tim Kucharzewski and Silvia Nicola, "Identity and the Far Right: People Talking about 'The People,'" in *Political Identification in Europe: Community in Crisis?* ed. Amanda Machin and Nadine Meidert (Bingley, UK: Emerald, 2021). In an interview a year earlier, he stated, "No, some church representatives may read [that the church and religion alone created the ethos that holds the state together], but it wasn't meant that way. Ideological, political or social movements can also promote the community spirit of the population and the willingness not always to look ruthlessly to one's own advantage, but rather to act in a community-oriented and solidarity-based manner." See "Freiheit ist ansteckend," https://taz.de/!5155667/. As a meta-theoretical statement, Böckenförde's argument is similar to mine, though his case is made weaker by focusing only on the surface artifacts of culture. My emphasis in this book is on the deep structures of culture as a framework of solidarity, one powerful enough to contain and mediate profound difference and conflict.
28. Philip Rieff, "By What Authority?" in *The Feeling Intellect* (Chicago: University of Chicago Press), 345.

29. Washington, Hamilton, and others spoke of the idea of American democracy as an experiment, though the notion of it as a "great experiment" is attributed to Alexis de Tocqueville at the end of the first chapter of *Democracy in America:* "In that land the great experiment was to be made, by civilized man, of the attempt to construct society upon a new basis; and, it was there, for the first time, that theories hitherto unknown, or deemed impracticable, were to exhibit a spectacle for which the world had not been prepared by the history of the past." The passage is actually mistranslated from the original French: "C'est là que les hommes civilisés devaient essayer de bâtir la société sur des fondements nouveaux. . . ." Directly translated, Tocqueville writes, "Here, civilized men would attempt to build. . . . " The word *experiment* is not used, though the general idea is there.

Chapter Two. The Boundaries of Solidarity

1. The ways in which human beings perhaps "instinctively" draw lines, form boundaries, or make distinctions are fundamental to the generation and maintenance of culture. The theoretical literature is extensive, though there is no better starting place than Mary Douglas, *Purity and Danger* (London: Routledge & Kegan Paul, 1966); and Eviatar Zerubavel, *The Fine Line* (New York: Free Press, 1991).

2. Originally called the Supreme Sacred Congregation of the Roman and Universal Inquisition.

3. The term was originally introduced in "Erinnern, Wiederholen und Durcharbeiten" in 1914. In English, the essay is published online as "Remembering, Repeating and Working-Through," http://marcuse.faculty .history.ucsb.edu/classes/201/articles/1914FreudRemembering.pdf.

4. Freud, "Remembering," 155.

5. Freud, "Remembering," 155.

6. Theodor W. Adorno, "The Meaning of Working through the Past," in *Critical Models: Interventions and Catchwords* (New York: Columbia University Press, 1998), 89–103.

7. John Patrick Diggins and Mark E. Kann, "Authority in America: The Crisis of Legitimacy," in *The Problem of Authority* (Philadelphia: Temple University Press, 1981), 6.

Chapter Three. The Sources of Solidarity

1. John Adams to Zabdiel Adams, June 21, 1776. Earlier that year, he wrote, "Public virtue cannot exist in a nation without private, and public virtue is the only foundation of republics" (John Adams to Mercy Otis Warren, April 16, 1776); George Washington, *Farewell Address*, September 19, 1796; James Madison, "Judicial Powers of the National Government, [June 20,]

1788," *Founders Online*, National Archives, http://founders.archives.gov
/documents/Madison/01-11-02-0101. (Original source: Robert A. Rut-
land and Charles F. Hobson, eds., *The Papers of James Madison*, vol. 11, *7
March 1788–1 March 1789* [Charlottesville: University Press of Virginia,
1977], 158–65.)

2.   Alexis de Tocqueville and Henry Reeve, *Democracy in America* (London:
     Saunders & Otley, 1835), 98, 26.

3.   Political theorists will find this debate old hat, while nonspecialists may
     find its intricacies tedious. Those who have an interest will find an elabo-
     ration of some of the complexities of this debate in the endnotes that
     follow.

4.   Iran's revolution in 1978 was, in aspiration, a "democratic" revolution, the
     result of which was an Islamic republic that sought to combine demo-
     cratic involvement (of an elected president and legislature) with theo-
     cratic oversight. In practice, the two elements often clash, with unelected,
     unaccountable officials holding the most power. This points to an inher-
     ent tension within Islamic regimes that claim to be democratic. What
     makes this tension inherent, of course, is the attempt to make a direct and
     literal implementation of Qur'anic law in society. In this version of foun-
     dationalism, even the act of human *interpretation* of divine principles intro-
     duces too much of human frailty and failure into the work of conforming
     to the immutable decrees of the divinity. Proponents believe, in varying
     degrees, that the divine law has been given in self-interpreting form and
     that the work of government is simply to implement it. In brief, rulers are
     bound by the very letter of the law. This was the view of the Ayatollah
     Khomeini, for example—the instigator of the Iranian Revolution. See
     Ayatollah Ruhollah Khomeini, "The Religious Scholars Led the Revolt"
     as well as "Part I: *Islamic Government*," both in *Islam and Revolution: Writ-
     ings and Declarations of Imam Khomeini*, trans. Hamid Algar (Berkeley, CA:
     Mizan, 1980). It was also the view held by Sayyid Qutb, founder of the
     Muslim Brotherhood. See Sayyid Qutb, *Milestones* (Riyadh: International
     Islamic Publishers, 1981), 158.

5.   This school of thinking is called Christian theonomy, the belief of a Cal-
     vinist theological sect that the Old Testament law (with the exception of
     the ceremonial law) should be put into practice in contemporary society
     precisely as given. Greg Bahnsen and R. J. Rushdoony were the leading
     thinkers of this perspective. See Greg Bahnsen, "The Theonomic Re-
     formed Approach to Law and Gospel," in *Five Views on Law and Gospel*,
     ed. Greg Bahnsen (Grand Rapids, MI: Zondervan, 1999), 93–143; Greg
     Bahnsen, *Theonomy in Christian Ethics* (Nacagdoches, TX: CMP, 2002);
     and Rousas John Rushdoony, *Christianity and the State* (Vallecito, CA: Ross
     House Books, 1986).

6.   Within theological progressivism, a telling case is found in the liberation
     theology of Gustavo Gutiérrez. For Gutiérrez, Christians must look to

salvation history for justification for political engagement. "Salvation," he writes, "embraces all persons and the whole person; the liberating action of Christ—made human in this history and not in a history marginal to real human life—is at the heart of the historical current of humanity; the struggle for a just society is in its own right very much a part of salvation history." See Gustavo Gutiérrez, *A Theology of Liberation* (Maryknoll, NY: Orbis Books, 1973), 97. The need to address "the immense suffering of the poor," the "misery and despoliation" of the fruits of human labor, the "exploitation of human beings," "the confrontation between social classes," and "liberation from oppressive structures" makes it difficult to maintain that the church can be expected to remain aloof from politics (40). Politics "must in the first place be enlightened by faith" (102). Gutiérrez's insistence that the church must take up a political role, then, makes his position *foundationalist in practice*. Without faith, the struggle for political liberation is necessarily misdirected. But this doesn't mean that the church should exercise temporal power. Rather, temporal power should proceed within the limits given by faith.

Among the most erudite of the theological foundationalists are Oliver O'Donovan, *The Desire of the Nations* (Cambridge: Cambridge University Press, 1996); and John Milbank, "The Politics of the Soul," *Revista de filosofía*, Open Insight 6, no. 9 (2015), https://www.redalyc.org/pdf/4216/421639456006.pdf. See also John Milbank and Adrian Pabst, *The Politics of Virtue* (London: Rowman & Littlefield, 2016). For O'Donovan, "It is not . . . that Christian political order is a *project* of the church's mission, either as an end in itself or as a means to the further missionary end. The church's one project is to witness to the Kingdom of God. Christendom is a *response* to mission, and as such a sign that God has blessed it. It is constituted not by the church's seizing alien power, but by alien powers becoming attentive to the church" (195). This means that despite the strict institutional separation, rulers must necessarily remain obedient to the content of revelation as proclaimed by the church. "The service rendered by the state to the church is to facilitate its mission" (217). Among the criteria he gives for the legitimacy of human authority is its alignment with its divine origins: "That any regime should actually come to authority, and should continue to hold it, is a work of divine providence in history, not a mere accomplishment of the human task of political service" (46). This criterion clearly gives human authority its origin and raison d'être in divine authority, not any instrumental considerations like life, health, security, or *virtù*. For Milbank and Pabst, the political community is also regarded as finally answerable to the spiritual (see Milbank and Pabst, *Politics of Virtue*, 30). By their account, the standards of the spiritual are found in a comprehensive account of the nature and destiny of human persons. As Milbank put it, "There can be no art of politics, defined as an exercise of justice, irreducible to either natural necessity or an individual will to power, if the soul that rules itself or other souls is not guided by the transcendent reality of the true, good, and beautiful. In practical terms this means that the just ruler does not *merely* ensure that the social realities of brute force and material need are kept in their spatial places by reason . . . but rather that he continuously tries to ensure through time and on differently arising occasions that these subordinate things, and all different things are harmoniously and proportionately blended in such a way as to participate in the transcendent *kalon* which is both goodness and beauty" ("The Politics of the Soul," 97).

7. Finnis goes on to say, "Those moral norms justify (*a*) the very institution of positive law, (*b*) the main institutions, techniques, and modalities within the tradition (e.g. separation of powers), and (*c*) the main institutions regulated and sustained by law (e.g. government, contract, property, marriage, and criminal liability)." John Finnis, *Natural Law and Natural Rights* (Oxford: Oxford University Press, 2011), 290.

8. As often discussed, natural law operates within a three-tiered structure, which includes a foundational set of basic human goods, a set of intermediary practical principles, and a number of "fully specific moral norms." See Robert P. George, *In Defense of Natural Law* (Oxford: Clarendon, 1999), 102. Finnis writes: "What truly characterizes the tradition is that it is not content merely to observe the historical or sociological fact that 'morality' thus affects 'law,' but instead seeks to determine what the requirements of practical reasonableness really are, so as to afford a rational basis for the activities of legislators, judges, and citizens (Finnis, *Natural Law*, 290). Natural law precisely gives the requirement that legislators and regulators should bring their own prudential reason to bear on most political questions—including very fundamental ones, like the organization of the best regime attainable under a given set of circumstances. In practice natural lawyers proceed by consulting human reason in accordance with reasonably established political procedures. As Finnis writes, "To be, itself, authoritative in the eyes of a reasonable man, a *determinatio* must be consistent with the basic requirements of practical reasonableness, though it need not necessarily or even usually be the *determinatio* he would himself have made had he had the opportunity; it need not even be one he would regard as 'sensible'" (289–90). The emphasis in natural law theory on *determinatio*, that is, morally neutral choice among political alternatives on purely practical grounds, also makes it a relatively pragmatic theory. But those choices are, importantly, always subject to the authority of the basic goods—that is, to a transcendent but entirely rationally accessible order that preexists their deliberations and binds them with normative force. Formally, then, the natural law theory also posits a strong, procedure-independent political foundation; but in practice it gives substantially more latitude to the reasoning legislator, who need merely follow his own

lights. At the end of the day, the theory's reference to a transcendent authority makes it decidedly foundationalist.

9. John Rawls, *Political Liberalism* (New York: Columbia University Press, 1993), 4.

10. John Rawls, *A Theory of Justice* (Cambridge, MA: Harvard University Press, 1971), 10.

11. John Rawls, "Justice as Fairness: Political, Not Metaphysical," *Philosophy and Public Affairs* 14, no. 3 (Summer 1985): 229, http://www.jstor.org /stable/2265349.

12. "In his own words, the aim of justice as fairness as a political conception is practical, not metaphysical or epistemological. That is, it presents itself not as a conception of justice that is true, but [as] one that can serve as a basis of informed and willing political agreement between citizens viewed as free and equal persons. . . . Thus, justice as fairness deliberately stays on the surface, philosophically speaking" (Rawls, "Justice as Fairness," 230). By extension, it is only natural that he rejects settled metaphysical concepts of human nature. The description of the parties may seem to presuppose some metaphysical conception of the person, for example, that the essential nature of persons is independent of and prior to their contingent attributes, including their final ends and attachments, and indeed, their character as a whole. But this is an illusion caused by not seeing the original position as a device of representation. The veil of ignorance, to mention one prominent feature of that position, has no metaphysical implications concerning the nature of the self; it does not imply that the self is ontologically prior to the facts about persons that the parties are excluded from knowing. He adds, "We can, as it were, enter this position any time simply by reasoning for principles of justice in accordance with the enumerated restrictions" (239).

13. John Rawls, "The Priority of the Right and Ideas of the Good," *Philosophy and Public Affairs* 17 (1988): 261–62 (emphasis added). This consensus of conviction serves as "provisional fixed points which any conception of justice *must account* for if it is to be reasonable for us. We look, then, to our public political culture itself, including its main institutions and the historical traditions of their interpretation, as the shared fund of *implicitly recognized basic ideas and principles*" (Rawls, "Justice as Fairness," 22, emphasis added).

14. Rawls, "Justice as Fairness," 247. He further writes, "It should also be stressed that justice as fairness is not intended as the application of a general moral conception to the basic structure of society, as if this structure were simply another case to which that general moral conception is applied" (224–25). In other words, for justice as fairness to become a comprehensive doctrine would defeat the purpose entirely. "Persons can accept [the liberal] conception of themselves as citizens and use it when

discussing questions of political justice without being committed in other parts of their life to comprehensive moral ideals often associated with liberalism" (245).

15. Habermas defined two decision principles that he said would ensure a fair and normatively binding outcome: the principle of universalization (U) and the discourse principle (D). (U): "All affected can accept the consequences and the side effects [a norm's] general observance can be anticipated to have for the satisfaction of everyone's interests (and these consequences are preferred to those of known alternative possibilities for regulation)." (D): "Only those norms can claim to be valid that meet (or could meet) with the approval of all affected in their capacity *as participants in a practical discourse.*" Jürgen Habermas, "Discourse Ethics: Notes on a Program of Philosophical Justification," in *Moral Consciousness and Communicative Action* (Cambridge, MA: MIT Press, 1990), 65–66 (emphasis added).

16. Other proceduralist accounts can be seen in part as pulling back (if only a bit) from the premises of the anti-metaphysical position. Here we find procedural theorists who believe that the authoritative footing of procedure is not so much constructed as discovered and so should be self-evidently appealing to everyone. This group of proceduralists begins with a minimal anthropology, arguing that those aspects of human nature that are the proper objects of politics are strictly limited in number and scope. These theorists can thus be said to believe that the basis for political authority is situated in particular aspects of the human condition that can be defended in public. Judith Shklar, for example, argued that the foundation of liberalism is placed in the universality of fear—the fear of cruelty. Judith Shklar, "The Liberalism of Fear," in *Liberalism and the Moral Life,* ed. Nancy L. Rosenblum (Cambridge, MA: Harvard University Press, 1989), 21–38. For Robert Audi, it is the universality of human intuition as the source of liberal democratic norms. Robert Audi, "Moral Foundations of Liberal Democracy, Secular Reasons, and Liberal Neutrality toward the Good," *Notre Dame Journal of Law, Ethics, and Public Policy* 19, no. 1 (2005): 197–218. On the surface, Rawls and Audi are similar in their view of intuition, but for Audi, intuitions are universal and naturally proper to us as citizens, whereas for Rawls, they are conditioned by our historical and material circumstances and *this*, rather than their basis in human nature, is precisely the source of their authority.

17. Sandel continues:

> To imagine a person incapable of constitutive attachments such as these is not to conceive an ideally free and rational agent, but to imagine a person wholly without character, without moral depth. For to have character is to know that I move in a history I neither summon nor command, which carries consequences nonetheless for my choices and conduct. It draws me closer to

some and more distant from others; it makes some aims appropriate, others less so. As a self-interpreting being, I am able to reflect on my history and in this sense to distance myself from it, but the distance is always precarious and provisional, the point of reflection never finally secured outside the history itself. But the liberal ethic puts the self beyond the reach of its experience, beyond deliberation and reflection. Denied the expansive self-understandings that could shape a common life, the liberal self is left to lurch between detachment on the one hand, and entanglement on the other.

Michael Sandel, "The Procedural Republic and the Unencumbered Self," *Political Theory* 12, no. 1 (February 1984): 90–91.

18. Communitarians accept this claim while arguing that these deliberations must take into account un-chosen or nonrationally determined aspects of the human condition. See Charles Taylor, "Cross-Purposes: The Liberal Communitarian Debate," in *Liberalism and the Moral Life*, ed. Nancy L. Rosenblum (Cambridge, MA: Harvard University Press, 1989), 159–82. Taylor argues that liberal proceduralism, "ontologically disinterested liberalism," is defined precisely by its rejection of comprehensive doctrines (164). He then argues that this form of liberalism is not *viable* because it is parasitic on the very preexisting foundations at which it is constantly eating away: "Every political society requires some sacrifices and demands some disciplines from its members: they have to pay taxes, or serve in the armed forces, and in general observe certain restraints. In a despotism, a regime where the mass of citizens are subject to the rule of a single master, or a clique, the requisite disciplines are maintained by coercion. In order to have a free society, one has to replace this coercion with something else. This can only be a willing identification with the polis on the part of the citizens, a sense that the political institutions in which they live are an expression of themselves" (165). The liberal society that tries to secure freedom without permitting (or, in fact, encouraging) that kind of self-identification with the laws will soon cease to be free. "The very definition of a republican regime as classically understood requires an ontology different from atomism, and which falls outside atomism-inflected common sense. It requires that we probe the relations of identity and community, and distinguish the different possibilities, in particular, the possible place of we-identities as against merely convergent I-identities, and the consequent role of common as against convergent goods" (170). Moreover, insofar as our societies do still continue to function, it is precisely because, despite their atomist premises, they retain some of the cultural habits of constitutive republics.

19. Taylor, "Cross-Purposes," 159–82.

20. Dwight Eisenhower, address at the Freedoms Foundation, Waldorf-Astoria,

New York City, December 22, 1952, https://www.eisenhowerlibrary.gov
/eisenhowers/quotes#Religion.

21. Taylor, for one, suggested that patriotism contains thicker resources for
    funding democratic politics. Commenting on the American response to
    Watergate, he wrote: "What generates the outrage is . . . neither egoism
    nor altruism, but a sense of patriotic identification. [In the United States],
    there is a widespread identification with 'the American way of life,' a
    sense of Americans sharing a common identity and history, defined by a
    commitment to certain ideals, articulated famously in the Declaration of
    Independence, Lincoln's Gettysburg Address, and such documents, which
    in turn derive their importance from their connection to certain climactic
    transitions of this shared history. It is this sense of identity, and the pride
    and attachment which accompanies it, that is outraged by the shady do-
    ings of a Watergate, and this is what provokes the irresistible reaction"
    (Taylor, "Cross-Purposes," 174).

22. A useful overview can be found in Shane Courtland, Gerald Gaus, and
    David Schmidtz, "Liberalism," in *The Stanford Encyclopedia of Philosophy*,
    ed. Edward N. Zalta (Spring 2022), https://plato.stanford.edu/entries
    /liberalism/.

23. Craig Calhoun, "Secularism, Citizenship, and the Public Sphere," *Hedge-
    hog Review* 10, no. 3 (Fall 2008): 14.

24. J. I. Mackey refers to the idea that virtue exists as dispositions about what
    is "to-be-done" and "not-to-be-done" in his critique of moral objectivism.
    See his *Ethics: Inventing Right and Wrong* (New York: Penguin, 1977).

25. Rawls, "Justice as Fairness," 228. Robert Audi psychologizes these deep
    structures by calling them "intuitions," but the intuitions human beings
    develop are formed within and out of the habitus of a culture and never
    independent of it. Political will formation is inextricable from the work-
    ings of a culture. Audi, "Moral Foundations."

26. Jürgen Habermas, *Between Facts and Norms: Contributions to a Discourse
    Theory of Law and Democracy* (Cambridge, MA: MIT Press, 1998). In an-
    other context, Habermas makes the case that the legitimacy of law de-
    pends upon "the democratic ethos of citizens," an ethos that inclines cit-
    izens to leave the role of private individuals and adopt that of participants
    in the formation of the common good. See Jürgen Habermas, "Postscript
    (1994)," chapter 40 in Mary Vogel, *Crime, Inequality, and the State* (Lon-
    don: Routledge, 2007). Rosati summarizes this observation: "The stabil-
    ity of the procedural legal paradigm of Habermas and, above all, the sta-
    bility of the democratic rule of law, depend—in the end—on an element
    that is not possible to produce in a procedural manner, namely they de-
    pend on the political culture of democratic citizens, on their democratic
    ethos. Every hope for a radical democracy rests on the presence of this
    political culture. The normative conception of the public sphere, i.e. the
    place where this democratic ethos is located, can be said to play a role

analogous to the sacred—a role that by transitivity necessarily reverberates on Habermas's idea of social solidarity in contemporary democracies." Massimo Rosati, "Solidarity and the Sacred: Habermas's Idea of Solidarity in a Durkheimian Horizon," *Durkheimian Studies* 6 (2000): 93–103. Habermas, in the end, affirms the Durkheimian insight into the nonrational foundations of his rationalist discursive project.

27. Sandel, *Democracy's Discontent*, 4 (emphasis added).
28. Abigail Adams to John Quincy Adams, March 20, 1780, in *The Letters of Mrs. Adams, the Wife of John Adams*, 3rd ed., ed. Charles Francis Adams (Boston: Charles Little & James Brown, 1841), http://nationalhumanities center.org/pds/livingrev/equality/text4/aadamstojqadams.pdf.

Chapter Four. America's Hybrid-Enlightenment

1. A useful overview of the plurality within the Enlightenment can be found in Roy Porter and Mikulas Teich, eds., *The Enlightenment in National Context* (Cambridge: Cambridge University Press, 1981).
2. This wonderfully textured description comes from John Ellis's *Founding Brothers* (New York: Knopf, 2001), 216. He, in turn, drew from John A. Schutz and Douglass Adair, eds., *The Spur of Fame: Dialogues of John Adams and Benjamin Rush, 1805–1813* (San Marino, CA: Huntington Library, 1966). The particular letters from which these statements are taken are Adams to Benjamin Rush, June 12 and August 17, 1812 (225, 242).
3. I draw heavily from Seligman in the pages that follow. See Adam Seligman, *The Idea of Civil Society* (New York: Free Press, 1992), 3, 29, 30.
4. Cicero, *The Republic*, III.2, cited in George Sabine, *A History of Political Thought* (New York: Rinehart & Winston, 1950), 164.
5. Seligman, *Civil Society*, 18–19.
6. A key part of the hybridity of the natural law tradition was made by Wolterstorff, who traced what are erroneously thought to be Enlightenment ideals of justice as "inherent rights" back to the Hebrew and Christian Scriptures. See Nicholas Wolterstorff, *Justice: Rights and Wrongs* (Princeton, NJ: Princeton University Press, 2008).
7. On the British variant, see Roy Porter, *The Creation of the Modern World: The Untold Story of the British Enlightenment* (New York: Norton, 2000).
8. Arguably, the greatest theologian America has produced is Jonathan Edwards. He is also, perhaps, the nation's most important Enlightenment thinker. From his youth, he was immersed in the literature of the British Enlightenment, and throughout his life, he wrestled with its implications for the Calvinist tradition. To understand Edwards in his own time, one can do no better than consult the most important biography of the man: George Marsden, *Jonathan Edwards: A Life* (New Haven, CT: Yale University Press, 2004).
9. Steven Pinker, *Enlightenment Now* (New York: Viking, 2018).

10. Henry May, *The Enlightenment in America* (New York: Oxford University Press, 1976), xiii–xvi.

11. Andrew Eliot, "A Discourse on Natural Religion" (1771), quoted in May, *Enlightenment*, 57.

12. Nathan Hatch, *Sacred Cause* (New Haven, CT: Yale University Press, 1977), 14.

13. Hatch, *Sacred Cause*, 2. Hatch is quoting *A Concert of Prayer Propounded to the Citizens of the United States of America* (Exeter, NH, 1787), 4, 9.

14. This letter was reproduced in the 1902 version of *The Jefferson Bible*, http://uuhouston.org/files/The_Jefferson_Bible.pdf (12). Of this work, he wrote to Mr. Charles Thompson, "A more beautiful or precious morsel of ethics I have never seen."

15. May, *Enlightenment*, 353.

16. Seligman, *Civil Society*, 23.

17. Seligman, *Civil Society*, 24.

18. Seligman, *Civil Society*, 35.

19. Seligman draws from David Hume's *Treatise of Human Nature* (book III, part 2) in *Civil Society*, 38.

20. Seligman, *Civil Society*, 74.

21. Adam Ferguson, *An Essay on the History of Civil Society* (1782), quoted in Seligman, *Civil Society*, 31.

22. Seligman, *Civil Society*, 126.

23. Sean Wilentz, *Chants Democratic* (New York: Oxford University Press, 1984), 61.

24. This was the argument of Nathan Hatch in *The Democratization of American Christianity* (New Haven, CT: Yale University Press, 1989). Hatch writes, "Amidst such acute uncertainty, many humble Christians in America began to redeem a dual legacy. They yoked strenuous demands for revivals, in the name of George Whitefield, with calls for the expansion of popular sovereignty, in the name of the Revolution. Linking these equally potent traditions sent American Christianity cascading in many creative directions in the early republic" (7).

25. Hatch, *Democratization*, 5. Hatch notes that the unique nature of this transformation in America is highlighted by the difference between British Methodism and American Methodism. Against the backdrop of the French Revolution and the discontent of industrial workers in England, English Methodists were forced to make a choice between being radical or loyal to the church. By 1819, the Methodist bishops made it impossible to be both. As Hatch put it, "Victorian Methodism in England took every opportunity to diminish popular expression and disown populist leadership" (8). This was not at all the case in America.

26. Hatch, *Democratization*, 3.

27. The antinomian impulse was already deep within American history and

culture at this point. Historically, antinomianism was a theological heresy, and in Puritan New England, it was illustrated most famously in the expulsion of Anne Hutchinson and her supporters from the Massachusetts Bay Colony for espousing it. (For those interested, antinomians denied the abiding validity of the moral law as a means or reflection of salvation. Rather, once pardoned and forgiven by the free grace of God, one is no longer obligated to follow the moral law as laid out, say, in the Ten Commandments; one's behavior had no bearing on one's spiritual condition. In its time, this implied a consent to behavior that was considered immoral or heterodox. As an antinomian, Hutchinson went so far as to argue that personal revelation from the Holy Spirit was equal in authority to Scripture.) But as a broader cultural dynamic, the antinomian ethos was characterized, on the one hand, by the rejection of institutional and cultural authority and, on the other, by the priority given to personal choice and personal moral righteousness. Antinomianism is the deep structure of American individualism, and it takes expression first as a predilection toward sectarianism, both religious and political, and second as a radical egalitarianism that flattens moral distinctions. Though always performed as an act of individual conscience, it is, perhaps inherently, subversive of both authority and solidarity.

28. Timothy Smith, *Revivalism and Social Reform* (Nashville: Abingdon, 1957).
29. See Hatch, *Democratization*, 62 n41.
30. In France, there was even a new calendar to mark this new age.
31. May, *Enlightenment*, 164.
32. Thomas Paine, *Common Sense*, https://www.learner.org/workshops/primary sources/revolution/docs/Common_Sense.pdf.
33. Paine, *Common Sense*.
34. The longer passage reads:

> What then is the American, this new man? He is either an European or the descendant of an European, hence that strange mixture of blood, which you will find in no other country. I could point out to you a family whose grandfather was an Englishman, whose wife was Dutch, whose son married a French woman, and whose present four sons have now four wives of different nations. *He* is an American, who leaving behind him all his ancient prejudices and manners, receives new ones from the new mode of life he has embraced, the new government he obeys, and the new rank he holds. He becomes an American by being received in the broad lap of our great *Alma Mater.*
>
> Here individuals of all nations are melted into a new race of men, whose labors and posterity will one day cause great changes in the world. Americans are the western pilgrims, who are carrying along with them that great mass of arts, sciences, vigor, and

industry which began long since in the East; they will finish the great circle. The Americans were once scattered all over Europe; here they are incorporated into one of the finest systems of population which has ever appeared, and which will hereafter become distinct by the power of the different climates they inhabit. The American ought therefore to love this country much better than that wherein either he or his forefathers were born. Here the rewards of his industry follow with equal steps the progress of his labor; his labor is founded on the basis of nature, self-interest; can it want a stronger allurement? Wives and children, who before in vain demanded of him a morsel of bread, now fat and frolicsome, gladly help their father to clear those fields whence exuberant crops are to arise to feed and to clothe them all; without any part being claimed, either by a despotic prince, a rich abbot, or a mighty lord. Here religion demands but little of him; a small voluntary salary to the minister, and gratitude to God; can he refuse these? The American is a new man, who acts upon new principles; he must therefore entertain new ideas, and form new opinions. From involuntary idleness, servile dependence, penury, and useless labor, he has passed to toils of a very different nature, rewarded by ample subsistence.—This is an American.

J. Hector St. John de Crèvecoeur, *Letters from an American Farmer,* letter 3, 1782, http://web.utk.edu/~mfitzge1/docs/374/creve.pdf.

35. Rodney was the first governor of Delaware and a signer of the Declaration of Independence. Quoted in May, *Enlightenment,* 164.

36. Hatch, *Sacred Cause,* 22.

37. David Hackett Fischer, *Albion's Seed* (New York: Oxford University Press, 1989).

38. May, *Enlightenment,* 160.

39. Hatch, *Sacred Cause,* 7–9.

40. May, *Enlightenment,* 189–90.

41. Paine, *Common Sense.*

42. Bernard Bailyn, *The Barbarous Years: The Peopling of British North America: The Conflict of Civilizations, 1600–1675* (New York: Vintage, 2012).

43. See May, *Enlightenment,* xv.

44. Bernard Bailyn, *The Ideological Origins of the American Revolution* (Cambridge, MA: Harvard University Press, 2017), 53–54.

45. Peter Gay acknowledged the point, but ultimately rejected it. See his *Enlightenment* (New York: Vintage, 1968), 322.

46. See Robert N. Bellah, Richard Madsen, William M. Sullivan, Ann Swidler, and Steven M. Tipton, *Habits of the Heart* (Berkeley: University of California Press, 1985); and Michael J. Sandel, *Democracy's Discontent: America*

in Search of a Public Philosophy (Cambridge, MA: Harvard University Press, 1996).

47. Gordon Wood, *Friends Divided: John Adams and Thomas Jefferson* (New York: Penguin, 2017), 277–78.

48. Wood, *Friends*, 114, 236, 250–51.

49. Wood, *Friends*, 375.

50. Wood, *Friends*, 182–85.

51. Wood, *Friends*, 378.

52. Wood, *Friends*, 326.

53. Wood, *Friends*, 114.

54. May, *Enlightenment*, 350.

55. John Patrick Diggins, "The Three Faces of Authority," in *The Problem of Authority in America*, ed. J. P. Diggins and Mark Kann (Philadelphia: Temple University Press, 1981), 35.

56. John Adams to Thomas Jefferson, October 9, 1781, in *The Papers of Thomas Jefferson*, vol. 12, ed. Julian Boyd (Princeton, NJ: Princeton University Press, 1950), 221. Also cited in Hannah Arendt, *On Revolution* (New York: Penguin, 2006), 143.

57. See May, *Enlightenment*, 97.

58. Adams to Jefferson.

59. Arthur Mann, *The One and the Many* (Chicago: University of Chicago Press, 1979), 68.

Chapter Five. Mythos and Nation-Building

1. John Adams, *A Dissertation on the Canon and Feudal Law* (1765), https://www.masshist.org/publications/adams-papers/index.php/view/PJA01dg2.

2. Adams, *A Dissertation*, 1765.

3. See Ernest Lee Tuveson, *Redeemer Nation* (Chicago: University of Chicago Press, 1980), 25.

4. John Quincy Adams, "An Address . . . Celebrating the Declaration of Independence," July 4, 1821, https://teachingamericanhistory.org/library/document/speech-on-independence-day/.

5. Adams, "An Address" (emphasis added).

6. Lyman Beecher, *A Plea for the West* (New York: Leavitt, Lord, 1835), 10–11, https://openlibrary.org/books/OL7046013M/A_plea_for_the_West.

7. Lyman Beecher, *The Memory of Our Fathers* (Boston: T. R. Marvin, 1828). All quotations in this section derive from this sermon.

8. See Leroy Froom, *The Prophetic Faith of Our Fathers*, vol. 4 (Washington, DC: Review & Herald, 1954). The nearly thirteen hundred pages of Froom's work provide hundreds of references to the end times and how Americans during the eighteenth and nineteenth centuries understood this and their own place within it. https://documents.adventistarchives

.org/Search/Pages/results.aspx/Results.aspx?k=prophetic%20faith%20 of%20our%20fathers.

9. The Reverend Thomas Barnard (1795), quoted in Tuveson, *Redeemer Nation*, 31.

10. Horace Bushnell, *Barbarism the First Danger* (New York: American Home Missionary Society, 1847), 32, https://archive.org/details/barbarismfirst daoobush/page/n1/mode/2up.

11. Daniel Walker Howe, "The Evangelical Movement and Political Culture in the North during the Second Party System," *Journal of American History* 77, no. 4 (March 1991): 1216–39.

12. These observations draw from Bernard Bailyn, "Sources and Traditions," in *The Ideological Origins of the American Revolution* (Cambridge, MA: Harvard University Press, 2017), 22–26.

13. Christopher Grasso, "Skepticism and American Faith: Infidels, Converts, and Religious Doubt in the Early Nineteenth Century," *Journal of the Early Republic* 22, no. 3 (Autumn 2002): 273–76.

14. Locke goes on to say, "As for other practical opinions, though not absolutely free from all error, if they do not tend to establish domination over others, or civil impunity to the Church in which they are taught, there can be no reason why they should not be tolerated." John Locke, *Letter concerning Toleration*, https://core.ac.uk/download/pdf/7048692.pdf.

15. See Bernard J. Kohlbrenner, "Religion and Higher Education: An Historical Perspective," *History of Education Quarterly* 1, no. 2 (June 1961): 45–56.

16. Francis J. Grund, *The Americans, in Their Moral, Social and Political Relations* (Boston: Marsh, Capen, & Lyon, 1837), 158, https://archive.org /details/americansintheiroogrun/page/n7/mode/2up.

17. Robert Handy, *A Christian America* (New York: Oxford University Press, 1984), 24.

18. Martin Marty, *Righteous Empire* (New York: Harper, 1970), 16.

19. This observation is from Donald Mathews, *Religion in the Old South* (Chicago: University of Chicago Press, 1977), 4.

20. John Murrin, "No Awakening, No Revolution? More Counterfactual Speculations," *Reviews in American History* 11 (June 1983): 161–71, cited in Howe, "The Evangelical Movement," 1216.

21. Connecticut in 1818, New Hampshire in 1819, and Massachusetts in 1833.

22. Howe, "The Evangelical Movement," 1222.

23. Grund, *The Americans*, 163.

24. Grund, *The Americans*, 163–64.

25. "True Sources of National Prosperity," sermon delivered in 1814, in *The Works of Jesse Appleton*, vol. 2 (Andover: Gould & Newman, 1836), 305, https://archive.org/search.php?query=jesse+appleton.

26. Winthrop Hudson, *The Great Tradition of the American Churches* (New York: Harper, 1953), 108.

27. Julian M. Sturtevant, *The Lessons of Our National Conflict: An Address to the Alumni of Yale College*, July 24, 1861 (New Haven, CT: Thomas Stafford, 1861), https://archive.org/details/lessonsofournatioostur/page/6/mode/2 up?q=social%2C+political+and+moral.

28. This is documented extensively in Timothy Smith, *Revivalism and Social Reform* (Nashville: Abingdon, 1957).

29. Grant Brodrecht highlighted this important element of Protestant theology in his *Our Country: Northern Evangelicals and the Union during the Civil War Era* (New York: Fordham University Press, 2018).

30. There is an abundance of good scholarship on this topic beyond Smith, *Revivalism*. See Charles Foster, *An Errand of Mercy: The Evangelical United Front, 1790–1837* (Chapel Hill: University of North Carolina Press, 1960); Clifford Griffin, *Their Brothers' Keepers: Moral Stewardship in the United States, 1800–1865* (New Brunswick, NJ: Rutgers University Press, 1960); Joel Bernard, "Between Religion and Reform: American Moral Societies, 1811–1821," *Proceedings of the Massachusetts Historical Society* 105 (1993): 1–38; and Howe, "The Evangelical Movement," 1216–39.

31. Michael Young, *Bearing Witness against Sin: The Evangelical Birth of the American Social Movement* (Chicago: University of Chicago Press, 2006), provides a smart and empirically based study of the organizations that constituted the benevolent empire.

32. This section on Phoebe Palmer draws from the biography by Charles Edward White, *The Beauty of Holiness* (Grand Rapids, MI: Francis Asbury, 1986).

33. White, *Beauty of Holiness*, 208.

34. White, *Beauty of Holiness*, 209.

35. Jacob Rush, *Charges and Extracts of Charges on Moral and Religious Subjects* (Philadelphia, 1804), quoted in Bernard, "Between Religion and Reform." NB: Jacob was Benjamin Rush's brother.

36. Thomas Jefferson, "A Bill for the More General Diffusion of Knowledge" (June 18, 1779), National Archives, Founders Online, https://founders .archives.gov/documents/Jefferson/01-02-02-0132-0004-0079.

37. Thomas Jefferson, "Notes on the State of Virginia" (1781), https://www .thefederalistpapers.org/wp-content/uploads/2012/12/Thomas-Jefferson -Notes-On-The-State-Of-Virginia.pdf (168).

38. Benjamin Rush, "Thoughts upon the Mode of Education Proper in a Republic" (1786), Explore PA History, https://explorepahistory.com/odocu ment.php?docId=1-4-218#:~:text=Our%20schools%20of%20learning %2C%20by,for%20uniform%20and%20peaceable%20government.

39. Noah Webster, "On the Education of Youth in America" (1790), https:// www.commonlit.org/en/texts/on-the-education-of-youth-in-america.

40. The commitment to public education for the cultivation of republicanism did not wane through the middle of the nineteenth century. "The establishment of a republican government," wrote the iconic educational re-

former Horace Mann in 1848, "without well-appointed and efficient means for the universal education of the people, is the most rash and fool-hardy experiment ever tried by man. . . . It may be an easy thing to make a Republic; but it is a very laborious thing to make Republicans; and woe to the republic that rests upon no better foundations than ignorance, selfishness, and passion. . . . Such a republic, with all its noble capacities for beneficence, will rush with the speed of a whirlwind to an ignominious end; and all good men of after-times would be fain to weep over its downfall, did not their scorn and contempt at its folly and its wickedness, repress all sorrow for its fate."

Never one to mince words, Mann argued that without an educated public, a republican form of government "must be, on a vast scale, what a mad-house, without superintendent or keepers, would be, on a small one;—the despotism of a few succeeded by universal anarchy, and anarchy by despotism with no change but from bad to worse." Horace Mann, *Twelfth Annual Report of the Board of Education* (Boston: Dutton & Wentworth, 1949), 78–79, 76, https://www.google.com/books/edition/Annual_report_of_the_Board_of_Education/eURNAAAAcAAJ?hl=en&gbpv=1.

41. Seven years later, Benjamin Rush echoed the point, contending in his "Thoughts upon the Mode of Education Proper in a Republic" that "the form of government we have assumed has created a new class of duties to every American," first among them the education of its citizen: "Producing one general and uniform system of education, will render the mass of the people *more homogeneous* and thereby fit them more easily for uniform and peaceable government" (emphasis added). Through its educational system, the state would come to monopolize legitimate public culture. And so it was that the growth of a system of universal education would become coterminous with the emergence and growth of the modern nation-state. Rush and Jefferson were not alone. Noah Webster prominently added his voice to the chorus, declaring in 1790 that "education should . . . be the first care of a Legislature; not merely the institution of schools, but the furnishing of them with the best men for teachers." Webster, "On the Education of Youth."

42. Rush, "Thoughts upon the Mode of Education."

43. Rush, "Thoughts upon the Mode of Education."

44. Rush, "Thoughts upon the Mode of Education." Noah Webster was of a similar mind. For example, he had no objection to the use of the Bible since that was the one book that most families had in their homes. He thought it would be useful "as a system of morality and religion," though he was concerned with the way certain passages were used "to strike terror to the mind." Webster, "On the Education of Youth."

45. The common and interdenominational Protestant character of the common school was a function of demographic realities. Except in large cities, the number of Baptists, Methodists, Episcopalians, or Presbyterians

in any community were never enough for any denomination to have its own school. They came together out of need, agreeing to set aside sectarian differences in favor of the beliefs and practices they shared.

46. I draw heavily from two landmark articles in the field: David Tyack, "The Kingdom of God and the Common School: Protestant Ministers and the Educational Awakening in the West," *Harvard Educational Review* 36, no. 4 (1966): 447–69; and Timothy Smith, "Protestant Schooling and American Nationality, 1800–1850," *Journal of American History* 53, no. 4 (1967): 679–95.

47. Alexis de Tocqueville, *Democracy in America*, trans. Harvey Mansfield and Delba Winthrop (Chicago: University of Chicago Press, 2000), 283. There were limits to Protestant hegemony in education. Lutherans and the Dutch Calvinists, for example, were holdouts in Protestantism, a dissent that was enabled and reinforced by language and ethnic heritage. With the great influx of Irish, Germans, Italians, and eastern Europeans in the 1830s through the 1860s, Catholics also—against much opposition— established their own schools. And yet even here, education was religiously infused and, as a rule, overseen by the clergy.

48. This was before Harrison became president. Henry Warner Bowden, *American Indians and Christian Missions* (Chicago: University of Chicago Press, 1981), 166, quoted by John F. Cady in "Western Opinion and the War of 1812," *Ohio Archaeological and Historical Society Publications* 33 (1924): 435–36.

49. https://www.ourdocuments.gov/doc.php?flash=false&doc=8.

50. A compilation of these treaties was made by Charles J. Kappler, *Indian Affairs: Laws and Treaties*, vol. 2 (Washington, DC: Government Printing Office, 1904), https://digitalcommons.csumb.edu/cgi/viewcontent.cgi?article=1062&context=hornbeck_usa_2_e.

51. The land cessions are listed in Charles C. Royce, *Indian Land Cessions in the United States*, Bureau of American Ethnology, annual report of 1899, https://www.gutenberg.org/files/17148/17148-h/17148-h.htm. An illustrated cartography of these cessions can be found at https://ic.pics.live journal.com/the_sun_is_up/13064998/82417/original.jpg.

52. U.S. Census Bureau, *The Population of the United States in 1860*, https://www.census.gov/library/publications/1864/dec/1860a.html.

53. Josiah Strong, *Our Country: Its Possible Future and Its Present Crisis* (New York: Baker & Taylor, 1885), 30.

54. Martin Marty quoted the collective opinion of the American bishops who, in 1844, declared that "Romanism is now laboring, not only to recover what it lost of its former supremacy in the Reformation, but also to assert and establish its monstrous pretensions in countries never subject either to its civil or ecclesiastical authority." See Marty, *Righteous Empire*, 129.

55. See Samuel F. B. Morse, *Foreign Conspiracies against the Liberties of the*

United States (New York: Chapin, 1841,) 11, https://archive.org/details /foreignconspiracyoomors/page/112/mode/2up?q=separate.

56. Beecher, *A Plea for the West*, 85–86.

57. Perhaps the most comprehensive work on this subject is Ray A. Billington, *The Protestant Crusade, 1800–1860* (New York: Macmillan, 1938).

58. The founding documents of the American Protestant Association can be found here: https://babel.hathitrust.org/cgi/pt?id=umn.31951001508384m &view=1up&seq=1.

59. Bushnell, *Barbarism*, 24.

60. See J. Spencer Fluhman, "Anti-Mormonism and the Question of Religious Authenticity in Antebellum America," *Journal of Religion and Society* 7 (2005).

61. Stephen LeSueur, *The 1838 Mormon War in Missouri* (Columbia: University of Missouri Press, 1987). LeSueur argues that Mormon militancy was as much to blame as anti-Mormon prejudice.

62. The text of this order can be found here: https://archive.org/details/Boggs ExterminationOrder44/page/n1/mode/2up.

63. Jefferson's opinion was typical of the opinion of other European Enlightenment figures. See Emmanuel Chukwudi Eze, ed., *Race and the Enlightenment: A Reader* (Oxford: Blackwell, 1997). David Hume, for example, wrote that he was "apt to suspect the Negroes, and in general, all other species of men to be naturally inferior to whites." See John Immerwahr, "Hume's Revised Racism," *Journal of the History of Ideas* 53, no. 3 (July–September 1992): 481–86. Kant was no less racist. See Dieter Schönecker, "How White Is Kant's White Race, After All?" *Telos*, February 23, 2021, https:// www.telospress.com/how-white-is-kants-white-race-after-all/.

64. J. D. B. De Bow, "Slavery and the Bible," *Southern and Western Review*, September 9, 1850, 281–86, https://archive.org/details/debowsreviewo2proj goog/page/n292/mode/2up; A. T. Holmes, *The Duties of Christian Masters* (Charleston, SC: Southern Baptist Publication Society, 1851), https:// archive.org/details/dutiesofmastersto1mcty/page/130/mode/2up?q =Holmes; Edmund Ruffin, *The Political Economy of Slavery* (Virginia: Lemuel Towers, 1853), https://babel.hathitrust.org/cgi/pt?id=loc.ark:/13960 /t3zs2vh6z&view=1up&seq=7; Thornton Stringfellow, *Scriptural and Statistical Views in Favor of Slavery* (Richmond: J. W. Randolph, 1856), https:// archive.org/details/scripturalstatisoostri; Thos. R. R. Cobb, *An Inquiry into the Law of Negro Slavery* (Philadelphia: T. & J. W. Johnson, 1858), 1, https:// archive.org/details/inquiryintolawofo1cobbiala/page/n232/mode/1up.

65. Samuel A. Cartwright, "Report on the Diseases and Physical Peculiarities of the Negro Race," *New Orleans Medical and Surgical Journal* 7 (May 1851): 691–715. All quotations in this section are derived from the online version of this report: https://ia803203.us.archive.org/7/items/TheNew OrleansMedicalAndSurgicalJournal/The%20New%20Orleans%20 medical%20and%20surgical%20journal.pdf.

66. Cartwright, "Report," 693.
67. Cartwright, "Report," 694.
68. Cartwright, "Report," 695–97.
69. Cartwright, "Report," 715.
70. Cartwright, "Report," 715.
71. Scientific racism reduced racial difference and Black humanity in particular to mere biology. The biologization of race allowed for the classification of race into a rigid hierarchy of higher and lower, better and worse. It laid the groundwork for a hardening racism before and after the Civil War and for a theory of eugenics and policies of "racial hygiene" in the early twentieth century. It was reflected in Darwin's work, both in *On the Origin of Species* (the subtitle of which was "By Means of Natural Selection, or the Preservation of Favoured Races in the Struggle for Life") and in *The Descent of Man*, and in textbooks, such as the one used by John Scopes of the infamous Scopes trial—George W. Hunter, *A Civic Biology: Presented in Problems* (New York: American Book Company, 1914). As Hunter put it, "At the present time there exist upon the earth five races or varieties of man, each very different from the other in instincts, social customs, and, to an extent, in structure. There are the Ethiopian or negro type, originating in Africa; the Malay or brown race, from the islands of the Pacific; the American Indian; the Mongolian or yellow race, including the natives of China, Japan, and the Eskimos; and finally, the highest type of all, the Caucasians, represented by the civilized white inhabitant of Europe and America" (196). Scientific racism was one of the reasons why racial separation became worse after the Civil War.
72. "Testimony of the Rev. William Allan, Late of Alabama," in *American Slavery as It Is: Testimony of a Thousand Witnesses*, ed. Theodore Dwight Weld (New York: American Anti-Slavery Society, 1839), 61, https://archive.org/details/americanslaverya1839weld2/page/61/mode/2up?q=Allan.
73. Weld, *American Slavery*, 46. In Samuel Johnson's 1755 dictionary, the word *brute* is defined as "senseless," "irrational," "savage," "bestial," "ferine," "undomesticated," "uncivilized."
74. Bushnell, *Barbarism*, 29.
75. The literature on the accomplishments of reform in this period is extensive, but the groundbreaking work was done by Smith, *Revivalism*.
76. Timothy Flint, *Indian Wars of the West, Biographical Sketches of Those Pioneers Who Headed the Western Settlers in Repelling the Attacks of the Savages, Together with a View of the Character, Manners, Monuments, and Antiquities of the Western Indians* (Cincinnati: E. H. Flint, 1833), 36, https://archive.org/details/indianwarsofwestooflin/page/n11/mode/2up?q=unchangeable+order+of.
77. U.S. Census, 1860, introduction, ix, https://www2.census.gov/library/publications/decennial/1860/population/1860a-02.pdf.
78. Strong, *Our Country*, 175.

79. Strong, *Our Country,* 225.
80. The quote, from a missionary agency in 1823, is in Bowden, *American Indians and Christian Missions,* 168.
81. Quotations from this section come from Beecher, *A Plea for the West,* 67, 85, 130, 63ff., 87, 166.
82. On Native American removal policy, for example, American Protestants differed over its effects. Some, Flint argued, saw "nothing in their removal, but oppression, violation of treaties, and of the faith of the United States, cruelty and perfidy on our part, and on theirs, banishment from their homes and the graves of their fathers, poverty, famine, degradation and utter extinction, chargeable to the ingratitude and tyranny of the whites." Others, however, saw "the race perpetuated in opulence and peace in the fair prairies of the west, . . . where they are to grow up distinct red nations, with schools and churches, the anvil, the loom, and the plough—a sort of Arcadian race . . . , standing memorials of the kindness and good faith of our government." Flint, *Indian Wars of the West,* 242.

Chapter Six. The Unmaking of the Christian Republic

1. David Walker, *Walker's Appeal, in Four Articles; Together with a Preamble, to the Coloured Citizens of the World . . .* , ed. Paul Royster (Boston, 1830), 39, 37, Zea E-Books in American Studies, book 15, https://digitalcommons .unl.edu/cgi/viewcontent.cgi?article=1014&context=zeaamericanstudies.
2. Johann Neem, *Democracy's Schools* (Baltimore: Johns Hopkins University Press, 2017), 3n6.
3. A cursory review of these laws and restrictions can be found in Neem, *Democracy's Schools,* 162–66.
4. Walker, *Walker's Appeal,* 20.
5. Charles M. Wiltse, introduction to *David Walker's Appeal, in Four Articles* (New York: Hill & Wang, 1965), vii.
6. Walker, *Walker's Appeal,* 20.
7. Walker, *Walker's Appeal,* 73–74.
8. In his conclusion, he asks rhetorically, "[Have] the Antideluvians—the Sodomites—the Egyptians—the Babylonians—the Ninevites—the Carthagenians—the Persians—the Macedonians—the Greeks—the Romans—the Mahometans—the Jews—or devils ever treated a set of human beings as the white Christians of America do us, the blacks, or Africans?" Walker, *Walker's Appeal,* 84.
9. Walker, *Walker's Appeal,* 49.
10. Walker, *Walker's Appeal,* 78.
11. Walker, *Walker's Appeal,* 85–86.
12. Walker is referring to Jefferson's *Notes on the State of Virginia* in which Jefferson observed that "the blacks, whether originally a distinct race, or

made distinct by time and circumstances, are inferior to the whites in the endowments both of body and mind. It is not against experience to suppose that different species of the same genus, or varieties of the same species, may possess different qualifications. Will not a lover of natural history then, one who views the gradations in all the races of animals with the eye of philosophy, excuse an effort to keep those in the department of man as distinct as nature has formed them? This unfortunate difference of colour, and perhaps of faculty, is a powerful obstacle to the emancipation of these people." https://www.thefederalistpapers.org/wp-content/up loads/2012/12/Thomas-Jefferson-Notes-On-The-State-Of-Virginia.pdf 12, 17, 31.

13. Quotations come from Walker, *Walker's Appeal*, 12, 19, 30, 82, 74–75, 79–81.
14. Walker, *Walker's Appeal*, 75.
15. Walker, *Walker's Appeal*, 62, 73.
16. Walker, *Walker's Appeal*, 13, 41, 43, 49. As he put it elsewhere, "It is surprising to think that the Americans, having the Bible in their hands, do not believe it" (78).
17. I rely heavily on Donald Mathews's insightful reading of Southern evangelicalism in his book *Religion in the Old South* (Chicago: University of Chicago Press, 1977).
18. Mathews, *Religion in the Old South*, 67.
19. Mathews, *Religion in the Old South*, 68; John Wesley, *Thoughts upon Slavery* (London: Joseph Cruikshank, 1774), 38, https://archive.org/details/thoughts uponslavoowesl/page/n103/mode/2up?q=.
20. Allen is quoted in *Walker's Appeal*, 65 (emphasis added).
21. E. Thomas, *A Concise View of the Slavery of the People of Colour in the United States; Exhibiting Some of the Most Affecting Cases of Cruel and Barbarous Treatment of the Slaves by Their Most Inhuman and Brutal Masters; Not Heretofore Published* (Philadelphia, 1834), 69, https://archive.org/details/concise viewofslaoothom.
22. Michael Young, *Bearing Witness against Sin: The Evangelical Birth of the American Social Movement* (Chicago: University of Chicago Press, 2006), 135–39.
23. Two biographies of the Grimké sisters are noteworthy: Catherine H. Birney, *The Grimké Sisters: Sarah and Angelina Grimké* (Boston: Lee & Shepard, 1885); and more recently, Gerda Lerner, *The Grimké Sisters from South Carolina* (Chapel Hill: University of North Carolina Press, 2004).
24. Angelina Grimké, *An Appeal to the Christian Women of the South* (Boston: American Anti-Slavery Society, 1836), https://archive.org/details/appeal tochristia1836grim.
25. Grimké writes, "I know you do not make the laws, but I also know that you are the wives and mothers, the sisters and daughters of those who do;

and if you really suppose you can do nothing to overthrow slavery, you are greatly mistaken." Grimké, *An Appeal*, 16. All quotations expositing on her argument in the *Appeal* come from this pamphlet (2–12).

26. Grimké, *An Appeal*, 2.
27. Her knowledge of the system of slavery and its cultural logics was both passionate and comprehensive in a lawyerly sense. Her fourteen-point distillation was masterful. See Grimké, *An Appeal*, 11–12.
28. Grimké, *An Appeal*, 11, 12.
29. Grimké, *An Appeal*, 3.
30. Grimké, *An Appeal*, 26.
31. Birney, *The Grimké Sisters*, 146–49.
32. Lerner, *The Grimké Sisters from South Carolina*, 143.
33. Angelina Grimké, *An Appeal to the Women of the Nominally Free States* (New York: Wm. S. Dorr, 1837), https://archive.org/details/DKC0122.
34. Theodore Dwight Weld, ed., *American Slavery as It Is: Testimony of a Thousand Witnesses* (New York: American Anti-Slavery Society, 1839), https://archive.org/details/americanslavery a1839weld2.
35. Frederick Douglass, "Oration," delivered in Corinthian Hall, July 5, 1852, https://archive.org/details/Douglass_July_Oration/page/16/mode/2up.
36. In 1861, the Southern theologian James Henley Thornwell gave a clear voice to this conviction when he wrote that "as a Church, let it be distinctly borne in mind that the only rule of judgment is the written word of God. The Church knows nothing of the intuitions of reason or the deductions of philosophy, except those reproduced in the Sacred Canon. She has a positive Constitution in the Holy Scriptures and has no right to utter a single syllable upon any subject, except as the Lord puts words in her mouth. She is founded, in other words, upon express *revelation*. Her creed is an authoritative testimony of God, and not a speculation; and what she proclaims, she must proclaim with the infallible certitude of faith, and not with the hesitating assent of an opinion." Quoted in Mark Noll, *The Civil War as a Theological Crisis* (Chapel Hill: University of North Carolina Press, 2006), 62.
37. Noll, *Civil War*, 6.
38. Noll, *Civil War*, 39.
39. Noll, *Civil War*, 4, 19.
40. David Brion Davis, "Slavery and Sin: The Cultural Background," in *The Antislavery Vanguard: New Essays on the Abolitionists*, ed. Martin Duberman (Princeton, NJ: Princeton University Press, 1965), 3; for the entire text, see 3–31.
41. George M. Stroud, *A Sketch of the Laws relating to Slavery in the Several States of the United States of America* (Philadelphia: Kimber & Sharpless, 1827), 23–24, https://archive.org/details/sketchoflawsrela1827stro/page/n13/mode/2up?q=.
42. Thomas, *A Concise View of the Slavery*, 71.

43. Abraham Lincoln, "Speech at Cincinnati, Ohio," September 17, 1859, in *The Collected Works of Abraham Lincoln*, ed. Ray Basler (New Brunswick, NJ: Rutgers University Press, 1953), 3, 445, quoted in Noll, *Civil War*, 56.

44. John Fee, *The Sinfulness of Slaveholding Shown by Appeals to Reason and Scripture* (New York: John A. Gray, 1851), 29.

45. James Pendleton, a Baptist preacher from Kentucky, argued that "[i]f then it could be established that slavery promotes the holiness and happiness of slaves, it would follow that as it does not promote the holiness and happiness of the white population, it would be well for white people to be enslaved in order to their holiness and happiness." Quoted in Noll, *Civil War*, 55.

46. This statement was made in 1862 by Alexander Crummell, a free African American educated at Cambridge University. See David Brion Davis, "Blacks Damned by the Bible," a review of *The Curse of Ham: Race and Slavery in Early Judaism, Christianity, and Islam*, by David Goldenberg, *New York Review of Books*, November 16, 2006.

47. Douglass, "Oration."

48. "Report of the Decision of the Supreme Court of the United States, and the Opinions of the Judges Thereof, in the Case of Dred Scott versus John F. A. Sandford," December Term, 1856. By Benjamin C. Howard, from the Nineteenth Volume of *Howard's Reports* (Washington, DC: Cornelius Wendell, 1857), 9–10, https://www.google.co.uk/books/edition/Re port_of_the_Decision_of_the_Supreme_Co/JOMSAAAAYAAJ?hl=en &gbpv=1&pg=PA4&printsec=frontcover.

49. "Report of the Decision of the Supreme Court of the United States, and the Opinions of the Judges Thereof, in the Case of Dred Scott versus John F. A. Sandford," 16.

50. "Report of the Decision of the Supreme Court of the United States, and the Opinions of the Judges Thereof, in the Case of Dred Scott versus John F. A. Sandford," 13, 16.

51. Alexander H. Stephens, "Cornerstone Address," March 21, 1861, http://teachingamericanhistory.org/library/document/cornerstone-speech/.

52. I'm grateful for the insightful treatment of this subject given by Grant Brodrecht in *Our Country: Northern Evangelicals and the Union in the Civil War Era* (New York: Fordham University Press, 2018).

53. Samuel Harris, *The Kingdom of Christ on Earth* (Andover, MA: Warren Draper, 1874), 190. In his magnum opus *The History of the Great Republic* (Boston: Levering, 1877), published just after Reconstruction, Jesse T. Peck wrote a very similar theological justification for the Civil War. "The religion of Jesus allows no personal resentments: it requires love for hatred and meekness under suffering. Nor will it permit national injustice or unrighteous retribution; but it requires the magistrate to protect the right, and punish aggressors who seek to destroy civil government. . . . When, therefore, liberty is assailed, the executive justice of the nation must defend it, and destroy the power which would overthrow it" (666–67).

Indeed, he argued, "the new nation is more *humane* for its justice," for "no deeper sympathy, no truer love, has ever honored the manhood of man than that, which, in the might of Christian justice, arose to strike off the fetters of slavery, and which, in the spirit of Jesus, is now endeavoring to 'beat our swords into ploughshares, and our spears into pruning-hooks'" (695). See https://archive.org/details/historyofgreatreoopeck_o.

54. J. David Hacker, "A Census-Based Count of the Civil War Dead," *Civil War History* 57, no. 4 (December 2011): 307–48.

55. Numbers are provided by https://famous-trials.com/sheriffshipp/1084 -lynchingsyear. See also https://lynchinginamerica.eji.org/report/.

56. Eric Foner, *Reconstruction: America's Unfinished Revolution, 1863–1877* (New York: HarperPerennial, 1988), 190ff., 171ff.

57. C. Vann Woodward, *The Strange Career of Jim Crow* (New York: Oxford University Press, 2001).

58. Made clearer by the further establishment of scientific racism and eugenics through the end of the nineteenth century. See chapter 5, note 71 above.

59. Isabel Wilkerson, *The Warmth of Other Suns* (New York: Random House, 2010), 40–44. See also Richard Wormser, *The Rise and Fall of Jim Crow* (New York: St. Martin's, 1999).

60. W. E. Burghardt Du Bois, *Black Reconstruction* (New York: Free Press, 1962), chapter 4.

61. See Ernest Lee Tuveson, *Redeemer Nation* (Chicago: University of Chicago Press, 1980), chapter 6.

62. The Reverend Marvin R. Vincent in a sermon entitled "The Lord of War and of Righteousness," quoted in Tuveson, *Redeemer Nation*, 203.

63. A comprehensive and helpful guide of the archival literature on this subject can be found in Timothy E. Fulop, "The Future Golden Day of the Race: Millennialism and Black Americans in the Nadir, 1877–1901," *Harvard Theological Review* 84, no. 1 (January 1991): 75–99.

64. R. H. Cain, "The Negro Problem of the South," *A.M.E. Church Review* 2 (January 1886): 145. Centuries of slavery were reconciled through the language and purposes of millennial thinking (92).

65. J. Augustus Cole, "The Negro at Home and Abroad: Their Origin, Progress and Destiny," *A.M.E. Church Review* 4 (April 1886): 401. For AME bishop W. J. Gaines, slavery under the white man had been the means by which God would achieve progress for all. "Providence, in wisdom," he wrote, "has decreed that the lot of the negro should be cast with the white people of America. Condemn as we may the means through which we were brought here, recount as we may the suffering through which, as a race, we passed in the years of slavery, yet the fact remains that today our condition is far in advance of that of the negroes who never left their native Africa. We are planted in the midst of the highest civilization man-

kind has ever known, and are rapidly advancing in knowledge, property and moral enlightenment. We might, with all reason, thank God even for slavery, if this were the only means through which we could arrive at our present progress and development." See W. J. Gaines, *The Negro and the White Man* (Philadelphia: A.M.E. Publishing House, 1897), 65.

66. Theophilus Steward, *The End of the World—or, Clearing the Way for the Fullness of Gentiles* (Philadelphia: A.M.E. Church Book Rooms, 1888).

67. Harris, *The Kingdom of Christ on Earth*, lecture 7, 255.

68. Josiah Strong, *Our Country: Its Possible Future and Its Present Crisis* (New York: Baker & Taylor, 1885). His thesis was reprised eight years later in *The New Era; or, the Coming Kingdom* (New York: Baker & Taylor, 1893). Once again, the themes of these books were commonplace long before Strong wrote them. In its day, *Our Country* was wildly successful, selling 158,000 copies in its first printing and after its revision following the 1890 census, it sold tens of thousands of copies more.

69. Above all, he was committed to improving the conditions of cities and of factories for ordinary people. His vision of America, then, was not political or military but rather theological, refracted through the prism of "home missions" and the longing for the kingdom of heaven. As he put it, the growth of a Christian and Anglo-Saxon world was "no war of extermination," "not one of arms, but of vitality and of civilization" (175–77). For further background on Strong and nuances of his thought, see Dorothea R. Miller, "Josiah Strong and American Nationalism: A Reevaluation," *Journal of American History* 53, no. 3 (December 1966): 487–503, as well as Christina Littlefield and Falon Opsahl, "Promulgating the Kingdom: Social Gospel Muckraker Josiah Strong," *American Journalism* 34, no. 3 (August 2017): 289–312.

70. Strong, *The New Era*, 81.

71. Strong, *Our Country*, 179–80, 15.

72. Strong, *Our Country*, 4, 5.

73. Strong, *Our Country*, 4–5.

74. See his argument on pages 160ff. "It was no accident that the great reformation of the sixteenth century originated among a Teutonic, rather than a Latin people. It was the fire of liberty burning in the Saxon heart that flamed up against the absolutism of the Pope."

75. Strong, *Our Country*, 179.

76. Strong, *Our Country*, 170. Strong is taking this passage from Darwin's *The Descent of Man*, 1:172, https://archive.org/details/descentmanoodarwgoog/page/n4/mode/2up.

77. Strong, *Our Country*, 176; citing *The Descent of Man*, 1:154. The association of race and nationalism and divine destiny was never more explicit, and it created even greater moral urgency to pursue policies of eugenics.

78. Strong, *Our Country*, 180.

79. Quoted in Tuveson, *Redeemer Nation*, 129.

80. Albert Jeremiah Beveridge, *Congressional Record* (56th Cong., 1st sess.), 33:705, 711. Beveridge was a thirty-seven-year-old Republican senator from Indiana. The issue Beveridge was addressing was the question of the relationship of the United States to the Philippines, and while the wisdom of the policy was debated, the framework for justifying America's territorial expansion was unexceptional. The Founders of the nation, he goes on to say,

> were not provincial. Theirs was the geography of the world. They were soldiers as well as landsmen, and they knew that where our ships should go our flag might follow. They had the logic of progress, and they knew that the republic they were planting must, in obedience to the laws of our expanding race, necessarily develop into the greater republic, which the world beholds today, and into the still mightier republic which the world will finally acknowledge as the arbiter, under God, of the destinies of mankind. . . .
>
> Blind indeed is he who sees not the hand of God in events so vast, so harmonious, so benign. Reactionary indeed is the mind that perceives not that this vital people is the strongest of the saving forces of the world; that our place, therefore, is at the head of the constructing and redeeming nations of the earth; and that to stand aside while events march on is a surrender of our interests, a betrayal of our duty as blind as it is base. Craven indeed is the heart that fears to perform a work so golden and so noble; that dares not win a glory so immortal.

    To our ears, the arrogance of his claims is, in turn, astonishing, fascinating, and repugnant. We want to imagine that he was a reactionary and fringe figure on the American political landscape, but this wasn't at all the case. Beveridge was not a conservative but a progressive who would go on to lead the establishment of the Progressive Party in 1912.

81. George Thomas, *Revivalism and Cultural Change* (Chicago: University of Chicago Press, 1989), 6–7. In short, the market, republican polity, and revivalism shared a similar ideological structure and were therefore mutually reinforcing. This was not because they were in any way similar in content, but rather that they shared a common cultural foundation in the commitment to the autonomy of the individual as a rational decision maker, a belief in the importance of individual action and rational calculation, and a predilection to demystify nature.

82. I am grateful to Mark Noll's work for pointing me in this direction. Noll, *Civil War*, 161.

83. Alfred Kazin, "Lincoln: The Almighty Has His Own Purposes," in *God and the American Writer* (New York: Knopf, 1997), 120–41.

Chapter Seven. A Secular Turn

1. August Meier, *Negro Thought in America, 1880–1915* (Ann Arbor: University of Michigan Press, 1988), 23. In the same paragraph, Meier wrote that "Negroes never abandoned their emphasis upon the Christian and humanitarian and democratic elements in the American tradition."

2. Empirical evidence for this is found in the famous studies of Muncie, Indiana, by Robert and Helen Lind in 1919 and a decade later in 1929. See their books *Middletown: A Study of Modern Culture* (New York: Harcourt, Brace, 1929) and *Middletown in Transition: A Study of Cultural Conflict* (New York: Harcourt, Brace, 1937). It is also worth quoting H. Richard Niebuhr from his *Social Sources of Denominationalism* (New York: Holt, 1929): "The only center [of immigrant unity] which was available, as a rule, was religion; the only leaders, with few exceptions, who had braved the difficulties of a new orientation along with the migrating artisans and farmers were the clergy; the only organization which was readily at hand for maintaining the unity of the group was the church" (223).

3. See Gary Dorrien, *The New Abolition: W. E. B. Du Bois and the Black Social Gospel* (New Haven, CT: Yale University Press, 2015). Though light (for my tastes) on the theological currents of the time, Dorrien does provide a masterful history of the key leaders of the Black social gospel movement.

4. These theological adaptations were crystallized in the Pittsburgh Platform of 1885. In this document, progressives argued that a rabbinical Judaism based on the law and tradition had lost its hold on the contemporary Jew. The only viable course, it maintained, was to reinterpret the meaning of Judaism in light of new historical developments. See J. D. Hunter, *Culture Wars: The Struggle to Define America* (New York: Basic Books, 1991), 81.

5. The story is elegantly and comprehensively told in George Marsden, *Fundamentalism and American Culture* (New York: Oxford University Press, 1980).

6. J. Gresham Machen, *Christianity and Liberalism* (New York: Macmillan, 1923), 17.

7. Hunter, *Culture Wars*, chapter 3.

8. In this entire section, I am beholden to the carefully researched work of Christian Smith in *The Secular Revolution* (Berkeley: University of California Press, 2003).

9. Thorstein Veblen, *The Higher Learning in America* (Stanford, CA: Academic Reprints, 1918), cited in Smith, *The Secular Revolution*, 78.

10. Smith, *The Secular Revolution*, 76.

11. I'm referring to the "commonsense realist" epistemology and Baconian philosophy of science that derived from the early Scottish and English Enlightenment and that was largely compatible with theism. Mill's work that I referred to was called *Auguste Comte and Positivism*, published in

1865. Spencer's reputation as a social Darwinist is disputed, but it draws mainly from his book *Man versus the State*, published in 1885, as well as some other essays.

12. Michael Schudson, *Discovering the News: A Social History of American Newspapers* (New York: Basic Books, 1978); and Michael Schudson, "The Profession of Journalism in the United States," in *The Professions in American History*, ed. Nathan Hatch (Notre Dame, IN: University of Notre Dame Press, 1988), 145–61.

13. Bruce Kimball, quoted in Richard Flory, "Promoting a Secular Standard: Secularization and Modern Journalism, 1870–1930," in Smith, *The Secular Revolution*, 414. See also David Mindich, *Just the Facts: How "Objectivity" Came to Define American Journalism* (New York: NYU Press, 1998).

14. T. J. Jackson Lears, "From Salvation to Self-Realization: Advertising and the Therapeutic Roots of the Consumer Culture, 1880–1930," in *The Culture of Consumption: Critical Essays in American History, 1880–1930*, ed. Richard Wightman Fox and T. J. Jackson Lears (New York: Pantheon, 1983), 1–38. See too Lears's remarkable book *Fables of Abundance: A Cultural History of Advertising in America* (New York: Basic Books, 1994).

15. Carroll Smith-Rosenberg, "The Cross and the Pedestal: Women, Anti-Ritualism and the American Bourgeoisie," in *Disorderly Conduct: Visions of Gender in Victorian America* (New York: Oxford, 1985), 129–64.

16. Stanton's observation about the Bible was made in her memoirs, *Eighty Years and More* (New York: European Publishing, 1898), 396. Her observation about the clergy was made in *The Women's Bible* (1895; repr., Boston: Northeastern University Press, 1993), 133, https://archive.org/details/WomansBibleElizabethCadyStanton/mode/2up.

17. Susan B. Anthony, quoted in Donna Nowak, "Women, the Church, and Equality: The Religious Paradox," history thesis, 38, p. 50, https://digital commons.buffalostate.edu/cgi/viewcontent.cgi?article=1039&context =history_theses/38.

18. Links to all of Mencken's essays on the Scopes trial and its aftermath are at https://famous-trials.com/scopesmonkey/2132-menckenaccount.

19. In addition to the primary sources of Dewey's, several secondary sources have been helpful in this review, among them Steven C. Rockefeller, *John Dewey: Religious Faith and Democratic Humanism* (New York: Columbia University Press, 1991); Alan Ryan, *John Dewey and the High Tide of American Liberalism* (New York: Norton, 1995).

20. Henry Steele Commager, *The American Mind: An Interpretation of American Thought and Character since the 1880s* (New Haven, CT: Yale University Press, 1950), 100.

21. John Dewey, "Liberty and Equality," *Social Frontier* 2 (January 1936): 105–6. This citation can be found in *The Later Works of John Dewey, 1925–1953*, ed. Jo Ann Boydston (Carbondale: Southern Illinois University Press, 1989), 11:370.

22. John Dewey, *Reconstruction in Philosophy* (New York: Dover, 1920), 212–13.

23. Dewey, *Later Works*, 14:225.

24. Dewey, "The Crisis in Culture," in *Later Works*, 5:108 (emphasis added), though he speaks of creating culture in other places in this essay as well.

25. John Dewey, "Individualism Old and New: The Crisis in Culture," *New Republic*, March 19, 1930, 126.

26. Robert B. Westbrook, *John Dewey and American Democracy* (Ithaca, NY: Cornell University Press, 1991), 365.

27. John Dewey, "Experience, Knowledge and Value: A Rejoinder," in *The Philosophy of John Dewey*, ed. Paul Arthur Schlipp (Evanston, IL: Northwestern University Press, 1939), 595.

28. John Dewey, *A Common Faith* (New Haven, CT: Yale University Press, 1934), 31 (emphasis added). The text of *A Common Faith* can be accessed through https://archive.org/details/in.ernet.dli.2015.90386/page/n7/mode/2up?q=A+comm.

29. Dewey, *A Common Faith*, 28.

30. Dewey, *A Common Faith*, 84.

31. The Conference on Science, Philosophy, and Religion and Their Relation to the Democratic Way of Life, Inc. was one important source of this opposition. In its own historical description, the gathering was founded in 1940 by such leading American intellectuals as Louis Finkelstein, Harold D. Lasswell, Mortimer J. Adler, Paul Tillich, Robert M. MacIver, Van Wyck Brooks, Franz Boas, Enrico Fermi, I. I. Rabi, and Pitirim Sorokin. Later participants included Hannah Arendt, Daniel Lerner, Perry Miller, and Bayard Rustin. Originating in a meeting of academics and seminary presidents called by Jewish Theological Seminary president (later chancellor) Louis Finkelstein in November 1939, the conference constituted a response to the rise of totalitarianism in Europe. Its founding members and their successors sought to create a framework for the preservation of democracy and intellectual freedom through the collaboration of scholars from a wide variety of disciplines in the sciences and humanities. Conference members, many of whom blamed the development of "value-free" scholarship for the rise of European fascism, additionally hoped to synthesize traditional values and academic scholarship. The conference met on a regular basis from 1940 to 1968. See Proceedings of the Conference on Science, Philosophy and Religion, JTSA, Conference on Science, Philosophy, and Religion Records, the Library of the Jewish Theological Seminary, New York, https://digitalcollections.jtsa.edu/islandora/object/jts%3A418345.

32. G. K. Chesterton, *What I Saw in America* (New York: Dodd, Mead, 1922), 293, 296 (emphasis added).

33. John Dewey, "Anti-Naturalism in Extremis," *Partisan Review* 10 (January–February 1943): 24–39, in John Dewey, *Later Works*, 15:54, https://archive.org/details/johndewey15john/page/54/mode/2up.

Notes to Pages 155–158

34. A point made by Richard Bernstein in his book *John Dewey* (New York: Washington Square, 1966), 161.
35. Dewey, *A Common Faith*, 8.
36. Dewey, *A Common Faith*, 54.
37. Dewey, *A Common Faith*, 87.
38. Dewey, *A Common Faith*, 48.
39. John Dewey, *Liberalism and Social Action* (New York: G. P. Putnam's Sons, 1935), https://archive.org/stream/dewey_liberalism/dewey_liberalism_djvu .txt, 93.
40. This was Bernstein's argument in *John Dewey*, chapter 11. Alan Ryan echoed the point, arguing that while Dewey should not be considered a religious humanist in any traditional sense, he did espouse "something one might call religious humanism . . . [yet] Dewey's 'religious' outlook illuminates his politics very much more vividly than it does the philosophy of religion as ordinarily conceived." Ryan, *John Dewey and the High Tide of Liberalism*, 12.
41. Dewey, *A Common Faith*, 25.
42. In his final report to the Massachusetts legislature, he wrote, "No student of history, or observer of mankind, can be hostile to the precepts and the doctrines of the Christian religion, or opposed to any institutions which expound and exemplify them; and no man who thinks, as I cannot but think, respecting the enduring elements of character, whether public or private, can be . . . opposed to religious instruction, and Bible instruction for the young." Horace Mann, *Twelfth Annual Report of the Board of Education* (Boston: Dutton & Wentworth, 1949), 104, https://www.google.com /books/edition/Annual_report_of_the_Board_of_Education/eURNAAAA cAAJ?hl=en&gbpv=1.
43. See Mann, *Twelfth Annual Report*, 116–17 (emphasis added), https://www .google.com/books/edition/Annual_report_of_the_Board_of_Education /eURNAAAAcAAJ?hl=en&gbpv=1&dq=inculcates+all+Christian+morals %3B+it+founds+its+morals+on+the+basis+of+religion&pg=PA117& printsec=frontcover.
44. As Mann put it,

> I believe in the existence of a great, immutable principle of natural law, or natural ethics,—a principle antecedent to all human institutions and incapable of being abrogated by any ordinances of man,—a principle of divine origin, clearly legible in the ways of Providence as those ways are manifested in the order of nature and in the history of the race,—which proves the absolute right of every human being that comes into the world to an education; and which, of course, proves the correlative duty of every government to see that the means of that education are provided for all. . . . The will of God, as conspicuously manifested in the

order of nature, and in the relations which he has established among men, places the right of every child that is born into the world to such a degree of education as will enable him, and, as far as possible will predispose him, to perform all domestic, social, civil and moral duties, upon the same clear ground of natural law and equity, as it places a child's right, upon his first coming into the world, to distend his lungs with a portion of the common air.

Tenth Annual Report to the Massachusetts Board of Education (1847), cited in *Children and Youth in America*, vol. 1, ed. Robert Bremner, John Barnard, and Temara Hareve (Cambridge, MA: Harvard University Press, 1970), 456.

45. Mustafa Kemal Emirbayer, "Moral Education in America, 1930–1990: A Contribution to the Sociology of Moral Culture" (PhD. diss., Harvard University, 1989), 100, Ann Arbor, MI: UMI Dissertation Services. It is important to note that the reforms advocated by Mann were mirrored in the evolution of the *McGuffey Readers*, the best-selling and most widely read schoolbooks of the nineteenth century: a series responsible, as one observer put it, "for the making of the American mind." According to Johann Neem, there were over 1.2 million copies of the *Readers* printed between 1836 and 1920, and they were widely used in the Midwest, the North, the South, and the expanding West (Neem, *Democracy's Schools* [Baltimore: Johns Hopkins University Press, 2017], 40n37). In line with the broadening ethos advocated by Mann, the foundations of this republican spirit shifted in the *Readers* from the theology and sectarianism of Calvinism (in the 1836 edition) to a more encompassing and certainly less sectarian ethical romanticism (found in the 1879 edition). The works mirrored the values that in home, neighborhood, and country appeared to be the ground of ultimate reality.

46. Dewey's manifesto "My Pedagogic Creed" was published in *School Journal* 54 (January 1897): 77–80.

47. John Dewey, *Human Nature and Conduct* (New York: Henry Holt, 1922), 127.

48. Dewey, "My Pedagogic Creed," 79, 80. He reiterated the point in *The School and Society*: "The chief means of continuous, graded, economical improvement and social rectification lies in utilizing the opportunities of educating the young to modify prevailing types of thought and desire." John Dewey, *The School and Society* (Chicago: University of Chicago Press, 1907), 44.

49. John Dewey, "Education and Social Change," *Bulletin of the American Association of University Professors* 23, no. 6 (1937): 474.

50. "There is a great deal of indoctrination now going on in the schools, especially with reference to narrow nationalism under the name of patriot-

ism, and with reference to the dominant economic regime." Dewey, "Education and Social Change," 472.

51. John Dewey, *Ethical Principles for Education* (Chicago: University of Chicago Press, 1897), 12.

52. Underwriting his experiential, pragmatic, and scientific educational theory was Dewey's naturalism, upon which well-being derived from the human capacity to learn from life. In this, process was primary; results were secondary. "Since the process of experience is capable of being educative, faith in democracy is all one with faith in experience and education." See John Dewey, "Creative Democracy: The Task before Us." This was originally delivered as a speech by philosopher Horace Kallen on October 20, 1939, at a dinner in honor of Dewey's eightieth birthday that he was unable to attend. See https://www.philosophie.unimuenchen.de/studium/das_fach/warum_phil_ueberhaupt/dewey_creative_democracy.pdf.

53. Biographers note that he collaborated with Catholic and Black communities to resist a resurgent Ku Klux Klan and that he even confronted Henry Ford for unfair labor practices.

54. Dewey, quoted in *Reinhold Niebuhr on Politics*, ed. Harry Davis and Robert Good (Eugene, OR: Wipf & Stock, 2007), 16. Niebuhr's concerns with the disproportionate inequalities generated by modern capitalism are present through much of his work. A fairly concise statement, however, can be found in Reinhold Niebuhr, "After Capitalism—What?" *World Tomorrow*, March 1, 1933, 203–5.

55. Reinhold Niebuhr, *The Children of Light and Children of Darkness* (Chicago: University of Chicago Press, 2011), 6.

56. Reinhold Niebuhr, *Moral Man and Immoral Society* (Louisville, KY: Westminster John Knox, 2013), xii (emphasis added).

57. Reinhold Niebuhr, "Ten Years That Shook My World," *Christian Century*, April 26, 1939, 543.

58. Niebuhr, introduction to *Moral Man*.

59. Niebuhr, *Moral Man*, 214.

60. Reinhold Niebuhr, *An Interpretation of Christian Ethics* (New York: Meridian Books, 1956), 99. See also Davis and Good, *Niebuhr on Politics*, 16.

61. Niebuhr's critique amplified that of others at that time, including Randolph Bourne and Waldo Frank. The term "cult of technique" was Bourne's.

62. The Kellogg-Briand Pact was an agreement to outlaw war signed on August 27, 1928. The pact, named after the secretary of state Frank Kellogg and the French minister of foreign affairs Aristide Briand, was one of a number of international efforts to prevent another world war. It was popular among the educated elite, but clearly ridiculous in the face of the expanding militarism of the 1930s. See Charles F. Howlett, "John Dewey and the Crusade to Outlaw War," *World Affairs* 138, no. 4 (Spring 1976).

63. John Dewey, *Philosophy and Civilization* (New York: Minton, Balch, 1932),

328, https://archive.org/details/philosophycivilioodewe/mode/2up?ref=ol
&view=theater&q=slogans.

64. See Niebuhr, *An Interpretation of Christian Ethics.*

65. Niebuhr, *Moral Man*, xiii.

66. Niebuhr, *An Interpretation of Christian Ethics*, 138.

67. Niebuhr, *Children of Light*, 22.

68. Alden Whitman, "Reinhold Niebuhr Is Dead; Protestant Theologian, 78,"
New York Times, June 2, 1971, 1.

69. Niebuhr, *Moral Man*, xv–xvi.

70. Niebuhr, *An Interpretation of Christian Ethics*, 32. Christopher Lasch is
an invaluable guide for me here. See his book *The True and Only Heaven:
Progress and Its Critics* (New York: Norton, 1991), 372.

71. Davis and Good, *Niebuhr on Politics*, 66.

72. Niebuhr, *Moral Man*, 231.

73. This section draws from chapter 9 of Niebuhr, *Moral Man*, 248–55.

74. Niebuhr, *Moral Man*, 255.

75. Niebuhr, *An Interpretation of Christian Ethics*, 204.

76. This draws from Christopher Lasch's discussion of Niebuhr in *The True
and Only Heaven*, 275–76.

Chapter Eight. A Fragile Humanism

1. Arthur M. Schlesinger Jr., *The Vital Center* (1949; repr., New Brunswick,
NJ: Transaction, 1998). Citations come from this later version.

2. Schlesinger, *Vital Center*, xii.

3. Schlesinger, *Vital Center*, 255.

4. Schlesinger, *Vital Center*, 206.

5. Schlesinger, *Vital Center*, 248, 10, 254.

6. Schlesinger, *Vital Center*, 248–49 (emphasis added).

7. Schlesinger, *Vital Center*, 255, 251, 256, 245.

8. Schlesinger, *Vital Center*, 245 (emphasis added).

9. Schlesinger, *Vital Center*, 246.

10. Walter Lippmann, *The Public Philosophy* (Boston: Little, Brown, 1955), 15,
63 (emphasis added).

11. Ronald Steele, *Walter Lippmann and the American Century* (Boston: Little,
Brown, 1980), 484.

12. Steele, *Lippmann and the American Century*, 267.

13. Walter Lippmann, *Drift and Mastery* (New York: Mitchell, 1914), 285. The
text was accessed through https://archive.org/details/driftmasteryatteoo
lipp.

14. Lippmann, *Drift and Mastery*, 285–86.

15. Accessible through https://archive.org/details/in.ernet.dli.2015.188702
/page/n3/mode/2up.

16. Lippmann, *The Public Philosophy*, 123.
17. Lippmann quotes F. de Zulueta, "The Science of Law," in *The Legacy of Rome*, ed. Cyril Bailey (Oxford: Clarendon, 1928), 202, in Lippmann, *The Public Philosophy*, 107n14.
18. Lippmann, *The Public Philosophy*, 107–8, 166–68.
19. Lippmann, *The Public Philosophy*, 104ff., 160ff.
20. Lippmann, *The Public Philosophy*, 138ff.
21. Lippmann, *The Public Philosophy*, 101, 123, 135, 172. Speaking of the freedom of speech, he writes that "on the postulate that there was a universal order on which all reasonable men were agreed, . . . it was safe to permit, and it would be desirable to encourage, dissent and dispute" (100).
22. Lippmann, *The Public Philosophy*, 109, 160–61.
23. Lippmann, *The Public Philosophy*, 176ff., 179. In this observation, Lippmann is approvingly quoting Bertrand Russell.
24. For a representative sample of Adler's views, see Mortimer Adler, *The Great Ideas: A Lexicon of Western Thought* (New York: Macmillan, 1992).
25. Russell Kirk, *The American Cause* (1957; repr., Wilmington, DE: ISI Books, 2014).
26. John Courtney Murray, *We Hold These Truths: Catholic Reflections on the American Proposition* (New York: Sheed & Ward, 1960).
27. See George Marsden, *The Twilight of the American Enlightenment* (New York: Basic Books, 2014), 53–54.
28. James Bryant Conant, ed., *General Education in a Free Society: Report of the Harvard Committee* (Cambridge, MA: Harvard University Press, 1950), https://archive.org/details/generaleducation032440mbp/page/n15/mode/2up.
29. Conant, *General Education in a Free Society*, xv.
30. Conant, *General Education in a Free Society*, 46, 39, 4.
31. Conant, *General Education in a Free Society*, 39–41.
32. Conant, *General Education in a Free Society*, 50–51.
33. Conant, *General Education in a Free Society*, 59, 4.
34. Conant, *General Education in a Free Society*, 76.
35. Conant, *General Education in a Free Society*, 45ff., 48.
36. Conant, *General Education in a Free Society*, 40 (emphasis added).
37. Theodore Blegen reaffirmed the point: "The central value of the humanities to American culture" is that they train an individual "to perform his duties in a democratic society, as important even as acquaintance with the persons and the current events on which he is called to pass. There is no substitute for an open mind enriched by reading and the arts. . . . The humanities are essential to political wisdom." Theodore C. Blegen, "The Prospect for the Liberal Arts," *Quarterly Journal of Speech* 40, no. 4 (December 1954). In his own manifesto, *One Great Society: Humane Learning in the United States* (New York: Harcourt, Brace, 1959), Howard Mumford Jones, the president of the American Council of Learned Societies,

stressed how the humanities are useful for American progress on the international scene as they help with American defense, the containment of communities, forming good diplomatic relations, and international business, in large part because they cultivate "political wisdom," "informed sympathy," and "personal detachment," all of which tend to curb provincialism (76–78).

38. *Report of the Commission on the Humanities* (New York: American Council of Learned Societies, 1964), 1–3, https://publications.acls.org/NEH/Report-of-the-Commission-on-the-Humanities-1964.pdf.

39. *Report of the Commission on the Humanities*, 4.

40. National Foundation on the Arts and the Humanities Act of 1965 (P.L. 89-209), https://www.neh.gov/about/history/national-foundation-arts-and-humanities-act-1965-pl-89-209.

41. Given on January 9, 1961, to the Massachusetts legislature. See https://www.jfklibrary.org/node/11516.

42. See Robert Wuthnow's review of the literature on this subtle transformation in his book *The Restructuring of American Religion* (Princeton, NJ: Princeton University Press), 1989.

43. Sinclair Lewis, *Main Street*, chapter 1, accessed at https://www.gutenberg.org/files/543/543-h/543-h.htm.

44. "Norman Rockwell: A Brief Biography," Norman Rockwell Museum, https://www.nrm.org/about/about-2/about-norman-rockwell/.

45. Cited from Dwight D. Eisenhower Presidential Library, Museum, & Boyhood Home website, https://www.eisenhowerlibrary.gov/eisenhowers/quotes.

46. Will Herberg, *Protestant, Catholic, Jew* (New York: Doubleday, 1955), 38–39.

47. Herberg, *Protestant, Catholic, Jew*, 257–58.

48. See Joel Carpenter, *Revive Us Again: The Remaking of American Fundamentalism* (New York: Oxford University Press, 1997), for a comprehensive historiography of this period in American conservative Protestantism.

49. Herberg, *Protestant, Catholic, Jew*, chapters 1 and 2.

50. Steven K. Green, *The Bible, the School, and the Constitution* (New York: Oxford University Press, 2012).

51. Herberg, *Protestant, Catholic, Jew*, 258.

52. This data is summarized in Susan Hansen, *Religion and Reaction* (Lanham, MD: Rowman & Littlefield, 2011), 26–27. See also Clyde Wilcox and Ted Jelen, "Evangelicals and Political Tolerance," *American Politics Research* 18 (1990): 25–46.

53. Mark Greif, *The Age of the Crisis of Man* (Princeton, NJ: Princeton University Press, 2016). Greif's masterful book highlights the intellectual side of this humanism, focusing on fiction and nonfiction writing during this period. Given the focus of the book, it is not unreasonable that he didn't address the elective affinities within popular religious culture. At this point

it should be clear that though they drew from different sources, they were part of the same fabric.

54. Martin Luther King Jr., "The Christian Doctrine of Man," sermon delivered at the Detroit Council of Churches' Noon Lenten Services, March 12, 1958, in *The Papers of Martin Luther King, Jr.*, vol. 6, *Advocate of the Social Gospel*, ed. C. Carson, S. Carson, Susan Englander, Troy Jackson, and Gerald Smith, https://kinginstitute.stanford.edu/king-papers/documents /christian-doctrine-man-sermon-delivered-detroit-council-churches -noon-lenten#ftnref6. This section draws from the helpful archival research in William G. Thompson, "An Experiment in Love: Martin Luther King and the Re-imagining of American Democracy," (PhD. diss., Department of Religious Studies, University of Virginia, 2015).

55. From King's "I Have a Dream" address, https://kinginstitute.stanford .edu/king-papers/documents/i-have-dream-address-delivered-march -washington-jobs-and-freedom.

56. See Martin Luther King, "Six Talks Based on Beliefs That Matter by William Adams Brown," https://kinginstitute.stanford.edu/king-papers /documents/six-talks-based-beliefs-matter-william-adams-brown#ftn ref2; Clayborne Carson et al., eds., *The Papers of Martin Luther King, Jr.*, vol. 1, *Called to Serve* (Berkeley: University of California Press, 1991), 281.

57. He used this term in a talk to a group of students at Barratt Junior High School in Philadelphia on October 26, 1967, available at https://projects .seattletimes.com/mlk/words-blueprint.html.

58. Carson et al., *The Papers of Martin Luther King, Jr.*, vol. 1, 109–11.

59. Martin Luther King Jr., in *A Testament of Hope: The Essential Writings and Speeches of Martin Luther King, Jr.*, ed. James M. Washington (San Francisco: Harper, 1986), 17.

60. King, "I Have a Dream."

61. Martin Luther King Jr., "The Negro and the Constitution," https://king institute.stanford.edu/king-papers/documents/negro-and-constitution.

62. Martin Luther King Jr., *Where Do We Go from Here?* (Boston: Beacon, 1968), 196, https://archive.org/details/wheredowegofromhooking_0.

63. These observations are derived from a 1967 speech by the same name, "Where Do We Go from Here?" See https://kinginstitute.stanford.edu /where-do-we-go-here#:~:text=where%20we%20are.-,Where%20 do%20we%20go%20from%20here%3F,be%20ashamed%20of%20 being%20black.

64. King, "Where Do We Go from Here?"

65. King, "Where Do We Go from Here?"

66. King, "I Have a Dream."

67. Martin Luther King Jr., "The Man Who Was a Fool," sermon delivered at the Detroit Council of Churches' Noon Lenten Services, March 6, 1961, https://kinginstitute.stanford.edu/king-papers/documents/man-who -was-fool-sermon-delivered-detroit-council-churches-noon-lenten.

68. Clayborne Carson et al., eds., *The Papers of Martin Luther King, Jr.*, vol. 4 (Berkeley: University of California Press, 2000), 318–19.

69. King, "I Have a Dream."

70. This was from his lecture "The Power of Non-violence," in King, *A Testament of Hope*, chapter 3.

71. King, "Where Do We Go from Here?" 84.

72. King, "I Have a Dream."

73. United States Congress, House Committee on Education and Labor, Select Subcommittee on Labor, *To Establish a National Commission on Negro History and Culture: Hearing, Ninetieth Congress, second session, on H.R. 12962. March 18, 1968* (Washington, DC: U.S. Government Printing Office).

74. See James Baldwin, "The Nigger We Invent," *Integrated Education* 7, no. 2 (March–April 1969): 15–22. A transcript of this testimony can also be found at http://johnshaplin.blogspot.com/2011/01/james-baldwins-testimony.html.

75. An observation made by Charles Taylor in "Cross-Purposes: The Liberal Communitarian Debate," in *Liberalism and the Moral Life*, ed. Nancy L. Rosenblum (Cambridge, MA: Harvard University Press, 1989), 174.

Chapter Nine. The Evolving Culture War

1. Martin Luther King Jr., "Loving Your Enemies," sermon delivered at the Detroit Council of Churches' Noon Lenten Services, March 7, 1961, https://kinginstitute.stanford.edu/king-papers/documents/loving -your-enemies-sermon-delivered-detroit-council-churches-noon -lenten (emphasis added). Elsewhere, he argued that "We are called to speak for the weak, for the voiceless, for victims of our nation *and for those it calls enemy*, for no document from human hands can make these humans any less our brothers. . . . Have they forgotten that my ministry is in obedience to the one who loved his enemies so fully that he died for them?" King, quoted in *A Testament of Hope: The Essential Writings and Speeches of Martin Luther King Jr.*, ed. James M. Washington (San Francisco, CA: Harper, 1986), 234.

2. The architects of neoliberalism are well known: Ludwig von Mises, Friedrich Hayek, James Buchanan, and Milton Friedman, and their combined scholarly *corpora* is voluminous. Among the secondary works of note are Thomas Biebricher, *The Political Theory of Neoliberalism* (Stanford, CA: Stanford University Press, 2018); Wendy Brown, *Undoing the Demos* (New York: Zone Books, 2015), as well as *In the Ruins of Neoliberalism* (New York: Columbia University Press, 2019); David Harvey, *A Brief History of Neoliberalism* (New York: Oxford University Press, 2005); and Quinn Slobodian, *Globalists: The End of Empire and the Birth of Neoliberalism* (Cambridge, MA: Harvard University Press, 2018).

3. Friedrich Hayek, *The Road to Serfdom* (London: Routledge, 1944), 10, https://archive.org/details/in.ernet.dli.2015.46585/page/n5/mode/2up. The iconic statement in which he makes the relationship clear was put as

a warning: "We have progressively abandoned that freedom in economic affairs without which personal and political freedom has never existed in the past."

4. Milton Friedman, "The Relationship between Economic and Political Freedom," in *Capitalism and Freedom* (Chicago: University of Chicago Press, 1982), 17.

5. As Hayek put it, coercion is "when one man's actions are made to serve another man's will, not for his own but for the other's purpose." By contrast, liberty is when "coercion of some by others is reduced as much as possible in society." See F. Hayek, *The Constitution of Liberty*, vol. 17 (1960; repr., Chicago: University of Chicago Press, 2011), 133 and 11, respectively. Milton Friedman made the same point, arguing that he "define[d] freedom as the absence of coercion of one person by another." See his essay "Free Markets and Free Speech," *Harvard Journal of Law and Public Policy* 10, no. 1 (Winter 1987): 1–9, keynote address given at the Federalist Society National Symposium held at Stanford University Law School on March 7, 1986.

6. I say "in all its forms" because Hayek recognized that socialism did not take form in only one movement or one political party. His dedication in *The Road to Serfdom* is "To the Socialists of All Parties."

7. Kevin Vallier, "Neoliberalism," in *The Stanford Encyclopedia of Philosophy*, ed. Edward N. Zalta and Uri Nodelman (Winter 2022), https://plato.stanford.edu/archives/win2022/entries/neoliberalism/.

8. Hayek, *The Road to Serfdom*, 177.

9. Friedman, "Free Markets and Free Speech," 8. In his book on political philosophy *The Limits of Liberty* (Chicago: University of Chicago Press, 1975), chapter 1, James Buchanan, in his radical and anarchic individualist framework, argued that there was and is no morality except what individuals happen to agree to.

10. Friedman, "The Relationship between Economic and Political Freedom," 18.

11. Robert N. Bellah, Richard Madsen, William M. Sullivan, Ann Swidler, and Steven M. Tipton, *Habits of the Heart* (Berkeley: University of California Press, 1985).

12. The sum and substance of this paragraph comes from Buchanan's opening chapter in *The Limits of Liberty*, 2, 3, 4, 6, 10.

13. A point made by Hayek in *The Constitution of Liberty*, 140.

14. Friedman, "The Relationship between Economic and Political Freedom," 16, 15 (emphasis added).

15. Ruth Ellen Wasem, "How a 1965 Immigration Law Forever Changed the Makeup of America," *The Hill*, October 3, 2020, https://thehill.com/opinion/immigration/519189-how-a-1965-immigration-law-forever-changed-the-makeup-of-america/.

16. Thomas Nagel, "Rawls on Justice," *Philosophical Review* 82, no. 2 (1973): 220–34, reprinted in Norman Daniels, ed., *Reading Rawls* (Oxford: Blackwell, 1975); Michael Sandel, *Liberalism and the Limits of Justice* (Cambridge: Cambridge University Press, 1982); Michael Teitelman, "The Limits of Individualism," *Journal of Philosophy* 69 (1972): 545–56.

17. Jim Wallis, "Post-American Christianity," *Post-American* (Fall 1971). In 1975, the magazine changed its name to *Sojourners*.

18. Philip Gorski, *American Covenant* (Princeton, NJ: Princeton University Press, 2017), 180.

19. Robert Wuthnow, "Recent Pattern of Secularization: A Problem of Generations?" *American Sociological Review* 41 (1976): 850–67; Robert Wuthnow, *The Restructuring of American Religion* (Princeton, NJ: Princeton University Press, 1988), 155–58.

20. Ronald Steele, *Walter Lippmann and the American Century* (Boston: Little, Brown, 1980), 592.

21. Martin Marty, "Tensions within Contemporary Evangelicalism: A Critical Appraisal," in *The Evangelicals: What They Believe, Who They Are, Where They Are Changing*, ed. David Wells and John Woodbridge (Nashville: Abingdon, 1976), 170–88.

22. Robert Wuthnow, "The Political Rebirth of American Evangelicalism," in *The New Christian Right: Mobilization and Legitimation*, ed. Robert Liebman and R. Wuthnow (New York: Aldine, 1983), 168–87.

23. I make no pretense to catalogue all of the disputes and organizations involved in this period. They were myriad. My main concern is to point to what was at stake institutionally. I draw liberally from prior work of mine on the subject. See J. D. Hunter, *Culture Wars: The Struggle to Define America* (New York: Basic Books, 1991); and J. D. Hunter and Alan Wolfe, *Is There a Culture War?* (Washington, DC: Brookings Institution Press, 2006).

24. Press citations are taken from Hunter, *Culture Wars*, 179–80.

25. National Organization for Women (NOW) Statement of Purpose, adopted on October 29, 1966, at its organizing conference. See https://web.archive .org/web/20150117134328/http://coursesa.matrix.msu.edu/~hst306 /documents/nowstate.html.

26. This account was told in Jonathan Zimmerman's wonderful treatment of conflict in education, *Whose America? Culture Wars in the Public Schools* (Chicago: University of Chicago Press, 2022), 98–99, 240.

27. When the Gallup Organization first asked the question in the early to mid-1970s, between two-thirds and three-fourths of the general public responded that they had a great deal or fair amount of trust in the media as a source of news and information. By 2019, the national average had declined to 41 percent. The partisan divide was revealing. Among Republicans, the figure was 15 percent, among independents, it was 36 percent,

and among Democrats, it was 69 percent. Megan Brenan, "Americans' Trust in Mass Media Edges Down to 41%," Gallup, https://news.gallup .com/poll/267047/americans-trust-mass-media-edges-down.aspx.

28. Tim LaHaye, National Right to Life Committee, direct mail appeal, May 1988.

29. Cited in Patrick Buchanan, "CBS: 'Conservative Broadcasting System,'" *Human Events*, February 16, 1985, 137.

30. Kennedy is quoted in James Reston, "Washington; Kennedy and Bork," *New York Times*, July 5, 1987, section 4, 15, https://www.nytimes.com /1987/07/05/opinion/washington-kennedy-and-bork.html.

31. William T. Cavanaugh, "A Nation with the Church's Soul: Richard John Neuhaus and Reinhold Niebuhr on Church and Politics," *Political Theology* 14, no. 3 (2013): 386–96.

32. Neuhaus had long been an advocate of a strong relationship between Christianity and Judaism, and his commitment to a strong relationship with evangelicalism was cemented by his leadership in producing the statement "Evangelicals and Catholics Together: Christian Mission in the Third Millennium," *First Things*, May 1994.

33. Daniel McCarthy, "Richard John Neuhaus," *New York Times*, March 26, 2015.

34. Randy Boyagoda, *Richard John Neuhaus: A Life in the Public Square* (New York: Image, 2015), 163.

35. Richard John Neuhaus, "Our American Babylon," *First Things*, December 2005, https://www.firstthings.com/article/2005/12/our-american-babylon.

36. Neuhaus, "Our American Babylon."

37. Neuhaus, "Our American Babylon."

38. Neuhaus, "Our American Babylon."

39. James Madison, *A Memorial and Remonstrance on the Religious Rights of Man* (Washington, DC: S. C. Ustick, 1828), 4. See https://archive.org/details /amemorialandremoomadigoog/mode/2up.

40. Neuhaus, "Our American Babylon." See also R. J. Neuhaus, "Turning the First Amendment on Its Head," *First Things*, September 26, 2008, https:// www.firstthings.com/web-exclusives/2008/09/turning-the-first-amend ment-on.

41. Richard John Neuhaus, *The Naked Public Square* (Grand Rapids, MI: Eerdmans, 1984).

42. Michelle Boston, "How a Russian Jewish Kid from Shanghai Came to Take on the American President," https://dornsife.usc.edu/news/stories /2667/how-a-russian-jewish-kid-from-shanghai-came-to-take-on-the -ameri/.

43. Laurence Tribe, *The Invisible Constitution* (New York: Oxford University Press, 2008).

44. Tribe, *Invisible Constitution*, 28–29, 188.

45. Tribe, *Invisible Constitution*, 52, 46.

46. Tribe, *Invisible Constitution*, 40, 46, 188.
47. Tribe, *Invisible Constitution*, 55.
48. Tribe, *Invisible Constitution*, 42.
49. Tribe, *Invisible Constitution*, 42.
50. Tribe, *Invisible Constitution*, 42.
51. Tribe, *Invisible Constitution*, 42, 58.
52. Tribe, *Invisible Constitution*, 45.
53. Tribe, *Invisible Constitution*, 203, 120, 169–70, 124–25, 147.
54. The question of authority was key to my earlier work *Culture Wars*. An important empirical observation in my argument about the centrality of authority was recognition of the ways in which competing conceptions of authority cut across the age-old divisions between Protestants and Catholics and Jews: the orthodox traditions in these faiths now have much more in common with one another than they do with progressives in their own faith tradition and vice versa. The polarity of *this* axis seemed to better account for variation of opinions and positions on a wide range of popular domestic disputes—abortion, sexuality, the changing role of women and the evolving nature of the family, church-state issues, funding for the arts, and so on—than did traditional axes such as religious affiliation, gender, socioeconomic standing, and race/ethnicity.
55. R. J. Neuhaus, "The Upside Down Freedom," *Christianity Today*, December 9, 1988, 24. See also Neuhaus, "Turning the First Amendment on Its Head."
56. Laurence H. Tribe, *American Constitutional Law* (St. Paul, MN: Foundation, 1978), section 14-4, 823.
57. Laurence H. Tribe, "Forward: Toward a Model of Roles in the Due Process of Life and Law," *Harvard Law Review* 87, no. 1 (1973): 21–23.
58. See L. Tribe, *Abortion* (New York: Norton, 1992) as well as Kermit Roosevelt III, "The Indivisible Constitution," Faculty Scholarship at Penn Law, 286, https://scholarship.law.upen.edu/faculty_scholarship/286; and Neuhaus, "Our American Babylon."
59. I made this comparison in an earlier work, *Before the Shooting Begins* (New York: Free Press, 1994). I cite Tribe here, but compare his statement to one made by the novelist Walker Percy. Percy also wrote about the principle of destroying human life "for what may appear to be the most admirable social reasons." The power of the principle, he noted, could be illustrated by the book published in the 1920s by Karl Binding (a prominent jurist) and Alfred Hoche (a prominent psychiatrist) entitled *The Justification of the Destruction of Life Devoid of Value* (Leipzig: Felix Meiner, 1920). The book made a case for improving the lot of the German population, socially and genetically, by getting rid of the unfit and the unwanted. All of this occurred in the Weimar Republic, long before the Nazis and Hitler came to power, but it is well known what use the Nazis eventually made of these ideas. Percy's statement was written as a letter to the *New*

York Times, which did not publish it. His letter and a follow-up letter were published in Walker Percy, *Signposts in a Strange Land*, ed. Patrick Samway (New York: Noonday, 1991).

60. Richard John Neuhaus, "The Way We Are, The Way They Were: Bioethics and the Holocaust," *First Things*, March 1990, https://www.first things.com/article/1990/03/the-way-they-were-the-way-we-are-bioethics -and-the-holocaust.

61. Tribe, *Abortion*, 58.

62. Others have made this observation as well. See Michael Kelly, "You Ain't Seen Nothing Yet," *New Yorker*, April 25, 1995, 40–46.

63. André LeDuc, "The Ontological Foundations of the Debate over Originalism," *Washington University Jurisprudence Review* 263 (2015), https:// openscholarship.wustl.edu/law_jurisprudence/vol7/iss2/7/.

64. See, for example, Steven Brint, "What If They Gave a War . . . ?" *Contemporary Sociology* 21, no. 4 (1992): 438–40; Christian Smith et al., "The Myth of Culture Wars," *Culture: Newsletter of the Sociology of Culture, American Sociological Association* 11, no. 1 (1996): 1, 7–10; Paul DiMaggio, John Evans, and Bethany Bryson, "Have Americans' Social Attitudes Become More Polarized?" *American Journal of Sociology* 102, no. 3 (1996): 690–755; Nancy Davis and Robert V. Robinson, "Are the Rumors of War Exaggerated? Religious Orthodoxy and Moral Progressivism in America," *American Journal of Sociology* 102, no. 3 (1996): 756–87; Nancy Davis and Robert V. Robinson, "Religious Orthodoxy in American Society: The Myth of a Monolithic Camp," *Journal for the Scientific Study of Religion* 35, no. 3 (1996): 229–45; Randall Balmer, "Culture Wars: Views from the Ivory Tower," *Evangelical Studies Bulletin* 10, no. 1 (1993): 1–2; Jeremy Rabkin, "The Culture War That Isn't," *Policy Review*, no. 96 (1999): 3–19; Alan Wolfe, *One Nation, After All: What Middle Class Americans Really Think about God, Country, Family, Racism, Welfare, Immigration, Homosexuality, Work, the Right, the Left, and Each Other* (New York: Viking Penguin, 1998), 320–21; Wayne Baker, *America's Crisis of Values* (Princeton, NJ: Princeton University Press, 2005), 109; Morris Fiorina, "What Culture War?" *Wall Street Journal*, July 22, 2004, A14.

65. Morris Fiorina, *Culture War? The Myth of a Polarized America* (New York: Pearson, Longman, 2005).

66. See the timelines for the legalization of gay rights nationally and internationally provided by Equaldex: https://www.equaldex.com/timeline /2000s.

67. The timeline of the founding of gay rights organizations nationally and internationally can be found here: https://www.equaldex.com/organizations /timeline.

68. The term *#MeToo* was introduced by the sexual assault survivor and activist Tarana Burke in 2006. The Black Lives Matter movement emerged

after the shooting death of Trayvon Martin in 2012 and Michael Brown and Eric Garner in 2014. Critical race theory, of course, which fueled BLM intellectually, traces back to the early 1970s.

69. Matt Stoller, "How Democrats Killed Their Populist Soul," *Atlantic*, October 24, 2016.

70. Data from Mark Muro and Jacob Whiton, "America Has Two Economies and They Are Diverging Fast," Brookings Institution, https://www.brookings.edu/blog/the-avenue/2019/09/10/america-has-two-economies-and-theyre-diverging-fast. From 2008 to 2018, gross domestic product increased by 36 percent in Democratic districts and declined by 2.1 percent in Republican districts. Likewise, household income grew 13 percent in Democratic districts and sank by 3.6 percent in Republican districts. In educational attainment, the number of adults with a college degree grew from 28.4 percent to 35.6 percent in Democratic districts compared to 26.6 percent to 27.8 percent in Republican districts. These data can be found in Adam Bonica and Howard Rosenthal, "The Wealth Elasticity of Political Contributions by the Forbes 400," September 26, 2015, https://ssrn.com/abstract=2668780 or http://dx.doi.org/10.2139/ssrn.2668780. See also Adam Bonica, Nolan McCarty, Keith T. Poole, and Howard Rosenthal, "Why Hasn't Democracy Slowed Rising Inequality?" *Journal of Economic Perspectives* 27, no. 3 (2013): 103–24.

71. See Muro and Whiton, "America Has Two Economies"; Thomas Edsall, "Has the Democratic Party Gotten Too Rich for Its Own Good?" *New York Times*, June 1, 2017, https://www.nytimes.com/2017/06/01/opinion/democratic-party-rich-thomas-edsall.html.

72. Kofi Lomotey, quoted in Arthur Schlesinger Jr., *The Disuniting of America: Reflections on a Multicultural Society* (New York: Norton, 1998), 67.

73. From the report "A Curriculum of Inclusion, Report of the Commissioner's Task Force on Minorities: Equity and Excellence," July 1989, referenced in Schlesinger, *The Disuniting of America*, 72, 187.

74. Maulana Karenga, referenced by Schlesinger, *The Disuniting of America*, 67.

75. Schlesinger, *The Disuniting of America*, 13, 14, 23. It was in the radical versions of multiculturalism that early efforts were made to "decenter" white culture and to recenter the cultures of all those who have been oppressed: most importantly, people of African, Hispanic, and Asian heritage and women. In the late 1980s and 1990s, this conclusion led to arguments and policies in favor of "Black English" or "Ebonics"; new histories that argued for the placement of Africa as the source of Western civilization and its achievements in science and philosophy; Afro-, ethno-, and feminist curricula; and resegregation of schools, fraternities, businesses, and neighborhoods (as in the proposed city of Mandela, Massachusetts, in 1986 and 1988). In their net effect, these arguments tended to sanction separate racial and ethnic identities.

76. Schlesinger, *The Disuniting of America*, 19–21. Schlesinger was referring to the *idea* of the melting pot, not so much its *reality*. Bourne described an America whose recent immigrants were resisting assimilation rather than complying with it. See Randolph Bourne, "Trans-National America," *Atlantic* 118, no. 1 (1916): 86–97.

77. Wendy Brown, "Wounded Attachments," *Political Theory* 21, no. 3 (August 1993): 394–95.

78. Stephen Hawkins, Daniel Yudkin, Miriam Juan-Torres, and Tim Dixon, *Hidden Tribes: A Study of America's Polarized Landscape* (New York: More in Common, 2018).

79. On the rifts within progressive organizations, see Ryan Grimm, "The Elephant in the Room," *Intercept*, June 13, 2022, https://theintercept .com/2022/06/13/progressive-organizing-infighting-callout-culture/; John Harris, "The Left Goes to War with Itself," *Politico*, June 23, 2022, https://www.politico.com/news/magazine/2022/06/23/the-new-battles -roiling-the-left-00041627; Molly Redden, "Inside the Left's Post-Trump Reckoning," *HuffPost*, June 17, 2022, https://www.huffpost.com/entry /aclu-trump-presidency-turmoil_n_62aa0e54e4b06169ca93c6a2; and Zack Colman, "Justice or Overreach?" *Politico*, June 19, 2022, https://www .politico.com/news/2022/06/19/big-green-justice-environment-00040148.

80. Ruy Teixeira, quoted in Thomas Edsall, "Democrats Can't Just Give the People What They Want," *New York Times*, October 13, 2021, https://www .nytimes.com/2021/10/13/opinion/david-shor-biden-democrats.html. Teixeira writes for the center-left Substack *The Liberal Patriot*.

81. At an LGBT campaign fundraising event in New York City on September 9, 2016, Clinton gave a speech in which she said:

> I know there are only 60 days left to make our case—and don't get complacent; don't see the latest outrageous, offensive, inappropriate comment and think, "Well, he's done this time." We are living in a volatile political environment. You know, to just be grossly generalistic, you could put half of Trump's supporters into what I call the basket of deplorables. (Laughter/applause) Right? (Laughter/applause) They're racist, sexist, homophobic, xenophobic, Islamophobic—you name it. And unfortunately, there are people like that. And he has lifted them up. He has given voice to their websites that used to only have 11,000 people— now have 11 million. He tweets and retweets their offensive hateful mean-spirited rhetoric. Now, some of those folks—they are irredeemable, but thankfully, they are not America.

Hillary Clinton, CBS News, https://en.wikipedia.org/wiki/Basket_of _deplorables—cite_note-10. Listening to the speech, one is struck as much by the spontaneous eruption of laughter and applause as by the verbal characterization itself.

82. J. D. Hunter, Carl Desportes Bowman, and Kyle Puetz, *Democracy in Dark Times* (Charlottesville, VA: Finstock & Tew, 2020).

83. A leader in the Charismatic movement, Lance Wallnau, published two books laying out this case: *God's Chaos Candidate: Donald J. Trump and the American Unraveling* (Keller, TX: Killer Sheep Media, 2016); and *God's Chaos Code: The Shocking Blueprint That Reveals 5 Keys to the Destiny of the Nation* (Keller, TX: Killer Sheep Media, 2020). And then there was a film that dramatized this message: *The Trump Prophecy* was produced in 2018. According to its description, "When Mary Colbert hears Mark's message she feels called to start a national prayer movement across the nation for the leadership of America and a return to the godly principles they were founded upon" (https://www.imdb.com/title/tt8235296/).

84. And yet the leader of Israel at the time, Benjamin Netanyahu, on a visit to Washington, called Trump Cyrus's heir, and the Mikdash Educational Center minted a commemorative "Temple Coin" depicting Trump and Cyrus side by side in honor of Trump's decision to move the American embassy in Israel to Jerusalem. See Tara Isabella Burton, "The Biblical Story the Christian Right Uses to Defend Trump," *Vox*, March 15, 2018, https://www.vox.com/identities/2018/3/5/16796892/trump-cyrus-christian-right-bible-cbn-evangelical-propaganda.

85. Mary Eberstadt, "Dangerous to Believe: Religious Freedom and Its Enemies," *Time*, June 29, 2016, https://time.com/4385755/faith-in-america/.

86. "American Views of Intolerance and Religious Liberty in America," Lifeway Research, September 14–28, 2015, https://research.lifeway.com/wp-content/uploads/2016/03/American-Views-on-Intolerance-and-Religious-Liberty-Sept-2015.pdf; Robert Jones, Daniel Cox, E. J. Dionne, William Galston, Betsy Cooper, and Rachel Lienesch, "How Immigration and Concern about Cultural Changes Are Shaping the 2016 Election," PRRI/Brookings Immigration Survey, June 23, 2016; National Association of Evangelicals, "Most U.S. Evangelicals Expect Persecution in Coming Years," November 28, 2016, https://www.nae.org/u-s-evangelical-leaders-expect-persecution-coming-years/.

87. Andrew R. Lewis, "The Transformation of the Christian Right's Moral Politics," *Forum* 17, no. 1 (2019): 25–44, https://doi.org/10.1515/for-2019-0001.

88. So far as I can tell, the Left's framing of politics as identity was adopted by the Right, but once adopted, it hardened lines on the left, furthering, in turn, a dialectic of antagonistic dependency.

89. According to one survey of evangelical leaders in late 2016, 32 percent indicated that they had already been persecuted socially, financially, and politically for their faith, and 76 percent expected that they would be persecuted in the future. This survey was reported by the National Association of Evangelicals, "Most U.S. Evangelicals Expect Persecution in Coming Years." See https://www.nae.org/u-s-evangelical-leaders-expect-persecution-coming-years/.

Chapter Ten. Exhaustion

1. Criticisms of the Enlightenment can be found across the intellectual spectrum. The iconic critique of the Frankfurt School was Max Horkheimer and Theodor Adorno, *Dialectic of Enlightenment* (Stanford, CA: Stanford University Press, 2002). Among post-structuralists and postmodernists, there was Jean-François Lyotard, *The Postmodern Condition* (Minneapolis: University of Minnesota Press, 1984); and Michel Foucault, *Discipline and Punishment* (New York: Vintage, 1979), along with his essay "Tomb of the Intellectual," in *Political Writings* (Minneapolis: University of Minnesota Press, 1993). Among Black scholars, there was Charles Mills, *The Racial Contract* (Ithaca, NY: Cornell University Press, 1977); and Cornel West, *Prophesy Deliverance! An Afro-American Revolutionary Christianity* (Louisville, KY: Westminster John Knox, 2002). Among feminists there was Jane Flax, "Is Enlightenment Emancipatory?" in *Disputed Subjects: Essays on Psychoanalysis, Politics, and Philosophy* (New York: Routledge, 1993); and Susan Hekman, *Gender and Knowledge* (Boston: Northeastern University Press, 1990). Among communitarians, the most prominent criticism came from Alastair MacIntyre, *After Virtue* (South Bend, IN: University of Notre Dame Press, 1984); and Charles Taylor, *Sources of the Self* (Cambridge, MA: Harvard University Press, 1989). Among conservatives, one can point to Isaiah Berlin, "The Counter-Enlightenment," in *The Proper Study of Mankind*, ed. Henry Hardy and Roger Hausheer (New York: Farrar, Straus & Giroux, 1998), 243–46; Michael Oakeshott, "The New Bentham," in *Rationalism in Politics and Other Essays* (Indianapolis: Liberty Fund, 1991); Leo Strauss, "Progress or Return? The Contemporary Crisis in Western Civilization," in *An Introduction to Political Philosophy: Ten Essays by Leo Strauss*, ed. Hilail Gildin (Detroit: Wayne State University Press, 1989); and Eric Voegelin, *From Enlightenment to Revolution* (Durham, NC: Duke University Press, 1975).

2. R. Rorty, "Trotsky and the Wild Orchids," *Common Knowledge* 1, no. 3 (1992): 140–53.

3. Rorty's attempt to construct an anti-metaphysical Dewey has been the subject of fierce debate in the main organ of American pragmatist thought, the *Transactions of the Charles S. Peirce Society*, with most of the pragmatists coming down against Rorty. While we can safely let the minutiae lie, it is worth summarizing where Rorty's Dewey and Dewey himself seem to part company. To begin, in *Philosophy and the Mirror of Nature*, the book in which Rorty broke publicly with analytic philosophy, Dewey made up one of a trinity of twentieth-century philosophers (the others being Wittgenstein and Heidegger) whom Rorty described as post-metaphysical, as having "broke[n] free of the Kantian concept of philosophy as foundational" in favor of "work [that] is therapeutic rather than constructive, edifying rather than systematic, designed to make the reader question his

own motives for philosophizing rather than to supply him with a new philosophical program." Richard Rorty, *Philosophy and the Mirror of Nature* (Princeton, NJ: Princeton University Press, 1981), 5–6. According to Rorty's account, Dewey saw knowledge as *socially* justified: "We will not imagine that there are enduring constraints on what can count as knowledge, since we will see 'justification' as a social phenomenon rather than a transaction between 'the knowing subject' and 'reality'" (9). Moreover, Rorty argued, Dewey's refusal of metaphysics was motivated not so much by the will to truth as by "a vision of a new kind of society" in which "culture is no longer dominated by the ideal of objective cognition but by that of aesthetic enhancement" (13). By this account, Dewey's pragmatism refuses any concept of the objective or natural in favor of a purely *social* understanding of truth. Inquiry aims not at the objective interpretation of reality but at satisfying social and aesthetic needs. Dreams for a shared future, not rigorous investigations of Being, give philosophy its task. In *Achieving Our Country* (Cambridge, MA: Harvard University Press, 1998), a short book about politics published seventeen years after *Philosophy and the Mirror of Nature*, Rorty invoked Dewey in a more practical context. "Late in his life," Rorty wrote, "Dewey tried to 'state briefly the democratic faith in the formal terms of a philosophical proposition.' The proposition was that democracy is the only form of moral and social faith which does not 'rest upon the idea that experience must be subjected at some point or other to some form of external control: to some "authority" alleged to exist outside the processes of experience'" (28–29). In this passage, Rorty identified Dewey's rejection of such an external authority with his "opposition to the correspondence theory of truth: the idea that truth is a matter of accurate representation of an antecedently existing reality." He continued: "For Dewey, the idea that there was a reality 'out there' with an intrinsic nature to be respected and corresponded to was not a manifestation of sound common sense. It was a relic of Platonic otherworldliness" (29). This is certainly a coherent view, but it does not appear to be Dewey's view. In the very next paragraph of "Creative Democracy," the lecture Rorty is citing, Dewey goes on to give an account of the basis for argument that differs quite sharply from Rorty's. "If one asks what is meant by experience in this connection," Dewey explains, "my reply is that it is that free interaction of individual human beings with surrounding conditions, especially the human surroundings, which develops and satisfies need and desire by increasing knowledge of things as they are. Knowledge of conditions as they are, is the only solid ground for communication and sharing; all other communication means the subjection of some persons to the personal opinion of other persons. Need and desire—out of which grow purpose and direction of energy—go beyond what exists, and hence beyond knowledge, beyond science. They continually open the way into the unexplored and unattained truth." John Dewey, "Creative

Democracy," in *America's Public Philosopher: Essays on Social Justice, Economics, Education, and the Future of Democracy*, ed. Eric Thomas Weber (New York: Columbia University Press, 2021), 65.

In this paragraph we can see both poles of Dewey's theory of experience: the radical contingency that Rorty stressed, but also a firm insistence on the grounding of social progress in "knowledge of things as they are." Dewey even seemed to be warning that a total unmooring from reality opens the way to inequality and domination, "the subjection of some persons to the personal opinion of other persons." While noting that Dewey certainly departed from neo-Kantian theories about the supreme authority of a unitary reason, Dewey nevertheless placed a heavy stress on the subject-independent authority of an intersubjectively shared "experience," a concept with no corresponding importance in Rorty's system. Dewey placed special trust in scientific methodology, and while he acknowledged that the methods of science were subject to improvement, he did not see them as arbitrary emanations of human will. In *A Common Faith*, for example, Dewey praised "faith in the possibilities of continued and rigorous inquiry" that "trusts that the natural interactions between man and his environment will breed more intelligence and generate more knowledge provided the scientific methods that define intelligence in operation are pushed further into the mysteries of the world, being themselves promoted and improved in the operation." For Dewey, science takes on such importance and power that it even begins to substitute for the objects of religious devotion: he wrote immediately after that, "There is such a thing as faith in intelligence becoming religious in quality—a fact that perhaps explains the efforts of some religionists to disparage the possibilities of intelligence as a force. They properly feel such faith to be a dangerous rival" (John Dewey, *A Common Faith* [New Haven, CT: Yale University Press, 1934], 6). It is not we who bend intelligence to the ends we choose for ourselves; intelligence determines our course for us. Rorty, by contrast, advises that "like Dewey, we give up the correspondence theory of truth and start treating moral and scientific beliefs as tools for achieving greater human happiness, rather than as representations of the intrinsic nature of reality" (Rorty, *Achieving Our Country*, 96). Dewey's avowedly religious faith in the dynamic but nevertheless directive methods of science, and their independence from the arbitrary will, is nowhere to be found in Rorty.

4. Rorty, *Achieving Our Country*, 11.

5. Richard Rorty, *Contingency, Irony, and Solidarity* (Cambridge: Cambridge University Press, 1989), 44.

6. Richard Rorty, "The Priority of Democracy to Philosophy," in *The Virginia Statute of Religious Freedom: Its Evolution and Consequences for American History*, ed. Merrill Peterson and Robert Vaughn (Cambridge: Cambridge University Press, 1998), 272.

7. Rorty, "The Priority of Democracy to Philosophy," in *Prospects for a Common Morality*, ed. John Reeder and Gene Outka (Princeton, NJ: Princeton University Press, 1992), 266–67.

8. Rorty, "Trotsky and the Wild Orchids," in *Philosophy and Social Hope* (New York: Penguin, 1999), 16–17.

9. Dewey, "Creative Democracy," 65.

10. Richard Rorty, "The Unpatriotic Academy," *New York Times*, February 13, 1994, section 4, 15.

11. Rorty, *Achieving Our Country*, 100.

12. Rorty, *Achieving Our Country*, 90.

13. Rorty, *Achieving Our Country*, 91–92.

14. In "Language: A Key Mechanism of Control," *FAIR*, February 1, 1995, https://fair.org/home/language-a-key-mechanism-of-control/.

15. Steven Gillon, *The Pact: Bill Clinton, Newt Gingrich, and the Rivalry That Defined a Generation* (New York: Oxford University Press, 2008).

16. "Attitudes on Same-Sex Marriage," Pew Research Center, May 14, 2019, https://www.pewforum.org/fact-sheet/changing-attitudes-on-gay-marriage/.

17. "Growth and Opportunity Project," 2012, https://www.documentcloud.org/documents/624581-rnc-autopsy.html.

18. According to tax documents posted on the website of the nonprofit information service GuideStar: https://pdf.guidestar.org/PDF_Images/2016/953/443/2016-953443202-0df7cc84-9.pdf.

19. "The Heritage Foundation and Affiliates: Consolidated Financial Statement," December 31, 2016, http://thf-reports.s3.amazonaws.com/2017/Heritage%20Foundation_16FS_Final.pdf.

20. Jon Baskin, "The Academic Home of Trumpism," *Chronicle of Higher Education*, March 17, 2017, https://www.chronicle.com/article/the-academic-home-of-trumpism/.

21. Charles Kesler, *Crisis of the Two Constitutions* (New York: Encounter, 2021), 19–20.

22. Kesler, *Crisis*, 68.

23. Kesler, *Crisis*, 94.

24. Kesler, *Crisis*, 183.

25. Kesler, *Crisis*, 151.

26. Kesler, *Crisis*, xii.

27. Abraham Lincoln, "To Henry L. Pierce and Others," in *Collected Works of Abraham Lincoln*, vol. 3, ed. Roy P. Basler (New Brunswick, NJ: Rutgers University Press, 1953), 375.

28. Kesler, *Crisis*, 43.

29. Michael Anton, *The Stakes* (Washington, DC: Regnery, 2020), xi. Relations among the Claremont institutions are complex; the Institute has no formal relation to either Claremont McKenna College or Claremont Graduate University, which are themselves two separate members of the

Claremont Colleges consortium. However, several CMC faculty, including Kesler, are also Institute affiliates, and CGU PhD students can work closely with CMC professors. Consequently, doctoral study at CGU gives sympathetic students an opportunity to pursue graduate study in the orbit of the Institute. Anton is one of several prominent conservative intellectuals who have taken this path.

30. Peter Maass, "Dark Essays by White House Staffers Are the Intellectual Source Code of Trumpism," *Intercept*, February 12, 2017, https://web .archive.org/web/20170307052317if_/https:/theintercept.com/2017/02 /12/dark-essays-by-white-house-staffer-are-the-intellectual-source-code -of-trumpism/.

31. Hillsdale president Larry Arnn studied with Jaffa at CGU (then Claremont Graduate School) and was among the founders of the Claremont Institute. Under his leadership, Hillsdale has become a center of Claremont-influenced thought; given its open sectarian bent, the college is a more natural home for a conservative school of political thought than Claremont McKenna, which has traditionally leaned to the right of its peer institutions but where conservatives must still contend with the strong progressive default in elite American higher education.

32. This is difficult to say with a straight face, when even Senator Mitch McConnell explicitly stated, at the outset of the Obama administration, that his main goal was to thwart Obama and prevent him from achieving anything.

33. Publius Decius Mus, "The Flight 93 Election," *Claremont Review of Books*, September 5, 2016, https://claremontreviewofbooks.com/digital/the-flight -93-election/. "Publius" was Anton's pseudonym.

34. Publius Decius Mus, "The Flight 93 Election."

35. Publius Decius Mus, "The Flight 93 Election."

36. Anton, *The Stakes*, 200.

37. Anton, *The Stakes*, 201.

38. Anton, *The Stakes*, 220.

39. Anton, *The Stakes*, 187.

40. Anton, *The Stakes*, 195.

41. Anton, *The Stakes*, 394.

42. Anton, *The Stakes*, 329–30.

43. See Laura Field, "What the Hell Happened to the Claremont Institute?" *Bulwark*, July 13, 2021, https://thebulwark.com/what-the-hell-happened -to-the-claremont-institute/.

44. Michael Anton, "The Coming Coup," American Mind, September 4, 2020, https://americanmind.org/salvo/the-coming-coup/.

45. "The Fight Is Now," American Mind, November 5, 2020, https://american mind.org/salvo/the-fight-is-now/.

46. "Rudy Giuliani Speech Transcript at Trump's Washington, D.C. Rally: Wants 'Trial by Combat,'" Rev.com, https://www.rev.com/blog/transcripts

/rudy-giuliani-speech-transcript-at-trumps-washington-d-c-rally-wants
-trial-by-combat.

47. Peter Baker, Maggie Haberman, and Annie Karni, "Pence Reached His
Limit with Trump. It Wasn't Pretty," *New York Times*, January 12, 2021,
https://www.nytimes.com/2021/01/12/us/politics/mike-pence-trump
.html.

48. See Michael Anton, "The Continuing Crisis," *Claremont Review of Books*
(Winter 2020/21), https://claremontreviewofbooks.com/the-continuing
-crisis/: "But extraordinary claims demand extraordinary evidence, of
which none was provided." However, Anton maintains that "no one really
knows for sure how much and what kind of fraud was committed, whether
it was of sufficient magnitude to change the election result, and, thus, who
truly won." Charles R. Kesler, "After January 6th: The Future of Trump
and Trumpism," *Claremont Review of Books* (Winter 2020/21), https://clare
montreviewofbooks.com/after-january-6th/.

49. Home page of NewFounding.com.

50. Benjamin Wallace-Wells, "Cass Sunstein Wants to Nudge Us," *New York
Times*, May 13, 2010, https://www.nytimes.com/2010/05/16/magazine/16
Sunstein-t.html.

51. Richard H. Thaler and Cass R. Sunstein, *Nudge: Improving Decisions about
Health, Wealth, and Happiness* (New York: Penguin, 2008).

52. The American Founders, with their Lockean concern for the ideals of
personal freedom and responsibility and republican political participation,
might or might not approve of the vast administrative and regulatory
apparatus that their successors in government have built, but there is no
question that times have changed. The degree to which we and our fellow
citizens are besieged by salespeople today would have been unimaginable
in the early days of the hybrid-Enlightenment, as would the scope and
scale of the administrative apparatus required to secure a basic level of
subsistence for a third of a billion people. Under these conditions, Sunstein and Thaler's claims about the inevitability of some form of nudging
seem impossible to dispute. The old ideal of responsibility may simply be
an outdated concept.

53. Sunstein also admitted in 2020's *Too Much Information* that he had been
too optimistic about the power of information disclosure in the halcyon
early days of progressive paternalism and during his tenure as President
Obama's administrator of the Office of Information and Regulatory Affairs. "Sometimes less is more," he explained. "What is needed, for the
future, is much more clarity about what information is actually doing or
achieving. If we focus insistently on that question and on how to answer
it, we will be able to make people's lives happier, freer, longer, and better."
Sunstein, *Too Much Information* (Cambridge, MA: MIT Press, 2020), 9.
Sunstein goes on to assess the extent to which various disclosures interact
with human cognitive biases to generate beneficial or harmful social ef-

fects. Many public information disclosures, he argues, come out unfavorably on a cost-benefit analysis.

54. Sunstein, *This Is Not Normal* (New Haven, CT: Yale University Press, 2021), 119–20.

55. See Robert Post and Reva Siegel, "Originalism as a Political Practice: The Right's Living Constitution," *Fordham Law Review* 75, no. 2 (2006): 545–74, http://ir.lawnet.fordham.edu/flr/vol75/iss2/5.

56. Donald Trump, for example, invoked "equal justice under law" in condemning George Floyd's killing. See Kathryn Watson and Grace Segers, "Trump Hails Improvement in Employment Numbers and Says It's a 'Great Day' for Equality and George Floyd," CBS News, June 5, 2020, https://www.cbsnews.com/news/trump-press-conference-may-un employment-rate-numbers-great-day-george-floyd/.

57. For a standard version of this argument, see Charles J. Cooper, "Confronting the Administrative State," *National Affairs*, Fall 2015, https://www.nationalaffairs.com/publications/detail/confronting-the-adminis trative-state. See Adrian Vermeule, *Law's Abnegation* (Cambridge, MA: Harvard University Press, 2016).

58. See Adrian Vermeule, *The Constitution of Risk* (Cambridge: Cambridge University Press, 2014), 190.

59. See Adrian Vermeule, "Optimal Abuse of Power," *Northwestern University Law Review* 109, no. 3 (2015): 673–94.

60. Eric Posner and Adrian Vermeule, *The Executive Unbound: After the Madisonian Republic* (New York: Oxford University Press, 2011), chapter 6.

61. See, for example, Eric Posner and Adrian Vermeule, "Demystifying Schmitt," in *The Oxford Handbook of Carl Schmitt*, ed. Jens Meierhenrich and Oliver Simons (New York: Oxford University Press, 2016); and Adrian Vermeule, "Our Schmittian Administrative Law," *Harvard Law Review* 122, no. 4 (2009): 1095–149.

62. See, for example, Adrian Vermeule, "Emergency Lawmaking after 9/11 and 7/7," *University of Chicago Law Review* 75, no. 3 (2008): 1155–90.

63. Adrian Vermeule, "Finding Stable Ground," *First Things*, November 4, 2016, https://www.firstthings.com/blogs/firstthoughts/2016/11/finding -stable-ground.

64. Steve Eder, "Neomi Rao, the Scholar Who Will Help Lead Trump's Regulatory Overhaul," *New York Times*, July 9, 2017, https://www.nytimes .com/2017/07/09/business/the-scholar-who-will-help-lead-trumps -assault-on-rules.html; Adrian Vermeule, "Bureaucracy and Mystery," *Mirror of Justice*, March 22, 2019, https://mirrorofjustice.blogs.com/mirrorof justice/2019/03/bureaucracy-and-mystery-.html.

65. See "A Christian Strategy," *First Things* (November 2017), 41–46; and "Integration from Within," *American Affairs* 2, no. 1 (Spring 2018).

66. "Ralliement: Two Distinctions," *The Josias*, March 16, 2018, https://the josias.com/2018/03/16/ralliement-two-distinctions/.

67. Vermeule, "Integration from Within."

68. Jackie Gu, "The Employees Who Gave Most to Trump and Biden," *Bloomberg*, November 2, 2020, https://www.bloomberg.com/graphics/2020 -election-trump-biden-donors/.

69. Vermeule, "Integration from Within."

70. Adrian Vermeule, "Beyond Originalism," *Atlantic Monthly*, March 31, 2018, https://www.theatlantic.com/ideas/archive/2020/03/common-good -constitutionalism/609037/.

71. Carl Schmitt, *The Crisis of Parliamentary Democracy*, trans. Ellen Kennedy (Cambridge, MA: MIT Press, 1988), 49–50.

72. Adrian Vermeule, "According to Truth," *The Josias*, July 19, 2018, https:// thejosias.com/2018/07/19/according-to-truth/.

73. Jonathan Allen, "Trump Says 'Get Out and Vote for Roy Moore' at Florida Rally," *NBC News*, December 8, 2017, https://www.nbcnews.com /politics/politics-news/trump-says-get-out-vote-roy-moore-florida -rally-n828021.

74. Tom Edsall, "No Hate Left Behind," *New York Times*, March 13, 2019.

75. J. D. Hunter, Carl Desportes Bowman, and Kyle Puetz, *Democracy in Dark Times* (Charlottesville, VA: Finstock & Tew, 2020), 35, https://iasculture .org/research/publications/democracy-in-dark-times.

76. See Jason Stanley, *How Fascism Works* (New York: Penguin, 2018); Timothy Snyder, *On Tyranny: Twenty Lessons from the Twentieth Century* (New York: Crown, 2017); and Madeline Albright, *Fascism: A Warning* (New York: Harper, 2018).

77. See Lane Cuthbert and Alexander Theodoridis, "Do Republicans Really Believe That Trump Won the 2020 Election?" *Washington Post*, January 7, 2022; Ashley Parker and Marianna Sotomayor, "For Republicans, Fealty to Trump's Election Falsehood Becomes Defining Loyalty Test," *Washington Post*, May 3, 2021.

78. Santi Ruiz, "PayPal and the ADL Are Hiding Their Partners in an Effort to Fight Extremism," *Washington Free Beacon*, July 28, 2021, https://free beacon.com/latest-news/paypal-and-the-adl-are-hiding-their-partners -in-an-effort-to-fight-extremism/.

79. See Kerrington Powell and Vinay Prasad, "The Noble Lies of COVID-19," *Slate*, July 28, 2021, https://slate.com/technology/2021/07/noble-lies -covid-fauci-cdc-masks.html.

80. See Freddie Sayers, "How Facebook Censored the Lab Leak Theory," *UnHerd*, May 31, 2021, https://unherd.com/2021/05/how-facebook-cen sored-the-lab-leak-theory/.

Chapter Eleven. A Great Unraveling

1. Jeffrey Stout, *Ethics After Babel* (Boston: Beacon, 1988).

2. Stout, *Ethics*, 291.

3. Stout, *Ethics*, 213.
4. See The Reunited States, "The #HealAmericaPledge," https://reunited states.tv/pledge.
5. Braver Angels, "What We Do," https://braverangels.org/what-we-do/.
6. Stout, *Ethics*, 242.
7. Eli Finkel et al., "Political Sectarianism in America," *Science* 370, no. 6516 (2020): 533–36;, https://www.science.org/doi/10.1126/science.abe1715 #con1; Jay Van Bavel, Steve Rathje, Elizabeth Harris, Claire Robertson, and Anni Sternisko, "How Social Media Shapes Polarization," *Trends in Cognitive Science* 25, no. 11 (2021): 913–16. A nice distillation of this research can be found in an article by Paul Barrett, Justin Hendrix, and Grant Sims: "How Tech Platforms Fuel U.S. Political Polarization and What Government Can Do about It," Brookings Institution, Strengthening American Democracy Initiative, September 27, 2021, https://www .brookings.edu/blog/techtank/2021/09/27/how-tech-platforms-fuel-u-s -political-polarization-and-what-government-can-do-about-it/.
8. Gerald M. Pomper, "The 2000 Presidential Election: Why Gore Lost," *Political Science Quarterly* 116, no. 2 (Summer 2001): 201.
9. Quote from an address by McAuliffe to Democratic GAIN (Grassroots Action Institute and Network) given on July 24, 2004. The speech is recorded on C-SPAN: https://www.c-span.org/video/?182870-1/democratic -youth-training-fundraising.
10. Jeff Horwitz, "It Ain't Over till It's Over," *Salon*, December 13, 2004, https://www.salon.com/2004/12/13/ohio_28/.
11. Presidential debate between Barack Obama and John McCain, October 7, 2008, Belmont University, https://www.youtube.com/watch?v=Voppj ZvvgDU.
12. See, for example, Alan Taylor, "'Not My President': Thousands March in Protest," *Atlantic*, November 10, 2016, https://www.theatlantic.com/photo /2016/11/not-my-president-thousands-march-in-protest/507248/.
13. Colby Itkowitz, "Hilary Clinton: Trump Is an 'Illegitimate' President," *Washington Post*, September 26, 2019, https://www.washingtonpost.com /politics/hillary-clinton-trump-is-an-illegitimate-president/2019/09/26 /29195d5a-e099-11e9-b199-f638bf2c340f_story.html.
14. See chapters 4 and 5 of this text.
15. Charles Taylor, *A Secular Age* (Cambridge, MA: Harvard University Press, 2007).
16. In the symposium "Religion and the Intellectuals" published in the *Partisan Review*, Dewey observed how far the prestige of science had declined since the late nineteenth century, but particularly after the world wars, in which antagonists had used science in the service of "vastly increased destructiveness" and the propaganda that justified such violence. See *Partisan Review* 17, no. 2 (February 1950): 129–33.

17. Jean-François Lyotard, *The Postmodern Condition* (Minneapolis: University of Minnesota Press, 1984).

18. An eloquent case in point is a commencement address given by George Will at the College of William and Mary, May 15, 1994, https://www .rjgeib.com/thoughts/george-will/george-will.html.

19. A superb treatment of this is found in Jonathan Rauch, *The Constitution of Knowledge* (Washington, DC: Brookings Institution Press, 2021).

20. Stanley Fish, "'Transparency' Is the Mother of Fake News," *New York Times*, May 7, 2018.

21. Farhad Manjoo, *True Enough* (Hoboken, NJ: John Wiley, 2008).

22. A very helpful meta-analysis can be found in Nathan Walter, Jonathan Cohen, R. Lance Holbert, and Yasmin Morag, "Fact-Checking: A Meta-Analysis of What Works and for Whom," *Political Communication* 37, no. 3 (2020): 350–75; Oscar Barrera, Sergei Guriev, Emeric Henry, and Ekaterina Zhuravskaya, "Facts, Alternative Facts, and Fact Checking in Times of Post-Truth Politics," *Journal of Public Economics* 182 (February 2020), https://www.sciencedirect.com/science/article/pii/S0047272719301859 ?via%3Dihub-aep-article-footnote-id1.

23. See "Fake News: You Ain't Seen Nothing Yet," *Economist*, July 1, 2017, for an account of these developments. https://www.economist.com/science -and-technology/2017/07/01/fake-news-you-aint-seen-nothing-yet.

24. Andrew Higgins, Mike McIntire, and Gabriel Dance, "Inside a Fake News Sausage Factory: 'This Is All about Income,'" *New York Times*, November 25, 2016. See also Rauch, *The Constitution of Knowledge*, chapter 5.

25. "Harry Reid Justifies Lying about Romney from Senate Floor: 'He Didn't Win, Did He?'" Grabien.com, https://grabien.com/story.php?id=25351.

26. Newt Gingrich, Feelings vs Fact—Newt Gingrich—RNC Topic on Violent Crime, CNN Interview, https://www.youtube.com/watch?v=xnh JWusyj4I.

27. Christopher Lasch, *The True and Only Heaven: Progress and Its Critics* (New York: Norton, 1991), 30–31.

28. Lasch, *The True and Only Heaven*, 30–31.

29. Soroush Vosoughi, Deb Roy, and Sinan Aral, "The Spread of True and False News Online," *Science* 359, no. 6380 (2018): 1146–51.

30. In the early years of the twenty-first century, the Right has certainly been more conspicuous than the Left in the active use of "fake news," but both sides indulge in the practice. Thus, a study conducted in 2016 by Buzz-Feed showed that three big right-wing Facebook pages published false or misleading information 38 percent of the time during the period analyzed, and three large left-wing pages did so in nearly 20 percent of posts. Craig Silverman, "Hyperpartisan Facebook Pages Are Publishing False and Misleading Information at an Alarming Rate," *BuzzFeed*, October 20, 2016, https://www.buzzfeednews.com/article/craigsilverman/partisan-fb -pages-analysis.

31. The Pew Research Center, "News Consumption across Social Media in 2021," https://www.pewresearch.org/journalism/2021/09/20/news-con sumption-across-social-media-in-2021/.

32. See Georges Sorel, *Reflections on Violence* (1908; repr., New York: B. W. Huebsch, 1912), https://archive.org/details/reflectionsonviooosoreuoft; Karl Mannheim, *Ideology and Utopia* (1929; repr., New York: Harcourt, 1936), https://archive.org/details/in.ernet.dli.2015.276580/page/n1/mode/2up.

33. This argument draws from Peter Berger and Thomas Luckmann, *The Social Construction of Reality* (New York: Doubleday, 1966). An insightful application of this "Bergerian" perspective can be found in a brilliant piece by Nicolas Guilhot, "Bad Information," *Boston Review*, August 23, 2021, a shrewd and perceptive reflection on the January 6, 2021, riots in Washington, DC. See https://bostonreview.net/articles/bad-information/.

34. For my own account of this failure, see J. D. Hunter and Paul Nedelisky, *Science and the Good: The Tragic Quest for the Foundations of Morality* (New Haven, CT: Yale University Press, 2018).

35. Stout, *Ethics*, 216.

36. Alasdair MacIntyre, *After Virtue* (South Bend, IN: University of Notre Dame Press, 1984), 8.

37. MacIntyre, *After Virtue*, 10.

38. J. D. Hunter, *Culture Wars: The Struggle to Define America* (New York: Basic Books, 1991), chapters 5 and 6.

39. Alasdair MacIntyre, *A Short History of Ethics* (New York: Macmillan, 1966), 266.

40. MacIntyre, *After Virtue*, 39.

41. MacIntyre's account of this can be found in *After Virtue*, chapter 3.

42. Arguably, the roots of emotivism can be found in the subversive tendencies of antinomianism. See chapter 4 of this manuscript, note 27.

43. MacIntyre, *After Virtue*, 8.

44. F. Nietzsche, *The Gay Science* (New York: Cambridge University Press, 2001), Section 335.

45. Both Mumford and Dawson are quoted in Lasch, *The True and Only Heaven*, 41.

46. The contradictions in the ways these issues are packaged are explored in the insightful book by James Mumford, *Vexed* (London: Bloomsbury, 2020).

47. MacIntyre, *After Virtue*, 203.

48. Wendy Brown, "Wounded Attachments," *Political Theory* 21, no. 3 (August 1993): 404.

49. Hans Gerth and C. W. Mills, *From Max Weber* (New York: Oxford University Press, 1957), 215–16.

50. Following Weber, the more "pure" the bureaucracy, the more dehumanizing it is; that is, the more bureaucracy "succeeds in eliminating love, hatred, and all purely personal, irrational, and emotional elements" from

its calculated efficiencies, the more alienating it is for those who work and live within its shadow. See Gerth and Mills, *From Max Weber*, 216. On the specific matter of identity, it is important to highlight the highly reductive power of bureaucracy. As in all work, people working or operating within bureaucracies are understood and understand themselves intersubjectively through the specialized role they play or the functions they perform in an environment defined by repetitive tasks as well as strict rules, abstract procedures, and emphasis on efficiencies and outcomes. Individuals working within and living among large-scale bureaucracies are, as a rule, not perceived *as* individuals in the richness and complexity of their lives, nor do they experience themselves as such. Surrounded by those who are similarly replaceable and limited in power, people experience bureaucracies as impersonal and often uncaring, disconnected if not hostile to those things that are most personally and professionally fulfilling. See Peter Berger, Brigitte Berger, and Hansfried Kellner, *The Homeless Mind* (New York: Vintage, 1974), chapter 2.

51. See, for example, Charles M. Bonjean and Michael D. Grimes, "Bureaucracy and Alienation: A Dimensional Approach," *Social Forces* 48, no. 3 (March 1970): 365–73.

52. As Ortega observed in the 1920s, a "mass culture" is an undifferentiated culture and "mass men" are generic in their identity and self-understanding. José Ortega y Gassett, *The Revolt of the Masses* (New York: W. W. Norton, 1957).

53. Berger, Berger, and Kellner, *The Homeless Mind*, chapter 3.

54. C. Wright Mills, *The Power Elite* (New York: Oxford University Press, 1956), 323.

55. Which is why the analogy to religion can't be pushed too hard.

56. There are other forces that frame common life as well—most notably the ubiquitous market—but these are not autonomous from the state but linked integrally with its extensive instrumentalities.

57. See, for example, Shanto Iyengar and Masha Krupenkin, "Partisanship as Social Identity: Implications for the Study of Party Polarization," *Forum* 16, no. 1 (2018), https://doi.org/10.1515/for-2018-0003; Sean J. Westwood, Shanto Iyengar, Stefaan Walgrave, Rafael Leonisio, Luis Miller, and Oliver Strijbis, "The Tie That Divides: Cross-National Evidence of the Primacy of Partyism," *European Journal of Political Research* (August 2017), https://doi.org/10.1111/1475-6765.12228.

58. The reference is to Michel Foucault's famous statement in *The Order of Things* (New York: Random House, 1994), 386–87, that man, being a "recent invention" promised to an imminent "death," is threatened with erasure like a "face drawn in the sand at the edge of the sea." French and German anti-humanism began in the postwar period with Heidegger's *Letter on Humanism* and proliferated through the works of the key existentialists and the structuralists.

59. Thomas Kuhn, *The Structure of Scientific Revolutions* (Chicago: University of Chicago Press, 1996), 125–27.

60. Data on the growing distrust of institutions (up to the 1980s) can be found in Seymour Martin Lipset and William Schneider, *The Confidence Gap* (Baltimore: Johns Hopkins University Press, 1987). In recent decades, the Institute for Advanced Studies in Culture has conducted successive installments of the Survey on American Political Culture that have updated many of these trends. These include *The State of Disunion* (1996), *The Politics of Character* (2000), *The Culture of American Families* (2012), *The Vanishing Center* (2016), and *Democracy in Dark Times* (2020), all available at https://iasculture.org/research/survey-lab#publications.

61. In *The Vanishing Center* survey (2016), the data showed that over half of all Democrats and Republicans held this view, but three out of four independents are especially adamant that the party system isn't working.

62. A quick internet search for journalistic fraud demonstrates the point. See https://www.thoughtco.com/the-top-journalism-scandals-2073750; and https://longreads.com/2014/01/22/famous-cases-of-journalistic-fraud -a-reading-list/.

63. On the replication crisis, see https://www.sciencemag.org/news/2018/08/ researcher-center-epic-fraud-remains-enigma-those-who-exposed-him. For a list of cases in scientific misconduct, Wikipedia provides a start: https://en.wikipedia.org/wiki/List_of_scientific_misconduct_incidents.

64. Glenn Kessler, Salvador Rizzo, and Meg Kelly, "Trump's False and Misleading Claims Total 30,573 over Four Years," *Washington Post,* January 24, 2021, https://www.washingtonpost.com/politics/2021/01/24/trumps -false-or-misleading-claims-total-30573-over-four-years/; David Leonhardt and Stuart A. Thompson, "Trump's Lies: The Definitive List," *New York Times,* December 14, 2017, https://www.nytimes.com/interactive/2017/06 /23/opinion/trumps-lies.html; Libby Cathey, "Legacy of Lies: How Trump Weaponized Mistruths during His Presidency," ABC News, January 20, 2021, https://abcnews.go.com/Politics/legacy-lies-trump-weaponized-mis truths-presidency/story?id=75335019.

65. Goldwater's observations come from his memoir: Barry Goldwater and Jack Casserly, *Goldwater* (New York: Doubleday, 1988). He elaborated, saying that Nixon "lied to his wife, his family, his friends, longtime colleagues in the U.S. Congress, lifetime members of his own political party, the American people, and the world." Quotes are from Richard M. Nixon's resignation speech, August 8, 1974, https://www.pbs.org/newshour/spc /character/links/nixon_speech.html.

66. "Takeaways from Day 3 of Jan. 6 Hearings: Lawyer Eastman Told Trump Election Plot Wasn't Legal," https://www.nbcnews.com/politics/congress /takeaways-day-3-jan-6-hearings-lawyer-eastman-told-trump-election -plot-rcna34034. The threat to Vice President Mike Pence is well known. Between 2016 and 2022, there was a surge in concrete threats to elected

officials (75 indictments, though to members of Congress alone, there were 902 threats in 2016, 3,939 threats in 2017, and 9,600 threats in 2021). These were threats of every sort: Republicans against Democrats, Democrats against Republicans, Republicans against Republicans, and Democrats against Democrats. See Catie Edmondson and Mark Walker, "One Menacing Call after Another: Threats against Lawmakers Surge," *New York Times,* February 9, 2022. Trump himself leveraged violence against specific officials. For example, Philadelphia city commissioner Al Schmidt and his family were doxed and then threatened multiple times after Trump tweeted him by name for defending the integrity of the vote. See Abe Asher, "Images Reveal Threats against Republican Official's Family after Trump Named Him in Election Tweet," *Independent,* June 15, 2022, https://www.independent.co.uk/news/world/americas/al-schmidt-trump-threats-election-tweet-b2100047.html.

67. Steve Lagerfeld, "America, the Exceptional?" *Hedgehog Review* (Fall 2020): 92.

68. This state of affairs puts America back in the situation feared by Schlesinger in the 1950s, but more so. In his terms, we have fewer cultural resources with which to respond to external threat.

Chapter Twelve. Nihilism and Its Cultural Logics

1. Friedrich Nietzsche, *The Will to Power* (New York: Vintage, 1968), 14–15, https://archive.org/details/FriedrichNietzscheTheWillToPower.

2. Nietzsche, *Will to Power,* 9.

3. Nietzsche, *Will to Power,* 7, 13.

4. Nietzsche, *Will to Power,* 37.

5. This is one of the hallmarks of the Durkheimian school of social theory: that social reality is a social fact. It exists sui generis and thus has a thing-like quality. As such, it can't be wished away. It follows that social reality has a coercive power of its own, independent of the will or intent of the people it affects. See Émile Durkheim, *The Rules of the Sociological Method* (New York: Free Press, 1982).

6. Nietzsche himself made the distinction between passive and active nihilism, though I mean something quite different by the distinction. For Nietzsche, passive nihilism is a "decline and recession of the power of the spirit." It is "a weary nihilism," "a sign of weakness." He offered Buddhism as its most famous expression. Active nihilism is "a sign of increased power of the spirit." At its fullest expression, it is "a violent force of destruction." See Nietzsche, *Will to Power,* 17–18.

7. These citations come from Nietzsche, *Will to Power,* #12A, 11–12. Nietzsche observed the normality of nihilism (#23, 17), as did Martin Heidegger in *The Quest for Being* (New York: Twayne, 1956), 47.

8. Karen L. Carr, *The Banalization of Nihilism* (Albany, NY: SUNY Press, 1992).

9. In this passage, I prefer the phrasing from Anthony Ludovici's translation of Nietzsche, *The Will to Power* (London: T. S. Foulis, 1914), #24, 22, https://archive.org/details/NIETZSCHETHEWILLTOPOWER12 /mode/2up.

10. The classic statement on this matter is the pathbreaking essay by Nancy Fraser, "Rethinking the Public Sphere: A Contribution to the Critique of Actually Existing Democracy," *Social Text* 25/26 (1990): 56–80. In her account, the concept of "subaltern counterpublics" is invoked as a solution to the "bourgeois masculinist" hegemony over the centralized public sphere. In this section, I draw heavily from her discussion, but in ways that seek to generalize the concept.

11. Wendy Brown, "Wounded Attachments," *Political Theory* 21, no. 3 (August 1993): 398.

12. Fraser, "Rethinking the Public Sphere," 67.

13. Jean Améry made this case convincingly in his extraordinary book, *At the Mind's Limits: Contemplations of a Survivor on Auschwitz and Its Realities* (Bloomington: Indiana University Press, 1966). See also Thomas Brudholm's treatment in *Resentment's Virtue: Jean Améry and the Refusal to Forgive* (Philadelphia: Temple University Press, 1995). The idea of an off-point comes from a helpful essay by Philip A. Powe, "A Short Explanation of *Ressentiment*," https://www.academia.edu/37027563/Ressentiment_Final _docx.

14. Most of what Nietzsche wrote about ressentiment can be found in *The Genealogy of Morals* (New York: Cambridge University Press, 2006), https:// philosophy.ucsc.edu/news-events/colloquia-conferences/Geneologyof Morals.pdf.

15. Max Scheler, *Ressentiment*, https://hscif.org/wp-content/uploads/2018 /04/Max-Scheler-Ressentiment.pdf. This was the version translated by Lewis Coser from the 1915 edition, published by Marquette University Press.

16. Nietzsche, *The Genealogy of Morals*, 94.

17. Nietzsche, *The Genealogy of Morals*, 93.

18. Nietzsche, *The Genealogy of Morals*, 48.

19. Friedrich Nietzsche, *Thus Spake Zarathustra* (New York: Cambridge University Press, 2006), 111, https://yale.imodules.com/s/1667/images/gid6 /editor_documents/life_worth_living/nietzsche_-_thus_spoke_zarathustra .pdf?sessionid=38e7969f-118d-474d-ac98–75cc6c980f3f&cc=1.

20. Scheler, *Ressentiment*, 8–9.

21. In this section, I draw heavily upon my essay "The Discourse of Negation and the Ironies of Common Culture," *Hedgehog Review* (Fall 2004), https:// hedgehogreview.com/issues/discourse-and-democracy/articles/the -discourse-of-negation-and-the-ironies-of-common-culture. Quotations below are drawn from the interviews cited there.

22. These justifications are not new. See Adam Goodman, "Producing TV: A Survival Game," *Campaigns and Elections* (July 1995): 22–24.

23. Peter Sloterdijk, *Rage and Time* (New York: Columbia University Press, 2010).

24. Jonathan Rauch, *The Constitution of Knowledge* (Washington, DC: Brookings Institution Press, 2021), chapter 5.

25. The historic turn toward subjectivity and moral autonomy has been underway for centuries, a turn recognized early in the nineteenth century by Hegel and many others since then. In 1821, Hegel wrote, "The right of the subject's particularity . . . or in other words the right of subjective freedom, is the pivot and center of the difference between antiquity and modern times. [It] has become the universal effective principle of a new form of civilization." G.W.F. Hegel, *The Philosophy of Right* (New York: Oxford University Press, 1952), 124.

26. Nietzsche, *The Genealogy of Morals*, 93.

27. No one is more insightful on this subject than Wendy Brown, and I draw heavily on her work in this section (Brown, "Wounded Attachments"). Brown's insightful piece is an extended but also subtle treatment of the limits and ironies of identity politics. She develops this argument in an equally powerful analysis in *States of Injury* (Princeton, NJ: Princeton University Press, 1995).

28. Brown, "Wounded Attachments," 395.

29. Brown, "Wounded Attachments," 400.

30. Brown, "Wounded Attachments," 390. Brown points out another irony. While the politics of ressentiment does lead to a recognition of a sort, in the process, recognition is obscured if not undermined altogether. The distinctions of race, ethnicity, color, national origin, gender, sexual orientation, marital status, disability, physical appearance, and the like, all listed in the efforts to ban discrimination in housing, employment, and public accommodations, in fact enumerate every difference as no difference but part of a seamless regulatory whole. As Brown put it, every potentially subversive rejection of culturally enforced norms is placed within a framework in which those aims and identities are normalized through law (399). This means that through the definitional, procedural, and remedial elements of the law, persons are reduced to the abstract bureaucratic categories of observable attributes and practices. As she notes, this ensures that persons describable according to these administrative categories are now regulated by them. What, she asks, do we make of a law "that renders as juridical equivalents the denial of employment to an African American, an obese man, and a white middle-class youth festooned with tattoos and fuchsia hair?" In the end, the distinctions that might make a difference are flattened out by the very efforts to ensure the legal recognition and acceptance of those distinctions.

31. There will be some who think that the problem of active nihilism is mainly one of the secular Left, perhaps especially conspicuous among secular intellectuals. There are reasons for that, but those tempted to think that way may also imagine that active nihilism among the religious—or, more particularly, the Christian Right—is muted or nonexistent. In reality, Nietzsche traced the origins of ressentiment in the Jewish inversion of the ancient aristocratic values that had equated the good with power and privilege. They replaced the "master morality" with a "slave morality," one that venerated the powerless, the poor, the suffering, but also condemned the noble and powerful as cruel and evil. (His treatment can be found in the first essay of *The Genealogy of Morals*, 34.) But if Jews introduced this inversion, it was refined and perfected by Christians, and today it is present among some of the most well-known Christian leaders and organizations in America. As I have documented elsewhere, the logics of revenge as a weapon to usurp the powerful is found both on the Christian right and the Christian left. Hunter, *To Change the World* (New York: Oxford University Press, 2010), essay 2. As I concluded in that work, by nurturing their various resentments and sustaining them through a discourse of negation toward outsiders, many Christians have become "functional nihilists" who, tragically, participate in the very cultural collapse they so ardently strive to resist (175).

32. Empirical work on this can be found in J. D. Hunter, Carl Desportes Bowman, and Kyle Puetz, *Democracy in Dark Times* (Charlottesville, VA: Finstock & Tew, 2020).

33. Nietzsche, *Will to Power*, #2, 3.

Chapter Thirteen. The Authoritarian Impulse

1. Oliver Wendell Holmes, "Letter to Frederick Pollock, February 1, 1920," in *Holmes-Pollock Letters: The Correspondence of Mr. Justice Holmes and Sir Frederick Pollock, 1874–1932*, ed. Howe Mark DeWolfe (Cambridge, MA: Harvard University Press, 1961), 36.

2. I have made this case in an earlier work: J. D. Hunter, *Before the Shooting Begins* (New York: Free Press, 1994).

3. Hannah Arendt, "What Is Authority?" in *Between Past and Future: Six Essays on Political Thought* (New York: Viking, 1961), 98.

4. Umberto Eco, "Ur-Fascism," *New York Review of Books*, June 15, 1995, https://www.nybooks.com/articles/1995/06/22/ur-fascism/.

5. Arendt, "What Is Authority?" 97.

6. Richard Rorty, *Contingency, Irony, and Solidarity* (Cambridge: Cambridge University Press, 1989), 189.

7. All quotations in this section are taken from *First Things* 57 (November 1996).

8. This debate was carried on in many different fora, but it came together in a concise form in an issue of the *New Criterion:* 40, no. 5 (January 2022).

9. Statements are from Glenn Ellmers, "Conservatism Is No Longer Enough," American Mind, March 24, 2021, https://americanmind.org/salvo/why-the -claremont-institute-is-not-conservative-and-you-shouldnt-be-either/. Sentiments like this are widely expressed—for example, in the National Conservatism Conference in November 2021. See the coverage provided by David Brooks, "The Terrifying Future of the American Right," *Atlantic*, November 18, 2021, https://www.theatlantic.com/ideas/archive /2021/11/scary-future-american-right-national-conservatism-conference /620746/.

10. Josh Hammer, "Common Good Originalism: Our Tradition and Our Path Forward," *Harvard Journal of Law and Public Policy* 44, no. 3 (2021): 925.

11. Hammer, "Common Good Originalism," 925.

12. Josh Hammer, "Yesterday's Man, Yesterday's Conservatism," *New Criterion* 40, no. 5 (January 2022): 24–27.

13. Cass Sunstein, *On Freedom* (Princeton, NJ: Princeton University Press, 2019), 91.

14. Sunstein, *On Freedom*, 112.

15. Adrian Vermeule, "Beyond Originalism," *Atlantic*, March 2020, https:// www.theatlantic.com/ideas/archive/2020/03/common-good-consti tutionalism/609037/.

16. Vermeule, "Beyond Originalism."

17. Vermeule, "Beyond Originalism."

18. Vermeule, "Beyond Originalism."

19. See Eric A. Posner and Adrian Vermeule, *The Executive Unbound* (New York: Oxford University Press, 2010), especially chapter 4. I'm grateful for the reference to this book found in Jason Blakely's fine essay, "The Integralism of Adrian Vermeule: Not Catholic Enough," *Commonweal*, October 20, 2020, https://www.commonwealmagazine.org/not-catholic -enough.

20. See Matthew Crawford's insightful essay "Algorithmic Governance and Political Legitimacy," *American Affairs* 3, no. 2 (May 2019). See also Frank Pasquale, *The Black Box Society* (Cambridge, MA: Harvard University Press, 2016).

21. Quoted in "Facebook's War on Free Will," *Guardian*, September 19, 2017. Zuckerberg elaborated upon his observation in an interview with Ezra Klein published on Vox. *See* https://www.vox.com/2018/4/2/17185052 /mark-zuckerberg-facebook-interview-fake-news-bots-cambridge.

22. There are other important voices in this emerging tradition, most notably William Connolly, *Identity/Difference* (Minneapolis: University of Minnesota Press, 2001); Bonnie Honig, *Political Theory and the Displacement of Politics* (Ithaca, NY: Cornell University Press, 1993); Bonnie Honig,

"What Is Agonism?" in "The Agonistic Turn," ed. Lida Maxwell, *Contemporary Political Theory* 18, no. 4 (December 2019).

23. Carl Schmitt, *The Concept of the Political*, trans. G. Schwab (1932; repr., Chicago: University of Chicago Press, 1996).

24. Chantal Mouffe, *Agonistics: Thinking the World Politically* (London: Verso, 1993), 9.

25. Mouffe, *Agonistics*, 6. By "the role played by affects in their community," she is not only critiquing rationalism but valorizing the emotivist nature of identity groups. On the larger contextual point, she tracks with the leftist tradition of seeing ideas as justifications for all sorts of vested interests, not least the interests of identity groups. But departing from the old-fashioned leftism that argues that liberalism is the political expression of capitalism and thus that liberalism and capitalism are inseparable, she has argued that this relationship "is not a necessary one." Chantal Mouffe, *Dimensions of Radical Democracy* (London: Verso, 1992), 2. This allows her to critique capitalism but defend liberal democracy.

26. Chantal Mouffe, *The Return of the Political* (London: Verso, 2020), 2.

27. Chantal Mouffe, *On the Political* (London: Routledge, 2005), 32.

28. Mouffe, *Dimensions of Radical Democracy*, 1.

29. Chantal Mouffe, *The Democratic Paradox* (London: Verso, 2000), 104 (emphasis added).

30. Mouffe, *The Democratic Paradox*, 103.

31. Mouffe, *Agonistics*, 9. Other agonistic theorists, like Connolly, also contend for an agonism limited by generosity and mutual respect for differences.

32. Mouffe, *The Return of the Political*, 151.

33. Mouffe, *Agonistics*, 9 (emphasis added). Mouffe reiterates this position in *The Return of the Political*: "It is . . . essential to establish a certain number of mechanisms and procedures for arriving at decisions and for determining the will of the state within the framework of a debate on the interpretation of these principles" (130).

34. George Crowder, "Chantal Mouffe's Agonistic Democracy" (paper presented at the Australasian Political Studies Association conference, University of New Castle, September 25–27, 2006), 13.

35. Mouffe, *The Democratic Paradox*, 97. She cites Ludwig Wittgenstein, *Culture and Value* (Chicago: University of Chicago Press, 1980), 64.

36. Stephen K. White, "Agonism, Democracy, and the Moral Equality of Voice," *Political Theory* 50, no. 1 (2021): 59–85. See also Mary F. Scudder and Stephen K. White, *The Two Faces of Democracy: Decentering Agonism and Deliberation* (New York: Oxford University Press, 2023).

37. The text of Winthrop's sermon "A Modell of Christian Charity," written on board the ship *Arbella*, can be found here: https://history.hanover.edu/texts/winthmod.html.

38. The scholarly literature on this is extensive and rich, beginning with works by Perry Miller. A lovely introductory summary of Miller's scholarly sig-

nificance can be found in a brief essay by Abram Van Engen, "How America Became a City on a Hill," *Humanities* 41, no. 1 (Winter 2020).

39. George Santayana, *Character and Opinion in the United States* (1920; repr., New York: Braziller, 1955), 4.

40. Even in the deconstructionist theories of Berger and Luckmann, Berger argues that "the most important function of society is nomization. The anthropological presupposition for this is a human craving for meaning that appears to have the force of instinct. Men are congenitally compelled to impose a meaningful order upon reality." Peter L. Berger, *The Sacred Canopy* (New York: Doubleday, 1967), 22.

41. In *Twilight of the Idols,* trans. Duncan Large (Oxford: Oxford University Press, 1998), 3:6, 19, Nietzsche declares that "the characteristics which have been given to the 'true being' of things are the characteristics of non-Being, of nothingness." This was why he could claim that the Platonists, the architects of the ancient utopia, were actually the real nihilists.

42. Friedrich Nietzsche, *The Will to Power* (New York: Vintage, 1968), #11, 1, https://archive.org/details/FriedrichNietzscheTheWillToPower.

43. Hunter, *Before the Shooting*, chapter 1.

44. For a brief account of this dynamic at the state level, see David French, "Don't Let the Culture War Degrade the Constitution," *New York Times*, March 12, 2023, https://www.nytimes.com/2023/03/12/opinion/newsom-desantis-walgreens-constitution.html.

45. All of this is alarming, but in the case of the Right, it is considerably more alarming because in a world as deconstructed as ours, there is nothing that would inhibit national conservatism from evolving into blood-and-soil nationalism. This is reflected in the attraction of the extreme Right to the authoritarian regimes of Russia and Hungary.

46. Kevin Townsend, "Radio Atlantic: How to Stop a Civil War," *Atlantic,* November 14, 2019. This was a podcast of a conversation with Danielle Allen, Jeffrey Goldberg, and Adam Serwer. The quotation is from the published version: Jeffrey Goldberg, "A Nation Coming Apart," *Atlantic,* December 2019.

47. The figures that follow are taken from reports produced by the Center for Strategic and International Studies. See Seth G. Jones, Catrina Doxsee, and Nicholas Harrington, "The Tactics and Targets of Domestic Terrorists," Center for Strategic and International Studies: CSIS Briefs, July 2020, https://www.csis.org/analysis/tactics-and-targets-domestic-terrorists; and Catrina Doxee, Seth G. Jones, Jared Thompson, Grace Hwang, and Kateryna Halstead, "Pushed to Extremes," Center for Strategic and International Studies: CSIS Briefs, May 2022, https://www.csis.org/analysis/pushed-extremes-domestic-terrorism-amid-polarization-and-protest.

48. Catie Edmondson and Mark Walker, "One Menacing Call after Another: Threats against Lawmakers Surge," *New York Times*, February 9, 2022.

49. Marjorie Taylor Greene, Republican member of Congress from Georgia,

declared on October 27, 2020, "If this generation doesn't stand up and defend freedom, it's gone. And once it's gone freedom doesn't come back by itself. The only way you get your freedoms back is it's earned with the price of blood. . . . This is it. November 3, freedom is on the ballot. You have a choice of either voting for freedom by voting for Donald J. Trump for president again for four more years, . . . or you're going to vote for socialism and vote to completely end America as we know it." See https://www.youtube.com/watch?v=J4rY-KL2JHI. On Congressman Paul Gosar's threat, see https://www.npr.org/2021/11/18/1056761894/rep-paul-gosar-is-censured-over-an-anime-video-depicting-him-of-killing-aoc. He neither regretted the video nor apologized. He was censured by the House on November 17, 2021.

50. Larry Diamond, Lee Drutman, Tod Lindberg, Nathan Kalmoe, and Lilliana Mason, "Americans Increasingly Believe Violence Is Justified if the Other Side Wins," *Politico*, October 1, 2020.

51. The actual percent was 34 percent. *Washington Post*–University of Maryland Poll, December 27–29, 2021, https://www.washingtonpost.com/politics/2022/01/01/1-3-americans-say-violence-against-government-can-be-justified-citing-fears-political-schism-pandemic/. This was the highest level measured since 1995. https://www.washingtonpost.com/politics/2022/01/01/post-poll-january-6/.

52. The percent was 62 percent. From a CBS-YouGov Poll conducted December 27–29, 2021, https://s3.amazonaws.com/drupal8mediamatters.org/static/D8File/2022/01/04/cbsnews_20211228_jan6_all-updated-with%20changes.pdf?VersionId=lg1MVUGm1VGk7zsm8P7Uh_9Qq2.XoRSl.

53. And, as Philip Rieff put it, "With the end of authority, there is no violence that cannot be justified." See Rieff, *Fellow Teachers* (Chicago: University of Chicago Press), 50.

Chapter Fourteen. Whither Liberal Democracy?

1. The first part of this sentence is a paraphrase of a lyrical observation about Europe made in the last paragraph of Milan Kundera's short book, *The Art of the Novel* (New York: Grove, 1988), 78.

2. In the *Journal of the Twenty-second Quadrennial session of the African Methodist Episcopal Church* (1904): 74.

3. Richard Rorty, "Solidarity," in *Contingency, Irony, and Solidarity* (Cambridge: Cambridge University Press, 1989), 194.

4. Danielle Allen, "What I Learned When I Ran for Governor of Massachusetts," *Wall Street Journal*, May 6, 2022.

5. For example, see J. D. Hunter and Carl Desportes Bowman, *The Vanishing Center* (Charlottesville, VA: Institute for Advanced Studies in Culture, 2016); and J. D. Hunter, Carl Desportes Bowman, and Kyle Puetz, *De-*

mocracy in Dark Times (Charlottesville, VA: Finstock & Tew, 2020), Both of these surveys can be found at https://iasculture.org/research/survey -lab#publications.

6. For those who have skipped ahead, I covered this point in the early pages of chapter 11.

7. In this respect, democratic politics proves a much better teacher, for it fosters public deliberation where actors must reason in public for their positions. There is at least the possibility of analyzing and disputing that reasoning in public by the public.

8. John Owen, *The Ecology of Nations: American Democracy in a Fragile World Order* (New Haven, CT: Yale University Press, 2023).

9. Owen, *Ecology of Nations*, describes these developments in the international order as a "democratic recession." It is marked by the success of populist leaders and parties winning elections, chipping away at constitutional restraints, and meeting with the approval of large portions of their citizens for doing so. Populists, he argues, present themselves as democratic but seek to erode constitutional restraints, regarding them as tricks emplaced by self-serving nefarious elites to thwart the will of the "real people." Statistics he cites from Freedom House, which has reported on democracy around the world since the 1940s, reported the fifteenth consecutive year of "decline in global freedom" in 2021.

10. Arthur M. Schlesinger Jr., *The Vital Center* (1949; repr., New Brunswick, NJ: Transaction, 1998), 245.

11. Friedrich Nietzsche, *The Genealogy of Morals* (New York: Cambridge University Press, 2006), 15.

Coda

1. These were reviewed in chapter 1.

2. This would be an expression of nihilism proper: a will to nothingness manifest as the utter destruction of the world. Its roots are Christian, but the apocalyptic has also survived its secularization.

3. Christopher Lasch, "Optimism or Hope? The Ethic of Abundance and the Ethic of Limits," *Sacred Heart University Review* 10, no. 2 (Spring 1990): 3–14.

4. As defined by the American Psychological Association, hope is "the expectation that one will have positive experiences or that a potentially threatening or negative situation will not materialize or will ultimately result in a favorable state of affairs." Camille Preston, "The Psychology of Hope," *Psychology Today*, October 24, 2021, https://www.psychologytoday .com/us/blog/mental-health-in-the-workplace/202110/the-psychology -hope.

5. It does this through, among other things, "set[ting] clear goals," "cultivat[ing] a growth mindset," and "tak[ing] perspective at regular intervals"

because "being able to see one's progress is a great way to foster hope for the future." Preston, "The Psychology of Hope."

6. Lasch, "Optimism or Hope?" 13.

7. I wrote these pages as my colleague Jay Tolson (editor) and the editorial team put together *Hedgehog Review* 24, no. 3 (Fall 2022), entitled "Hope Itself." My indebtedness to Tolson, his team, and the contributors to this issue is extensive.

8. Martin Luther King Jr., "The Three Dimensions of a Complete Life," sermon delivered at the Chicago Sunday Evening Club, March 14, 1965, 5–6, quoted in David J. Garrow, "Martin Luther King, Jr., and the Spirit of Leadership," *Journal of American History* 74, no. 2 (September 1987): 438–47.

9. These quotations come from King's sermon "Shattered Dreams," given in 1959 at the Dexter Avenue Baptist Church in Montgomery, Alabama. Published in Clayborne Carson et al., eds., *The Papers of Martin Luther King, Jr.*, vol. 4 (Berkeley: University of California Press, 2000), https:// kinginstitute.stanford.edu/king-papers/documents/draft-chapter-x -shattered-dreams.

10. Lasch, "Optimism or Hope?" 13–14.

11. Jonny Thakkar, *Plato as Critical Theorist* (Cambridge, MA: Harvard University Press, 2018), 330. The materialist bias within the social sciences orients scholars to downplay the symbolic element of agency. Thakkar's argument provides a counterpoint to these tendencies by demonstrating the indispensable role of ideals and idealism in the work of criticism.

12. See the discussion in chapter 13 under the heading "From America's Deep Structure."

13. The musings that follow are aspirational, though few if any will find them adequate. Perhaps, then, this could be a starting point for a longer and more fruitful conversation.

14. Reinhold Niebuhr, *Moral Man and Immoral Society* (Louisville, KY: Westminster John Knox, 2013), 249.

15. Hannah Arendt, *The Human Condition* (Chicago: University of Chicago Press, 1998), 237. MLK was of the same conviction: "We must develop and maintain the capacity to forgive. He who is devoid of the power to forgive is devoid of the power to love." In Martin Luther King Jr., *A Gift of Love* (1963; repr., Boston: Beacon, 2012), 46.

16. The notion of "passing by" comes from Nietzsche. As he put it, "Where one can no longer love, there should one—pass by!" It is a way of tempering ressentiment. *Thus Spake Zarathustra* (New York: Modern Library, 1917), 198, https://archive.org/details/thusspokezarathuoonietuoft/page /198/mode/2up. An even more compelling case was made in his book *The Genealogy of Morals* (New York: Vintage, 1974), 39: "To be incapable of taking one's enemies, one's accidents, even one's misdeeds seriously for very long—that is the sign of strong, full natures in whom there is an

excess of the power to form, to mold, to recuperate and to forget. . . . Such a man shakes off with a single shrug many vermin that eat deep into others; here alone genuine 'love of one's enemies' is possible—supposing it to be possible at all on earth. How much reverence has a noble man for his enemies!—and such reverence is a bridge to love."

17.   Niebuhr, *Moral Man*, 255.

Acknowledgments

THOUGH AUTHORS WRITE IN solitude, we never write in isolation. We write in conversation—with predecessors from generations past and with contemporaries, often in community. I have had the very good fortune of enjoying and benefiting from a wonderful community of family, friends, and colleagues, and I am indebted to them all for their help on this project.

At Yale, my long-standing editor Bill Frucht came alongside me from the conception of the project with tough questions and great encouragement. He persuaded six anonymous reviewers to engage the argument, and thanks to the gift of their time and critical reading, the book is significantly better. My dear friend Susan Arellano, who edited an earlier book of mine, *Culture Wars: The Struggle to Define America*, now decades ago, also came on board with wise counsel, helping to shepherd the book to completion.

Friends and colleagues at the Institute for Advanced Studies in Culture—including Jay Tolson, John Owen, Jackson Lears, Isaac Reed, Matt Crawford, Stephen White, Malloy Owen, and Joe Davis—came together for a manuscript workshop and pushed me at every point of the argument to correct, clarify, and expand. I cannot adequately thank them for their exacting standards. I especially want to thank three from this group: the incomparable Jay Tolson, editor of *The Hedgehog Review*, who read multiple drafts of the manuscript and edited it not only for substantive coherence but also line by line; my learned friend and colleague John Owen, with whom I have the great privilege of editing Yale's Politics and Culture Series; and Malloy Owen, not only a skilled and astute research scholar on the project but a brilliant conversation partner who widened the horizons of the literature I needed to work through. My friend, the late Tim Keller, as well as Carl Bowman, Steve Lagerfeld, and Ethan Podell, also suffered through the manuscript and provided very helpful commentary, and to them I am much obliged.

I also owe a profound debt to other friends and colleagues at the Institute and its supporting foundation—Ryan Olson, who orchestrated the time and resources to allow me to write; Ty Buckman and Paul Nedelisky, who juggled the myriad duties of the Institute while I was in hiding; along with John Moon, Jim Seneff, Don Flow, Jeff Wright, Phoebe Miles, Richard Gilliam, Frank Batten, and David Turner, who have been unstinting in their encouragement.

Less proximate, but every bit as important, are my intellectual debts to Peter L. Berger, Robert Wuthnow, Philip Rieff, Christopher Lasch, Jean Bethke Elshtain, Robert Bellah, Nick Wolterstorff, and Charles Taylor. These towering intellects and the intellectual vitality of such friends as Philip Gorski, Angel Parham, Isaac Reed, Tal Brewer, Jeff Olick, Krishan Kumar, Christian Smith, Charles Mathewes, Jennifer Geddes, and Hans Joas have all enriched my scholarly vocation and, in direct and indirect ways, informed this work.

Through all of this, I am enduringly grateful for my family— my father, Robert Lorin Hunter, a stalwart of wisdom, care, and support, and my children, Whit, Colin and Margaret, Kirsten and Matt, and their children—Peter, Jack, Thomas, Honor, Isabella, and Henrietta. I am sustained through the complexities of life by their love. Most of all, I am grateful for my wife, best friend, and long-suffering partner, Helen Stehlin Hunter, the love of my life, to whom this book is dedicated.

Index